Staging O'Neill

RONALD H. WAINSCOTT

Staging O'Neill

The Experimental Years,
1920–1934

Yale University Press
New Haven and London

Designed by James J. Johnson
and set in Fairfield Medium types by
the Composing Room of Michigan, Grand Rapids, Michigan.
Printed in the United States of America by
Braun-Brumfield, Inc., Ann Arbor, Michigan.

Library of Congress Cataloging-in-Publication Data

Wainscott, Ronald Harold, 1948–
    Staging O'Neill.

    Bibliography: p.
    Includes index.
    1. O'Neill, Eugene, 1888–1953—Stage history—
1800–1950. 2. Experimental theater—United States.
I. Title.
PS3529.N5Z888 1988   812'.52   87–34056
ISBN 0–300–04152–7

The paper in this book meets the guidelines for
permanence and durability of the Committee on
Production Guidelines for Book Longevity of the
Council on Library Resources.

10 9 8 7 6 5 4 3 2

For Kathy Fletcher

Contents

Illustrations

Preface

The sheer extensiveness of published O'Neill scholarship is firm testimony to the mania which has possessed numerous biographers, critics, and historians who have pursued the life and meaning of Eugene O'Neill and his plays, especially since the revival of interest sparked in 1956 by the emergence of *Long Day's Journey into Night*. When faced with book-length bibliographies of O'Neill studies, one is inclined to assume that the history of the production of O'Neill's plays has been well documented and thoroughly explored. If, however, one eliminates the extensive biographies which explore his mysterious life and drama, and the profusion of critical interpretations which "explain" O'Neill, approach his plays as literature, or examine the plays in terms of the dramatist's fascinating experiences and relationships, one is left with just a handful of books, articles and dissertations—a meager collection of material which is concerned only in part with the production of O'Neill's plays. In these biographies and critical works accounts of the original productions, directors, designers, and actors of O'Neill's theatrical experiments are often reduced to minor anecdotes.[1] There is no historical survey of the stage direction of the O'Neill dramatic canon. Timo Tiusanen addressed the deficiency with *O'Neill's Scenic Images* in 1968, but his work is primarily theoretical, utilizing O'Neill's published stage directions, not the plays as produced.

1. Although Louis Sheaffer, for example, wrote an excellent two-volume biography of O'Neill, he gave less than two pages to the production of *The Straw* and less than a paragraph to *The Ancient Mariner* experiment. Louis Sheaffer, *O'Neill: Son and Artist* (Boston: Little, Brown, 1973), pp. 69–71, 137–38.

Important historical studies of the Provincetown Players, the Theatre Guild, American theatrical activity between the world wars, and individual analyses of theater practitioners appear periodically, but only one study deals exclusively with some of O'Neill's plays, an unpublished dissertation which concentrates primarily on textual alterations made during the rehearsal process.[2] None of the production studies includes all of O'Neill's professionally produced plays, or even all of his plays staged in the experimental era of the 1920s. Also, there are some remarkable omissions in the area of individual artists. No full-length study, for example, has been written on James Light, a director of important new plays by O'Neill as well as being a driving force in the Provincetown Players, and no book has emerged on Philip Moeller, one of the most dynamic directors of the 1920s and a very successful director of five O'Neill plays.[3] Furthermore, there is no study of the production problems confronting all of O'Neill's American professional directors as they grappled with original O'Neill plays amid the exciting innovations of the New Stagecraft designers in the 1920s or beyond.[4]

Most scholarship which explores American production history concentrates either on acting, design, specific directors, or general theatrical development and trends of a given period. Individual studies, for example, have been written on a few of O'Neill's directors—George Cram Cook, Robert Edmond Jones, Arthur Hopkins, Rouben Mamoulian, and Philip Moeller[5]—but only one work examines a director or designer working exclusively with O'Neill.[6] All other scholarly evaluations of directors or designers pertinent to this research survey the practitioners' entire careers.

The challenges besetting O'Neill's directors and designers must have been overwhelming at times, and it is the purpose of this book to explore

2. Mary Hedwig Arbenz, "The Plays of Eugene O'Neill as Presented by the Theatre Guild," Diss., University of Illinois, 1961.

3. An interesting unpublished dissertation by David W. Wiley, "Philip Moeller of the Theatre Guild: An Historical and Critical Study," Indiana University, 1973, surveys Moeller's entire career (though by necessity does not linger long with the O'Neill productions).

4. My own dissertation, "A Critical History of the Professional Stage Direction of the Plays of Eugene O'Neill, 1920–1934," Indiana University, 1984, was the first attempt to bridge this gap in research. The present book developed from it.

5. Most of this work is in unpublished dissertations (see Bibliography). A notable exception is *Jig Cook and the Provincetown Players* by Robert Karoly Sarlos, an important contribution to O'Neill scholarship, though it provides few details for O'Neill's productions, a task beyond the scope of the book.

6. Sweet's dissertation unfortunately discusses just three productions. Jones designed the three productions but directed only one, whereas he directed three other O'Neill plays and designed several more. Harvey Sweet, "Eugene O'Neill and Robert Edmond Jones: Text into Scene," University of Wisconsin, 1974.

their problems and reconstruct historically and critically the theatrical experiments of O'Neill's professional work in order to expand the scholarship dedicated to the development of American stage direction. Additionally, the intent here is to represent fairly a collected body of directorial accomplishment which complements the familiar corpus of the playwright's written work as well as the wealth of dramatic analysis and biographical study already dedicated to O'Neill and his era.

This book examines the accomplishments, failures, problems, and solutions of the professional directors in league with designers who produced the first performances of O'Neill's plays from 1920 to 1934. It starts with *Beyond the Horizon*, the first professional production of a new O'Neill play. The amateur production work from 1916 to 1920 usually lacked organization and sometimes even a director, was often slipshod scenically, featured very inexperienced actors, and yielded no promptbooks, few photographs and designs, and a dearth of reviews. Also, all of the early plays are one-acts, mostly mood pieces such as *Moon of the Caribbees* (1918) or romantic realism like *Bound East for Cardiff* (1916), which include little of significance as theatrical experimentation other than a few immature attempts with monologue (*Before Breakfast* in 1916) and the supernatural (*Fog* in 1917 and *Where the Cross Is Made* in 1918).

Until 1934 O'Neill's plays appeared in a virtually unbroken line of professional productions; after *Days Without End* came a hiatus of twelve years with no new plays. To examine the direction of the plays after this break requires a different methodology than is utilized here, and I intend to pursue these productions in a future study. All of O'Neill's drama from 1946 onward (*The Iceman Cometh* to *More Stately Mansions*) falls into the genre of realism; his experiments in style and staging were over. By the 1930s the New Stagecraft had ceased to be an innovative element because its tenets were so fully absorbed by the theater that they were essentially a part of all professional work.[7] Finally, although O'Neill was involved in the rehearsals of only two plays after 1934, his last plays have received more critical attention both as dramatic literature and as productions than nearly all of his earlier drama.[8] The period covered in my study, then, was one marked by creative collaboration and struggles between the playwright and his fellow theater artists who endeavored with varying degrees of success to cope with rapidly shifting dramaturgical forms, methods,

7. The spare simplification of the New Stagecraft designs was an important influence on the visual style of selective realism which has dominated so much of American stage design from the 1930s to the present.

8. O'Neill was present for the rehearsals of *The Iceman Cometh* in 1946 and *A Moon for the Misbegotten*, which closed out of town in 1947. There were no more new productions until after O'Neill's death.

techniques, and devices. The impact of these experiments on American theater and drama was enormous.

Most of O'Neill's works from 1920 to 1934 reflect a curious admixture of forms and methods within single plays and, by extension, suggest the free reign of eclecticism during the artistic maturation of America's leading dramatist. For fourteen years he extensively investigated realism, romantic melodrama, symbolism, and expressionism, as well as numerous devices such as masks, sound effects, music, simultaneous settings, internal monologues, and split characterizations. Due to their concurrence, however, these techniques and styles cannot be used authoritatively as divisions to mark artistic periods in the development of the playwright. In consequence, 1920–1934 can be considered O'Neill's age of serious, professional experiment. With only one exception the productions of this era are examined here chronologically.[9]

In order to focus both on what was most difficult for directors and on what was unusual, innovative, and historically significant in production, this study emphasizes O'Neill's experimental theatrical devices, characters, and forms as well as the interpretations and treatments of these experiments by the directors. It explores possible lines of development, regression, recurring problems, and the relationship and work of the directors with their actors, designers, and O'Neill, closely examining the directors' approaches to stage composition and the resultant use of the performance space, an extremely important element of theatrical production in the 1920s.

Of the twenty-three plays produced in this fourteen-year period, one by necessity is omitted and a few receive considerably less attention than the rest. Only *Exorcism*, a poorly produced one-act of 1920, scarcely reviewed, never published, and long ago destroyed by O'Neill, cannot be discussed. All the rest, however, successes and failures, are examined in various degrees of detail determined by the extent and nature of available evidence, importance of staging experiment, and contribution to the ongoing theater. Each play's value as dramatic literature is not a criterion for judging the importance of production.

From the time of *The Hairy Ape* onward surviving materials in support of the productions are generally more plentiful, and beginning with *Desire Under the Elms* surviving promptbooks offer a wealth of information and answer many questions (while raising intriguing new ones). Furthermore, production procedures become clearer to the historian almost in direct proportion to O'Neill's growing prominence as the leading Ameri-

9. *Lazarus Laughed*, which was not produced professionally and was written two years before the Pasadena Playhouse production, is discussed in the chapter dealing with *Marco Millions*, which shares much stylistically with the Dionysian epic.

can playwright. From about 1924 O'Neill's collaborators became more exacting with production record keeping, thus avoiding large gaps of information or missing graphic materials, the absence of which clouds the history of several early productions.

Major sources for this book include numerous unpublished materials. Invaluable were photographs, manuscript notes, ground plans, scenic elevations, technical plots, letters, telegrams, and six promptbooks held by the Beinecke Rare Book and Manuscript Library of Yale University; programs, photographs, clippings, publicity materials, drawings, and one promptbook in the Theatre Collection of the Museum of the City of New York; clippings, scrapbooks, technical plots, ground plans, and nine promptbooks in the Billy Rose Theatre Collection of the New York Public Library at Lincoln Center, Astor, Lenox and Tilden Foundations; letters, account books, and contracts held by the William Seymour Theatre Collection of the Firestone Library of Princeton University; seven unpublished O'Neill typescripts held by the Rare Book Collection of the Library of Congress; and one letter held by the Harry Ransom Humanities Research Center of the University of Texas at Austin. Other important unpublished sources were eleven doctoral dissertations which were very useful for their inclusion of interviews with and letters from now deceased directors, designers, actors, and other production personnel.

Acknowledgments

I must first of all express my sincere gratitude to the National Endowment for the Humanities for a summer grant to complete the revision of this book. I am also pleased to acknowledge the Collection of American Literature of the Beinecke Rare Book and Manuscript Library of Yale University, the Billy Rose Theatre Collection of the New York Public Library at Lincoln Center, Astor, Lenox and Tilden Foundations, the Theatre Collection of the Museum of the City of New York, the Theatre Collection of the Princeton University Library, the Rare Book and Manuscript Division of the Library of Congress, and the Harry Ransom Humanities Research Center of the University of Texas at Austin for permission to quote from and refer to unpublished materials in their collections. Without access to these materials this book could not exist. I also wish to thank Ron Engle, editor of *Theatre History Studies*, and Frederick C. Wilkins, editor of the *Eugene O'Neill Newsletter*, for their kind permission to reprint material from my articles on *Mourning Becomes Electra* and *Dynamo* which appeared in those periodicals in the issues of 1987 (volume VII) and Winter 1986 respectively.

Many scholars, teachers, colleagues, and librarians have given important assistance, support, and suggestions throughout the preparation and writing of this study, which began as dissertation research in 1979. I offer thanks especially to Walter J. Meserve, Richard Moody, and Howard Jensen of Indiana University, Marvin Carlson of the City University of New York, Rosemarie K. Bank of Kent State University, David Schoonover and Patricia C. Willis of the Beinecke Library, Faith Coleman and

Acknowledgments

Wendy Warnken of the Museum of the City of New York, Dorothy L. Swerdlove of the New York Public Library, Mary Ann Jensen of the Princeton University Library, Nan Edgerton and Annette Chappell of Towson State University, and Travis Bogard of the University of California at Berkeley. Most of all I am indebted to my wife and colleague Kathy Fletcher, for her suggestions, acute analytical eye, understanding, patience, and unwavering support.

CHAPTER I

Hitching Pegasus and Harnessing Furies

Excuse me for not being nice, but I've just returned from hell.[1]

Eugene O'Neill's plays produced between 1920 and 1934 presented a multitude of imposing problems for their directors. Here were not only plays which offered complicated characterization, weighty symbolism, gritty language, and intriguing situations but plays which were bold, new (and occasionally poor) experiments in form and theatricalism as well as vibrant displays of emotional skyrocketing—personal, extravagant voyages of psychological anguish.

Exploring the themes of alienation, pipe dreams, materialism, the role of the artist in society, and the relationship of humankind with undefined, mystical life forces, O'Neill pondered, plotted, suffered, and bled, and after a difficult birth presented each new dramatic offering to a director. Often the play demanded an unusual use of space, sound, language, or character, but whatever the challenge, each director was harnessed with a further, personal burden, an onus of responsibility which was hard to ignore when faced with O'Neill's quiet but emotionally ravaged countenance and deep, dark, brooding eyes which could so easily plead, suffer, and accuse. With each new script came a pronouncement (sometimes uttered, often implied) from the country's leading playwright: "This is the best play I have ever written."[2]

1. Benjamin de Casseres' impression of O'Neill's countenance reported in Barrett H. Clark, *Eugene O'Neill: The Man and His Plays* (New York: Dover, 1947), p. 40.
2. This quotation and variations of it appear time and again in the O'Neill biographies and numerous letters from O'Neill to friends and coworkers; e.g., O'Neill letter to George C. Tyler, Sept. 29, 1919, regarding *The Straw*, in George C. Tyler Papers, William Seymour

The heyday of O'Neill, the 1920s, was a season of stage experiment, cultural rebellion, and economic and artistic prosperity for the American theater. Throughout the decade New Yorkers witnessed professional play production maturing both quantitatively and qualitatively. In the season of 1927–1928 the numbers of new professional productions (264) and legitimate theatres (76) peaked just as O'Neill entered his last great phase of experiment with the Theatre Guild.[3] While important plays vied for critical and popular attention, the excellence of dramatic content and stage presentation steadily escalated; successful little theaters like the Washington Square and Provincetown Players bloomed into professional, full-time organizations with impressive staffs; innovative American playwrights, led by O'Neill, not only built solid local reputations but also entered the international market; and the position of the stage director enjoyed a new admiration, both within and outside the theatrical world.

"The director and the set designer were finally acknowledged in the twenties," Emory Lewis observed, "with Broadway profoundly influenced by the off-Broadway rebels. . . . Before this time, the director was seldom mentioned on Broadway or in the press, hiding behind the mask of producer, artistic manager, or some other title."[4] These rebellious experimenters of off-Broadway were part of a revolution in morals and manners which swept not just Bohemian outposts like Greenwich Village but the entire country's "lost generation." Openly flouting authority and tradition, the flaming youth and flappers abandoned heavy, confining garments, invented wild dances, swung to jazz music, professed hedonism, swilled bathtub gin, and threw petting parties. More lasting, however, were the ideas which accompanied the flagrant symbols of recklessness: women's emancipation and suffrage, Freudian psychology, religious skepticism, and political disillusionment.

Although the social rebels who led the way had been sermonizing and experimenting in the preceding decade, it was not until after the horror of "the War to End All Wars" that the downtown amateurs of Greenwich Village became prominent uptown professionals. In 1915 (the founding year of the Washington Square Players and the Provincetown Players) a

Theatre Collection, Princeton University Library; O'Neill letter to Kenneth Macgowan, May 14, 1926, regarding *Lazarus Laughed*, in Jackson R. Bryer, ed., *"The Theatre We Worked for": The Letters of Eugene O'Neill to Kenneth Macgowan* (New Haven and London: Yale University Press, 1982), p. 112; O'Neill letter to John Peter Toohey, Dec. 6, 1920, regarding *Diff'rent*, in Sheaffer, *Artist*, p. 42.

3. Jack Poggi, *Theatre in America: The Impact of Economic Forces, 1870–1967* (Ithaca: Cornell University Press, 1968), pp. 47–48.

4. Emory Lewis, *Stages: The Fifty-Year Childhood of the American Theatre* (Englewood Cliffs, N.J.: Prentice-Hall, 1969), p. 41.

columnist in *Current Opinion* declared that "the amateur is violating theatrical neutrality. He is rushing in and winning, where the experienced theatrical producer has feared to tread."[5] The little theaters challenged their commercial cousins and eventually helped to establish a cultural environment which welcomed a host of European movements, many promising young American artists, and myriad experiments in direction, design, and playwriting.

With the arrival of the 1920s the theatrical profession had just passed through a bitter actors' strike which severely weakened the stranglehold of unsympathetic management.[6] The Theatre Guild arose from the ashes of the Washington Square Players, and the little Provincetown Players collective finally mounted a production which stunned the New York theatrical community.

Of course, Broadway's penchant for escapist drama and titillating sensation could never be smothered by iconoclastic experiment and serious modern drama. A Broadwayite could always pass up *The Hairy Ape* for *The Demi-Virgin*, *Desire Under the Elms* for *Artists and Models*, or *Anna Christie* for *Getting Gertie's Garter*. Although some Broadway producers like David Belasco sometimes teased downtown companies, most professional producers did not seem to recognize the little theater movement as a serious commercial threat and in consequence did not fight it. The art theaters, however, through playwriting, directing, and design, eventually made a dynamic impact on Broadway which did not recognize its own transformation until it was an accomplished fact. Thus, the "Great Trite Way"[7] welcomed, but never yielded popularity to, the art theater movement which, with Sheldon Cheney as guru, loudly heralded the advent of the artist-director.[8]

"The American director is a new development, a post-war product. He has sprung into being because the development of atmosphere and personality in American drama necessitated another type of staging than the old," wrote a *New York Times* correspondent in 1928.[9] Certainly, the influence of a changing American drama was pivotal to the artistic methods of directors who forged careers in the 1920s, and the plays of O'Neill in particular attracted much critical attention to the new drama, thereby

5. "The Violation of Theatrical Neutrality by the Experimental Amateur," *Current Opinion* 66 (May 1915): 334.

6. In August 1919 the newly formed Actors' Equity struck for thirty days.

7. Edmond Gagey, *Revolution in American Drama* (New York: Columbia University Press, 1947), p. 19.

8. Sheldon Cheney, *The Art Theatre* (New York: Alfred A. Knopf, 1917), pp. 58–59.

9. William Leon Smyser, "A Temporary Expatriate Again Views Broadway," *New York Times*, July 1, 1928, sec. 8, p. 1.

spotlighting the burgeoning talents of American directors and designers.

Responsibility for the direction of O'Neill's twenty-two major productions during 1920–1934 fell to fourteen men of distinctly different backgrounds, but they can be roughly assembled into four theatrical camps. Richard Bennett, Charles O'Brien Kennedy, Homer Saint-Gaudens, Frederick Stanhope, and George C. Tyler all belonged to the old professional line whose training predated the arrival of New Stagecraft designs in America inspired by Gordon Craig and other European innovators. Representing the art theater movement, which bore a kinship to the teachings of George Pierce Baker at Harvard and Yale, and which readily employed experimental staging and designs, were Gilmor Brown, George Cram Cook, Augustin Duncan, Arthur Hopkins, Robert Edmond Jones, James Light, and Philip Moeller. Rouben Mamoulian suggested a new wave of rhythmic staging influenced by the Russians and popularized in American large scale productions, especially musicals. Stark Young was emblematic of the theater critic as director. John D. Williams directed none of these plays, but his involvement as problematic producer of *Gold* and *Beyond the Horizon* necessitates serious attention. Although Kenneth Macgowan also never directed an original play by O'Neill, as a frequent correspondent with O'Neill as well as being managing director of Experimental Theatre, Incorporated (the successor to the Provincetown Players which was commonly called "the Triumvirate"), he was a tremendous influence on the productions from 1924 to 1926.

Each of these directors usually had to cope with a company of actors untrained to deal with experimental drama, a cramped or antiquated stage space, an unusual, innovative, or inadequate set design, an experiment in dramaturgy, a brooding and tortured playwright, and an at first unsuspecting and later suspicious audience. Centering on these problems, but most of all on the use of space when evidence allows, what follows is description and analysis of the productions as they were rehearsed and mounted in the theater for which O'Neill was writing—not productions as they might be, but as they were, confronting audiences which never knew what novel and exciting experiments or dreary ordeals O'Neill would hurl at them next.

Of course, each director had to combat many acting problems caused by O'Neill's dark plays and characters, not to mention his special aversion to the acting profession. The son of James O'Neill, a popular melodramatic actor, Eugene O'Neill did not trust actors and almost always thought them inadequate as his characters. Since actors in turn were frequently confused by O'Neill's creations, directors were sometimes faced with enormous difficulties in casting and rehearsal.

In the 1920s American actors were in a transitional period, as Travis

Bogard has observed.[10] Growing out of the sophisticated and somewhat artificial presentation common on the Broadway stage since the mid-nineteenth century, the style of acting was most effective in comedy of manners or the slick productions of Augustin Daly and David Belasco. What lay ahead was a new psychological realism which would erupt forcefully in the 1930s with the Group Theatre. Since the 1890s, however, a few actors like James Herne and Minnie Maddern Fiske had been preparing the American theater for the change, but O'Neill's actors were never such innovators. Emblematic of this 1920s passage, O'Neill's casts were usually peopled with competent journeyman actors, although a few stars like George M. Cohan, Pauline Lord, and Lynn Fontanne occasionally led the ranks. The casting of such actors undoubtedly affected the degree of the director's control, as well as important rehearsal decisions and discoveries, and contributed to each director's interpretation, whether by intention or accident.

Because stage design was important to O'Neill, who felt it was often critical to the meaning and effectiveness of the play, it is important to examine the settings executed for these productions and each director's use of the stage space.[11] Therefore, this study explicates physical composition, movement, picturization, ground plans, and the director's contribution to or failure to understand the physical design of the play—both O'Neill's and the designer's. In *Creative Play Direction*, for example, Robert Cohen and John Harrop note that the importance of the ground plan "is enormous insofar as it determines the visual shape of the play's action." They go on to say that "stage composition is a fluid enterprise that . . . creates exciting stage pictures throughout a production, not just at its crucial moments."[12] Design as an integral part of direction was also recognized in the 1920s. Lee Simonson, who designed three O'Neill productions, wrote that design is inseparable from directing, that "stage design is part and parcel of the job of [directing] a play." Furthermore, Simonson said that his designs and those of Robert Edmond Jones, who designed nine of these productions under examination, were dependent upon the director's interpretation and that designs in turn determine much of what a director can and cannot do.[13]

10. Travis Bogard, *Contour in Time: The Plays of Eugene O'Neill* (New York: Oxford University Press, 1972), pp. xvii–xviii.

11. O'Neill wrote very careful, often exacting stage directions and descriptions of the settings. In addition, he frequently made drawings of settings (as for *Desire Under the Elms* and *Dynamo*), which he shared with directors and designers.

12. Robert Cohen and John Harrop, *Creative Play Direction*, 2d ed. (Englewood Cliffs, N.J.: Prentice-Hall, 1984), pp. 87, 97.

13. Lee Simonson, in Walter Prichard Eaton, *The Theatre Guild: The First Ten Years* (New York: Brentano's, 1929), p. 191.

Most of these productions incorporated original set designs, fourteen of which were created by a group of artists who emerged as the standard-bearers of America's first wave of the New Stagecraft which dominated the most important American design work from 1915 until World War II. Chief among O'Neill's New Stagecraft designers were Robert Edmond Jones, Lee Simonson, Cleon Throckmorton and Jo Mielziner. When this movement, along with the recognition of the artist-director, was getting underway in the United States, Harley Granville-Barker's visiting British productions suggested the mixture of artistic tasks which fell to both director and designer when staging the new forms: "The new art of the theater is a thing of subtle esthetic values, of the control of decorative movement, of the studied juxtaposition of colors, groupings that follow geometric laws, and an attempt at an effect that synthesizes emotion, produces a mood, and wrenches essentials from the cold forms in which they are embodied."[14] New Stagecraft, as the European movement was christened in the United States, was an exciting environmental change from realistic, predictable designs which had dominated the American stage for decades. The new, often spare, selective designs created a new focus on space: empty space as a design element and a new challenge for directors.

Theories of space and design were important concepts to the artist-directors, but a more immediate pedestrian problem often confounded creative fancy. Directors in New York in the 1920s often found themselves working with very little stage depth. As Lee Simonson lamented in 1929, "The shallow stages current in New York, 20 and 22 feet deep, flout even the minimum needs of the average play, make rehearsals a needlessly long agony for every one involved, and add, needlessly, to the production expense."[15]

The coeval rise of directors and designers with O'Neill is not merely symptomatic of the growing importance and merit of drama and production; it reflects the interdependence and mutual influence of these disciplines. The New Stagecraft, along with expressionism, which together dominated innovative set design in the 1920s, created unexplored liberties and restrictions for the performance space while placing exciting new demands on the directors, just as the latter's increasing independence and authority placed a multitude of requirements on the designers. As a result, any study of direction in this period presupposes a concurrent examination of design.

Beyond the technical and imaginative demands of space, however,

14. "Granville Barker, the New Art of the Theater and the New Drama," *American Review of Reviews*, Apr. 1915, p. 498.
15. Lee Simonson, in Eaton, *Theatre Guild*, pp. 201–02.

most of the directors had to deal with O'Neill's ever-shifting theatrical experiments, sometimes brilliant, often erratic, which were built into nearly every submitted script. Most of the playwright's· experiments reflected a mixture of forms and styles. At times he seemed to toy with a device simply for the sake of novelty, because he would abandon it with the next play, even when it was successful. These radical, often unpredictable shifts must have been both unsettling and exciting for O'Neill's directors and designers. Repeatedly, O'Neill bequeathed to his directors the trappings of expressionism cohabiting with realism, or self-conscious symbols and allegory unleashed in a modern, Freudian world, or oversize characters confronting grotesque masks, choral hymns, marathon length, strident sound, chanted speeches, primitive dreams, antique memories, tragic muses, cosmic groping. In short, what he provided was a dynamic, imaginative world replete with theatricalism.

Behind each experiment, however, was a personal, autobiographical struggle which often caused O'Neill to be intractable with his directors, who were occasionally but not ordinarily aware of O'Neill's almost Strindbergian angst imbedded in each page of wounded dialogue. His moody presence in rehearsal, exacerbated by his sometimes unbearable conflict and torment, caused some directors no end of difficulty. Others seemed to relish the anguish.[16]

O'Neill often seemed to ignore deliberately what his producers believed their audiences sought: "O'Neill is conspicuously a writer more aware of himself than his audience."[17] Although he thought that an audience could be made to accept anything so long as it was presented with commitment and authority, his plays always seemed to demand a strong audience response. It was easy for auditors to love or hate, to be shocked, surprised, disgusted, or even amused by his plays, but it was difficult to be indifferent to O'Neill's drama. The vision, sounds, distortions, and anguish substantially denied neutrality and insisted upon immediate reaction. Anticipation and fear of this response recurred as if they were the director's task of Sisyphus.

Perhaps one reason for the wide diversity of his experiments and the vast number of failures among the hits is in part a lack of consistent production discipline, a condition which is typical of the avant-garde in general and twentieth-century movements in the United States in particular. By closely examining the unsuccessful endeavors along with the enduring efforts, one can more clearly understand historically, intellec-

16. Both extremes, for example, can be found at different times in the direction of Robert Edmond Jones and Philip Moeller.

17. Robert E. Spiller et al. *Literary History of the United States*, vol. 1 (New York: Macmillan, 1974), p. 1243.

tually, and artistically the problems, enthusiasms, fears, and growth of O'Neill and his directors. Study of O'Neill's plays in production not only helps to disclose the emerging ascendant role of the director in the modern American theatre; it also reveals the new directors, along with O'Neill, upsetting the dramaturgical status quo and assisting O'Neill in carrying the theater along in his breakneck flight beyond the horizon.

CHAPTER II

Altar Building:
Beyond the Horizon and *Chris Christophersen*

> God blast 'em, how I hate to see a play in that stage of
> development![1]

On a cool, brisk, Tuesday afternoon in the winter of
1920 the grand drape of the Morosco Theatre on West Forty-fifth Street
rose on a hastily assembled, stock exterior which resembled many other
forgettable settings seen on the rounds of jaded New York theatergoers
and critics. What the audience experienced from 2:20 until 5:50 P.M.,
however, left the settings almost superfluous and marked February 3,
1920, as a special day in American theater history.[2] This underfinanced,
marginally advertised matinee was the Broadway premiere of Eugene
O'Neill and his first produced full-length play, *Beyond the Horizon*.[3] One
would think such a watershed date would be indelibly etched in historical
accounts, but surprisingly, the date of this famous matinee is quoted
frequently throughout histories, biographies, critical texts, and articles as
February 2 rather than the following day.[4]

Arriving in the wake of the Eighteenth Amendment (undoubtedly
O'Neill's least favorite legislation) and the aftershock of World War I (still

1. Eugene O'Neill letter to Agnes Boulton, Jan. 27, 1920, in Louis Sheaffer, *O'Neill: Son
and Playwright* (Boston: Little, Brown, 1968), p. 475.

2. Curtain time was originally scheduled for 2:15 P.M. but was changed to 2:20 on the
first day of performance. Advertisement, *New York Times*, Feb. 3, 1920, p. 18; Alan Dale, "With
Alan Dale at the New Play," *New York American*, February 8, 1920, sec. CE, p. 7; Eugene
O'Neill letter to Agnes Boulton (c. Feb. 4, 1920), in Sheaffer, *Playwright*, p. 480.

3. *In the Zone*, a one-act, had received professional production in vaudeville in 1918, but
Beyond the Horizon was O'Neill's first play produced in a legitimate house.

4. In the Gelb biography of O'Neill, for example, both dates appear. The actual date is
not difficult to resolve, however, because newspaper advertisements of production week an-

monopolizing the headlines when *Beyond the Horizon* opened), the play joined an array of Broadway entertainment dominated by melodrama, farce, and musical revue. As Brooks Atkinson declared, "Broadway has never been the same since."[5] Only Arthur Hopkins and the Theatre Guild were at that time exploring serious drama by playwrights like Maxim Gorky and Leo Tolstoy.[6] Such plays which presented tragic themes or utilized modern theatrical devices, however, reached the New York stage via Europe. O'Neill's "new American tragedy,"[7] on the other hand, "became the great divide between the provincial theater of ready-made plays and modern American drama."[8]

Many research problems regarding the direction and production period of *Beyond the Horizon* are not easily resolved. When attempting to reconstruct and evaluate the theater artists' preparations, one is struck by an intriguing question: "Who is in charge here?" Again, when consulting standard sources, various candidates appear to claim credit for directing the O'Neill first.

No one doubts that the producer of *Beyond the Horizon* was John D. Williams, but evidence of direction can be found in support of Williams as well as Homer Saint-Gaudens and actor Richard Bennett. After reviewing the available evidence it seems almost certain that the play was virtually codirected in a modern sense by Bennett (acting and interpretation) and Saint-Gaudens (blocking and stage management), with Williams maintaining a strong final approval.

The original program announces that *Beyond the Horizon* was presented by Williams and "staged under the direction of Homer Saint-Gaudens."[9] The leading role of Robert Mayo was played by Richard Bennett, a forty-seven-year-old irascible star who took a strong hand in his productions with Williams.[10]

Letters and personal accounts attest to O'Neill having worked di-

---

nounce the first matinee as Feb. 3. In addition, all first-performance reviews began to appear on Wednesday, Feb. 4, and Alexander Woollcott's review along with Heywood Broun's of Feb. 4 states specifically that the play opened on Tuesday afternoon, Feb. 3. The confusion probably arose from the Burns Mantle yearbook of 1919–1920, which erroneously reports the Broadway opening as Feb. 2.

5. Brooks Atkinson, *Broadway* (New York: Macmillan, 1970), p. 195.

6. Gorky's *Night Lodging* [*The Lower Depths*] opened under the direction of Arthur Hopkins on Dec. 22, 1919; Tolstoy's *The Power of Darkness* opened at the Theatre Guild on Jan. 19, 1920.

7. Advertisement, *New York Times*, Feb. 2, 1920, p. 10.

8. Atkinson, *Broadway*, p. 195.

9. Program, *Beyond the Horizon*, Theatre Collection, Museum of the City of New York, (MCNY).

10. Louis R. Reid, "Beyond the Horizon," *Dramatic Mirror* 81 (Feb. 14, 1920): 258.

rectly with Williams and Bennett when the playwright was involved with production preparation like cutting and rehearsals. Saint-Gaudens has program credit, yet O'Neill never mentions him. It seems likely, therefore, that Saint-Gaudens, who was kept as a house director by Williams in much the same way that Charles Frohman[11] kept directors to stage but not necessarily interpret productions, blocked and coordinated the physical staging problems and collected the stock scenery and saw to all stage management functions.

Saint-Gaudens, a forty-year-old Harvard man and a native of Massachusetts (many of the important figures who mounted O'Neill's plays shared with him a New England background) was not destined to become an important figure in the American theater, but ahead of him lay a significant managerial career in the visual arts. A bright, resourceful man and the son of the renowned sculptor Augustus Saint-Gaudens, Homer worked in stage management in New York, often under Charles Frohman, from 1908 until the outbreak of the Great War. He later married a painter and left the theater for the Carnegie Institute in Pittsburgh, where he became director of fine arts the following year.

Strangely enough, Saint-Gaudens had unusual military training and experience which, coupled with his artistic background, may have equipped him for large-scale theatrical staging. As a U.S. Army captain during World War I, he was assigned to a camouflage unit. "I found myself," he wrote, "guiding the emotional destinies of 400 temperamentalities in the form of artists, plumbers, carpenters, and other eccentrics, who ultimately won the War by spreading scenery over the gory fields of the A.E.F."[12] Therefore, in Europe and the army until 1919, he was involved with movement and "decoration" on a grand scale. Perhaps the comparatively narrow physical confines and lack of discipline he found in the commercial theater upon his return in 1919 and the limited praise for his staging, which rarely extended beyond acknowledgement of competence, led to his loss of interest. Whatever the reason, his directorial career after the war was short lived.

Saint-Gaudens' position under Williams is to be expected, since Williams was also trained by Charles Frohman and did not set out on his own until Frohman perished aboard the torpedoed *Lusitania* in 1915. Before his Frohman apprenticeship the Boston-born Williams, like Saint-Gaudens, matriculated at Harvard, where he encountered George Pierce

---

11. Charles Frohman was a leader of the Theatrical Syndicate, a conservative theater owner, and a very successful producer of popular entertainment on Broadway from c. 1888 to 1915.

12. Homer Saint-Gaudens, in *Current Biography* (New York: H. W. Wilson, 1941), p. 747.

Baker.[13] This exposure helped to instill an interest in new drama, and Williams went on to work with John and Lionel Barrymore as well as Minnie Maddern Fiske; yet Williams' production techniques remained firmly entrenched in the old Frohman school.

At the time of production Williams was approximately thirty-four years old, near in age to O'Neill (thirty-one) and, like him, something of a recluse. Agnes Boulton, O'Neill's wife at the time, wrote that Williams had "a strange desire for secrecy and aloofness. There were periods when he seemed to disappear from the earth and, no matter how urgent the matter, was incommunicado."[14] His unpredictable personality, coupled with an alcohol problem[15] (common also to O'Neill and a number of his fellow creators), apparently left the tiller much of the time in the hands of others. In early 1920 the responsibility fell to Bennett and Saint-Gaudens.

Nevertheless, just twelve days after opening *Beyond the Horizon* Williams told an interviewer that he did his own directing: "It is a wonderful part of my work. I believe in leaving the acting to the actors, not in leaving them as putty in the hands of the stage manager. They are all allowed to work out their own interpretations of the parts they play."[16] What Williams meant by directing, then, must be akin to production management and staging, not interpretation. In addition, since *Beyond the Horizon* was receiving much positive critical attention, he may have decided to take credit for a job he apparently did not do.

In the area of interpretation Richard Bennett entered the production with considerable force. He not only exerted a strong influence through the performance of his own role but was also involved in cutting and interpreting the text, and even in making the decision to produce *Beyond the Horizon*.

This volatile actor, whom Daniel Blum described as "dynamic, caustic and temperamental"[17] and who was known occasionally to harangue an impolite audience, had been acting professionally for more than twenty-eight years and had been a star for fourteen when he initiated a year of work under Williams' producing organization, described by a reviewer as "Richard Bennett's repertory season under the direction of John D. Williams."[18] The preeminence of the star and producer is implicit in this line; Saint-Gaudens is designated a subordinate assistant in this and other

13. Philip Mindil, "Behind the Scenes," *New York Tribune*, February 15, 1920, sec. 3, p. 1; Gelbs, *O'Neill*, p. 375.

14. Agnes Boulton, *Part of a Long Story* (Garden City, N.Y.: Doubleday & Company, 1958), p. 214.

15. Sheaffer, *Playwright*, p. 423.

16. John D. Williams in Mindil, Feb. 15, 1920, p. 1.

17. Daniel Blum, *Great Stars of the American Stage* (New York: Greenberg, 1952), p. 59.

18. Reid, "Beyond," p. 258.

reviews which mention him. In 1920 directors who were not also their own producers were rarely acknowledged as significant theater artists.

Before his season with Williams, with the exception of a run in George Bernard Shaw's *Man and Superman* (1905), Bennett's production work was confined to melodrama and sentimental fare under conservative Syndicate and independent producers like Marc Klaw, Abraham Erlanger, and Augustin Daly, and opposite lovely, popular actresses such as Grace Elliston and Maude Adams. Thus, this new play was exciting to Bennett because it not only provided a large, serious role but also enabled him to exploit a tragic situation within the American idiom, an opportunity virtually unique in the modern New York theater of his time.

According to Burns Mantle, Williams decided to produce *Beyond the Horizon* "partly to quiet the pleading of Richard Bennett . . . who, having read the play, insistently demanded a chance to play the chief male role."[19] Bennett's urging is reiterated by his daughter, who reports that he chanced upon the script in Williams' office sometime in 1919 and launched a campaign to mount it, "although he had some strong reservations about its length and awkwardness."[20] Since Williams had been holding the play and promising production since 1918 (causing O'Neill considerable frustration), Bennett's offer to appear in the leading role probably seemed to Williams some kind of insurance against loss. Nonetheless, Williams would not commit himself beyond trial matinees. In fact, all actors were selected from casts of running Broadway productions of *For the Defense* by Elmer Rice, a struggling Williams production which starred Bennett, and Langdon McCormick's *The Storm*, a successful melodrama under the aegis of George Broadhurst.[21]

In a letter written the month following the opening of *Beyond the Horizon*, Bennett told a friend that "very few besides Williams believed in it and even he got cold feet. I had to do it all, cast it, cut it, and produce it. Still I owe the finding of it to him."[22] This is very likely exaggeration, but it reinforces the probability of the actor's significant directorial contributions.

Bennett's attraction to the play is not difficult to understand. He saw in Robert Mayo (described by O'Neill as having "a touch of the poet")[23] a

19. Burns Mantle, ed., *The Best Plays, 1919–20; and the Year Book of the Drama in America* (Boston: Small, Maynard, 1920), p. 30.

20. Joan Bennett and Lois Kibbee, *The Bennett Playbill* (New York: Holt, Rinehart and Winston, 1970), p. 63.

21. Advertisement, *New York Times*, Feb. 1, 1920, sec. 8, p. 5; "The New Plays," *New York Times*, Feb. 1, 1920, sec. 8, p. 2.

22. Bennett, *Bennett*, p. 66.

23. Eugene O'Neill, *Beyond the Horizon* typescript, Rare Book Collection, Library of Congress, 1918, p. 1.

dynamic character quite unlike any previous American creation, a tragic character whose suffering was complemented in subdued counterpoint by his brother Andrew. Recalling the production some thirteen years later for Brooks Atkinson, George M. Cohan asked, "Do you remember the first act? I never saw such contrast in characters as [O'Neill] got in those two brothers, and I knew right way he had the goods."[24]

O'Neill's promise, recognized by many besides Cohan, lay in his ability to combine prosaic realism and poetic, romantic fervor, struggle, and symbolism, all of which were presented earnestly and seriously. When reviewing the published play the next winter, Lola Ridge called O'Neill "a romanticist who takes one by the scruff of the neck and holds one's nose to reality."[25] O'Neill was not, therefore, just another Broadway playwright who requested a hearing, and who hoped to be acknowledged finally in marquee bulbs and Sunday supplements, but a demanding dramatist who insisted on attention and response.

This romantic realism, this "lyric use of realistic brutal detail,"[26] which would in later plays burst forth in cosmic struggles between humankind and whatever forces O'Neill found stirring the trifling affairs of men, was manifested in *Beyond the Horizon* in the bitter, ironic struggle of Robert Mayo, confined to the land while lusting for the mysteries of travel and exploration. The earth of the deteriorating farm, the distant sea, and the natural horizon provided the principal symbols which accented the crumbling life of Mayo and his misalliance with a disenchanted wife.

Although Williams eagerly optioned *Beyond the Horizon*, which he later called "the most honest tragedy I have ever seen,"[27] he did not produce it for two years. After critic George Jean Nathan took him to see *The Moon of the Caribbees* which opened at Provincetown in December 1918, Williams signed a contract with O'Neill for all future full-length work.[28] By May 1919, however, O'Neill was already weary of "Williams' dilatory tactics,"[29] and the playwright began to wonder if his play, completed since at least August 1917, would ever get a commercial production.

When rehearsals were finally announced to begin in early January 1920, Williams began asking for cuts in the protracted script. Throughout O'Neill's career, cutting was always a difficult struggle, and he often

24. George M. Cohan in Brooks Atkinson, "George M. Cohan at Home," *New York Times*, Sept. 10, 1933, sec. 10, p. 1.

25. Lola Ridge, "Beyond the Horizon," *New Republic* 25 (January 5, 1921): 173.

26. Stark Young, *Immortal Shadows* (New York: Hill and Wang, 1948), p. 61.

27. John D. Williams in Mindil, Feb. 15, 1920, p. 1.

28. Isaac Goldberg, *The Theatre of George Jean Nathan* (New York: Simon and Schuster, 1926), p. 144; Mindil, Feb. 15, 1920, p. 1; Bennett, *Bennett*, p. 63.

29. O'Neill letter to George Jean Nathan, May 1, 1919, in Goldberg, *Theatre*, p. 144.

seemed to take such requests as personal attacks. This problem may have grown out of his independence at Provincetown when assisted or directed by George Cram Cook, Ida Rauh, and Nina Moise. The Playwrights' Theatre organization on Macdougal Street allowed him to do exactly what he wanted with his plays. The sudden shift to commercial theater after four full years of production freedom was probably a difficult shock.

As early as November 1919 Richard Bennett was looking for cuts. In a letter dated that month the actor wrote, "I started to blue pencil day before yesterday and, God knows, it needs blue penciling. As I read it now, it seems terribly stretched out, and a lot of words with little active material."[30] Apparently O'Neill was unaware of Bennett's activity and the playwright corresponded only with Williams during the preproduction period. After his arrival in New York, however, O'Neill found himself arguing with both men who were asking for much line cutting. Not to be denied by a stubborn playwright, Bennett took O'Neill home with him, and over a series of drinks long into the night and early morning of January 15–16 the experienced actor convinced the inebriated dramatist to make considerable manuscript cuts.[31]

Despite the new streamlining, however, the play was still very long by Broadway standards. The opening performance ran for three and a half hours. Granted, there were long waits due to unwieldy scene changes, but many critics, even while praising O'Neill's work, also complained of an overlong text. Louis de Foe, for example, observed that O'Neill "has not yet learned that brevity is a virtue. . . . He will yet discover that, however minutely he aims to analyze his characters, he must respect mechanical necessity and must not write his plays in what amounts to six acts."[32] O'Neill would later make theatergoers accept many more acts than six.

From the beginning of preproduction Bennett asserted that if only O'Neill would agree to enough cutting "a great play can be made out of *Beyond the Horizon*."[33] He certainly cut the script considerably, and his son Shane reported that his father later cut the play by another 20 percent for publication.[34] Unfortunately, just what cuts or how much alteration was made for production will probably never be known since no promptbook has yet surfaced.

What *is* clear, though, about rehearsal is the indisputable shortage of preparation time. All of the cast except the child, Elfin Finn, were already in regular runs of two other productions, giving eight performances per

30. Bennett, *Bennett*, p. 64.

31. Bennett, *Bennett*, p. 64; Sheaffer, *Playwright*, pp. 472–73.

32. Louis V. de Foe, in "An 'American Tragedy,'" *Literary Digest*, Feb. 28, 1920, p. 33.

33. Bennett, *Bennett*, p. 64.

34. Croswell Bowen and Shane O'Neill, *The Curse of the Misbegotten: A Tale of the House of O'Neill* (New York: McGraw-Hill, 1959), p. 100.

week. Therefore their available rehearsal time was severely limited. The Bowen biography reports that rehearsals commenced in January,[35] and the total rehearsal period according to Williams was four weeks.[36] So rehearsals probably began on or about Monday, January 4. How frequently the cast met thereafter remains unknown. It is likely, however, that the amount of time devoted was minimal, for Towse asserted that "it had not been too carefully rehearsed,"[37] while Arthur Hornblow pointed to very specific evidence of insufficient preparation: "Richard Bennett," he wrote, " . . . could tug more effectively at the heartstrings if he had his part letter perfect, for his frequent [stumbling with] his lines destroys illusion."[38] The actors needed more time and a controlling hand.

Discipline, however, was not forthcoming from O'Neill, who was of little help through most of the rehearsal period. Although he worked with Williams and Bennett on script changes, O'Neill's letters indicate that he was in New York for two weeks before attending his first rehearsal on January 27. Four days earlier he wrote to his wife that the actors, whom he had not yet met, would be incapable of capturing his characters. "I'd never go near a rehearsal if I didn't have to. . . . Those people will never—can never—be my Robert, Ruth, and Andy."[39] Such negative assumptions could be attributed to nerves, but it is typical O'Neillian hyperbole which appeared frequently when performances of new plays grew near.

In his frequent letters to Agnes during his six days of rehearsal O'Neill related that he sat alone in the theater and watched the cast run scenes, after which Bennett called for suggestions from the playwright. It is curious that O'Neill never mentioned Williams, Saint-Gaudens, a stage manager, or even an assistant. He clearly identified himself as "the only man in the auditorium."[40] Assuming that O'Neill's letter is accurate, it could be that Bennett was in charge of late rehearsals after Saint-Gaudens defined the space and gave initial blocking. Perhaps during this final week Saint-Gaudens was busy coordinating scenery and properties, thus leaving the newly arrived O'Neill to baby-sit the rehearsals. Since he wrote letters daily, it is unfortunate that O'Neill did not start attending rehearsals sooner, especially during the formative period.

The single dress rehearsal of *Beyond the Horizon* began at 1:00 P.M. on Sunday, February 1, and continued for "twelve hours straight without a

35. Bowen, *Curse*, p. 113.

36. John D. Williams, in Mindil, Feb. 15, 1920, p. 1.

37. J. Ranken Towse, "Beyond the Horizon," *New York Evening Post*, Feb. 4, 1920, p. 11.

38. Arthur Hornblow, "Mr. Hornblow Goes to the Play," *Theatre Magazine*, March 1920, p. 185.

39. O'Neill letter to Agnes Boulton, Jan. 23, 1920, in Sheaffer, *Playwright*, p. 474.

40. O'Neill letter to Agnes Boulton, Jan. 28, 1920, in Sheaffer, *Playwright*, p. 476.

break for dinner."[41] The actors worked in the settings, and perhaps the costumes, for the first time. Therefore they had two days (including one tryout performance in Yonkers) to adjust to technical difficulties before performing for the first critical audience.

No notices appeared in New York newspapers announcing the Yonkers presentation on February 2, but the *Morning Telegraph* mentioned it on the day of the Morosco opening.[42] The single unadvertised matinee was performed at the Warburton Theatre the day before the Manhattan premiere. Although O'Neill was present for the performance on the third, he wrote that he could not bring himself to attend the Yonkers trial run.[43] The preview may have been done for a select, invited audience, but it remains a mystery why, with only twenty-four hours before the premiere, it was held away from the Morosco (were the scenery and properties moved?).

It was clear that O'Neill, viewing it as a theatrical experiment, had no qualms about breaking "some of the rules of dramatic technique,"[44] and what was most obvious about this play was its unorthodox length. This was a manifestation of O'Neill's struggle with the theater in which he demanded that the stage adapt itself to him.[45] While *Beyond the Horizon* was still running in New York, O'Neill wrote an open letter to the *New York Times*. When beginning work on this play, he explained, he "dreamed of wedding the theme for a novel to the play form in a way that would still leave the play master of the house. I still dream of it; and when audiences develop four-hour attention power and are able to visualize a whole set from one or two suggestive details, then!"[46] This dream would plague the playwright until he finally actuated the vision with *Strange Interlude* in 1928.

Meanwhile, most critics found it difficult to believe that such prolixity was necessary, especially when delivered at too slow a tempo.[47] J. Ranken Towse, for example, found the length, coupled with a relentless somber tone, a bit too trying for an audience, even though the play was "exceedingly

---

41. Dale Shaw, *Titans of the American Stage* (Philadelphia: Westminster, 1971), p. 147; Sheaffer, *Playwright*, p. 477.

42. "Beyond the Horizon Seen," New York *Morning Telegraph*, Feb. 3, 1920, p. 14.

43. O'Neill letter to Agnes Boulton (c. Feb. 2, 1920), in Sheaffer, *Playwright*, p. 477.

44. Louis Grady, "Eugene O'Neill's 'Beyond the Horizon' Is One of the Great Plays of the Modern American Stage," *New York Call*, Feb. 5, 1920, p. 4.

45. Joseph Wood Krutch, *The American Drama Since 1918* (New York: George Braziller, 1957), p. 290.

46. Eugene O'Neill, "A Letter from O'Neill," *New York Times*, April 11, 1920, sec. 6, p. 2.

47. "Tragedy of Great Power at Morosco," *World*, Feb. 4, 1920, p. 13.

promising juvenile work."[48] Likewise, Louis De Foe, after lamenting the length of *Beyond the Horizon*, remarked that "if its scenes were not absorbing, it might be complained of them that each is overladen. The last one is surely superfluous."[49] The critic of the *World* reinforced the charge: "The final act is too long-drawn and badly in need of compression."[50]

Echoed in nearly all reviews, this last criticism became a point of contention for O'Neill and many of his later champions. It was the overwhelming critical response to the retarding delay before the final brief scene which induced Williams and his directors to eliminate the closing scene and incorporate its essential dialogue and action into the preceding one. Although the Gelbs describe this decision as accession "to the critical carping,"[51] the carping makes a bit more sense when one recalls that all reviewers, without the benefit of having read the written play, were seeing a single performance which was presented in fits and starts with numerous long breaks in the action for set changes. Nonetheless, some critics did recognize that the play was "heavily handicapped by [the] production."[52]

O'Neill's ensuing outrage is understandable and probably justifiable, but it is very easy in retrospect to blame Williams for a decision made under pressure which many others might also have made when facing a production problem which could be solved so easily—even at the expense of the play. A satisfactory solution to the problem was found in a revival of 1926, but in 1920 the only way to avoid a big delay just before the climax (a situation all but intolerable in the theater), would have been to redesign the production. Of course, this problem could have been overcome in advance with an imaginative design.

The immediate problem was essentially this: O'Neill wrote a three-act play with two scenes per act. Each act had both an interior and exterior scene (but only three settings in all), with property changes made for each shift. The order of scenes was road exterior (I.1), farm house interior (I.2), interior (II.1), hill exterior (II.2), interior (III.1), and road exterior (III.2). Thus, four complete set changes were required, and each shift was time consuming. Virtually all reviewers grew weary of the delays which Woollcott gracefully described as "a certain clumsiness and confusion . . . in its too luxurious multiplicity of scenes."[53] O'Neill himself complained that "the waits were terrible."[54]

48. Towse, "Beyond," p. 11.
49. Louis De Foe, in "American Tragedy," p. 33.
50. "Tragedy of Great Power at Morosco," *World*, Feb. 4, 1920, p. 15.
51. Gelbs, *O'Neill*, p. 412.
52. Dale, "With," Feb. 8, 1920, p. 7.
53. Woollcott, "Eugene," Feb. 4, 1920, p. 12.
54. O'Neill letter to Agnes Boulton (c. Feb. 4, 1920), in Sheaffer, *Playwright*, p. 480.

Most importantly, however, the last set change occurred just after Andrew Mayo discovered that his dying brother, Robert, had crawled out through an open window, rushing toward the horizon, claiming freedom in his last gasps before collapsing and dying in a short scene with only seventeen speeches (approximately three to five minutes of playing time, perhaps more if Bennett milked his stage death). Heywood Broun found that the final scene "[compelled] a wait at a time when the tension [was] seriously impaired by the fall of the curtain."[55] Another long wait before this climactic scene was simply too much to bear after some three and one-half hours of intense drama.

Williams' solution (or Bennett's or Saint-Gaudens') seemed simple enough: consolidate the last two scenes and present all action, including the death, indoors. Woollcott's Sunday follow-up of his review verifies that "the third act was telescoped into a single scene" for the second performance, but he wishes "the same violence were done the other acts."[56] From a practical standpoint Woollcott and the production team were correct: the production was instantly rendered more manageable for performance and more tolerable for audiences.

From an artistic and interpretive viewpoint, however, the alteration was a grave mistake. O'Neill was apparently attempting to establish a rhythmic struggle, symbolically representing Robert Mayo's spiritual dilemma. In an interview with Mary Mullett, O'Neill not only mentioned the relationship of rhythm and the play as staged but also dropped his first hints of how important the use of the stage space was becoming to his work. He explained that "one scene is out of doors, showing the horizon, suggesting the man's desire and dream. The other is indoors, the horizon gone, suggesting what has come between him and his dream. In that way I tried to get rhythm, the alternation of longing and of loss."[57] In fact, throughout his career O'Neill frequently referred to the importance of rhythm in his plays. Addressing the idea more broadly in the above interview, he said: "People do not know how sensitive they are to rhythm. You can actually produce and control emotions by that means alone."[58] Edmond Gagey, when reviewing dramatic experimentation of the 1920s, suggested that O'Neill's "tidelike rhythm" in *Beyond the Horizon* helped to "prepare the way for the then unconventional technique of *The Emperor*

55. Heywood Broun, "Beyond the Horizon by Eugene O'Neill a Notable Play," *New York Tribune*, Feb. 4, 1920, p. 9.

56. Alexander Woollcott, "Second Thoughts on First Nights," *New York Times*, Feb. 8, 1920, sec. 8, p. 2.

57. Eugene O'Neill, in Mary B. Mullett, "The Extraordinary Story of Eugene O'Neill," *American Magazine*, Nov. 1922, p. 118.

58. O'Neill, in Mullett, "Extraordinary," p. 118.

Jones and *The Hairy Ape*,"[59] the direction of which was considerably more successful than that of *Beyond the Horizon*.

According to Arthur Hobson Quinn in a 1922 article, "the scene closed in the sordid farmhouse, the voice of Andy Mayo denouncing Ruth."[60] When editing the play for an anthology in 1953, Quinn identified the closing moment more specifically as the line "'Damn you, you never told him' . . . as Andy entered Robert's room to find him dead."[61] If this is accurate, not only was Robert's hopeful speech in sight of the pictorial horizon undermined, but the final reconciliation of Andrew and Ruth was eliminated. Thus, the themes of aspiration and vision were overshadowed by the secondary love struggle.

O'Neill called for one more troublesome experiment with *Beyond the Horizon*. The dramatis personae included a two-year-old child Mary, the daughter of Robert Mayo and Ruth. Children beyond infancy but below school age usually pose a difficult production problem, but O'Neill complicated the predicament by including the toddler in two scenes and by giving her important dialogue and stage business. For example, at the opening of act II, scene 2, little Mary tried to get her father to play with her as she delivered fourteen lines alternating with Robert.[62] Naturally, a much older child had to be cast, an impracticality objected to by Woollcott as well as Heywood Broun, who noted that "the little actress is perhaps ten or twelve."[63] In consequence, Mary's infantile dialogue was incongruous with her physical appearance, which became a bit ridiculous. O'Neill would return to the problematic use of child actors in both *The Straw* and *All God's Chillun Got Wings*, each time causing difficulties for his directors.

Although Williams never said so publicly, it may be that the foregoing difficulties posed by excessive length, alternating settings, and the role of Mary Mayo contributed to Williams' hesitance in presenting this play. As the production entered its third week and success seemed assured, Williams avoided problems and told an interviewer that what he admired in the play was its special realism. "The environment is the only villain," he said. "It is utterly devoid of 'stage English,' and is the only play by an American author I have ever seen which is."[64]

59. Edmond M. Gagey, *Revolution in American Drama* (New York: Columbia University Press, 1947), p. 46.

60. Arthur Hobson Quinn, "The Significance of Recent American Drama," *Scribner's Magazine* 72 (July 1922): 100.

61. Arthur Hobson Quinn, ed., *Representative American Plays*, 7th ed. (New York: Appleton-Century-Crofts, 1953), p. 933.

62. Eugene G. O'Neill, *Beyond the Horizon* (New York, Boni and Liveright, 1920), pp. 93–96.

63. Broun, "Beyond," p. 9.

64. Williams in Mindil, Feb. 15, 1920, p. 1.

The villainous environment, as it turned out, was an enemy not only to Robert Mayo but to the production as well. Most reviewers who mentioned the scenery did so with vociferous loathing. Apparently, the scenery was both inappropriate for the play and far beneath the usual standard for a Broadway production. "The scenery here is cheap and poor," Ludwig Lewisohn wrote in the *Nation*. "The backdrops in the out-of-doors scenes are daubs."[65] Woollcott's Sunday article more colorfully attacked "the conspicuously dinky expanses of nature. . . . The wrinkled skies, the portiere-like trees, the clouds so close you are in momentary expectation that a scrub lady will waddle on and wash them."[66] This critic's original review notes that two different exteriors were used, each dominated by "draperies (painted in the curiously inappropriate style of a German post card)."[67] The exteriors were reportedly so unsatisfactory that the play's efforts to escape the confining farmhouse for outdoor expanses became absurd.

Two surviving photographs of the road exterior, a close-up and a full stage shot, reveal that the foregoing descriptions are accurate,[68] and that this uninspired and uninspiring piece of work was probably constructed from stock scenic units (see illustration 1). O'Neill's winding road in the distance was present on a backdrop which was neither naturalistically nor impressionistically designed but seemed most appropriate for the background of an animated cartoon. The practical road was defined by a space between the backdrop, ground rows, and a rock fence (O'Neill asked for a "straggling line of piled rocks too low to be called a wall")[69] which the close-up reveals to be practical for sitting. All downstage space ranging below the wall to the footlights was a completely open acting area. Although O'Neill intended this as a triangular space representing an open field, the resultant stage space was a trapezoid.

This playing space was reasonably deep above the curtain line with more space center stage and stage left than stage right, where the wall crept downstage at an angle running from up right center to down right.[70] The playable area and the unimaginative design provided nothing to lead

65. Ludwig Lewisohn, "An American Tragedy," *Nation* 110 (Feb. 21, 1920): 242.

66. Woollcott, "Second," Feb. 8, 1920, p. 2.

67. Woollcott, "Eugene," Feb. 4, 1920, p. 12.

68. All photographs from the Theatre Collection, MCNY, and the Theatre Collection, Beinecke Library, Yale University.

69. O'Neill, *Beyond the Horizon*, p. 1.

70. It should be noted that when one compares published plays with production results, O'Neill always uses the audience's right and left rather than standard stage directions. I use standard stage directions which correspond to the plays as staged and are usually the reverse of corresponding directions found in the published plays when the directors tried to follow O'Neill's suggestions. The promptbooks used in later chapters also reverse O'Neill's directions.

the actor downstage, but instead trapped him or her along the road and wall or invited the actor to wander.

The second exterior, a hilltop with a boulder and a "purple-hazed"[71] vista which included the distant sea, has not survived in photographs except as background for a close-up of Richard Bennett sitting on the boulder in the opening pose of act II, scene 2. No details can be ventured except that a painted backdrop (out of focus in the photograph) is in evidence upstage. O'Neill wrote George Tyler in April that he hated the cheap exteriors but was appreciative of the detail of the interior scenes.[72]

In keeping with the simplicity of the exteriors, the single interior setting of the farmhouse sitting room was cheaply furnished and slightly cluttered with realistic detail within an ordinary box set. Unfortunately, none of the four photographs which provide useful detail shows the entire setting, only the central upstage wall, door, table, and surrounding chairs are visible. The stage picture (all four shots are from act I) was one of dull domesticity. O'Neill's request for "orderly comfort"[73] is not evident.

The set properties, however, were changed selectively in keeping with O'Neill's instructions. For act II, for example, Lewisohn reported that "in the cottage itself the indications of a sooty lamp and a broken chair suffice to give us that chill of loneliness and desolation of which we are already convinced by the speech and movements of the human souls before us."[74] Therefore, with a few substitutions of properties the production suggested deterioration of the interior as the play became progressively gloomier.

Intriguing differences appear in the four act I photos because two are from the original matinee run while the other two record scenes from the slightly revised setting after it was moved to a new theater in March. The differences suggest that after the opening Williams and his directors became more concerned with realistic detail and rougher presentation of the rural characters. Two original production poses which represent moments in act I, scene 2 (Robert's dreamy announcement to his family that he has decided to stay on the farm, and his fight with his father) have fewer books and dishes on the shelves, fewer clothes on the coat pegs, and Robert and Andrew are dressed more formally than in corresponding photographs from the later performance recreating the same moments. In the later photograph Robert is coatless, and Andrew (a new actor) is dressed more casually (no tie and rolled up sleeves) and has mussed hair.

71. Leo A. Marsh, "'Beyond Horizon' Stirring Drama," New York *Morning Telegraph*, Feb. 4, 1920, p. 14.

72. O'Neill letter to Tyler, Apr. 7, 1920, Tyler Papers, Princeton.

73. O'Neill, *Beyond the Horizon*, p. 29.

74. Lewisohn, "American," Feb. 21, 1920, p. 242.

Also, the two older men, the father and Captain Scott (a new actor), have white hair which is conspicuously absent from the first photos. The second set of corresponding act I photos which record the fight between Robert and his father reveal many of the same altered details.

Since O'Neill reported to his wife that only one very long, tedious dress rehearsal was held at the Morosco on Sunday, February 1, it seems likely that some production elements such as costumes, properties, and stage dressing were not finalized until the last minute, perhaps for the opening performance. According to the original program, responsibility for the execution of this haphazard scheme belonged to the corporate design firm of Hewlett & Basing, assisted with decorations by one Mrs. Sidney Harris, who contributed to other Williams productions as well including O'Neill's *Gold* in 1921. The Gelbs, however, assert that the scenery was "thrown together" by Saint-Gaudens.[75] It is probable that he was accountable for the procurement of the sets and almost certain that he was in charge of coordinating the inefficient scene shifts.

Writing in 1930 and comparing the original set changes with those of the 1926 revival, Samuel Selden reported that the last scene change of the original production could not be executed "in less than five minutes"[76] because the whole interior had to be carried off and all exterior pieces carried on. In 1926 Cleon Throckmorton, who would design important O'Neill productions such as *The Emperor Jones* and *All God's Chillun Got Wings*, created a new design which mounted the intact sets on wagons, which in turn allowed very rapid shifts throughout the play.

If the Selden estimate of the 1920 production is accurate, no extra time should have been added to the two major intermissions, but Towse complained that "the waits between acts were tedious beyond words."[77] Furthermore, at least a quarter of an hour (reviewers are not specific, but suggest much more time) was added to the running time of the play due to scene changes within the acts. Such logistical inefficacy compounded by "non-selective realism"[78] was diametrically opposite the New Stagecraft simplicity which some of O'Neill's plays would enjoy, beginning with *The Emperor Jones* in November.

In defense of Saint-Gaudens it must be noted that although he had at his disposal a standard Broadway house, the three-year-old Morosco Theatre, he must have had a very limited budget for a series of trial

75. Gelbs, *O'Neill*, p. 406.

76. Samuel Selden and Hunton D. Sellman, *Stage Scenery and Lighting* (New York: F. S. Crofts, 1930), pp. 195–96.

77. Towse, "Beyond," p. 11.

78. John Mason Brown, *Upstage: The American Theatre in Performance* (Port Washington, N.Y.: Kennikat, 1969), p. 139.

matinees.[79] A press release in March for the opening of the regular run declared: "The current congestion in the theatres had made it particularly difficult to obtain a house for this play, and John D. Williams . . . declared last night that the special matinee had been resorted to in this instance because it was felt that the booking managers would be particularly disinclined to provide a New York house for a tragic play until it had proved itself."[80] In addition, the Morosco had to house its scenery and properties for *Beyond the Horizon* along with *For the Defense*, a melodrama with three interior settings which was playing there at night. Since all but the largest spectacle houses had storage problems (an ongoing New York dilemma), it may be that flat, stowable, flyable scenery was the only practical solution at the Morosco.

Nevertheless, such a dismal presentation understandably disgusted O'Neill, who according to his wife Agnes had two years earlier carefully made "little drawings and plans for the sets" while composing the play in Provincetown, Massachusetts.[81] Luckily for O'Neill, however, the play, and to some degree the acting, overcame the scenery. As Lewisohn described it, "When Robert Mayo turns his eyes toward the horizon of his dreams, we do not see the wretched paint."[82]

Except for expert use of a wheelchair by Louise Hale as Mrs. Atkins, reviewers make no specific references to actors' movement or stage composition. Furthermore, it is unlikely that anything other than predictable, comfortable blocking was used, due to the traditional backgrounds of the artists involved, the lack of rehearsal time, and the absence of a strong, imaginative, controlling director. These same deficiencies may also have contributed to the production's difficulty with pace. "It is played much too slowly,"[83] complained Towse, who agreed with the *World*'s critic that "a quicker tempo in the acting would have greatly benefited the general performance."[84] The *Sun* was more specific. "Just why the drama was taken at such an exasperatingly slow tempo it is not easy to say. By the time the last act was reached Miss MacKellar and Mr. Bennett seemed to be pausing between every word a most unnecessary interval of time."[85] Unchecked self-indulgence on the part of Bennett and perhaps others was very likely the culprit.

79. A standard house seated between eight hundred and twelve hundred spectators, a typical capacity for nonmusical entertainment in New York. Mary C. Henderson, *The City and the Theatre* (Clifton, N.J.: James T. White, 1973), p. 199.

80. "O'Neill's Play Tonight," *New York Times*, Mar. 9, 1920, p. 18.

81. Boulton, *Part*, p. 101.

82. Lewisohn, "American," Feb. 21, 1920, p. 242.

83. Towse, "Beyond," p. 11.

84. "Tragedy," *World*, Feb. 4, 1920, p. 15.

85. "Eugene O'Neill's Tragedy Played," *Sun*, Feb. 4, 1920, p. 13.

Bennett's personality, voice, and presence were significant in maintaining audience interest in this play which, regardless of its innovation and merit as a dramatic work, would not have had a reasonable chance of surviving a professional Broadway run on its inherent qualities alone. Unevenness and inconsistency abounded among a cast casually assembled from two ongoing productions, but most of the actors relied on the standard character traits and tricks which had worked for them many times before. In short, the actors were following comfortable acting lines in order to present an unusual dramatization in an efficient manner. As one would expect, the actors' choices met with varying degrees of acceptance and response, but most acting attempts were satisfactory enough to maintain interest, empathy, and sometimes fascination with the struggles of the Mayo family and O'Neill's ironic and tragic scheme.

Although Bennett appears to have been in the position to coordinate acting decisions, he practiced a laissez-faire approach to the actor's freedom. "As Richard Bennett truly says," Williams told an interviewer, "'It is a great mistake to let the stage manager impose his will upon the actor.' The manager who does this paralyzes the actor and cheats himself out of much."[86] It seems, therefore, that the actors were given much freedom to develop as they wished.

Not surprisingly, the results of this methodology reaped mixed responses among critics. When synthesizing the collected criticism, however, one is struck by the lack of very strong positive or negative remarks for the collected cast. In fact, even when writing a damning phrase a reviewer usually provided a qualification or excuse because it is obvious that most reviewers appreciated some of the performances and that nearly all critics wanted their readers to witness this production, not just read the play.

At its most positive, for example, criticism claimed that the play "asked great things of the actors, and, for the most part, asked not in vain."[87] Kenneth Macgowan, on the other hand, lamented that, although worthwhile, "it is not as good a performance . . . as the play deserves,"[88] whereas the *World*'s critic suggested that the play was "produced . . . with what, under the circumstances, was an unusually fine cast."[89] It was clear that the actors were eager and spirited, but their "enthusiasm [outran] their discretion—or the discretion that the director should supply."[90]

86. John D. Williams, in Mindil, Feb. 15, 1920, p. 1.
87. Alexander Woollcott, *Shouts and Murmurs* (New York: Century, 1922), p. 151.
88. Kenneth Macgowan, "America's Best Season in the Theatre," *Theatre Arts* 4 (Apr. 1920): 100.
89. "Tragedy," *World*, Feb. 4, 1920, p. 15.
90. Kenneth Macgowan, "Curtain Calls," New York *Globe*, Feb. 7, 1920, p. 6.

Woollcott offered some of the strongest praise for the actors, using such words as "satisfying," "admirable," and "eloquent," but he also qualified his applause by condemning the inept performance of Mary Jeffrey (as did many critics) in the role of Robert's mother.[91] Jeffrey was said, for example, to have "much difficulty in hiding her youth behind her wig."[92] Lewisohn's more general evaluation, however, pointed to the waste of talent expended on nearly all Broadway fare until this time. "The production . . . illustrates once more the hidden possibilities of our actors."[93]

Such potential was perhaps most evident in the talent of Richard Bennett, who, although a bit old for the role of Robert and guilty of familiar stage trickery in his performance, was nonetheless important in getting a fair hearing for O'Neill's rustic tragedy. Most reviewers noted the power and vigor as well as the debility and languor in Bennett's representation, but Louis Reid noted an important key to Bennett's commitment to the role: "He must revel in it, for he hasn't had such an acting opportunity in years."[94] After many seasons of starring roles in forgettable melodramas, Bennett acquired an exciting character to meld with his volatile temperament and demands for acting freedom ("he counts the day lost when he doesn't add a new line to the play he happens to be in").[95] It is small wonder, therefore, that his stage product was engaging and emphatic, although occasionally wide of the tragic mark.

Bennett reportedly displayed "a delicate blending of intellectual virility and the elegiac grace of a conquered spirit."[96] Thus, with his expressive voice, commanding stage presence and melancholy eyes, the leading actor won over much of his audience as his character's fortunes inexorably declined. If anything, his mannered style was in part his undoing. He gave so much intellectual attention to "reality of detail"[97] that his performance reflected his study rather than apparent spontaneity.[98]

Bennett's deliberate style was probably most apparent in the last act when Robert was overcome with illness and ultimately died. Although several critics admitted to being caught up with his "adroit pathology,"[99] Bennett was often found to be striving for "'effects' when he should be content to move steadily, simply and honestly with the play along a road of

91. Woollcott, "Second," Feb. 8, 1920, p. 2
92. Grady, "Eugene," Feb. 5, 1920, p. 4.
93. Lewisohn, "American," Feb. 21, 1920, p. 242.
94. Reid, "Beyond," p. 258.
95. Sidney Skolsky, *Times Square Tintypes* (New York: Ives Washburn, 1930), p. 223.
96. Lewisohn, "American," Feb. 21, 1920, p. 242.
97. Lewisohn, "American," Feb. 21, 1920, p. 242.
98. Towse, "Beyond," p. 11.
99. O. W. Firkins, "Drama," *Review* 2 (Feb. 21, 1920): 186.

utter naturalism."[100] More specifically, Macgowan found that Bennett pushed his dying scene "of fevered suffering to the point where it becomes boyish dementia tinged with alcoholism—an excellent simulation of the wrong thing."[101] Broun agreed that Bennett was "much too deliberate in dying" and worked his audience for pathetic response.[102]

What Bennett had probably not counted on was a loss of definition, a movement toward vagueness with some of his carefully planned attitudes. He repeatedly smiled, for example, with "hesitating vacancy" which sometimes undermined "his finely sympathetic voice."[103] As a result, by concentrating on the dreamy, frail qualities of Robert, Bennett transformed predetermined definition to indistinct reverie.

In the midst of so much interesting but calculated pathos, Louise Closser Hale lent "a gleam of humor"[104] and entertaining movement as Ruth's paralytic mother who flitted about the stage and was "ever so agile in maneuvering her wheel-chair."[105] Describing her as "garrulous, uncharitable, impatient," Towse observed that Hale granted the production much needed stability because hers was "a type of character which she long ago made her own."[106] Despite the familiarity, however, such a performance provided the play with memorable physical detail, an important element for perpetuating a production's success. When describing her use of the wheelchair, for example, Woollcott noted that "she uses it as Mrs. Fiske uses a fan or a lorgnette, something to brandish, something wherewith to bridle and emphasize a thought or point a bit of wit."[107] It is unfortunate that specific descriptions of her blocking and positioning in stage pictures perished with the closing of the play.

Critical evaluations of the remaining actors make up a mixed bag of assessments ranging from "affected" and "adequate" to "deeply studied, graphic and finely felt" performances.[108] Helen MacKellar's Ruth received enough comment for one to realize that she had difficulty with the early, joyous, girlish scenes but felt at home with the suffering, complaining, frustrated wife of the last act. Firkins found her "soundest of all in the apathy of Act III with its alternate stripes of petulance and compas-

100. Macgowan, "America's," Apr. 1920, p. 100.
101. Macgowan, "Curtain," Feb. 7, 1920, p. 6.
102. Broun, "Beyond," Feb. 4, 1920, p. 9.
103. Firkins, "Drama," Feb. 21, 1920, p. 186.
104. Metcalfe, "Drama," *Life* (New York) 75 (Feb. 19, 1920): 322.
105. Reid, "Beyond," p. 258.
106. Towse, "Beyond," p. 11.
107. Woollcott, "Second," Feb. 8, 1920, p. 2.
108. "'Beyond the Horizon,' a Frank Tragedy, Is Very Interesting," *New York Clipper*, Feb. 11, 1920, p. 21.

sion."[109] Likewise, Lewisohn thought her "artificial in tone and gesture in the opening act. Later she rises magnificently to her opportunities."[110] Such demanding character growth was typical of most of O'Neill's important creations and became a special problem for actors of less than remarkable emotional endowments.

Without a strong director as go-between, especially when the leading actor on stage was the principal liaison between O'Neill and the other actors, the performers probably had difficulty getting insightful or objective advice concerning characterization. "O'Neill refused to mingle with actors and actresses. It was almost as if he had contempt for them, in spite of, or perhaps because of, the fact that it had been his father's profession."[111] This judgment by an early biographer collaborating with O'Neill's son is reinforced by O'Neill himself, who said, "The only thing I ever get out of seeing a presentation is the actors' faults, which never fail to set me in a rage."[112] O'Neill wrote these words only six weeks after *Beyond the Horizon* opened at the Morosco.

The newspaper advertisements of the first week proclaimed that *Beyond the Horizon* would be "installed regularly in a theatre when one is available."[113] This was duly done on February 23 at the Criterion Theatre, followed by another move on March 9 to the Little Theatre.[114] Because *The Storm* was still running successfully, the roles of Andrew, Ruth, and Captain Scott had to be recast, but Williams closed the struggling *For the Defense*. Woollcott, who attended the reopening of *Beyond the Horizon* in March, wrote that after the move to the Little Theatre, "the play and the mounting of it have been subjected since the first performance to several slight but important modifications, to the end that it is now considerably better looking and far more compact."[115] Unfortunately, more details concerning these improvements, other than those noted earlier in the photographs, are not available.

The collective directorial work of Williams, Bennett, and Saint-Gaudens was rather poor in its preparation for the play and especially weak in attempting to meet O'Neill's experiment with vacillating scenic units. Although the play was elongated by inordinate scene shift delays, the text was apparently cut to a serviceable playing length. Fortunately,

109. Firkins, "Drama," Feb. 21, 1920, p. 186.

110. Lewisohn, "American," Feb. 21, 1920, p. 242.

111. Bowen, *Curse*, p. 134.

112. O'Neill letter to George C. Tyler, March 17, 1920, Princeton.

113. "The New Plays," *New York Times*, Feb. 1, 1920, sec. 8, p. 2.

114. Advertisement, *New York Times*, Feb. 23, 1920, p. 11; "O'Neill's Play Tonight," *New York Times*, Mar. 9, 1920, p. 18.

115. Alexander Woollcott, "'Beyond the Horizon' Established," *New York Times*, Mar. 10, 1920, p. 9.

the production featured several acting performances which helped to maintain a reasonable run for *Beyond the Horizon*, but the production was weakest of all in its scenic investiture and the use of space, which seemed to be arbitrary and determined by the limitations of stock scenery and the invention of the actors fending for themselves. While O'Neill received important public attention because of Williams' efforts, the direction did not serve the playwright well. As De Casseres phrased it, the play was much "greater in conception than . . . in execution."[116] The first real exemplification of O'Neill's stage power lay nine months ahead.

The bestowing of the Pulitzer Prize on *Beyond the Horizon* came as quite a surprise to O'Neill and to everyone involved. O'Neill reported that after the opening performance he felt certain "that it was a rank failure,"[117] and Williams later surmised that the public seemed "to be turning to the more serious plays. I suppose the great war has had that effect."[118] When writing to Agnes after *Beyond the Horizon* opened, O'Neill exclaimed, "The first performance was hell!"[119] His next production, however, *Chris Christophersen*, never had the opportunity to disappoint him in New York. Nevertheless, O'Neill would have been correct in quoting his own Robert Mayo in proclaiming that with theatrical experiment he was just at "the start of my voyage."[120]

Chris Christophersen

Writing briefly of the aborted production fourteen years later, producer George C. Tyler lamented that *Chris*[121] "never got away from Atlantic City, and the great world never heard of it until it was revised.[122] Although Tyler had forgotten that his production also tried out for two weeks in Philadelphia beginning at the Broad Theatre on March 15, 1920, following its six days (March 8–13) at the Apollo Theatre in Atlantic City, the message is nonetheless clear. Few people saw *Chris*, and once it was severely rewritten as *Anna Christie*, few were able to read *Chris* until 1982 when it finally reached publication.

By May of 1919 Tyler had optioned the play, and like John D.

116. Benjamin De Casseres, in S. Jay Kaufman, "Round the Town," New York *Globe*, Mar. 1, 1920, p. 14.

117. Eugene O'Neill, in Philip Mindil, "Behind the Scenes," *New York Tribune*, Feb. 22, 1920, sec. 3, p. 1.

118. John D. Williams, in Mindil, "Behind," Feb. 15, 1920, p. 1.

119. O'Neill letter to Agnes Boulton (c. Feb. 4, 1920), in Sheaffer, *Playwright*, p. 480.

120. O'Neill, *Beyond the Horizon* typescript, p. 120.

121. The play was produced under the title of *Chris*.

122. George C. Tyler and J. C. Furnas, *Whatever Goes Up—*(Indianapolis: Bobbs-Merrill, 1934), p. 273.

Williams delayed production.[123] Although it was announced the following month that *Chris* would be produced in the fall as O'Neill's "first full-length play,"[124] Tyler waited until Williams had *Beyond the Horizon* in rehearsal before deciding to mount a production (the first significant production expenses for *Chris* were recorded in February 1920).[125] In consequence, less than five weeks after *Beyond the Horizon* premiered in New York, *Chris* opened before the "tango lovers and chewing-gum sweethearts"[126] at the Apollo Theatre in what O'Neill called the "frothy cesspool"[127] of Atlantic City, but without the blessing or full attention of the playwright who had grown dissatisfied with the text as well as with some of Tyler's production procedures.

Staged by Tyler's house director, British-born Frederick Stanhope, the production starred Emmett Corrigan, Arthur Ashley, and Lynn Fontanne (then virtually unknown). As it turned out, the play needed extensive revision, a necessity recognized by both O'Neill and Tyler; yet O'Neill would not commit enough of his time or presence to the production, due at least in part to a bad case of influenza in February and later the illnesses of his father and his wife. When surveying O'Neill's working and personal behavior before and after the rehearsal period, however, one is inclined to suspect that O'Neill simply was not very interested in dedicating himself to extensive production work so soon after finishing *Beyond the Horizon.* Using a slightly ill wife as an excuse, O'Neill left New York for Provincetown and missed all the late rehearsals and all out-of-town previews. Several future productions of contiguous or overlapping O'Neill productions also indicate a tendency of the playwright to choose one play and virtually abandon another.

In a flurry of often angry letters between O'Neill and Tyler during preproduction as well as rehearsal the two men argued (O'Neill usually with vehemence, Tyler with restraint) over cuts and revisions.[128] When Tyler reached an impasse in Philadelphia and refused to risk a New York opening without major alterations, O'Neill wrote, "Throw the present play in the ash barrel."[129] In this fashion he bowed out of a project in which he was never really an efficient participant.

123. Leslie Eric Comens, in O'Neill, *Chris Christophersen* (New York: Random House, 1982), p. v.

124. "What News on the Rialto?" *New York Times,* June 1, 1919, sec. 4, p. 2.

125. *Chris* account book, Tyler Papers, Princeton.

126. Tyler letter to O'Neill, Mar. 11, 1920, Princeton.

127. O'Neill letter to Tyler, June 6, 1920, Princeton.

128. O'Neill letters to Tyler and Tyler's office copies of letters to O'Neill (1919–1921), Tyler Papers, Princeton.

129. O'Neill letter to Tyler, Mar. 14, 1920, Princeton.

Although Stanhope (aged forty-five) was the assigned director and O'Neill had several preproduction conferences with him in New York during the rehearsal period of *Beyond the Horizon*, [130] George Tyler was in charge of casting and making all important production decisions, in much the same way that producers Charles Frohman and William A. Brady controlled all aspects of production when they so chose. Advertisements in Philadelphia, for example, denote "Direction of George C. Tyler. Staged by Frederick Stanhope."[131] Tyler, however, though very energetic, had a gentler disposition than the typical Broadway moguls. It is perhaps for this reason that he was unable to manipulate successfully an often stubborn O'Neill in order to get a workable play script.

When *Chris* entered production, Tyler was a fifty-three-year-old experienced producer and manager who had regularly mounted productions and organized touring companies since 1894 having earlier worked for years as an advance man. His productions had included performances by the visiting Irish Players and Eleanora Duse, the native talents of Viola Allen and Alfred Lunt, and, most significant for this study, the services of James O'Neill. Tyler and Eugene O'Neill's father were, in fact, old friends, a situation which helped to bring the plays of the younger O'Neill to Tyler's attention. Tyler and Eugene O'Neill, however, represented disparate generations, artistic ideals, and cultural values. In short, they typified different theaters. Tyler recognized the need for theatrical experiment when he could appreciate beauty in the artistic product (as in the acting of Duse), but he was primarily a preserver of the old and the cherished. O'Neill was an iconoclast.

Although Tyler optioned *Chris* after Williams had turned it down, the producer was aware of numerous textual problems which he assumed he could convince O'Neill to alleviate. Tyler's persuasive task, however, took the form of numerous letters from June 1919 until March 1920, a labor which for the most part went unrewarded. Tyler's major complaints attacked the play's length and denouement. O'Neill at last agreed to some cutting and altered the conclusion several times, but never to Tyler's satisfaction. Consequently, after O'Neill abandoned the production, Tyler took matters into his own hands and made severe internal cuts (he maintained all six scenes),[132] until he had what he believed was a manageable length. Nonetheless, Tyler realized that the play needed the hands of its original artist, and he appealed to O'Neill to return. Although O'Neill tardily agreed that the final scene was "weak and all wrong and must be

130. O'Neill letter to Tyler, Mar. 14, 1920, Princeton; Sheaffer, *Playwright*, pp. 473, 476.
131. Advertisement, *Philadelphia Press*, Mar. 21, 1920, sec. 4, p. 3.
132. "Chris," *Dramatic Mirror* 81 (Mar. 27, 1920): 577.

radically rewritten before the play has a New York showing,"[133] he refused to come to Philadelphia or write new material for the present production. Once all pleas and even demands were denied, Tyler was left with no choice but to close in Philadelphia.[134]

While *Chris* was still previewing in Philadelphia, O'Neill wrote to Barrett Clark blaming the play's failure on Tyler's alterations. "They cut it unmercifully in my enforced absence—on the strength of an adverse decision by an Atlantic City audience, at that!—and little play is left, I guess."[135] It is interesting that in the same week O'Neill's letter to Tyler acknowledged that his script was much too long and he apologized for "misjudging the length of the play so completely."[136] He asserted that he had mistaken the playing time of each page by one-third, which curiously turns out to be the same fractional difference in the lengths of *Chris* and its overhauled offspring, *Anna Christie*.[137]

Unfortunately, the exact cuts and alterations, even their nature, are lost due to the absence of a prompt book, but the performance criticism and plot summaries of the newspapers affirm that all written scenes were presented and that no characters or significant events were missing. The cutting must have been internal streamlining which may or may not have injured the rhythm, style, or language of the play. Because O'Neill's unhappy letter to Clark claimed that "the curtain rings down before 10:30—after the cutting,"[138] and 8:15 was the scheduled starting time,[139] the production script must have played in little more than two hours, certainly not a problematic length. Figuring in set changeovers, however, O'Neill was horrified to realize that each scene must have been on the stage little more than fifteen minutes.[140]

As a dramatic experiment, *Chris* did not break much significant new ground, but many reviewers were fascinated or disappointed by the play's kinship to an espisodic novel. Advertised as "a play of the sea and seafaring folk,"[141] *Chris* was described by many critics as an atmospheric piece which presented little dramatic conflict. "What little of real drama there

133. O'Neill letter to Tyler, Mar. 14, 1920, Princeton.

134. Tyler letters to O'Neill, Mar. 15 and 29, 1920, Princeton; Claude R. Flory, "Notes on the Antecedents of *Anna Christie*," *PMLA* 86 (Jan. 1971): 78.

135. O'Neill letter to Clark, in Barrett H. Clark, *Eugene O'Neill: The Man and His Plays* (New York: Dover Publications, 1947), p. 69.

136. O'Neill letter to Tyler, Mar. 17, 1920, Princeton.

137. *Chris* is approximately ten thousand words, or about one-third, longer than *Anna Christie*. Comens, in O'Neill, *Chris*, p. xi.

138. O'Neill to Clark, in Clark, *Eugene*, p. 69.

139. Advertisement, *Philadelphia Inquirer*, Mar. 14, 1920, sec. 2, p. 15.

140. O'Neill letter to Tyler, Mar. 26, 1920, Princeton.

141. Advertisement, *Philadelphia Press*, Mar. 16, 1920, p. 2.

is," the *Public Ledger* reported, "is crowded into the few closing moments, after one has been somewhat wearied by a too long establishment of atmosphere."[142] Similarly, the *Philadelphia Press* asserted that the play's action was secondary to atmosphere[143] and actually violated "the accepted and standard formula of play construction" with its episodic and sketchy presentation of events.[144] Linton Martin summed up the typical critical response to the play: "It is for all the world like a placidly ambling novel, with its plethora of scenes, its over-elaborate attention to the trivial and the inconsequential."[145]

O'Neill likewise insisted on regarding *Chris* as an experiment in dramatic construction in keeping with his aforementioned desire to transform the experience of the novel to the stage. For example, he wrote to Tyler after the play closed that *Chris* was "a technical experiment by which I tried to compress the theme for a novel into play form without losing the flavor of the novel. The attempt failed."[146] In letters to Clark and actor John Rogers, however, he stressed structure as his experiment,[147] perhaps because each of the play's six scenes takes place in a different location, and fifteen of the nineteen characters appear in only one scene each. As a result, these minor characters are closely aligned with environment, mood, and atmosphere but have little to do with the dramatic action of the play—a fact observed by many of the reviewers.

How the production was designed and how Stanhope and Tyler handled the space and logistical problems called for by the script are not clear. Undeniably, however, nearly every critic praised highly the six different settings and alternately gave either Tyler or Stanhope credit for creating very realistic, detailed settings and staging. Although no separate designer is credited in the program, the production account book lists Samuel Friedman (not the later theatrical press representative and publicist) as scene painter and Liberty Construction Company for building sets. Furthermore, no one provided any negative criticism of the direction or settings, a rare occurrence in the American theater of the 1920s. Although Tyler asked O'Neill to consider consolidating the six settings into three, ostensibly to mollify the episodic nature of the play and tighten the struc-

142. "Sea Story 'Chris' by Monte Cristo's Son," Philadelphia *Public Ledger*, Mar. 16, 1920, p. 9.

143. "Lounger in the Lobby," *Philadelphia Press*, Mar. 21, 1920, part 4, p. 1.

144. "'Chris' Sailor Play at Broad," *Philadelphia Press*, Mar. 16, 1920, p. 12.

145. Linton Martin, "Dramaless Drama," Philadelphia *North American*, Mar. 21, 1920, p. 6.

146. O'Neill letter to Tyler, Mar. 26, 1920, Princeton.

147. O'Neill letter to Clark, in Clark, *Eugene*, p. 69; O'Neill letter to John Rogers, Apr. 20, 1920, in Flory, "Notes," p. 77.

ture, O'Neill rejected the scheme.[148] As a result O'Neill was blamed for leaning "heavily upon the scenic artists."[149]

Like *Beyond the Horizon*, the play called for three acts, each divided into two scenes. The action moves from Johnny the Priest's saloon to the interior cabin of Chris' barge, to the exterior stern of the barge, to the interior cabin of the ocean steamer, to the interior of the steamer's forecastle, and concludes on the steamer's deck. All the action of *Anna Christie* would later be played in the first three settings (O'Neill finally taking Tyler's advice). It seems impossible, though, to maintain the basic action of *Chris* in those three locations. Perhaps Tyler wanted to eliminate the ship's forecastle and steamer-cabin settings, thus placing all ship scenes on the deck, the only common ground where all of the steamer action could ostensibly take place. The other likely candidate for exclusion is one of the barge settings, or perhaps Tyler meant to combine the interior and exterior scenes as one setting. This scheme does not cleanly reduce each act to one setting, thereby confining set changes to intermissions only, but no such scheme is possible without reordering the sequence of events.

"Scenically the production is perfect in every detail," the *Inquirer* exclaimed.[150] "George C. Tyler must be credited with one of the most complete productions in many years," echoed the *Press*.[151] Each of the six scenes was separately cited for excellence, elaborateness, solid construction, and "every accessory of detail necessary for realism,"[152] but rarely is any particularized description forthcoming. "The piece is staged with attention to detail that even a Belasco might consider to his credit,"[153] one is told. The opening saloon scene and the fog-enveloped barge of scene 3, however, seemed to capture the imagination of many viewers. The barge was said to create in a quiet, simple fashion "all the mystery and danger of the gray-black night. . . [as the] father and daughter are alone in the dense fog and there is heard the warning siren of a nearby steamer. There is a moment's vastly telling silence and the curtain falls."[154] This recaptures the tense, suspenseful wait before the collision at sea with the blind tramp ship. By contrast the opening scene was a faithful recreation of a pre-prohibition, roustabout waterfront dive. Reportedly a believable product of close observation and vivid depiction of depravity, the saloon scene

148. Tyler letter to O'Neill, Mar. 15, 1920; O'Neill letter to Tyler, Mar. 17, 1920, Princeton.

149. C. H. Bonte, "'Chris' and the Modernist School," Philadelphia *Public Ledger*, Mar. 21, 1920, sec. 1, part 2, p. 9.

150. "Broad," *Philadelphia Inquirer*, Mar. 21, 1920, sec. 2, p. 21.

151. "Lounger," p. 1.

152. "Lounger," p. 1

153. "Current Bills at the Theatres," Philadelphia *Evening Bulletin*, Mar. 16, 1920, p. 24.

154. Bonte, "Chris," p. 9.

convinced the audience not only by the physical verisimilitude of the locale but also by the human stage dressing of various intoxicated barflies. Whatever the exact detail of the designs, it was said that the settings, which were permeated with the atmosphere of the sea, went "far toward saving what would otherwise be a dreary, draggy play."[155]

No ground plan, designs, or set photographs survive. One close-up photograph of Lynn Fontanne as Anna and Emmett Corrigan as Chris indicates that they are probably dressed for their first meeting aboard the barge in act I, scene 2, though the background, which can be hazily discerned, may belong to a portion of the saloon scene (I.1) in an incomplete stage.[156] Therefore, the photograph was probably made for publicity and reveals nothing useful about the space.

Lynn Fontanne was a very different physical type than O'Neill wanted. Her thirty-three-year-old, 5'6", thin body, her dark hair, and her brown eyes hardly matched O'Neill's Anna, who in the text has blue eyes and "is a tall, blond, fully developed girl of twenty, built on a statuesque, beautifully moulded plan—a subject for a sculptor with the surprising size of her figure so merged into harmonious lines of graceful youth and strength as to pass unnoticed."[157] Miss Fontanne was at least graceful, but her physical inappropriateness may have been O'Neill's leading reason for complaining that the play was "miserably cast"[158] despite, or because of, the fact that the three leading actors garnered praise for their acting from nearly all of the newspaper critics, even as the play was condemned for its "slim plot and very little action."[159] It is curious by contrast that O'Neill was "tickled to death" when he first heard that Emmett Corrigan, "a corking actor," would be playing Chris.[160] Furthermore, all minor performers as sailors and derelicts were lauded for attention to realistic detail and helping immeasurably to create remarkable shipboard and barroom environments. The overall impression was of a "carefully selected and efficiently directed" cast.[161]

The *Dramatic Mirror* praised Fontanne's "refinement [which] did much to off-set the common coarseness of the coal-bargers."[162] Agnes Boulton likewise later remembered the written creation as "a very proper young lady . . . who spoke most correctly."[163] Nevertheless, Fontanne

155. "'Chris' at Broad," *Philadelphia Inquirer*, Mar. 16, 1920, p. 6.
156. Photograph, MCNY.
157. O'Neill, *Chris*, p. 37.
158. O'Neill letter to Clark, in Clark, *Eugene*, p. 69.
159. "Chris," *Dramatic*, p. 577.
160. O'Neill letter to Tyler, Sept. 25, 1919, Princeton.
161. "Current Bills at the Theatres," Philadelphia *Evening Bulletin*, Mar. 16, 1920, p. 24.
162. "Chris," *Dramatic*, p. 577.
163. Boulton, *Part*, p. 278.

recalled to a biographer that she "played Anna with a very slight cockney accent."[164] If this is accurate, the subtlety of the dialect escaped her American auditors.

Emmett Corrigan in the title role was thought by some to have achieved "the most perfect study in his whole career,"[165] and the failure of the play to continue into New York must have come as quite a disappointment to the fifty-one-year-old seasoned character actor. Capturing both the light-heartedness of the play's opening and closing scenes, and the superstitious fearfulness of the "ole davil sea," Corrigan utilized a thick but "well-assumed"[166] Scandinavian dialect to propel his awkward, heavy-footed barge captain. Alternately cheerful, embarrassed, morbid, and homicidal, his creation was an impressive emotional stage journey.

Almost nothing is known of the rehearsal period except that O'Neill was present for some early sessions and that he claimed to be disgusted with the casting and the lack of acceptable results. He complained to Tyler that he never got anything useful from rehearsals of his own plays.[167] It is interesting that O'Neill contradicted a previous letter he wrote to Agnes in which he talked about how much he learned from *Beyond the Horizon* rehearsals,[168] the only other professional production he had behind him when writing to Tyler.

The rehearsal period, however, was probably an uneasy one because of the struggle between Tyler and O'Neill over the script problems. Fontanne claimed that the "rehearsals went badly. The scenes dragged," and when O'Neill was present he "habitually sat in glum silence in the back of the theatre."[169]

When writing years later to Lawrence Langner and attempting to puncture the myth about his failure to attend rehearsals, O'Neill asserted that he was always present "except in cases where I saw that my play was being given no chance and it didn't matter whether I was there or not."[170] He then proceeded to list plays for which he was always on the job. *Chris Christophersen* was not on the list.

Despite O'Neill's flood of complaints, the work of Tyler and Stanhope seems to have been efficient in the execution of staging and fair

164. Lynn Fontanne in Maurice Zolotow, *Stagestruck: The Romance of Alfred Lunt and Lynn Fontanne* (New York: Harcourt, Brace & World, 1965), p. 66.

165. "'Chris' Sailor Play at Broad," *Philadelphia Press*, Mar. 16, 1920, p. 12.

166. "Sea Story 'Chris' by Monte Cristo's Son," Philadelphia *Public Ledger*, Mar. 16, 1920, p. 9.

167. O'Neill letter to Tyler, Mar. 14, 1920, Princeton.

168. O'Neill letter to Agnes Boulton, Jan. 31, 1920, in Sheaffer, *Playwright*, p. 476.

169. Lynn Fontanne, in Zolotow, *Stagestruck*, p. 67.

170. O'Neill letter to Lawrence Langner in "Eugene O'Neill," in Norman Nadel, *A Pictorial History of the Theatre Guild* (New York: Crown, 1969), p. 89.

to the world of the play, even if not innovative or particularly imaginative. The directors' insistence on absolute physical verisimilitude in the elaborate, detailed scenery lent the play a sense of authenticity but denied it the mystical, almost ethereal flavor which Robert Edmond Jones would give *Anna Christie* almost two years later. It was toward such selective, simple designs for locale that O'Neill's plays seemed to be gravitating despite the playwright's detailed stage directions, which the older directors like Tyler took literally, but which those close to O'Neill's age chose to treat figuratively. The younger group of directors and designers enjoyed much more success with both public and critics, perhaps because they realized that O'Neill was "a realist with a poet's vision."[171]

The chief difficulties in the presentation of *Chris* lay with the inability of the production to find a supportive audience among the critics and audiences of Atlantic City and Philadelphia. The gross receipts were low in both cities. Had O'Neill been willing to overhaul the final scene, however, Tyler would probably have risked a New York opening. Without playing there the production lost more than fourteen thousand dollars.[172] Obviously, O'Neill threw himself later into a severe reorganization and revision of the play in terms of structure, character, and dialogue. Yet he was undeniably stubborn with this old-line producer-director, who would attempt one more time to satisfy the demands of an O'Neill script. Although Tyler's efforts once again met with failure, in *The Straw* the primary fault lay with the director.

After two false starts, which nonetheless attracted much attention to the young playwright, O'Neill received a production which not only garnered extraordinary critical and popular attention but also ushered in a style and methodology which firmly associated the author with theatrical experiment while placing his Provincetown Players in the thick of professional activity in New York. Under the direction of Jig Cook, the pilgrimage of Brutus Jones into the heart of darkness signaled O'Neill's glorious leap into the exciting but dangerous fires of controversy and international fame.

171. "Seafaring Folk as They Really Are," *Philadelphia Record*, Mar. 21, 1920, part 5, p. 7.
172. *Chris* account book, Princeton.

CHAPTER III

First Flames:
The Emperor Jones

> If any writers in this country are capable of bringing down the
> fire from heaven to the stage, we are here to receive and help.[1]

Wwith his first two professional productions O'Neill
had found fortune and failure, notoriety and disenchantment. More importantly, however, he was becoming acutely aware of the limitations of
old-line producers handling his plays, which needed innovative and imaginative direction and design. Some of this new experimental territory was
successfully breached with the Provincetown Players' production of *The
Emperor Jones*.

When O'Neill finished writing *The Emperor Jones*, he returned to his
old friends the Provincetown Players rather than entrust his important
experiment to commercial producers. Since 1916 the Provincetown organization had given O'Neill a free hand with his long series of one-acts.
"No other American playwright," a Provincetowner wrote, "has ever had
such prolonged preliminary freedom with stage and audience alike."[2] He
was granted production of almost all of his submitted scripts and allowed
to have them staged in any way he wished—always, of course, limited by a
tiny budget.

Founded in the summer of 1915 under the spiritual and artistic
leadership of George Cram Cook, the Provincetown Players, an instrument of cultural revolt, dedicated themselves to fostering worthwhile
American playwriting—playwriting as an art, not as a commercial prod-

1. George Cram Cook, in Susan Glaspell, *The Road to the Temple* (New York: Frederick
A. Stokes, 1927), pp. 263–64.
2. Edna Kenton, "Provincetown and Macdougal Street," in George Cram Cook, *Greek
Coins* (New York: George H. Doran, 1925), p. 24.

uct. "To *cause* better American plays to be written—that is what [Cook] kept saying."[3] Jig Cook (as he was addressed by virtually all who encountered him) was a dynamic leader of the little-theater movement, who may have contributed little of artistic merit himself but inspired many others to produce important work, most notably his wife, Susan Glaspell, and Eugene O'Neill, who joined them in the summer of 1916 at Provincetown, Massachusetts.

The Provincetown constitution stated that "no play shall be considered unless the author superintend the production. . . . The author shall produce the play without hindrance according to his own ideas."[4] Here was a freedom which O'Neill relished and exploited, although most productions were cheaply produced and amateurishly staged and acted. O'Neill grew accustomed to having his way working under the aegis of Cook's philosophy, which insisted that "what playwrights need is a stage . . . their own stage."[5] Indeed, at O'Neill's suggestion the tiny Provincetown playhouse in Greenwich Village was officially christened the Playwrights' Theatre.

Given such production liberty, the Provincetowners mounted many strange projects in the name of experiment. As Floyd Dell later wrote of his own group, "nothing was too mad or silly to do in the Provincetown Theatre."[6] Experiment, however, was explored in a spirit of both frivolity and intense artistic endeavor. It is this endeavor which best characterizes the zeal with which O'Neill contributed twelve one-acts before offering his sensational *The Emperor Jones*.

"Try to realize the essential quality of a stage dedicated to 'experiment,'" Edna Kenton wrote soon after the Provincetown folded in 1922, "and you immediately eliminate all the essentials that make for so-called success."[7] The Provincetowners were accustomed to a small subscription audience, little attention from the press, and failure in abundance; yet the group persevered unabashed because it assigned to failure an artistic, qualitative value: "failures are the inevitable price of free experiment."[8] Herein lay the raison d'être of the impassioned company: to maintain a "stage for free dramatic experiment in the true amateur spirit!"[9] What

3. Glaspell, *Road*, p. 264.

4. Helen Deutsch and Stella Hanau, *The Provincetown: A Story of the Theatre* (New York: Farrar & Rinehart, 1931), pp. 38–39.

5. Cook, in Glaspell, *Road*, p. 256.

6. Floyd Dell, *Homecoming* (New York: Farrar & Rinehart, 1933), p. 266.

7. Edna Kenton, "The Provincetown Players and the Playwrights' Theater," *Billboard*, Aug. 5, 1922, p. 6.

8. Kenton, "Provincetown," *Billboard*, p. 6.

9. The first Provincetown public statement in New York, in Robert Karoly Sarlos, "The Provincetown Players: Experiments in Style," vol. 1, unpublished diss., Yale University, 1966, p. 76.

neither Cook nor his followers counted on with *The Emperor Jones* was a commercial hit.

The Provincetown Players opened their seventh season on November 1, 1920, with the new O'Neill play under the direction of Cook, who had taken a sabbatical from the theater during its sixth season.[10] Following a curtain raiser, *Matinata*, by Theatre Guild director Lawrence Langner, *The Emperor Jones* began what was expected to be a usual two-week run. The critical reception and subsequent demand for tickets, however, extended the Provincetown run to December 27 when Adolph Klauber, an independent producer and former theater critic, successfully negotiated the commercial rights and moved the play uptown to the Selwyn Theatre for special matinees, followed by a regular Broadway engagement at the Princess Theatre beginning January 29, 1921.[11]

When Cook first read *The Emperor Jones*, his excitement was hardly containable, for here was the play he had awaited so long—the worthy experiment which represented both mature playwriting and the promised yield of the Provincetown commitment. Cook was both ecstatic and frightened. With almost boundless energy he attacked the new project, but his free-spirited approach to direction had not prepared him for some of the demanding staging experiments of O'Neill's play.

Unfortunately, proper credit for this directing assignment is sometimes disputed. Although it was commonly assumed at the time that Cook was the director, and the programs (except for the first, which included no direction acknowledgment) list him as such,[12] a vague rumor arose that Arthur Hopkins may have been called in to stage the unusual play. This story was perpetuated by a confused article written in 1930 by Provincetowner Harry Kemp in which he substituted the dispute between O'Neill and Cook over *The Hairy Ape*, which actually took place in 1922, for the rehearsal period of *The Emperor Jones*.[13]

More confusion arose years later when seventy-year-old Jasper Deeter, who played Smithers in the production, told an interviewer in 1963 that it was actually he who directed *The Emperor Jones*, "sometimes with Jig's help."[14] This rash assertion can be dismissed, since Deeter, who

10. This date is sometimes quoted as Nov. 3, since the first reviews appeared on Nov. 4. Most critics, however, did not ordinarily review Provincetown productions, and those who did never attended opening night when a Broadway production opened on the same evening. Word of mouth brought many reviewers downtown to Greenwich Village beginning Nov. 3.

11. Klauber, who was once part of the Selwyn organization, later moved *Diff'rent* to Broadway as well.

12. Original programs for *The Emperor Jones*, Theatre Collection, MCNY.

13. Harry Kemp, "Out of Provincetown," *Theatre Magazine*, Apr. 1930, p. 66.

14. Robert Karoly Sarlos, *Jig Cook and the Provincetown Players* (University of Massachusetts Press, 1982), p. 134; Sarlos, "Provincetown," vol. 2, p. 345.

never liked Cook, joined Provincetown during Cook's year of rest and became with James Light a participant in the revolt against the old Provincetown principles.[15] Nevertheless, Deeter was certainly present for many production decisions, because the original program lists him under the company staff as stage manager.

Edna Kenton, when writing of her years of involvement with and dedication to the Provincetown Players, tried to lay to rest all disputes: "Jig directed the first production. . . . I know this because I was there and watched him do it."[16] I shall proceed as though Cook directed the production. Even if Cook *were* replaced sometime in rehearsal by Hopkins, who had never yet been associated in any way with the Provincetown and O'Neill, or even if Deeter actually gave direction in rehearsals, the Provincetown Players remained "under the direction of George Cram Cook."[17] It was definitely Cook who launched the production, and it was his ideology and presence which governed the spirit and methods of Provincetown.

Cook, who turned forty-seven just as rehearsals for *The Emperor Jones* commenced, ruled his company with a paternalistic, protective hand, but he exhibited such boyish energy and enthusiasm that his stark white hair often seemed to belie his years. O'Neill was Cook's leading discovery, and in their protean, love/hate relationship the labels of mentor and student were frequently switched. Cook and O'Neill were symbiotic forces which served as catalysts for the realization of each other's talents—a condition which culminated in *The Emperor Jones*.

Although Provincetown sent several productions to Broadway, including Cook's *Tickless Time* and *The Spring*,[18] the director-playwright was never really a part of mainstream theatrical activity. On the contrary, by "animating all the members of a clan" Cook tried to inculcate a group vivacity, a belief in the Dionysian spirit—"a spirit shared by all and expressed by the few for the all."[19] Seeking in the theater some kind of alternative to religion, Cook wanted to recapture the pristine conditions "out of which the Dionysian dance was born,"[20] recreating the theatrical event as celebration, exploration, and experiment for its own sake.

15. See also 1962 interview with Jasper Deeter, in William Warren Vilhauer, "A History and Evaluation of the Provincetown Players," unpublished diss., University of Iowa, 1965, p. 170.

16. Edna Kenton, in Travis Bogard, *Contour in Time: The Plays of Eugene O'Neill* (New York: Oxford University Press, 1972), p. 72.

17. *The Emperor Jones* program, MCNY.

18. *Tickless Time* accompanied *The Emperor Jones* as a curtain raiser on Broadway; *The Spring* was an abject failure in 1921.

19. Cook, in Glaspell, *Road*, p. 252.

20. Cook, in Glaspell, *Road*, p. 253.

A "strange erratic genius,"[21] Cook as director was moody, dreamy, mystical, idealistic, impractical, unsystematic, and impulsive—always on some ill-defined quest in search of an aesthetic phantom. He could, nevertheless, "inspire divergent minds to work together for one idea," even if it "was never quite clear to him."[22] Provincetowner Hutchins Hapgood wrote that Cook "was so intense that his esthetic creative excitement finally carried him into a nervous crisis."[23] Or as his friend Floyd Dell wrote, "It was as if he were being driven on by a daemon to some unknown goal."[24]

Not surprisingly, Cook seemed to see his own mission in the theater in Promethean terms. Casting his thoughts in verse intended for his daughter, Cook wrote:

> And I have been light-bringer
> To those around me
> Because light is born in me
> And is there as a gift to be given.[25]

Cook probably believed that *The Emperor Jones* was the play he had been awaiting to fulfill his gift of light.

When directing, Cook worked inspirationally and playfully; he sought dynamic and interesting results with little or no thought for the response of the audience. His directing methods "were chaotic, partly because they were so dependent upon the character of the people with whom he worked."[26] Drawing inspiration from his artistic clan, and in turn trying to inspire them, he insisted that "work done in the spirit of play has the only true seriousness."[27] As a consequence, the quality and duration of his work, and his attention to the company, were always erratic. He might celebrate collective creativity in one moment and become autocrat in the next. "Sometimes Jig was about as true as a hurricane to the group ideal."[28] He might work diligently for many hours or only a few minutes before suddenly stopping and dismissing the company.

In preparing *The Emperor Jones* Cook often would not or could not delegate authority: "he thought that nothing could get done without his

21. S. J. Woolf, "O'Neill Plots a Course for the Drama," *New York Times Magazine*, Oct. 4, 1931, p. 6.

22. Djuna Barnes, "The Days of Jig Cook," *Theatre Guild Magazine*, Jan. 1929, p. 32.

23. Hutchins Hapgood, *A Victorian in the Modern World* (Seattle: University of Washington Press, 1972), p. 397.

24. Dell, *Homecoming*, p. 267.

25. George Cram Cook, "Nilla Dear," *Greek Coins* (New York: George H. Doran, 1925), p. 113.

26. Deutsch, *Provincetown*, p. 42.

27. Cook, in Glaspell, *Road*, p. 245.

28. Glaspell, *Road*, p. 277.

doing it himself."[29] He drove himself to exhaustion and often un-necessarily carried emotional burdens which arose from his guiding the Provincetown company while also staging the production. As a result, while many parts of the production of *The Emperor Jones* bordered on brilliance, others were slipshod at best. Nonetheless, this proved to be the most exciting and appropriate production of an O'Neill play to date—and would remain so until *Anna Christie*. *The Emperor Jones*, however, would stand as O'Neill's most important theatrical experiment until *The Hairy Ape*.

O'Neill showed the play to Cook in Provincetown, Massachusetts, sometime in late summer or early fall of 1920, but since a handwritten draft is dated October 2, 1920,[30] he apparently continued to revise it until just before rehearsals began. Cook's enthusiasm over the script was reportedly unbounded, and in December O'Neill seemed satisfied with his working relationship with Cook, for he wrote to George Tyler that he was able to "rely on and demand . . . a new ingenuity and creative collaboration on the part of the producer" while mounting *The Emperor Jones*.[31]

After O'Neill read his play to Cook and Glaspell, the energetic director told his wife that O'Neill "wrote it to *compel* us to the untried, to the 'impossible.'"[32] He was inspired to return immediately to New York and prepare the company and the tiny theater for noble experiment in "theatre of pure space."[33] Yet once rehearsals began, O'Neill had little contact with the production and observed only very early and late rehearsals. The playwright chose instead to seclude himself in Provincetown, Mas-sachusetts, and complete the final draft of *Diff'rent*.[34] One brief descrip-tion of a rehearsal survives in the memoirs of Provincetowner Mary Heat-on Vorse: "I shall never forget the excitement there was in listening to a rehearsal of *The Emperor Jones*. The stark fear in Gilpin's voice. The creative quality of George Cram Cook's suggestions."[35] Although this may be accurate, the usual haphazard conditions of Provincetown rehearsals, and the part-time commitment of most Provincetowners, suggest a pro-duction whose fortunate results were at least in part serendipitous.

O'Neill was understandably proud of his stylistic experiment which explored some of the principles of German expressionism, Jungian psy-

29. Dell, *Homecoming*, p. 266.

30. Egil Tornqvist, *A Drama of Souls: Studies in O'Neill's Super-naturalistic Technique* (New Haven: Yale University Press, 1968), p. 260.

31. O'Neill letter to Tyler, December 9, 1920, Princeton.

32. Cook in Glaspell, *Road*, p. 287.

33. Sarlos, *Jig*, p. 52.

34. O'Neill finished a draft of *Diff'rent* on Oct. 19, 1920. Tornqvist, *Drama*, p. 260.

35. Mary Heaton Vorse, *Time and the Town: A Provincetown Chronicle* (New York: Dial, 1942), p. 126.

chology, racial memory, and atavistic primitive behavior.[36] His play may have inspired his later theatrical partner Kenneth Macgowan to write in 1923 that "the tribal legends of primitive man lead backward into buried history as well as forward into the theatre."[37] Macgowan was writing here of African masks, but he had been following O'Neill's plays critically for years and would soon embark on a theatrical journey with the playwright who was being heralded by many as America's best.

Meanwhile, in 1920 O'Neill seems to have been attempting to assault the senses of his audience with a frenzy of drumming, character disintegration, and reversion to primal drives. It was his intent to accomplish this with sound, light, and relentless focus on a single character whose importance as a dramatic device, a virtual mono-performance, somewhat resembled the complaining wife in his one-act *Before Breakfast* (1916). With *The Emperor Jones*, however, O'Neill replaced the almost static harangue of a carping wife with a constantly shifting, emotional display.

Perhaps of more importance, but less terrifying in prospect, the play required a powerful, realistic acting portrayal surrounded by a world of phantasmagoria, myriad shadows from the nether world of Brutus Jones' panicky imagination and genuine racial memory. It was difficult to imagine the small Playwrights' Theatre circumscribing Brutus Jones' all-night journey through an ever-changing jungle, a series of fantastic dumb shows, and an escalating tribal drumming rhythmically underpinning and driving the action to a colossal encounter of the subjective world with the objective. Cook's problem was finding a way to present O'Neill's sweeping nightmare on a stage the size of an ordinary living room.

Although John Gassner marked this play as the beginning of the American theater's "minor vogue of expressionism,"[38] the drama merely borrowed various expressionistic techniques and principles in order to satisfy O'Neill's urge to experiment with any technique which might serve his immediate dramatic purpose. O'Neill conceived an expressionistic journey, but his traveler was a very specific, individualized human being—not a generic, mechanical, foundering everyman.

When reviewing *Anna Christie* one year after *The Emperor Jones*, James Whittaker described O'Neill's general approach to style in the earlier play as well as many of his plays written before *Anna Christie*. O'Neill's characters, he said, were usually "tied to the tail of some overwhelming abstraction and moved dependently by the progress of an emo-

36. See David W. Sievers, *Freud on Broadway* (New York: Hermitage House, 1955), p. 105; Bogard, *Contour*, p. 135.

37. Kenneth Macgowan and Herman Rosse, *Masks and Demons* (New York: Harcourt, Brace, 1972), p. 81.

38. John Gassner, *Form and Idea in Modern Theatre* (New York: Dryden, 1956), p. 118.

tion."[39] Thus, it was the stylized elements surrounding and propelling realistic character which created numerous production problems for Cook.

O'Neill's character Brutus Jones undertook a journey, a flight from rebellion caused by his own corruption. Several critics have likened the emperor's progress and stops along the way to the structure of station drama,[40] a technique used both by German expressionists and writers of medieval morality plays and, most notably, August Strindberg, a major influence recognized by O'Neill himself. Like the expressionists, O'Neill "wanted to treat not one incident and one climax but a series."[41] In consequence, Jones encounters one phantom image after another, each time ending the short scene with an outburst of horror and a gunshot, as a native drumbeat advances.

O'Neill's journey and stations created a special production problem. The audience was to see not just reality distorted through the eyes of the central character (an expressionistic device) but distortions as creations of the terrified mind of Jones. His hallucinations, projections, visions, or whatever one chooses to call them, sprang not only from present fears but also from subliminal superstition, from unconscious, primordial, racial experience which rose to the surface in an abhorrent, living nightmare.

Each encounter called for stylized pantomimic action such as a noiseless chain gang or a silent American slave auction inexplicably appearing in the midst of a dense West Indian jungle. Such scenes, not unlike Elizabethan dumb shows, required well-planned, dynamic picturization and careful rehearsal. Cook was not entirely successful with this aspect of production.

O'Neill's deliberate intersection of the subjective world with the objective bore some resemblance to surrealism, and convincing an audience to accept both worlds was a task which the production accomplished with most of its audience. O'Neill and Cook had to make the audience share not only Jones' personal panic but also, on a symbolic level, "the terrors of [humanity's] collective unconscious"[42] in order to care about the plight of Jones, who was presented at the outset as a selfish rogue.

Cook and his company externalized graphically Jones' internal, crit-

39. James Whittaker, "O'Neill Has First Concrete Heroine," New York *Daily News*, Nov. 13, 1921, p. 21.

40. For example, Horst Frenz, *Eugene O'Neill*, trans. Helen Sebba (New York: Frederick Ungar, 1971), p. 33.

41. John Mason Brown, *Upstage: The American Theatre in Performance* (Port Washington, N.Y.: Kennikat, 1969), p. 14.

42. Mardi Valgemae, *Accelerated Grimace: Expressionism in the American Drama of the 1920s* (Carbondale: Southern Illinois University Press, 1972), p. 122.

ical turmoil in strong visual and aural terms. One of their most obvious and successful devices was the execution of offstage drums which O'Neill requested in the written play. The drumming began near the close of scene 1, and continued "at a gradually accelerating rate," as O'Neill wrote, "uninterruptedly to the very end of the play."[43] Actually, the drumming ceased when Jones was shot with rifles some ten speeches before the final curtain.[44]

O'Neill told an interviewer in 1924 that while reading of African drums played at tribal feasts, he was inspired to experiment with drumming which "starts at a normal pulse-beat and is slowly intensified until the heart-beat of every one present corresponds to the frenzied beat of the drum."[45] This normal pulse rate is identified in the play text as "72 to the minute,"[46] and its speed was increased eight times, usually at a dynamic moment such as lighting a match in the darkness or firing a pistol at a phantom image.

Although the drumming was effective from the beginning of production, delays in set changes interrupted the drumming in early performances, and this problem was probably not corrected for at least several days. O'Neill vaguely mentioned that "in the first presentation . . . the drum was not handled as skilfully as it might have been,"[47] but Florence Gilliam's review, while praising the play, specifically describes the delays: "One longed to see the eight scenes run through in quick succession with the house in continuous darkness and the beating of the drum uninterrupted."[48] By November 5, however, the shifting problems must have been solved, since Stephen Rathbun reported that the "incessant beating . . . continue[d] even during the brief intermissions."[49] Maida Castellun's enthusiastic report was more colorful. "Bang! Bang! Bang! Bang! goes the drum . . . for a steady hour and a half, through eight scenes and seven intermissions, until the brain throbs to its monotonous beat and the world of reality is forgotten."[50] Since Montrose Moses reported on February 12 that "the savage tom-tom . . . thuds thruout the scenes and in the intermis-

43. Eugene O'Neill, *The Emperor Jones* (Cincinnati: Steward Kidd, 1921), p. 25.

44. O'Neill, *Emperor Jones*, p. 53.

45. O'Neill, in Charles P. Sweeney, "Back to the Source of Plays Written by Eugene O'Neill," *World*, November 9, 1924, p. M-5.

46. O'Neill, *Emperor Jones*, p. 25.

47. O'Neill in Sweeney, "Back," p. M-5.

48. Florence Gilliam, untitled clipping, *Quill*, Nov. 1920, p. 26, in Provincetown Players scrapbook, Theatre Collection, Performing Arts Center of New York Public Library.

49. Stephen Rathbun, "In the Plays," *Sun*, November 6, 1920, p. 3.

50. Maida Castellun, "O'Neill's 'The Emperor Jones' Thrills and Fascinates," *New York Call*, Nov. 10, 1920, in Miller, *Playwright's Progress*, p. 22.

sions,"[51] the uninterrupted percussion must have been continued after the move to Broadway.

In a 1962 interview George Greenberg, a Provincetown stagehand and later stage manager (1921–1922) reported that the drums were kept in the cellar upstage and moved throughout the play until by the play's end they were placed directly beneath the middle of the house. [52] Unfortunately, it is not clear if Greenberg is referring to Provincetown or a Broadway theater. There was definitely basement space beneath the Provincetown stage, but it is not certain whether this extended beneath the audience area. If the drums were shifted at Provincetown, it is not likely that the movement in such a small house would have made a dynamic difference, but the possibilities of psychological manipulation are intriguing nonetheless.

The production of *The Emperor Jones* introduced to New York another inventive artist-craftsman who joined the ranks of the New Stagecraft designers led by Robert Edmond Jones and Lee Simonson. The program for *The Emperor Jones* includes the curious credit, "settings designed and executed with the assistance of Cleon Throckmorton."[53] It seems that Throckmorton was brought to Cook's attention when it was obvious that screens designed by the actor and painter Charles Ellis were inadequate.

A graduate of Carnegie Tech in engineering and architecture, twenty-three-year-old Throckmorton hastily drafted and built his first New York stage setting in a few days. His work was so impressive that he was invited to remain with the Provincetowners as their "first permanent technical director."[54] He later designed three more productions for O'Neill as well as many others for the Provincetown, the Theatre Guild and the Group Theatre.

When Throckmorton arrived at the Provincetown sometime in late October, he encountered an old converted stable at 133 Macdougal Street, where the Provincetowners had worked since 1918. Here they had more stage and storage space than at their former home a few doors away at number 139. Nonetheless, the stage area was still very limited, "a stage too small by one-half," it was reported, "for the purpose of [*The Emperor Jones*]."[55] It was not quite so constrained as is often reported, however.

51. Montrose J. Moses, "O'Neill and 'The Emperor Jones,'" *Independent*, 105 (Feb. 12, 1921): p. 159.

52. George Greenberg interview (Nov. 27, 1962), in Vilhauer, "History," p. 285.

53. *Emperor Jones* program, MCNY.

54. Deutsch, *Provincetown*, p. 69.

55. "Provincetown Players Stage Remarkable Play," *Brooklyn Daily Eagle*, Nov. 9, 1920, p. 5.

Edna Kenton was the only Provincetown Player who reported the stage dimensions, which she recorded as twelve feet by twenty-six feet, but without distinguishing width from depth.[56] When quoting Kenton's figures Sheaffer and Sarlos interpreted twelve feet as width, while the Gelbs read the smaller figure as depth.[57] Either interpretation, however, is problematic, since twenty-six feet exceeds the width of the lot of the building[58] and twelve feet falls far short of the proscenium-opening estimates determined for this study from surviving production photographs which include actors, box sets, and doorways for scale.[59] A conservative estimate of proscenium-opening width based on photographic evidence is sixteen feet.

Sarlos reproduces a Federal Theatre Project diagram of 1937 which lists the stage from wall to wall as twenty-two feet, ten inches.[60] This seems consistent with a lot width of twenty-four feet, six inches. In addition, the downstage proscenium opening is fifteen feet, six inches, which is reasonable, since the O'Neill-Jones-Macgowan triumvirate in 1924 remodeled much of the interior and reduced the proscenium opening by adding side masking and proscenium doors. Federal Theatre figures are further corroborated by measuring proportionally the one surviving photograph of the theater interior taken during the triumvirate period (1924–1926). If the proscenium opening is nine feet, five and one-half inches tall (the height indicated on the Federal Theatre diagram), then the proscenium opening in 1920 probably fell between sixteen and twenty feet.

The Provincetown audience sat on hard benches which accommodated approximately two hundred people, although many more often stood or sat on the raked floor, especially for *The Emperor Jones*. In her review Castellun described the "dingy hall, with its stiff benches and its dim lights and its thick atmosphere," where "people squat on their coats on the hard and not immaculate floors, or sit cheerfully on radiators, or stand patiently for two hours."[61] Here it was that Throckmorton, inspired by O'Neill's play and Cook's enthusiasm which "had made a virtue of the simplicity which the limited area and proscenium height imposed,"[62] provided a jungle from strips of cloth which stood in strong relief against Cook's theatrical coup, New York's first complete sky dome, built express-

56. Kenton, "Provincetown," *Billboard*, p. 14.

57. Sheaffer, *Playwright*, p. 439; Sarlos, *Jig*, p. 204; Gelbs, *O'Neill*, p. 385.

58. Bromley & Company Manhattan Land Book in Sarlos, *Jig*, pp. 203–04.

59. Photographs of interior settings for O'Neill's *Diff'rent* (1920) and Susan Glaspell's *Bernice* (1918) were especially helpful in making proscenium-width estimates. Theatre Collection, MCNY.

60. Sarlos, *Jig*, p. 127.

61. Castellun, "O'Neill's," p. 22.

62. Deutsch, *Provincetown*, p. 62.

ly for this production. Cook's daughter later wrote that her father "built a sky in the Provincetown Playhouse, a plaster dome flooded with blue light, before which bodies stood outlined against infinite light."[63] It was not without a fight, however, that Cook managed to erect his scenic marvel. Due to a shortage of funds (the Provincetown treasury had $530 as the new season was beginning),[64] Cook's suggestion for a dome for *The Emperor Jones* was rejected by the Provincetowners, but the director was unyielding. "The Emperor has *got* to have a dome to play against," he exclaimed,[65] and set about building it himself—although his efforts exhausted nearly all of the production money. This dictatorial maneuver was disturbing to many of the Players until they witnessed the beautiful results.

Based on the German *Kuppelhorizont*, Cook's dome was a permanent cyclorama built of concrete and iron. The dome was "in section a quarter of a sphere and semicircular in ground plan."[66] Its sand-finished surface described "a constant curve in every direction,"[67] and when lit provided an "illusion of distance," an "effect of infinite and intangible distance."[68] The new construction, however, eliminated much of the available stage space—eight feet of depth according to Deutsch and Kenton, the latter calling it a sacrifice of "eight feet of reality for an illusion of illimitable space."[69] It is difficult to determine the resultant depth. Using Kenton's twenty-six feet as a possible original stage depth, modified by the Federal Theatre measurements, an estimate is possible. At upstage center the dome's distance from the proscenium line may have been about twenty-two feet with the distance gradually growing smaller to perhaps eighteen feet (representing the eight-foot loss), or less as the dome approached the wings.[70] If the foregoing dimensions of width and depth are remotely accurate, the Provincetown, which had little space before the dome, afterward had an approximate eighteen-foot-square practical playing area, no shifting space, no usable wings except for actor passage, and a diminutive visual scope for its *boîte à illusions*. As a result, Throckmorton and

63. Nilla Cram Cook, *My Road to India* (New York: Lee Furman, 1939), p. 48.

64. Glaspell, *Road*, p. 289. Deutsch reports a much lower figure but goes on to agree with Glaspell that Cook spent about $500 on the dome.

65. Kenton, "Provincetown," *Greek*, p. 26.

66. Lee Simonson, *The Art of Scenic Design* (Westport, Conn.: Greenwood, 1950), p. 39.

67. James Light, in Deutsch, *Provincetown*, p. 61.

68. Sheldon Cheney, *The New Movement in the Theatre* (New York: Mitchell Kennerley, 1914), p. 133.

69. Kenton, "Provincetown," *Billboard*, p. 14.

70. Figures based on Kenton's twenty-six feet as original stage depth, Federal Theatre diagram which indicates maximum depth of dome as twenty-two feet, and the reported eight-foot depth loss.

Cook had to utilize considerable imagination to mount O'Neill's eight different vistas.

The sky dome was the key to their success. When describing its power, Macgowan wrote that "it is a property of this curving plaster to catch and mix light so deftly that, in the diffused glow that reaches the spectator, it is impossible to focus the eye with any degree of assurance upon the actual surface of the dome. . . . [Director and designer] have used this sky with such inspiring effect as has never been achieved in New York before."[71] While providing stunning effects, the dome created new lighting problems, since the stage was small. Such distortions as "the flitting of grotesque shadows across the dome sky at the entrance of each actor [and] the necessity of players passing through rays of light intended for the sky, producing for the moment blue or green faces,"[72] were undoubtedly caused by the short throw distance and low angle from lighting positions to stage and dome. Such problems, however, were surpassed by the new possibilities of the dome. It appears, then, that Cook made an excellent creative decision which contributed significantly to the success of *The Emperor Jones* as well as to the notoriety of the Provincetown Players.

Enhancing Cook's dome was Throckmorton's design cast in a style akin to fauvism, the simplified design of which shared many of the characteristics and values of the New Stagecraft in the theater. Fauvism utilized "rich surface texture, lively linear patterns, and boldly clashing effects of primary colors."[73] Likewise, the New Stagecraft designer often used broad splashes of color, flat, simple presentations of objects and surfaces, and plastic, pliable materials. Shadows were often created with objects and light rather than paint. The key was simplicity. As John Mason Brown described it, the New Stagecraft artist "invited judgment as much by what he left out as by what he put in."[74] Robert Hughes' list of the characteristics of fauvism, "its bright, dissonant colour, crude urgency of surface, distorted drawing, and love of brisk, raw-looking sensation,"[75] could well stand as a description of the setting for *The Emperor Jones*.

In a letter to George C. Tyler, O'Neill wrote that what the production team sought scenically was a very simple and flexible staging system which in concert with lights would allow numerous and rapidly changing scenic locations.[76] These changes were afforded by many pieces of hang-

71. Kenneth Macgowan, "The New Season," *Theatre Arts* 5 (Jan. 1921): 6.

72. Edward J. Powers, "What Next for the Small Theatre?" *Arts & Decoration* 15 (Oct. 1921): 374.

73. Helen Gardner, *Art Through the Ages*, 6th ed. (New York: Harcourt, Brace, Jovanovich, 1975), p. 722.

74. Brown, *Upstage*, p. 140.

75. Robert Hughes, *The Shock of the New* (New York: Alfred A. Knopf, 1980), p. 132.

76. O'Neill letter to Tyler, December 9, 1920, Princeton.

ing cloth—cut, painted, and molded in a variety of shapes—which were hung from the flies and arranged in divers ways to expose or conceal different parts of the dome. Thus, Throckmorton built a stylized jungle which was meant to allow much variance and transformation with little loss of time.

"The giant, forbidding trees," Throckmorton later wrote, "were merely chunks of old scene canvas hanging on lines from above."[77] A series of wires were hung in batten positions, and the strips of canvas which had screw eyes at the top could be easily pulled along the lines in any number of patterns.[78] In addition, cut drops were used upstage, above the trees, for additional depth, fill, and control of the dome. In a close-up photograph from scene 2, Jones' grub search, the tree hangings trail onto the floor and the cloth seems very coarse and heavy with paint—much like a house painter's drop cloth. The effect of the hangings is continued texturally by a ground cloth which appears to be in use in every scene.[79] Unfortunately, the floor was not "covered sufficiently to kill the sound of boards."[80] The creaky old surface of the stage would be expected to disturb much of the play's silent, pantomimic action, but the drumming should have rendered much of this negligible.

In many scenes the trees provided a silhouette effect against the dome as well as strong vertical lines towering over their human prisoner. Sometimes, however, the texture of the trees was revealed by direct, but limited, light. As Throckmorton wrote, "If enough light did not hit them, they were perfectly satisfactory."[81] Thus, the color and texture of the trees were an important part of the design, but their hazy, indistinct shapes and illumination lent a necessary sense of mystery and uncertainty to Jones' surroundings.

One of the most intriguing uses of the trees can be seen in a photograph of scene 4, Jones' confrontation with the chain gang (see illustration 2). Many narrow and wide strips of cloth were hung close together on either side of the stage, but much light reflected by the dome was allowed to filter through. In addition, an opening of some four or five feet at right center suggested a passage while providing a bright space for dynamic human silhouettes. The slave auction of scene 5, though, utilized even

77. Cleon Throckmorton, "Scenic Art," in Herschel L. Bricker, ed., *Our Theatre Today* (New York: Samuel French, 1936), p. 274.

78. Selden, *Stage*, pp. 130–31.

79. Photograph, Yale. There are a total of eleven different photographs from the Theatre Collection, Beinecke Library, Yale University, and five photographs from the Theatre Collection, MCNY. Unfortunately, there are no photographs of scene 3 (Jeff throwing dice) or the slave ship of scene 6.

80. Gilliam, *Quill*, p. 26.

81. Throckmorton, "Scenic," p. 274.

fewer trees and revealed more dome, thus stronger silhouettes than in the preceding scene. Although the photographs display a brighter glow, the human elements are darker and less distinct, except in outline.

Most of the dome was exposed in Jones' final meeting with his racial past, the witch doctor's dance of scene 7. The trees were still present right and left, but the central area was quite bare and radiant. This dark presence of animated bodies on an infinite field contrasted sharply with the next and final scene, a clearing on the edge of the forest. For scene 8 the dome was obscured completely by a collection of hangings and drops. The glow from the luminous void was gone, and with it the life of Jones, whose body lay at the feet of Smithers and the natives. This final mundane stage picture was completely without the magic and chiaroscuro of the previous scenes: an abrupt return to the real world.

Throckmorton surely had no time to draft ground plans, but Samuel Selden later drew approximate ground plans from memory.[82] The plan for scenes 2–8 includes three overhead lines for canvas hangings, a foliage border, and two cut drop positions. Offstage areas are masked with black flannel. The opening scene, however, the throne room, is totally different and was probably a major cause for delay in production.

Selden's ground plan for scene 1 presents standard wall flats creating a three-sided box set approachable by two archways, stage right and up left center. The production photographs verify the essential elements of Selden's plan but reveal that the upstage door was much farther stage right, and they indicate much more strongly that the audience was looking into a corner of the room where the throne rested, flanked by the two exits. The literal cornering of Jones (not specified in O'Neill's text) provided many opportunities for interesting diagonal blocking in the expository argument of Jones and Smithers. The floor treatment enhanced diagonal composition with a narrow floor runner of a brighter color than the ground cloth, which extended from down right through the up center archway and separated the throne from most of the playing space. In addition Throckmorton invigorated the throne room with dynamic lighting. The walls were a stark white, and apparently little color appeared anywhere except possibly in the floor runner and in the almost grotesque coloration of the throne ("eye-smiting scarlet" and "brilliant orange") and the emperor's uniform (light blue, gold, and bright red) if O'Neill's color scheme was followed strictly.[83] Yet this bright room was lit throughout much of the scene with pools of light creating strong chiaroscuro, obvious facial shadows, and intense fields of darkness. Macgowan complained that this

82. Selden, *Stage*, p. 50.
83. O'Neill, *Emperor Jones*, pp. 7, 11.

first scene was "so tediously directed that it seems longer and less skilful than it should." In the following seven scenes, however, "something akin to O'Neill's own pictorial genius enters the direction, and shows us . . . scenes of extraordinary expressiveness and beauty."[84]

Other reviews and the photographs verify that Cook created interesting and dynamic stage pictures with the actors against the dome and within Throckmorton's forests. Since the sets were redesigned and finished at the last moment, however, and since some reviewers complained of occasional disorganized movement and scene shifting in early performances, it is likely that much blocking was belatedly adjusted.

Cook's movement and composition appear to have been inspired by O'Neill's description of what he was seeking with this play: a "creative collaboration" with the director, "a new system of staging of extreme simplicity and flexibility which, combined with art in the lighting, will permit of many scenes and instantaneous changes, a combination of the scope of the [silent] movies with all that is best of the spoken drama."[85] The pantomimic action of silent film and expressionistic drama found its way into the staging of *The Emperor Jones* with a crap shooter who had the "regular, rigid, mechanical movements of an automaton;" with a chain gang whose tools made no sound as they worked and whose overseer's snapping whip cut the air noiselessly; with the dark, crawling, "little Formless Fears" nuzzling up to Jones; with a "stiff, rigid, unreal marionettish" slave auction; with a ship full of broken, swaying slaves; and with a wildly dancing Congo witch doctor. The pantomimic creatures moved inaudibly, and if they made noise at all it was usually groaning, wailing, chanting, or "melancholy murmur."[86]

Cook accentuated this stylization by producing strong silhouettes and contrasts. When moving actors close to the glowing dome, he enhanced the human silhouettes. The director removed actors from the sky field by bringing them far downstage, or created half-lit, half-shadowed figures by placing them at mid-stage. Several variations are evident in the photographs. In the slave auction, for example, Jones was on a block near the dome, creating a strong silhouette. The auctioneer and buyers, however, were farther downstage. As an actor approached the proscenium line, the costumes and features became more distinct. Jones' anonymity as a slave was thus dynamically reinforced.

In scene 7 the witch doctor first appeared as a dark silhouette far upstage from behind a tree close to the dome, while Jones was more clearly lit downstage. As the dance and incantation proceeded, Jones crawled

84. Kenneth Macgowan, "The New Plays," New York *Globe*, Nov. 4, 1920, p. 14.
85. O'Neill letter to Tyler, Dec. 9, 1920, Princeton.
86. O'Neill, *The Emperor Jones*, pp. 32, 35, 43, 46.

toward the native and the dome until both actors were in silhouette and Jones returned to his racial past.

Dark bodies set against the dome and forest received considerable praise from many reviewers. Heywood Broun found that Charles Gilpin as Jones "seems fairly painted into the scenic design,"[87] and Macgowan strongly praised the joint effort of Cook and Throckmorton in their handling of dome, lights, and space.[88] A few critics, however, while appreciating much in the production, complained of the amateurish disorganization which affected composition and movement. "The stage mechanics of his apparitions," according to *Outlook*, were less successful than "they might have been done on commercial Broadway."[89] Gilliam "wished the entrances, groupings, and gestures of the pantomimic figures might have been less confused and awkward."[90] Although the production obviously suffered from difficulties with organization and execution, a synthesis of the reviews supported by photographs substantiates that Cook used the small space imaginatively.

The Emperor Jones was not a full-length play; yet the playing time due to scene change delays was probably between ninety minutes and two hours.[91] Woollcott complained of "long, unventilated intermissions,"[92] a sentiment shared by Broun, who wrote that "the waits between . . . scenes are often several minutes in length. Each wait is a vulture which preys upon the attention. With the beginning of each new scene, contact must again be established."[93] Likewise, Gilliam longed for quicker scene shifts and a front curtain which "closed at the right moment without audible and repeated orders."[94] Throckmorton himself admitted to much disorganization. "On opening night," he wrote, "I had forgotten one scene entirely, and so we pulled everything off, leaving a bare stage and nothing but the blue sky dome."[95] Despite such problems, all the foregoing critics agreed with Woollcott that the production "weaves a most potent spell."[96] In fact, Macgowan asserted that if the shifting problems could be solved the pro-

87. Heywood Broun, "The Emperor Jones," New York *Tribune*, Nov. 4, 1920, in Cargill, *O'Neill*, p. 146.

88. Macgowan, "New Season," Jan. 1921, p. 6.

89. "Not as Others Are, But Still Worth While," *Outlook*, 126 (Dec. 22, 1922): 711.

90. Gilliam, *Quill*, p. 26.

91. Suggested by Castellun, "O'Neill's," p. 22.

92. Alexander Woollcott, "The New O'Neill Play," *New York Times*, Nov. 7, 1920, sec. 7, p. 1.

93. Broun, "Emperor," p. 145.

94. Gilliam, *Quill*, p. 26.

95. Unfortunately, Throckmorton does not identify the overlooked scene. Throckmorton, "Scenic," pp. 274–75.

96. Woollcott, *New York Times*, Nov. 7, 1920, p. 1.

duction "would be such a piece of pure terror and imagination as no American has ever put upon the stage."[97]

When Throckmorton and Cook redesigned and restaged the production for the move to Broadway, many of the earlier logistical problems were solved, and the play ran smoothly. At the Selwyn some critics found the larger performance space a boon to production, since Gilpin had more freedom to perform broadly.[98] Also, the hanging trees as evidenced in photographs were much taller and, at least in the witch doctor scene, not so striated. The Broadway production, however, was always less stirring than the Provincetown rendering because a traditional sky drop (obviously wrinkled in some photos) replaced the gleaming sky dome.

Given the focus of the play and the overpowering performance of Charles Gilpin as Jones, critics wrote little of the supporting actors. The witch doctor's dance was said to be "thrilling;"[99] Jasper Deeter as Smithers "acted well only at such times as he had to sneer."[100] Otherwise, critical remarks regarding acting were generalized or devoted to Gilpin's singular achievement.

The Emperor Jones required an actor with undeniable power and majestic presence. The actor had to have a voice of authority as well as the whine of petty lament. Furthermore, the role called for a black man. Cook did not have in his company an actor who could approach the part of the Pullman porter monarch. The director's decision to use a black actor in a leading dramatic role outside Harlem remains a landmark in American theater history. As a reviewer wrote at the time, "It is extremely doubtful whether Broadway would have afforded him the chance to play this part."[101] Just how the decision to cast Gilpin was reached remains vague. Susan Glaspell wrote that Cook insisted from the first that "the Emperor has got to be a black man. A blacked up white is not in the spirit of this production."[102] Burns Mantle wrote that a black actor was sought when "none of the white actors who were given a chance at it could read convincingly."[103] Likewise, Deeter much later told several interviewers that Charles Ellis, a Provincetown regular, who would later star in *Desire Under the Elms,* was the original choice but was found to be inappropri-

97. Macgowan, "New," Nov. 4, 1920, p. 14.
98. For example, "More Room Improves 'The Emperor Jones,'" *World*, Dec. 28, 1920, p. 11.
99. Gilliam, *Quill*, p. 26.
100. "Provincetown Bill Best They've Done for Long Time," *New York Clipper*, November 24, 1920, p. 19.
101. "Not as," *Outlook*, p. 711.
102. Glaspell, *Road*, p. 287.
103. Mantle, *Best Plays, 1920–21*, p. 299.

ate.[104] Predictably, Deeter went on to claim that he "was the one who insisted that a Negro play Jones."[105] However it may have happened, Cook or someone with his approval ventured into Harlem and came back to Greenwich Village with Charles Gilpin.

This temperamental, heavy-drinking, often depressed performer was approaching his forty-second birthday when he joined the Provincetown Players as their first salaried actor.[106] Incongruously surrounded by white actors in blackened faces and bodies (the contrast is sometimes amusing in close-up photographs), Gilpin "seemed to be made for the part."[107] He managed to harness much deep-seated anger and frustration in presenting, both realistically and expansively, a low-born Pullman porter who rose to magisterial heights of grandeur in "a performance of heroic stature,"[108] before plummeting to the excruciating "agony of the confused, half-crazed creature stumbling to his doom."[109] Both physically and vocally, Gilpin was mesmerizing.

Gilpin's stunning vocal support and power seemed effortless, and even at high volume "never once . . . sounded harsh on the ears of his auditors."[110] This ease and controlled strength was matched by his physical prowess. "Hence in moments of the severest strain he [was] never even on the edge of violence."[111] Yet, as Gilliam wrote, "the wailing in the forest left us limp from emotion."[112] Gilpin's believable suffering and rapid transformations through manifold moods and emotions helped to sustain the production even when the scene-shift delays threatened to retard the forward action.

Although laced with hyperbole, the following excerpt from a review by O. W. Firkins captures much of the excitement, surprise and enthusiasm which the audience experienced when Gilpin publicly unveiled his long-suppressed powers: "Mr. Gilpin is an actor of extraordinary alacrity, versatility, and resilience. We watched him lazily and gloatingly uncoil his sinuosities in the first scene with the stupefied recoil with which we might have watched the same process in the nodes of a boa-constrictor. . . . Mr. Gilpin can harmonize, can attemper, a transition; he imparts to an

104. Gelbs, *O'Neill*, p. 445; Sarlos, "Provincetown," vol. 2, p. 340.

105. Gelbs, *O'Neill*, p. 445; see also Sheaffer, *Artist*, p. 32; Sarlos, *Jig*, p. 134.

106. Gilpin received fifty dollars per week. Deutsch, *Provincetown*, p. 67.

107. Torrey Ford, "From Pullman Car Porter to Honor Guest of Drama League," New York *Tribune*, Mar. 13, 1921, sec. 7, p. 7.

108. Broun, "Emperor," p. 146.

109. Ford, "From," p. 7.

110. "Provincetown," *New York Clipper*, p. 19.

111. Ludwig Lewisohn, "Native Plays," *Nation* 112 (Feb. 2, 1921): 189.

112. Gilliam, *Quill*, p. 26.

angle the delicacy of a curve."[113] In the midst of all this control and intensity, however, there must have lurked a wry sense of humor, because in several production photographs one can discern Gilpin wearing a belt buckle bearing the initials "CSA," a relic from a military uniform of the Confederate States of America.

Just how much Cook had to do with Gilpin's performance is unknown, but it is likely that the actor was given considerable liberty to interpret as he saw fit. Cook was much less concerned with individual acting interpretation than with visual impact, large themes, and the spirit of communal creativity. Cook's dome and staging combined with Gilpin's stunning portrayal and Throckmorton's forests, however, provided O'Neill with a fitting production for his study in personal and racial anguish.

The Emperor Jones remains Cook's glorious moment in the sun. It was his last direction of an O'Neill play and a turning point for the Provincetown Players, who took several more productions to Broadway before dissolving in 1922. Although far less organized than Tyler with *Chris*, and with a tiny budget (even when compared to Williams' parsimonious contributions to the mounting of *Beyond the Horizon*), Cook managed not only to do justice to the spirit of *The Emperor Jones* but also to afford it an excitement and dignity not yet achieved in any previous production of an O'Neill play. The controlled turbulence inherent in the fragmenting world of Brutus Jones corresponded to the almost runaway theatrical mania of Cook and his followers, who conjured up a vision of midnight madness on the little Provincetown stage which not only captured the imagination of New York theatergoers but made modern American theater history.

As the Provincetown became a tributary for the commercial main stream, the little theater, wrote Hapgood, "grew to be what it had been a protest against."[114] Cook recognized this, as well as part of his own contribution to something much larger than himself. In a poem to his daughter he wrote:

> If you could see how by a hair's breadth
> I miss
> Being a transforming force
> In the theatre of our unrealized nation—[115]

113. O. W. Firkins, "Eugene O'Neill's Remarkable Play," *Weekly Review* 3 (Dec. 8, 1920): 568.

114. Hapgood, *Victorian*, p. 395.

115. George Cram Cook, *Greek Coins* (New York: George H. Doran, 1925), p. 111.

First Flames:

His sense of importance, his driving need to lead, to enthrall, most of all to inspire, had borne some rewards, but he left America in disappointment in 1922 bound for Greece and new hope in the residue of the classical world. Unfortunately, he died within two years. Edna Kenton later told his daughter that "the last thing [Cook] had done in America was to turn the blue light on the dome and stand looking at it in the empty theatre, alone."[116]

116. Nilla Cook, *Road India*, p. 48.

CHAPTER IV

Scattering Ashes:
Diff'rent and *Gold*

> Oh boy! There was nothing for me to do but a Pontius Pilate water cure![1]

Afternote the public notoriety of *Beyond the Horizon* and the fiery sensation of *The Emperor Jones* illuminated the star of O'Neill, the playwright coasted through two minor experiments. Although both were important to his development, neither generated much excitement in production with either the dramatist or his public. The first enjoyed a modicum of commercial and critical success; the second miscarried abominably. In both instances the direction was a significant factor in the outcome.

When *Diff'rent* was moved from Provincetown to the Times Square Theatre[2] for special matinees in February 1921, the Selwyn organization, in typical Broadway fashion, loudly trumpeted the play as a "daring study in feminine sex psychology" and a "daring study of a sex-starved woman."[3] Although these descriptions are not fallacious, they certainly refocus the central subject of the play which for O'Neill was an experiment in form: a study in contrasts and transformation (both physical and psychological).

The Provincetown Players were likewise undergoing change. *The Emperor Jones* was not their only production to leave the Playwrights'

---

1. O'Neill, commenting on *Gold* in a letter to Kenneth Macgowan, June 8, 1921, in Jackson R. Bryer, ed., *"The Theatre We Worked For:" The Letters of Eugene O'Neill to Kenneth Macgowan* (New Haven and London: Yale University Press, 1982), p. 26.

2. Advertisements and theatrical notes of the daily newspapers clearly locate the play in the Times Square Theatre under the Selwyn banner, but the production is often mistakenly reported as having begun its Broadway run at the Selwyn Theatre.

3. Advertisements, *New York Times*, Feb. 1, 1921, p. 14, and Feb. 5, 1921, p. 14.

Theatre in search of commercial glory. When *The Emperor Jones* began its special matinees on December 27, 1920, *Diff'rent* opened downtown to interested but unenthusiastic reviews.[4] Nonetheless, in little more than a month O'Neill's "sex-starved" Emma Crosby joined Brutus Jones uptown.

Like *The Emperor Jones*, *Diff'rent*, which was somewhat brief in its two acts, was preceded by a one-act curtain raiser, *What D'You Want* by Lawrence Vail. Together the two plays ran at approximately two hours, twenty minutes.[5] Once again O'Neill was granted the designs of Cleon Throckmorton, but his director was a moonlighting actor from the camp of Arthur Hopkins. Unluckily, Charles O'Brien Kennedy did not possess the creative powers of his mentor.

Nearly a decade older than O'Neill, Kennedy was an experienced utility actor whose arrival at Provincetown signaled a desire by many of the Provincetowners to install a more disciplined, professional approach to production. As Deutsch wrote, "The Provincetown was evolving from its early recreational purpose."[6] Kennedy had an appropriate background for serious and sensitive production, for he had worked as an assistant and actor with Arthur Hopkins and Robert Edmond Jones on several occasions at the Plymouth Theatre, most notably as a supporting actor in Tolstoy's *Redemption* (1918) and the reopening of Sem Benelli's *The Jest* (1919). It was also in these productions that Kennedy became associated with Edward J. Ballantine (an actor from the original cast of O'Neill's *Bound East for Cardiff*) and Thomas Mitchell (the first director of O'Neill's *The Moon of the Caribbees*). It was probably through Ballantine and Mitchell that both Kennedy and later Hopkins joined the work of the Provincetown and O'Neill. Unlike Jones and Hopkins, however, Kennedy was not an experimenter.[7]

Kennedy was, nevertheless, well-suited to O'Neill's personality in terms of cultural background and temperament, for the Irish-Catholic actor was quiet in speech, close-mouthed with the dramatist, somewhat austere and studied but gentle with people, and he had acted with John Barrymore, an actor who long held a poetic fascination for O'Neill. Because O'Neill, who shared the foregoing qualities, got along with Kennedy so well, he requested Kennedy's direction again for *The Hairy Ape* in 1922.[8] Fortunately for O'Neill and the production, Kennedy was unavailable.

4. The first reviews appeared Dec. 29, 1920.
5. Stephen Rathbun, "January Plays," *Sun*, Dec. 31, 1920, p. 5.
6. Deutsch, *Provincetown*, p. 54.
7. See Frank Leslie, "Letters from the Drama Mailbag," *New York Times*, Sept. 14, 1958, sec. 2, p. 5.
8. See "Charles Kennedy, Ex-Actor, 79, Dies," *New York Times*, Sept. 9, 1958, p. 35; Leslie, "Letters," p. 5.

A clue to Kennedy's inappropriateness for O'Neill's ironic, searching, tragic material may lie in his work as an actor. He seems to have been at his best in pleasant, gentle comedy like *Little Old New York*,[9] an adaptation of *Twelfth Night* in which Kennedy was appearing even as he was rehearsing *Diff'rent* (the latter presumably in the mornings).[10] Committed to a commercial run (evenings and regular matinees) of the Rida Johnson Young play at the Plymouth Theatre throughout the rehearsal period and run of *Diff'rent*, Kennedy's direction was complicated by split focus and restricted rehearsal and preparation time. This situation was not unlike the constraints placed on rehearsals of *Beyond the Horizon*, nearly the entire cast of which was performing in other full-time productions. Under similar limitations many important or unusual plays by the likes of Shaw and Ibsen often found their way to a stage that otherwise offered unfriendly reception, but few such productions were fully mounted or imaginatively staged. Although most critics said little or nothing about Kennedy's direction specifically, Towse found the directorial choices abominable.[11]

Kennedy approached *Diff'rent* as a realistic play which centered on psychological aberration and intense emotional development. He was not at all flamboyant in staging or interpretation, and his conservatism caused him to balk when O'Neill hinted that something more was intended for the production of this play. After one of the few rehearsals which he attended,[12] O'Neill suggested that when the word "diff'rent" appeared, it "should always be read in the same uninflected tone."[13] Naturally, such stylization would remove the audience from the emotional intensity and involvement, especially since the word is used so frequently. In the first seventeen speeches, for example, the word appears eleven times, and is spoken repeatedly thereafter throughout the play. In a single speech (an important confession near the end of act I), Caleb Williams utters "diff'rent" five times.[14] Kennedy demurred and preferred to interpret the lines as realistically and diversely as possible. It should be noted, however, that O'Neill's suggestion arose very late in the rehearsal period, probably too late to be incorporated effectively.

9. For a review which includes Kennedy see J. Ranken Towse, "The Play," *New York Evening Post*, Sept. 9, 1920, p. 9.

10. The Gelbs reported Kennedy as calling rehearsals for 10:00 a.m., Gelbs, *O'Neill*, p. 453.

11. Towse, "Play," Dec. 29, 1920, p. 9.

12. Sheaffer and the Gelbs report that O'Neill did not arrive for rehearsals until a few days before opening. Sheaffer, *Artist*, p. 42; Gelbs, *O'Neill*, p. 452.

13. Gelbs, *O'Neill*, p. 453.

14. Eugene O'Neill, *Diff'rent*, in *The Emperor Jones, Diff'rent, The Straw* (New York: Boni and Liveright, 1921), pp. 205–07, 235–36.

O'Neill's subtle departures from realism (inherent in the written play) extended much more deeply than a capricious or last-minute suggestion for a stage device. *Diff'rent* certainly had the trappings of realism, but—as in some of Strindberg's plays, notably *The Dance of Death*—the intense psychological struggle and inward exploration of the playwright carried the form to another stylistic plane. Likewise, *Diff'rent* treated personal compromise as a structural mechanism. Emma Crosby will not compromise her principles at all, and this fixation to be "diff'rent," this superhuman rigidity, is the instrument of her destruction in act II. Thus, O'Neill adorned his central character with a dehumanizing excess; yet the production, as evidenced by Mary Blair's performance, centered on emotional agitation. Whereas O'Neill tried to encapsulate and characterize, as he said, "the eternal, romantic idealist who is in all of us—the eternally defeated one,"[15] the production presented a small, emotional, brittle woman. Nevertheless, some aspects of the play suggested at first that O'Neill might be departing from his usual psychic anguish for a traditional, domestic tale. "We were almost misled at the opening of the first act," the *New York Clipper* reported. "When we discovered Caleb and Emma sitting on the couch, he holding her chastely in his arms. . . . it was all so sweet and tender that, for a moment, it occurred to us that here might be a play by Eugene O'Neill with a happy ending."[16] What followed of course was emotional exploration which reflected a tendency in O'Neill and the Provincetowners to "turn their stage into [as it was sometimes facetiously described] a Freudian clinic."[17]

Homer Woodbridge wrote that O'Neill's symbolism "often sacrifices the illusion of reality to the projection of an idea."[18] The idée fixe which drives act I of this play almost overwhelms the homespun, New England atmosphere, the local dialects, and rustic character relationships. It is surprising that few production reviews mention the incessant repetition of the word "diff'rent," while those who criticize the published play cannot avoid it. Perhaps Kennedy tried to suppress and disguise what Travis Bogard calls the "almost choric repetition"[19] by lack of stress and possibly by subtle cutting.

"Eugene O'Neill will not be dictated to in the matter of form," Towse wrote in his production review of *Diff'rent*.[20] Similarly, Lewisohn found it

15. O'Neill, in Deutsch, *Provincetown*, p. 73.

16. "Provincetowners Put on 'Diff'rent,' a Really Great Play," *New York Clipper*, Jan. 5, 1921, p. 19.

17. Rathbun, "January," p. 5.

18. Homer E. Woodbridge, "Beyond Melodrama," in Cargill, *O'Neill*, p. 310.

19. Bogard, *Contour*, p. 145.

20. J. Ranken Towse, "The Play," *New York Evening Post*, Dec. 29, 1920, p. 9.

not just psychologically, but "structurally . . . violent."[21] So it was that O'Neill experimented with a sudden time shift, an instantaneous thirty-year leap into the future from act I to act II. The characters were aged, the central character was garishly altered to "a painted lady with titian-dyed hair,"[22] a ridiculous parody of youth (another extreme character transformation so attractive to O'Neill), and the setting (although representing the same room), like its mistress, was given a tasteless costume to mask its age. Such radical time shifts would appear with mixed results in future O'Neill experiments such as *The Fountain, Marco Millions* and *Strange Interlude*.

After Emma's disguise was unsympathetically wrenched from her late in act II, she systematically denuded the room of its gauche "up-to-date"[23] accoutrements. Such obvious and pivotal symbolism, however, received no comment in the reviews, only verification that the event occurred. O'Neill describes this special moment in a half-page of directions. Emma mechanically removes curtains, pictures, cushions, rugs, and books, making a great pile on the floor. "She does all this without a trace of change in her expression—rapidly, but with no apparent effort."[24] This is a radical change from Emma's previous hysteria which reviewers frequently described in detail. The event probably lacked the power its image suggests in the imagination. The absence of reportage suggests that the actress may have been unable to shut down her passionate upheaval (thus there was no emotional shift at all), or perhaps the destruction was abbreviated to minor importance by the director. Woollcott also supplies a hint that this late event may have been upstaged by the "dull and conventional"[25] double suicide at the conclusion of the play.

The imagination which Throckmorton had demonstrated in capturing the visual essence of *The Emperor Jones* was not evident in *Diff'rent*. The smallness of the Playwrights' Theatre remained very obvious in the ordinary interior constructed for this New England drama of frustration. Only one full-stage photograph (from act II) survives (see illustration 3), along with a close-up from the same scene and one from act I.[26] Although much can be discerned about the space and general ground plan, the dynamics of the scenic transformation from act I to act II are very difficult to ascertain.

21. Ludwig Lewisohn, "Gold," *Nation* 112 (June 22, 1921): 902; this review of *Gold* includes a note on *Diff'rent*.

22. "Provincetowners," *New York Clipper*, Jan. 5, 1921, p. 19.

23. O'Neill, *Diff'rent*, p. 250.

24. O'Neill, *Diff'rent*, p. 284.

25. Alexander Woollcott, "A New O'Neill Play," *New York Times*, Dec. 29, 1920, p. 8.

26. Three photographs in Theatre Collection, MCNY.

The limitations of this setting may reflect the strain on the technical resources of the Provincetowners, who for the first time were attempting to mount and run two separate productions simultaneously. While realistic in detail, the setting had a rather flimsy appearance that undercut the solidity needed to convey age and tradition, which are stressed in the play.

Although O'Neill called for a small room (which Throckmorton had to provide due to space limitations), the playwright requested four windows on two walls.[27] Thus, the room could quite naturally be made to look open, sunny, and airy. Throckmorton, however, provided two windows along the upstage wall which also contained the front door up left, so that all natural light emanated from upstage (apparently using part of the dome for sky backing), giving a somewhat static appearance and dull lighting for the interior.

The already limited playing depth was further reduced by the fact that the upstage set wall ran parallel to the proscenium line and a porch area extended upstage beyond the front door. Furthermore, the very shallow room was complicated by a clutter of furniture which, though it lent an appropriate sense of period to the setting, left little room for movement. In fact, with a bulky table at center stage (requested by O'Neill),[28] Kennedy's only convenient movement pattern was circular, revolving about the obtrusive table. A narrow downstage strip just above the proscenium line, and anchored by chairs set in profile right and left, provided the only interesting alternative. The stage-right door was blocked by a sofa and was almost inaccessible. Business at the fireplace stage left was restricted, since it was partially masked by a chair down left. Although Kennedy and Throckmorton included much less furniture than is found in the published stage directions, the resultant space for act II was typified by congestion, and the dialogue of act II suggests that act I had even more furniture.

One close-up photograph suggests a probable method for the set transformation for act II. In the play O'Neill stipulates that not only are furnishings, curtains, and pictures changed, but even the brown wallpaper becomes "a cream color sprayed with pink flowers."[29] The flowered paper was present for act II, but in close-up the wall treatment is clearly wide strips of flowered cloth hung loosely against the flats. The drab walls of act I were apparently covered at intermission with the cloth. This method was certainly cheaper and more efficient than constructing two different sets, especially since offstage storage was so difficult at Provincetown.

27. O'Neill, *Diff'rent*, p. 203.
28. O'Neill, *Diff'rent*, p. 203.
29. O'Neill, *Diff'rent*, p. 241.

Although the performance space was cramped and crowded, Kennedy enjoyed moderate success with his actors even if most were very inexperienced. Kennedy's problems were complicated by *The Emperor Jones*, which used many Provincetown regulars including Charles Ellis, who appeared in both plays. Besides Ellis as Benny Rogers, Kennedy had a reasonably experienced performer in James Light as Caleb Williams, but the casting long shot was choosing twenty-five-year-old newcomer Mary Blair to play Emma Crosby.

Three weeks before opening, O'Neill conveyed some of his uneasiness to John Toohey, suggesting that the unseasoned downtown talent would probably appear weak indeed immediately following the tour de force of Charles Gilpin.[30] His apprehension was not unfounded, especially since Blair turned out to be a very fitful actress who depended on her own emotional tides. A small, frail, sometimes sickly performer, Blair had little experience but a wealth of feeling. When she was personally moved to passion, Blair acted rather well, but this early graduate of Carnegie Tech lacked the technique and control to shape effectively, modulate, and repeat her emotional work.[31] Nevertheless, she would later create two more of O'Neill's important characters: Mildred in *The Hairy Ape* and Ella in *All God's Chillun Got Wings*.

Despite inexperience, Blair and the rest of the cast managed to make their characters adequate for the dramatic moment, although some passages were "amateurishly played."[32] Kennedy's chief difficulty and outcome were suggested in passing by Woollcott, who wrote that "'Diff'rent' is no easy piece to play and it is creditably managed."[33] The play's troublesome, swiftly vacillating emotions and moods required a sophisticated approach to characterization on the part of Blair, Light, and Ellis who needed to carry the weight of such shifts. The actors seemed to find a way to cope with, rather than conquer, character difficulties.

Most critics described the performances in terms of adequacy, evenness, and regularity, at least within each act. Macgowan, for example, found the cast "pretty evenly effective,"[34] while Hornblow wrote that "Blair gave a seriously studied and in the main, consistent portrayal" and that Ellis "was to the life the degenerate, heartless, good-for-nothing"[35]

30. O'Neill letter to John Peter Toohey, Dec. 6, 1920, in Sheaffer, *Artist*, p. 42.

31. See "Mary Blair, Star of Stage for Years," *New York Times*, Sept. 19, 1947, p. 23; Edmund Wilson, *The Twenties*, ed. Leon Edel (New York: Farrar, Straus and Giroux, 1975), p. 147 (Wilson was married to Blair in the 1920s).

32. "Opening Nights," *Independent* 105 (Feb. 12, 1921): 153.

33. Woollcott, *New York Times*, Dec. 29, 1920, p. 8.

34. Kenneth Macgowan, "Diff'rent," in Cargill, *O'Neill*, p. 149.

35. Arthur Hornblow, "Mr. Hornblow Goes to the Play," *Theatre Magazine*, Apr. 1921, p. 261.

with no redeeming values. Macgowan enjoyed such two-dimensionality on this occasion and added that Ellis capably projected "spiritual degradation, cruelty, and lasciviousness by tone and glance."[36] Firkins, like Macgowan, found Blair credible and consistent within the first act but could not accept the monstrous transformation of act II (although consistent within the last act) as a logical or possible leap from act I.[37] Much of the difficulty, of course, lay with the play itself and the unexplained alteration of Emma. Nonetheless, Blair's diminutive, stiff, awkward physicalization and vivid, passionate upheaval were difficult for some reviewers like Stark Young to forget. "How pathetic it was," he wrote a year later, "and tense and withdrawn!"[38] Blair's performance, as erratic as it was, probably was as prominent as anything in sustaining the moderate run of *Diff'rent*.

Nearly all critics found Blair and the supporting cast seriously committed to their tasks. In this respect at least, Kennedy's discipline was effective. The reviewer for the *New York Clipper* adjudged performances as effective or not on the basis of commitment to what he found to be realistic, believable portrayal. After panning the stylization of *The Emperor Jones* he wrote of *Diff'rent*: "Never before have we seen a play so capably acted by the Provincetown Players."[39] So it was that under Kennedy's direction some Provincetown members began moving away from their playful, experimental amateurism and began to assimilate professional methods. One more sensational O'Neill experiment would be produced, however, by this group in *The Hairy Ape*.

There should be little doubt that Kennedy was instrumental in helping Blair and her fellow actors approach journeyman performances. O'Neill, in fact, is reported as crediting what success the play enjoyed to the "hard labor of Kennedy."[40] Yet this director was unremarkable as an interpreter of O'Neill, as an exponent of experimental production of the drama of a man who constantly "tried form after form, struggled valiantly with this bit of 'modern' psychology, played easily with that rag of old 'theatricalism.'"[41] A bit "old fashioned" in his approach to theatre,[42] Kennedy was not the experimenter O'Neill's plays required. Even so, it was already clear to Macgowan (and would eventually be to others) that the

36. Macgowan, "Diff'rent," p. 149.

37. O. W. Firkins, "Drama," *Weekly Review* 4 (Mar. 2, 1921): 208–09.

38. Young recalled Blair's Emma Crosby when reviewing *The Verge* at Provincetown. Stark Young, "Susan Glaspell's *The Verge*" in Montrose J. Moses and John Mason Brown, eds., *The American Theatre as Seen By Its Critics* (New York: W. W. Norton, 1934), p. 254.

39. "Provincetowners Put on 'Diff'rent,' a Really Great Play," *New York Clipper*, Jan. 5, 1921, p. 19.

40. Leslie, "Letters," p. 5.

41. Kenton, "Provincetown," *Greek*, p. 24.

42. Leslie, "Letters," p. 5.

future for O'Neill lay with obvious staging experiments akin to the theatrics of *The Emperor Jones* rather than those of *Diff'rent*.[43]

Gold

Less than five months after the opening of *Diff'rent*, O'Neill once again had a full-length play in rehearsal. This time, however, the unevenness and unsatisfactory elements of *Diff'rent* seemed minimal compared to the gross mismanagement, awkwardness, and insensitivity evident in the production of *Gold*, the least successful of all first-run O'Neill productions in New York.

Although *Gold*, labeled "a study in conscience" by a press release,[44] is admittedly one of the least gripping and most predictably structured of O'Neill's plays (and deservedly is rarely if ever revived), the playwright described several dynamic settings and images for it which in more capable hands could have been stunning in the theatre. Unfortunately, John D. Williams and Homer Saint-Gaudens accomplished even less with *Gold* than they had managed for *Beyond the Horizon*.

Williams' "half-hearted production"[45] was scheduled to open very late in the season on May 23, but it was rescheduled for May 30 and then postponed again until June 1, 1921.[46] Unlike his matinee trial with *Beyond the Horizon*, Williams mounted *Gold* as a full production intended for a regular run, but his decision to open in summer, the "transition period of the theatre season,"[47] indicates a lack of confidence on the part of the producer.[48] Despite Williams' desperate advertisements during the week after opening hailing the play as "Eugene O'Neill's greatest drama" and "the greatest dramatic event of the year!!,"[49] *Gold* closed quickly after only thirteen performances in ten days.[50]

Before he had finished his directing assignment with *Gold*, Saint-

43. Kenneth Macgowan, "The New Plays," New York *Globe*, Dec. 31, 1920, p. 7.

44. "The Week's New Plays," *New York Times*, May 29, 1921, sec. 6, p. 1.

45. Pierre Loving, "Eugene O'Neill," *Bookman* 53 (Aug. 1921): 516.

46. Advertisements, *New York Times*, May 18, 1921, p. 20; May 19, 1921, p. 10; *World*, June 1, 1921, p. 24; "Theatrical Notes," *New York Times*, May 26, 1921, p. 11.

47. Louis V. De Foe, "New O'Neill Play," *World*, June 2, 1921, p. 9.

48. Many of New York's theater practitioners and theatergoers habitually left the city for the summer; successful regular productions often closed for the summer months and reopened in the fall. George Tyler wrote O'Neill that Williams' plans for such a late opening in "almost the middle of summer" (at the time, May 23 was still scheduled) was ridiculous and a betrayal of management. Tyler letter to O'Neill, Apr. 27, 1921, Princeton.

49. Advertisements, *New York Times*, June 7, 1921, p. 20; June 5, 1921, sec. 6, p. 2.

50. Ten evening performances and three matinees. Newspaper advertisements through Saturday, June 11, 1921; Miller, *Eugene*, p. 53.

Gaudens, who reportedly did not have O'Neill's approval to direct,[51] had already decided to leave the theater and join the Carnegie Institute. *Gold* closed at the Frazee Theatre on June 11; by July 1 the forty-year-old director was working in Pittsburgh,[52] and no more productions were "staged under the direction of Homer Saint-Gaudens."[53]

It is likely, therefore, that the director's inability to control the leading actor Willard Mack's domineering personality, to interest the (at this time) perpetually inebriated John Williams, to procure better scenery than the ordinary designs of Joseph Physioc, or to prevent the horrified O'Neill from fleeing rehearsals, did not inspire Saint-Gaudens to commit all of his faculties to *Gold*. A saner job was awaiting him.

Williams' usual practice of gentle managerial control and minimal interference with creative personnel was in this production nonexistent. Just one year earlier Williams stated that "the manager must maintain his editorial prerogative, but the sensible manager is just like the sensible editor. He is there to listen or to read and to pass final judgment or to criticize, but the editor does not try to write all the stories; neither should the manager try to play all the parts."[54] When O'Neill and Agnes Boulton arrived for rehearsals sometime in May, however, they discovered that rehearsals were out of control, with Williams mysteriously absent and taking no evident part in production. Boulton apparently found the producer, whom she described as having "a strange desire for secrecy and aloofness,"[55] on a drinking spree, and he was incapable of, or unwilling to try, salvaging the ailing production.[56]

O'Neill completed this play early in 1920, but as with *Beyond the Horizon*, Williams held his option on the play until O'Neill again feared that a production would not materialize. It was reported that Williams was holding the play "in the expectation that Lionel Barrymore would act the leading role."[57] The eldest Barrymore, however, displayed no interest. O'Neill wrote Macgowan in July that "I had to wait so long for the production, and there were so many disagreeable incidents connected with that wait, that by the time rehearsal started I was 'fed up' and rather apathetic about its fate."[58] This defensive remark is not unusual in O'Neill, who sometimes quickly turned against a play which he once extolled. He pro-

51. Gelbs, *O'Neill*, pp. 470–71.

52. *National Cyclopedia*, vol. 48 (1965), p. 586; *Current Biography* (1941), p. 747; *Who's Who in America*, vol. 12 (1924–1925), p. 2797.

53. *Gold* program, Theatre Collection, MCNY.

54. Williams, in Mindil, "Behind," Feb. 15, 1920, p. 1.

55. Boulton, *Part*, p. 214.

56. O'Neill letter to Macgowan, June 8, 1921 in Bryer, *Letters*, pp. 25–26; Sheaffer, *Artist*, p. 56; Gelbs, *O'Neill*, p. 470.

57. "This Week's," *New York Times*, p. 1.

58. O'Neill letter to Macgowan, July 1, 1921, in Bryer, *Letters*, p. 26.

claimed *The First Man* and *Dynamo*, for example, as unworthy efforts soon after their failure.

With *Gold* most critics for the first time strongly attacked both production and play. "A talky, balky, tiresome and impossible play," quipped *Variety*.[59] Wondering why the play was produced at all, Lewisohn assumed "that it was due to Mr. O'Neill's reputation rather than to any commanding merit in the work itself."[60] Towse condemned the play even more harshly, claiming that "it came perilously close to the verge of utter fiasco. It was difficult to give full credit to the reputed authorship of a piece of melodrama so raw and imitative."[61] Because of bothersome repetitious material as elements of the story were related over and over, the play seemed "much too long for its subject matter. . . . And you have the feeling of having been cheated to the extent that your emotions have been played upon far beyond the worth and merit of the play."[62] In all fairness to the play, the first and fourth acts conjure up intriguing action and images, but the long periods of repetition and maudlin fussing which fall between make for tedious reading and in the theater fairly bored the audience.

Complaints to this effect were raised in several reviews[63] and in Macgowan's correspondence with O'Neill. "Yes, I think you are quite right about the middle part of 'Gold,'" O'Neill wrote in reply. "Certainly I would do it quite differently if I were writing it now."[64] In an earlier letter he acknowledged that the play needed "a highly imaginative artistic production that would hold the play up where I fell down. One glance at rehearsals showed me this was not to be hoped for."[65] Years later (1932) he admitted that the play was completely bungled and not worth revision.[66]

Although *Gold* was something new for O'Neill, he was in part reaching back in his own work and enlarging and domesticating a previous one-act experiment in insanity and the supernatural, *Where the Cross Is Made* (1918), a Provincetown production which was essentially act IV of *Gold* with a few changes.[67] Any time during his experimental period that

59. [Jack] Lait, "Gold," *Variety*, June 10, 1921, p. 15.

60. Lewisohn, "Gold," p. 902.

61. J. Ranken Towse, "The Play," *New York Evening Post*, June 2, 1921, p. 7.

62. "The Theatre," *Sun*, June 2, 1921, p. 14.

63. For example, "'Gold' O'Neil's [sic] New Play Interesting But Far from Writer's Best," *New York Clipper*, June 8, 1921, p. 19.

64. O'Neill letter to Macgowan, July 1, 1921 in Bryer, *Letters*, p. 26.

65. O'Neill letter to Macgowan, June 8, 1921, in Bryer, *Letters*, p. 26.

66. Eugene O'Neill, "Second Thoughts," in Cargill, *O'Neill*, p. 118.

67. Jordan Miller points out that *Gold* was actually written before *Where the Cross Is Made*, but *Gold* was not revised for production and copyrighted until after the one-act was performed successfully. Miller, *Eugene*, pp. 22, 53; see also Eugene O'Neill, *Where the Cross Is Made* in *Seven Plays of the Sea* (New York: Vintage, 1972), pp. 135–62.

O'Neill resurrected a previously successful experiment in subject matter, structure, or technique, (such as *Dynamo*), he usually failed.

While some reviewers recognized the source,[68] Towse did not. He shrewdly suspected *Gold* "of being an early experiment hastily retouched to supply a present demand."[69] The play desperately needed revision and cutting, but there is no evidence that O'Neill did any such work during the rehearsal period. After quickly abandoning rehearsals he returned to Provincetown to work on *The Fountain*,[70] a play which did not reach production until 1925.

Some of O'Neill's scenic demands for *Gold* were his most complex to date. He was perhaps at his most cinematic in this play. His "affinity for film techniques" were most evident in "the minute detail of O'Neill's stage directions, which only the camera could properly translate into visual terms."[71] In act I, for example, O'Neill described the coral island where shipwreck survivors have landed: "The island bakes. The intensity of the sun's rays is flung back skyward in a quivering mist of heat-waves which distorts the outlines of things, giving the visible world an intangible eerie quality, as if it were floating submerged in some colorless molten fluid."[72] Of course, only the suggestion of such effects was possible on the stage and probably could have been best approached through a selective New Stagecraft design and imaginative lighting. What was provided was at best four ordinary, possibly attractive, literal representations of the play's locations.

Responsible for these designs was Joseph Physioc, a fifty-six-year-old painter and set designer who grew up in Virginia and South Carolina before coming to New York and joining the staff of the Metropolitan Opera. Eventually, he designed realistic settings for professional theater, getting his first break with Richard Mansfield's production of Shaw's *Arms and the Man* (1894). He went on to design *The Climbers* (1901) for Clyde Fitch, *The Lion and the Mouse* (1905) with Richard Bennett, and the runaway Broadway hits *Peg o' My Heart* (1912) with Laurette Taylor and *Lightnin'* (1918) with Frank Bacon. Most of these settings are handsomely executed and all reflect a penchant for carefully rendered realistic detail, including an affinity for detailed ceilings.[73] In summarizing his career an obituary called him "a strong supporter of the traditional style of

68. For example, "Eugene O'Neill's 'Gold' Tells a Weird Tale," *New York Times*, June 2, 1921, p. 14.

69. Towse, "Play," June 2, 1921, p. 7.

70. Tornqvist, *Drama*, p. 261; O'Neill letter to Macgowan, June 8, 1921, in Bryer, *Letters*, pp. 25–26.

71. Frenz, *O'Neill*, p. 104.

72. Eugene O'Neill, *Gold* (New York: Boni and Liveright, 1920), p. 1.

73. See photographs in Stanley Applebaum, ed., *The New York Stage* (New York: Dover, 1976), pp. 14, 18, 28, 40.

stage design as opposed to symbolism or modernism."[74] Physioc, then, was a significant exponent of the old school of production led by Charles Frohman and David Belasco, not a suitable designer for the emotional expressions of O'Neill.

Unfortunately, there are no photographs to support the critical evaluations of the settings and performance space for this production. Physioc's designs were augmented by the decorations of Mrs. Sidney B. Harris, who also decorated *Beyond the Horizon*. The settings were mounted in the spacious Frazee Theatre, a sixteen-year-old standard house on Forty-second Street. This theater, while still called the Hackett, had accommodated Minnie Maddern Fiske's production of *Salvation Nell* (1908). Production photographs for the street exterior demonstrate that the stage area was generously endowed with height and depth, but had a small proscenium-opening width.[75]

Heywood Broun, who found the settings "cheap and tasteless,"[76] believed that less prosaic interpretations of the settings would have better served the fantastic excesses of Captain Bartlett's imagination which drives the action of the play. Similarly, Pollock and Macgowan found them poorly lit, "thoroughly old-fashioned and absurd."[77] Most others, however, thought the settings adequate, even ambitious or admirable in their literal renderings. The latter evaluations came from critics like Arthur Hornblow, who regularly responded favorably to conventional stagecraft, displaying skepticism for the new forms.

O'Neill's opening act called for "coral sand, blazing white under the full glare of the sun."[78] A small ridge of this sand was indicated as running from down left to up right, broken by "one stunted palm"[79] tree practical for climbing. With his literal interpretation, Physioc used "real sand,"[80] perhaps shaped with a ground cover, since Robert Benchley refers to dunes and wrote that "the members of the crew . . . are seen staggering about over the sand."[81] Also, because Hornblow describes the setting as a "desert sand spit,"[82] the elongated nature of the hummock in O'Neill's

74. "J. A. Physioc Dead; Stage Designer, 86," *New York Times*, Aug. 5, 1951, p. 73.

75. See illustration for act III of *Salvation Nell* (includes proscenium frame) in Archie Binns, *Mrs. Fiske and the American Theatre* (New York: Crown, 1955), following p. 278.

76. Heywood Broun, "'Gold' at Frazee Shows O'Neill Below His Best," *New York Tribune*, June 2, 1921, p. 6.

77. Arthur Pollock, "Another O'Neill Play," *Brooklyn Daily Eagle*, June 2, 1921, p. 6; Kenneth Macgowan, "The New Play," New York *Globe*, June 2, 1921, p. 16.

78. O'Neill, *Gold*, p. 1.

79. "'Gold' a Triumph for Willard Mack," *Journal of Commerce*, June 2, 1921, p. 7.

80. "Willard Mack Scores in New Drama," *New York Evening Journal*, June 2, 1921, p. 14.

81. Robert C. Benchley, "Drama," *Life* (New York) 77 (June 16, 1921): 876.

82. Arthur Hornblow, "Mr. Hornblow Goes to the Play," *Theatre Magazine*, Aug. 1921, p. 97.

description may have been followed. Given that Firkins described the "desolation and barren splendor"[83] of the opening setting, probably little other decoration was provided except a sky drop, which Broun complained was badly wrinkled.[84]

Unfortunately, the boat-shed interior of act II is described only as "cluttered up as such a place would naturally be,"[85] and the Bartlett house exterior with cliff is listed in reviews without specification. The land-locked ship's cabin with lookout post of act IV was only once described. The *New York Herald* reported that "the captain's eerie cabin-like garret"[86] was a ghostly environment, as the play required. Otherwise the appearance of the settings remains a mystery. This is especially disappointing since the exterior of act III as described in the play seems to be a miniature side-view version[87] of the green-shuttered, white-columned Mannon mansion of *Mourning Becomes Electra*, one of the most dynamic settings ever created for O'Neill. Saint-Gaudens' use of the space is addressed only in general terms such as finding the staging "curiously awkward at many moments."[88]

As in *Beyond the Horizon* the scene shifts were once again a major problem. Towse remarked that the play "suffered considerably . . . from the poor management which tested the patience of a friendly audience to the uttermost by intolerable delays in the raising of the curtain and between the acts."[89] De Foe complained that the production ran so late his review was hurriedly written.[90] The critic for *Variety*, however, was more specific. The production, which was scheduled to commence at 8:20 P.M.,[91] "staggered around until 11:45 and never got off the ground."[92] Thus, for well over three hours the audience sat through a play, the text of which can be read aloud, unrushed, in less than two.

When O'Neill saw a rehearsal, he was disgusted with Willard Mack and generally dissatisfied with the remaining cast despite the presence of

83. O. W. Firkins, "Drama," *Weekly Review* 4 (June 18, 1921): 584.

84. Broun, "Gold," p. 6.

85. "Willard," *New York Evening Journal*, p. 14.

86. "Eugene O'Neill's New Play, 'Gold,' Not Without Alloy," *New York Herald*, June 2, 1921, p. 9.

87. The descriptions and stage position of the house vary in the unpublished preproduction script and published text, but the essentials which suggest the Mannon house appear in both. Eugene O'Neill, *Gold*, typescript, Rare Book Collection, Library of Congress, 1920, act III, p. 1.

88. Macgowan, "New," June 2, 1921, p. 16.

89. Towse, "Play," June 2, 1921, p. 7.

90. De Foe, "New," June 2, 1921, p. 9.

91. Advertisements, *World*, June 1, 1921, p. 24; *New York Times*, June 1, 1921, p. 12.

92. [Jack] Lait, "Gold," *Variety*, June 10, 1921, p. 15.

his friend E. J. Ballantine in the supporting role of Nat Bartlett, the mad Captain's nearly possessed son. "Mack and the general stupid ensemble proved more than I could swallow," O'Neill wrote Macgowan.[93] Of course, the dramatist almost always had difficulty with actors. As he lamented just two months before rehearsals began when discussing artificiality in acting, "I can't help seeing with the relentless eyes of heredity, upbringing, and personal experience every little trick they pull as actors. . . . The actor stands revealed, triumphant in his egotistic childishness."[94] This could also stand as O'Neill's response to Willard Mack.

When the production opened, several critics found one or more minor performances (especially George Marion's Butler, the ship's cook who is murdered in act I) superior to the leading roles. The acting in general, however, was considered uninspired. For example, in the opening act on the waterless island the characters seemed "for men with parched and swollen throats and lips, strangely vigorous and eloquent."[95] *Variety* jibed that Katherine Grey as the Captain's longsuffering wife "grumbled and sighed, ditto, and died."[96] It appeared to some critics that a major difficulty with acting was "insufficient rehearsal,"[97] but it is more likely that Willard Mack's lack of discipline, coupled with Saint-Gaudens' inability to restrain him, led to erratic, haphazard performances on the part of Mack as well as many of those attempting to support him.

The forty-two-year-old Canadian-born Mack was a spirited actor, well experienced in melodrama and, as a director and playwright, accustomed to artistic control of his productions. The titles of some of his plays provide a clue to his personality: *Tiger Rose*, *Gang War*, *Men of Steel*, and *Honor Be Damned*. His deep voice (often punctuated with a "husky growl"),[98] forceful delivery, broad brow, and strong jaw, lent the performance a vibrancy it needed "to keep the audience alive during the middle of the play,"[99] as well as effectively characterize the tyrannical aspects of the role of Captain Bartlett.[100] Yet it was always the obvious which Mack emphasized. "The noisy sorrows of Mr. Mack could bludgeon you sometimes into yielding sympathy," James Whittaker explained.[101] Subtlety was not a staple ingredient of Mack's characterization. Nonetheless, his

93. O'Neill letter to Macgowan, June 8, 1921, in Bryer, *Letters*, p. 25.

94. O'Neill letter to Macgowan, March 18, 1921, in Bryer, *Letters*, p. 20.

95. Towse, "Play," June 2, 1921, p. 7.

96. [Jack] Lait, "Gold," *Variety*, June 10, 1921, p. 15.

97. Towse, "Play," June 2, 1921, p. 7.

98. "Eugene," *New York Herald*, June 2, 1921, p. 9.

99. Benchley, "Drama," June 16, 1921, p, 876.

100. S. Jay Kaufman, "Gold," *Dramatic Mirror* 83 (June 11, 1921): 1001.

101. James Whittaker, "All of O'Neil's [sic] Surplus Tragedy Utilized in Gold," New York *Daily News*, June 3, 1921, p. 15.

bravura and presence were said to represent "the sole figure that kept the audience from arising and walking out en masse."[102]

O'Neill claimed that Mack never learned his lines but kept going "by extemporizing every damn speech, and repeating the lines he liked best whenever he forgot."[103] Because the critic of the *New York Herald* complained of "Willard Mack's habit of repeating everything at least twice before he seems to feel the audience has caught up with him,"[104] it appears that the actor's substitutions and repetitions in rehearsals not only became ingrained but contributed to the production's excessive playing time. Sheaffer reports that Mack suddenly left rehearsals a few days before opening and did not return until dress rehearsal. George Marion, who would soon appear as the revamped Chris Christophersen in *Anna Christie*, was moved into the role of Captain Bartlett, but never played him.[105] This absence could account for the second delay, announced on May 26. Also, a curious note in a press release of May 29 relates that "as matters now fall, [Captain Bartlett] will be in the hands of Willard Mack."[106] Mack's unexplained holiday undoubtedly further undermined Saint-Gaudens' and the actors' confidence in the dismal presentation of *Gold*, the final production of O'Neill with either Saint-Gaudens or John D. Williams.

Without the help of Williams or O'Neill, plagued by a temperamental star, limited by unimaginative settings, and knowing that he would soon leave the theater, Saint-Gaudens could not, or at least did not, control this production with any degree of effectiveness. His use of the space is not reported, but his most obvious failures with this spiritless production were his inability to stimulate respectable acting performances, to manage reasonably efficient scene shifts, and to convince O'Neill to cut or revise the dull material which laced acts II and III. With the possible exception of *The First Man*, *Gold* was the worst first production of a full-length O'Neill play.

Since the triumph of *The Emperor Jones*, O'Neill had primarily been offering only minor experiments in domestic themes. It was as if he were scattering ashes half-heartedly from the fires of earlier dramatic ventures. The month of November, however, brought to New York two more O'Neill plays, one of which added greatly to the playwright's notoriety,

102. Lait, "Gold," p. 15.
103. O'Neill letter to Macgowan, June 8, 1921, in Bryer, *Letters*, p. 26.
104. "Eugene," *New York Herald*, June 2, 1921, p. 9.
105. Sheaffer, *Artist*, p. 56.
106. "The Week's," *New York Times*, p. 1.

thanks in no small way to the play's beautiful production. Although O'Neill claimed that the failure of *Gold* on stage did not bother him because "the thing was already such a failure in my own mind,"[107] he was at that moment comforted and hopeful because Arthur Hopkins had optioned *Anna Christie*.

107. O'Neill letter to Macgowan, July 1, 1921, in Bryer, *Letters*, p. 26.

CHAPTER V

Libation Bearers:
Anna Christie and *The Straw*

[O'Neill] was not interested in seeing the end product and rarely witnessed a public performance of his plays. But he nearly always attended rehearsals scrupulously, through the final dress rehearsal.[1]

O'Neill rarely attended rehearsals, and he generally avoided his first nights.[2]

Both *Anna Christie* and *The Straw*, which were in rehearsal at the same time, were important experiments in mood as well as engaging examinations of the plight of forlorn, sacrificing, desperate women. Although each play needed careful, sensitive direction to keep extensive pathos under control, the productions followed markedly different courses in preparation. The painstaking craftsmanship and perception of Arthur Hopkins and his production team contributed to the overwhelming critical and popular success of *Anna Christie*, while the serious but haphazard methods of George Tyler's production assisted the bitter failure which met *The Straw*. Nevertheless, O'Neill turned against both plays by eventually ignoring the existence of *The Straw* (his final venture with old-line commercial producers) and railing against *Anna Christie*, although the staging of the latter remains an important achievement in American directing and design.

The production of *Anna Christie* was another in a long line of collaborations between director-producer Arthur Hopkins and designer Robert Edmond Jones, which had begun in 1915 with *The Devil's Garden* by Edith Ellis and had peaked most recently with *Richard III* (1920) starring John Barrymore. While conducting rehearsals for *Anna Christie*, which opened on Wednesday, November 2, 1921, at the Vanderbilt The-

1. Gelbs, *O'Neill*, p. 325.
2. Sheaffer, *Playwright*, p. 395.

atre,[3] Hopkins and Jones opened Henri Bernstein's tragedy *The Claw* on October 17.[4] Director and designer had only fifteen days between openings.

Referring to Hopkins, Jones, and actress Pauline Lord, Brooks Atkinson wrote that the production of *Anna Christie* "represented the most perceptive talent in the New York theatre."[5] Certainly in the 1920s New York had no finer or busier director than Arthur Hopkins, who O'Neill reportedly said "brought more out of the play than even [I] had imagined was there."[6] Oliver Sayler, once a press agent to Hopkins, later described some of Hopkins' work at this time as "atmospheric and stylized romanticism" and "simplified and stylized realism."[7] Indeed, Hopkins had the ability to make the histrionic seem ordinary while subtly theatricalizing the naturalistic.

At forty-three, the former reporter and booking agent had nine years of Broadway direction (more than twenty-five productions) and had written several plays as well as a book on professional production entitled *How's Your Second Act?* The man whom critic George Jean Nathan lauded as representing "the finest ideals, the bravest ambitions and the most vigorous analytical and critical virtues to be found in the American dramatic theatre"[8] was a master of almost laissez-faire direction. He honestly and consciously attempted to *allow* the play, design, and acting to develop with minimal manipulation; he wanted to appear to do as little as possible while calmly guiding the actors and designers. "It is always my aim," he wrote, "to get a play completely prepared without anyone realizing just how it was done."[9] Naturally, such an approach was quite successful when Hopkins surrounded himself with very talented and experienced people, which during the 1920s he usually managed to do. *Anna Christie* was no exception.

In keeping with his policy of minimal dictatorial instruction, he endeavored to eliminate "all the nonessentials,"[10] adamantly insisting on simplicity in design and staging. "He has demonstrated," wrote Nathan,

3. Advertisement, *New York Times*, Nov. 2, 1921, p. 20; the first reviews appeared on Nov. 3. When *Anna Christie* opened, Hopkins was still running two other productions, *The Claw* at the Broadhurst and Zoe Akins' *Daddy's Gone A-Hunting* at his own Plymouth Theatre.

4. Advertisement, *New York Times*, Oct. 17, 1921, p. 18.

5. Brooks Atkinson and Albert Hirschfeld, *The Lively Years: 1920–1973* (New York: Association, 1973), p. 12.

6. Mantle, *Best Plays* (1921–22), p. 22.

7. Oliver M. Sayler, *Our American Theatre* (New York: Brentano's, 1923), p. 59.

8. George Jean Nathan, *The World in Falseface* (New York: Alfred A. Knopf, 1923), p. 103.

9. Arthur Hopkins, "Capturing the Audience," in Toby Cole and Helen Krich Chinoy, *Directors on Directing* (Indianapolis: Bobbs-Merrill, 1963), p. 207.

10. Hopkins, "Capturing," p. 210.

"that he places his trust entirely in a superlatively rigid simplicity of treatment . . . none of the excess baggage of the Broadway direction."[11] The setting designs and use of the performance space in *Anna Christie* reflected this simplicity which was typical of Hopkins when working with Jones before, during, and after this production.[12]

A "rotund, rosy, amiable little"[13] man, who allowed actors and designers abundant freedom, Hopkins nonetheless controlled rehearsals and made significant production decisions. The director managed his actors and production personnel with a soft manner and composure which had a calming effect on those who worked with him. As a director "he was," in the words of Percy Hammond, "foremost among the American apostles of repose."[14]

Only one review of the production of *Anna Christie* faulted the direction of the play.[15] Others who evaluated staging praised Hopkins' "complete understanding of [the play's] mood and feeling"[16] in his "most plausible, most effortless direction."[17] Pollock, who loved the play, rhapsodized that the scenes were "staged with a perfection commensurate with the worth of the play itself," and he went on to assert that "O'Neill has never been in better hands."[18] Hopkins reportedly gloried in the play's atmosphere,[19] using both "photographic methods"[20] and stylization to evoke a "pungent realism," modified by "something of the inner spirit"[21] which would have been missing from a strictly conventional, realistic approach so characteristic of the time.

When preparing *Anna Christie* for production, Hopkins used his well-developed "stage editorial skill,"[22] which was a boon to O'Neill, who

11. George Jean Nathan, foreword to Arthur Hopkins, *How's Your Second Act?* (New York: Alfred A. Knopf, 1918), p. 13.

12. See reviews, for example, of *The Jest* (1919) and *Hamlet* (1922). "After the Play," *New Republic*, May 10, 1919, p. 55; Stark Young, "'Hamlet' Reinterpreted," *New Republic*, Dec. 6, 1922 in Hewitt, *Theatre*, p. 348.

13. Nathan, *World*, p. 102.

14. Percy Hammond, *This Atom in the Audience* (New York: no publisher, 1940), p. 137. See also Arthur Hopkins, *Reference Point* (New York: Samuel French, 1948), p. 27.

15. Gilbert Seldes, "The Theatre," *Dial* 71 (Dec. 1921): 725.

16. Louis V. De Foe, "Two Plays," *World*, Nov. 6, 1921, p. M-2.

17. Kenneth Macgowan, "Year's End," *Theatre Arts Magazine* 6 (Jan. 1922): 6.

18. Arthur Pollock, "Anna Christie," *Brooklyn Daily Eagle*, Nov. 3, 1921, p. 6.

19. "Drab Life of the Sea in O'Neill's 'Anna Christie,'" *New York Herald*, Nov. 3, 1921, p. 15.

20. Percy Hammond, "'Anna Christie' by the Acrid Mr. O'Neill, Is Presented at the Vanderbilt," *New York Tribune*, Nov. 3, 1921, p. 10.

21. Macgowan, "Year's," Jan. 1922, p. 6.

22. Nathan, *World*, p. 104; Nathan in *How's*, p. 8; for an account of Hopkins' editing of Elmer Rice's *On Trial* see Mantle, *Best Plays (1909–1919)*, p. 203.

did not struggle with Hopkins over the Christophersen material as he had with George Tyler. After Hopkins optioned *Anna Christie,* for example, he informed O'Neill that he "thought the play was a half-hour too long." According to Hopkins, O'Neill trusted the director and "asked me to make the cuts."[23] Hopkins often warned, however, that a director should seriously hesitate before suggesting revisions to a playwright's work which at first reading seemed authentic.[24] Apparently his main concern with *Anna Christie* was length, although the play remained longer than usual Broadway drama. If Hopkins' account is accurate, O'Neill probably agreed with his close friend Nathan that this director centered "his attention first and last upon the manuscript of the play"[25] and serving the playwright, not upon scoring a commercial success.

During the preparation of *Anna Christie,* Hopkins and O'Neill got along famously, respecting one another's talents, tastes, and achievements. Perhaps of more importance to O'Neill was the fact that both men were quiet, often working or relaxing for long periods of time while communicating little or nothing with the spoken word. Precisely how actively, however, Hopkins and O'Neill worked together during preproduction and rehearsal remains arguable. Just as O'Neill's biographers disagree in reporting the playwright's usual involvement with the rehearsal process, so the first-hand accounts offer contradictory information regarding O'Neill's role in production preparation. Whereas O'Neill told Lawrence Langner in the late 1920s that he was "very much on the job" for *Anna Christie,*[26] and although O'Neill moved his family from Provincetown to New York during the rehearsal period of both *Anna Christie* and *The Straw,* Hopkins said that "Gene saw the play for the first time at the final dress rehearsal and was pleased."[27] O'Neill may have been pleased until he read the reviews—which were very positive but, from the playwright's point of view, for the wrong reasons.

Hopkins' memoirs which describe his rehearsal methods at the time of *Anna Christie* relate that his blocking rehearsals were designed to give the actors freedom to move as they felt motivated, virtually to block themselves, thereby solving much of the movement and business through spontaneous discoveries. Hopkins gently coached and suggested alternatives and possibilities, but he usually encouraged minimal movement and

23. Arthur Hopkins, *To a Lonely Boy* (Garden City, New York: Doubleday, Doran, 1937), p. 179.

24. Arthur Hopkins, "Producer and Play," in Herschel L. Bricker, ed., *Our Theatre Today* (New York: Samuel French, 1936), p. 180.

25. Nathan in *How's,* p. 11. See also Hopkins, *Lonely,* pp. 220–21.

26. O'Neill letter to Lawrence Langner, n.d., in Langner, "Eugene," p. 89.

27. Hopkins, *Lonely,* p. 179.

stressed that "emotion or destination" were the only legitimate motivations for stage movement.[28] Working from a posture of suggestion rather than instruction, Hopkins usually succeeded with such a *dégagé* system by casting experienced actors like Pauline Lord (Anna) and George Marion (Chris) who could work alone and respond to his patient personality. Using emotional performers like Lord also required Hopkins to work slowly and mete out criticism gently, an approach he preferred in any event.

About one year before the October rehearsals of *Anna Christie*, O'Neill was very enthusiastic as he completed a severe revision of *Chris Christophersen* and retitled it *The Ole Davil*.[29] He resubmitted his play in November to Tyler, who was not interested in a second solo attempt with this material. By the time Hopkins received the play in early summer after more changes, it had its final title, which signaled a significant shift in focus away from Chris to his daughter, Anna Christopherson.[30] The revision not only refocused the material but significantly altered the scenic requirements. O'Neill eliminated the barge wreck and extracted all three steamer settings which scenically had cluttered *Chris*.

Centering on a sympathetically presented fallen woman, this play would later be called by O'Neill his "most conventional" work, "although its subject matter was damned unconventional in our theatre of 1921."[31] Of course, the fallen woman was a very old device used extensively in much melodrama and realism long before O'Neill. It was in his manner of presentation, however, that O'Neill was experimenting. The playwright not only gave rugged language to Anna and the waterfront characters but also created explicit situations and revelations, especially in acts I and III.

Not surprisingly, this play attracted many curious sensation seekers who came to be shocked or titillated by language and situation, just as they flocked to the sex farce *The Demi-Virgin* by Avery Hopwood at the same time. Gilbert Seldes, for example, who saw the second performance of *Anna Christie*, exclaimed, "Destroy the audience!" He lamented that "every time Anna Christie spoke the vicious racy ugly slang of her past, every word of which should have fallen like sleet upon our stricken hearts,

28. Hopkins, *Reference*, pp. 14, 41, 53, 55; Hopkins, *How's*, pp. 28, 32.

29. *The Ole Davil* was completed in the fall of 1920 and received by the Library of Congress on Nov. 29. Eugene O'Neill, *The Ole Davil*, typescript, Rare Book Collection, Library of Congress, 1920; Tornqvist, *Drama*, p. 260; Jordan Y. Miller, *Eugene O'Neill and the American Critic* (Hamden, Conn.: Shoestring, 1973), p. 22.

30. After conferring with the American-Scandanavian Foundation O'Neill discovered after *Chris Christophersen* was written that the correct spelling was "Christopherson." O'Neill letter to Tyler, July 26, 1919, Princeton.

31. O'Neill letter to Theresa Helburn and Lawrence Langner, July 29, 1941, in Virginia Floyd, *Eugene O'Neill at Work: Newly Released Ideas for Plays* (New York: Frederick Ungar, 1981), p. 28.

the audience of which I was a part gathered itself with refreshment and laughed."[32] Seldes' experience was not an aberration. Percy Hammond, who reviewed opening night but returned for four subsequent performances, complained that although Hopkins' actors delivered the material very seriously, each audience laughed frequently at the harsh language.[33] This situation became an ongoing problem in the 1920s for several of O'Neill's directors who attempted to address rough language and sensitive social situations without catering to sensation-seeking audiences which so often gravitated to O'Neill's plays. The difficulty was especially evident in *The Hairy Ape*, *All God's Chillun Got Wings*, and *Desire Under the Elms*.

More troublesome to O'Neill at the time, however, was a subtle experiment which failed in his own estimation but which, like the language and dramatic situations, may have contributed to the commercial success of the play. Many months before production O'Neill sent a copy of *Anna Christie* to George Jean Nathan. The critic's major criticism of the play was its apparent happy ending. O'Neill took umbrage at this and insisted that the audience was meant to infer that the future for Anna and Mat was at best uncertain and probably arduous. In O'Neill's view the audience should sense that the play does not have a storybook finale.[34]

O'Neill did not act on Nathan's warning, and numerous critics of the production referred to the happy ending; several, such as Towse, De Foe, and Woollcott, objected to it as a contrivance.[35] The *Sun* wondered if O'Neill was "gradually degenerating into a Broadway playwright."[36] O'Neill privately attacked everyone's obtuseness ("either I am crazy, or they all are"),[37] but with more restraint explained in print what the audience was meant to discern: "In the last few minutes . . . I tried to show that dramatic gathering of new forces out of the old. I wanted to have the audience leave with a deep feeling . . . of a problem solved for the moment but by the very nature of its solution involving new problems."[38] As published, the inconclusive ending which O'Neill sought is subtly implied, but not strongly enough to negate the obvious optimism of Anna and

32. Seldes, "Theatre," Dec. 1921, p. 724.

33. Percy Hammond, *But—Is It Art* (Garden City, N.Y.: Doubleday, Page, 1927), pp. 66–67.

34. O'Neill letter to Nathan, Feb. 1, 1921 in Sheaffer, *Artist*, p. 67, and Gelbs, *O'Neill*, p. 436.

35. J. Ranken Towse, "The Play," *New York Evening Post*, Nov. 3, 1921, p. 9; De Foe, "Two," Nov. 6, 1921, p. M-2; Alexander Woollcott, "The New O'Neill Play," *New York Times*, Nov. 3, 1921, p. 22.

36. "'Anna Christie' Has Its Premiere at Vanderbilt," *New York Sun*, Nov. 3, 1921, p. 20.

37. O'Neill to Oliver Sayler in Gelbs, *O'Neill*, p. 480.

38. Eugene O'Neill, "The Mail Bag," *New York Times*, Dec. 18, 1921, sec. 6, p. 1. Letter dated Dec. 12, 1921.

Mat.[39] In production, however, Hopkins intended or allowed the final cheerful mood to dominate. Nevertheless, Woollcott's assessment of the production's conclusion suggests at least part of what O'Neill was seeking: "There is probably no end of misery for everybody [the characters] hidden just ahead in the enfolding mists of the sea. It is a happy ending with the author's fingers crossed."[40] Although in 1932 O'Neill tried to blame Hopkins for directing it as a "conventional happy ending,"[41] neither playwright nor director had stressed a problematic future for Anna. "I must have failed in this attempt" was O'Neill's public admission in 1921.[42]

Once again O'Neill, who seemed to be slowly edging toward experimental length, provided a production which lay outside standard duration, but few complaints arose in the criticism of production. Although the play text was reduced by a half-hour according to Hopkins' wishes, the production ran from 8:30 until approximately 11:30 P.M.[43] Audiences found the production engrossing enough to endure three hours easily. Unlike *Beyond the Horizon* and *Gold*, the scene shifts for *Anna Christie* did not contribute unnecessarily to the three-hour length of the performance.

The play's three settings, which received considerable attention in reviews, were the first designs for nine O'Neill productions which Jones created between 1921 and 1933.[44] This New Stagecraft designer, who had studied in Europe with Max Reinhardt, had been a marvel in the professional theatre since his rendering of *The Man Who Married a Dumb Wife*, which opened Harley Granville-Barker's remarkable New York season of 1915. Characteristically, the designs of Jones featured simplicity in line, liberal usage of open space as an important compositional element, strong contrasts in darks and lights, and occasional splashes of vibrant color which sometimes seemed to make his settings shimmer. To Jones lighting was always a compositional and atmospheric element, never just illumination.

Because Hopkins' own Plymouth Theatre was occupied with *Daddy's Gone A-Hunting*, the director, who produced all of the plays he directed at this time, provided Jones with the Vanderbilt Theatre, a three-year-old

39. Eugene O'Neill, *Anna Christie*, in *The Hairy Ape, Anna Christie, The First Man* (New York: Boni and Liveright, 1922), pp. 210–11.

40. Alexander Woollcott, "Second Thoughts on First Nights," *New York Times*, Nov. 13, 1921, sec. 6, p. 1.

41. O'Neill letter to Lawrence Langner, May 8, 1932, in Floyd, *Work*, p. 27.

42. O'Neill, "Mail," p. 1.

43. Advertisement, *New York Times*, Nov. 2, 1921, p. 20; Hammond, "Anna," Nov. 3, 1921, p. 10.

44. Jones also designed *The Iceman Cometh* when O'Neill emerged briefly from seclusion in 1946.

house which seated fewer than eight hundred.[45] Although small by Broadway standards, the Vanderbilt's stage was large enough to accommodate musicals. The record-breaking *Irene*, for example, ran there for almost two years just before the tenure of *Anna Christie*. Therefore, Jones was probably not unusually restricted in his use of space, although the production photographs and reviews suggest that the stage may have had quite limited depth. Photographs of *Anna Christie* and *Irene* reveal generous stage width but shallow settings.

When writing of the New Stagecraft, Walter Prichard Eaton insisted that such designs were at their best when they simplified as well as intensified the environment.[46] Such were the sentiments of Jones and Hopkins. Railing against naturalistic scenery, Hopkins asked, "Must we have intricate woodturning and goulash painting? If so, we have no right in the theatre. We have no imagination."[47] Although Hopkins planned and discussed the ideas for the play's environment, and noted the director's importance to the designer's task, he believed that "in execution the designer must have a free hand," because the imaginative "designer can, and usually does, surpass the director's conception by heightening the intent."[48] Thus, Hopkins encouraged Jones to provide believable, recognizable environments for *Anna Christie* but to transcend freely the play's apparent realism and "emphasize the unreality of the whole attempt"[49] through simplicity and economy.

Jones wrote that "a stage setting is not a background; it is an environment. Players act in a setting, not against it."[50] Hence, he tried to surround the performers physically with a keynote to the play's mood, to evoke "the spiritual ambience in which a play was to be immersed."[51] In a realistic or even "naturalistic" play, as O'Neill once labeled *Anna Christie*,[52] Jones "suggested mood by understatement and revealed the essence"[53] of the environment. With *Anna Christie* Jones' "battered, moody settings"[54] provided a strong semblance of reality stripped of some

45. Henderson, *City*, p. 278.
46. Walter Prichard Eaton, "The Economics of Experiment," *Shadowland*, Jan. 1923, pp. 26–27.
47. Hopkins, "Capturing," p. 213.
48. Hopkins, *Reference*, p. 125.
49. Mordecai Gorelik, *New Theatres for Old* (New York: E. P. Dutton, 1962), p. 179.
50. Robert Edmond Jones, *The Dramatic Imagination* (New York: Theatre Arts Books, 1941), pp. 23–24.
51. Harold Clurman, *On Directing* (New York: Macmillan, 1972), p. 53.
52. O'Neill, "Mail," p. 1.
53. Donald Oenslager, in Ralph Pendleton, ed., *The Theatre of Robert Edmond Jones* (Middletown, Conn.: Wesleyan University Press, 1958), p. 131.
54. Atkinson, *Lively*, p. 12.

details, relieved of distractions, but magnified in essentials. As a consequence, in Jones' renderings "the ugliest scenes in real life throbbed with
beauty,"[55] and critics left the theater talking of "great bales of atmosphere
and the salt of the seaspray"[56] which inundated the production.

O'Neill told Burns Mantle that "Jones' settings were strikingly true
to the atmosphere"[57] which he sought to capture in the written play. The
most completely preserved of these environments is Johnny-the-Priest's
waterfront saloon of the opening act. This long, somewhat shallow setting, more than thirty feet wide at the proscenium line,[58] represented a
divided barroom, with the male-only stand-up bar stage right countered
stage left by the back room with its "family entrance." The upstage wall,
which ran parallel to the proscenium line, served both rooms, each of
which was entered by an outside door on the upstage wall. The side walls
were raked, and a third thick wall with doorway which separated the
rooms was perpendicular, or nearly so, to the curtain line.

Jones made numerous changes in the scene as described by O'Neill.
He moved the long, straight bar from the upstage wall to the stage-right
wall and changed the bar to a wraparound design with a metal footrest. By
adding gritty windows to the back room's stage-left wall and up right
center as backing for the front door, he could take advantage of the late-
afternoon autumnal light to enhance most of the emotional action which
transpired in this room. Woollcott, for example, in April 1922 still recalled the "saloon . . . through whose grimy windows the light filtered on
the gaudy hair and cheerless face of Anna Christie."[59] Jones also simplified the rooms by eliminating large mirrors behind the bar as well as two
tables and numerous chairs (O'Neill called for twenty, Jones provided
five), leaving only two tables for the scene between Anna and Marthy
Owen.

Described by Francis Hackett as "a gray-lighted, somber barrel-
house,"[60] the saloon obviously displayed grime and wear; yet the walls
were strangely devoid of decorations or objects, appearing just as dark,
dirty, unpleasant walls. Nevertheless, Jones included a few naturalistic

55. John Mason Brown, *Dramatis Personae* (New York: Viking, 1963), p. 403.

56. Woollcott, "New," Nov. 3, 1921, p. 22.

57. Mantle, *Best Plays* (1921–22), p. 22.

58. As earlier for the Provincetown Playhouse, approximate scale measurements were
made for this setting based on a photograph which includes Pauline Lord (5'2") standing at the
bar close to the proscenium line. Photograph, Theatre Collection, MCNY. There are ten
different photographs at MCNY and Yale, but only one photograph (from act I) is a complete stage
shot.

59. Alexander Woollcott, "Second Thoughts on First Nights," *New York Times*, Apr. 16,
1922, sec. 6, p. 1.

60. Francis Hackett, "Anna Christie," *New Republic*, Nov. 30, 1921, in Cargill, *O'Neill*,
p. 152.

touches such as "flecked mosquito netting wrappers on the chandelier" hanging above the back room. As James Whittaker noted, "There never burned a barroom chandelier without them."[61] Despite such detail and murkiness, however, John Mason Brown insisted that this setting was "lustrous," that it captured "a luminosity . . . which made spectators at once aware that reality had been lifted into theatre, and theatre into art."[62] Responding to Brown's commendation, Jones wrote typically that "it is the occasion and not the setting which should be lustrous."[63] The choice of the critics to dwell on describing this barroom scene and its inhabitants, just as those in Philadelphia had done with *Chris*, was probably due in no small part to nostalgia for the bygone days preceding the much-loathed Prohibition years.

The occasion was marked by Hopkins's use of this setting, which featured interesting simultaneous staging. Although the principal action of the play shifted from room to room, the barroom space maintained its activity (usually secondary focus) stage right while the backroom (stage left) featured the important conversations of Chris with Marthy, Marthy with Anna, and finally Anna with Chris.[64]

The barge interior of acts III and IV can be viewed only in close-ups which provide some detail. A limited sense of the whole effect, however, which apparently was one of mean, constricted space, can be gleaned from photographs and reviews. Only two critics referred in passing to the "little cabin."[65] O'Neill called for "a narrow, low-ceilinged compartment" with light-brown walls and four "small square windows," two doors, and a few sticks of furniture.[66] Except for a gaudy pattern in the curtains, which contradicted O'Neill's directions, the photographs reinforce the play text by revealing crude wooden walls built or painted in vertical stripes, cheap table and chairs, small windows mounted rather high on the wall, and a wooden door to the main deck, which was elevated so that one stepped down into the living compartment.

It was in this cabin that Hopkins staged dynamically the fight of Chris and Mat struggling over possession of Anna. Presented "so that it resembled the conflict of two dogs fighting over a bone,"[67] the scene

61. James Whittaker, "O'Neill Has First Concrete Heroine," New York *Daily News*, Nov. 13, 1921, p. 21.

62. Brown, *Dramatis*, p. 403.

63. Jones, *Dramatic*, p. 121.

64. Whittaker, "O'Neill," Nov. 13, 1921, p. 21; Macgowan, "Year's," Jan. 1922, pp. 5–6; "Drab," Nov. 3, 1921, p. 15.

65. Hackett, "Anna," p. 154; "'Anna Christie' New Triumph for O'Neill," *New York Evening Journal*, Nov. 3, 1922, p. 18.

66. O'Neill, *Anna Christie*, p. 155.

67. Hammond, *But*, p. 66.

excited critics and audiences with an emotional and physical fight which culminated in the takeover by Anna, who "shove[d] both wrangling men from her in the little cabin and scream[ed] out her own story of what she really [was]."[68] The effect of the scene on the audience was both exhilarating and draining.

The most intriguing yet difficult to reconstruct of the three settings is the barge exterior in the night fog of act II. Photographs reveal only the actors' oilskin costumes and surrounding darkness. Nothing can be discerned about set size and shape or the use of fog. What Jones provided was described as "that part of a barge which is set back like an alcove with a long bench in it."[69] Jones modeled his design from life, for he made a special trip to Provincetown to sketch a wrecked barge washed up near O'Neill's beach house.[70]

O'Neill called for artificial light in this act from a lantern outside the cabin and from "misty windows glowing wanly" inside.[71] Hackett mentions "one solitary lamp glimmering around [the actors] through the fog,"[72] thus enhancing the mysterious evening of Mat Burke's arrival—a gift from the sea. Jones, who loved the opportunity to experiment with such effects, told Sayler that he chose light "not only to bring out elements of 'character' by a slightly unfamiliar color and value just below the threshold of conscious appreciation, but also to make the players swim in . . . the ideal poetic atmosphere."[73] Castellun recalled that Jones had "hidden the coal barge and its characters in a fog so beautifully mystifying that a breathless audience sat through one practically dark act without even coughing once."[74] According to the wry Robert Benchley, however, the very dim illumination of act II, which often did not clearly light the actors, caused him "to accept not only love at first sight but love at practically no sight at all."[75] Nevertheless, reviewers more sensitive to New Stagecraft methods, such as Macgowan, found not only "inspired [but] inspiring"[76] the selective illumination which was characteristic of Jones' work.

It was, however, the fog which lent this scene its special qualities. Described as "impressionistic" when compared to the other settings,[77] the

68. Hackett, "Anna," p. 154.

69. Hackett, "Anna," p. 153.

70. Gelbs, *O'Neill*, p. 476.

71. O'Neill, *Anna Christie*, p. 131.

72. Hackett, "Anna," p. 153.

73. Sayler, *Our*, p. 158.

74. Maida Castellun, "Eugene O'Neill's 'Anna Christie' Is Thrilling Drama, Perfectly Acted with a Bad Ending," *New York Call*, Nov. 4, 1921, p. 4.

75. Robert C. Benchley, "Drama," *Life* (New York), Nov. 24, 1921, p. 18.

76. Macgowan, "Year's," Jan. 1922, p. 6.

77. Whittaker, "O'Neill," Nov. 13, 1921, p. 21.

second act's "dense fog"[78] remained throughout the action and provided an almost magical atmosphere for many viewers. Whittaker wrote that "the unavoidable effect of [Jones'] idealized fog is that the people who move about in it begin to lose some of their reality."[79] Although this was not meant to be complimentary, it captures precisely the atmospheric effect which Hopkins and Jones were seeking.

The playwright was pleased, not only with the settings but also with Hopkins' casting and the actors' renderings of difficult characters whom O'Neill described as "a bit tragically humorous in their vacillating weakness."[80] He refers here to the three main roles of Anna, Chris, and Mat played by Pauline Lord, George Marion, and Frank Shannon. Most reviewers were ecstatic or at least pleased with the acting, which some found to be enriched by O'Neill's most effective and believable dialogue to date. Although a few critics took exception to some of the performances,[81] the audiences were convinced, often overwhelmed by the theatrical experience. "No other players this year, except Lionel Barrymore," De Foe reported, "have stampeded an audience to such unrestrained enthusiasm as these three did last Wednesday night."[82] The power and emotional fervor of these three actors controlled the audience as the trio held the stage alone in the drab barge interior of the final two acts of the play.

The part of Chris Christopherson, still a major role, but no longer central as in *Chris*, represented sixty-one-year-old Marion's second venture with O'Neill within five months, but yielded much happier results than did the ill-fated *Gold*. Reviews suggest that Marion was very consistent with his Swedish dialect and long-suffering anxiety, but that he occasionally bordered on the tedious. This problem, however, is evident in the written play and is not just an indication of the actor's performance. His broad gestures and expansive movement, which grew out of his extensive dance and musical background, provided Marion with the means to create something of a dichotomy on the stage: a "touchingly amusing and [physically] graceful,"[83] chubby old man whose emotional immaturity rendered him nonetheless awkward.

Pauline Lord's appearance, manner, and methods were not unlike those of emotional, fragile Mary Blair of *Diff'rent* (see illustration 4). With Lord, however, the results were much more consistent and finely tuned. Unlike the previously discussed actors, Lord was a regular from the

78. Benchley, "Drama," Nov. 24, 1921, p. 18.

79. Whittaker, "O'Neill," Nov. 13, 1921, p. 21.

80. O'Neill, "Mail Bag," p. 1; Mantle, *Best Plays (1921–22)*, p. 22.

81. See especially Jolo, "Anna Christie," *Variety*, Nov. 11, 1921, p. 17.

82. De Foe is referring to another Hopkins production, *The Claw*. De Foe, "Two," Nov. 6, 1921, p. M-2

83. Hopkins, *Lonely*, p. 180.

Hopkins stable who had been growing steadily in public stature since 1914. At thirty-one the captivating, diminutive actress had already been seen in serious and emotional roles in *On Trial, The Deluge, Night Lodging* [*Lower Depths*], and *Samson and Delilah.*

Hopkins said that immediately after reading *Anna Christie* he called Lord and informed her that "I've got your play."[84] Anna was virtually perfect for this actress, who, though not capable of a broad range of roles, had no superior on the American stage in the 1920s when playing an emotional, suffering, frightened, suppressing, and concealing character. Sensitive, intuitive, and "intensely subjective"[85] in preparation, Lord, according to Hopkins, "doesn't know where or how or when she gets what she does. . . . Her reading of a part has the absolute sureness of a hypnotized person."[86] Such a performer was ideal as the embodiment of the "badgered and inarticulate desperation"[87] which plagues O'Neill's Anna, and an excellent exponent of Hopkins' methods, which encouraged the actress to explore the emotional limits of the character with minimal instruction from the director.

Robert Parker felt that Lord's inarticulate portrayal actually heightened Anna's eloquence by exploiting suppression and the limitations of character and "by the suggested fatigue of her emotional expression."[88] With her "hesitant voice and that nervous, hunted manner,"[89] Lord seemed to betray rather than portray Anna's suffering, as though she were revealing emotion unwillingly.[90] Macgowan described this revelation as naturalistic: "minute, exact and subtle reproduction of emotion—absolutely at its best."[91]

Lord supplied the nervous, reticent, faltering nature of Anna almost habitually, since it appeared in much of her work. According to reviews, this actress lent the character a control and repeatability not evident in the emotionally moving but erratic performance of Mary Blair in *Diff'rent.* Pauline Lord projected "an introverted pride"[92] which provided both Anna and the play with a "quiet power"[93] they would otherwise lack. With her

84. Hopkins, *Lonely*, p. 179.

85. Elizabeth Shepley Sergeant, *Fire Under the Andes* (New York: Alfred A. Knopf, 1927), p. 151.

86. Hopkins in Sergeant, *Fire*, p. 154.

87. Macgowan, "Year's," Jan. 1922, p. 6.

88. Robert Allerton Parker, "An American Dramatist Developing," in Miller, *Playwright's Progress*, p. 30.

89. Brown, *Upstage*, p. 117.

90. Sergeant, *Fire*, p. 146.

91. Kenneth Macgowan, "Eugene O'Neill's 'Anna Christie' a Notable Drama Notably Acted at the Vanderbilt Theatre," New York *Globe*, Nov. 3, 1921, in Miller *Playwright's*, p. 28.

92. Atkinson, *Lively*, p. 12.

93. Ludwig Lewisohn, "Eugene O'Neill," *Nation* 113 (Nov. 30, 1921): 626.

characteristic "arrested phrase . . . and a flutter of speaking hands,"[94] she delivered her show-stopping as well as "desperate, forthright, forlorn and reluctant"[95] revelation in act III in a way that not only devastated the characters of Chris and Mat but nightly stunned audiences before they broke out in enthusiastic cheers and applause.[96] Lord's performance and the theatrics of the production often kept the spectators in "a state of receptive agitation,"[97] but Hopkins' repose always found its way into the presentation and prevented an emotional actress like Lord from losing control.[98]

Despite the fact that *Anna Christie* was a popular play in production and a Pulitzer Prize winner, O'Neill grew to despise his play, which he decided catered to "easy" popular tastes.[99] Nevertheless, Hopkins gave it and O'Neill's reputation a great boost following two disappointments by mounting *Anna Christie* with a well-orchestrated production featuring moving, emotional acting, effective, somber settings, and dynamic, atmospheric staging. "Mr. Hopkins," as the *Herald* summarized, "has put [*Anna Christie*] on the stage in a way to realize every one of its virtues and build up the atmosphere in which its faults would be obscured."[100] Together, Hopkins and O'Neill would go much further artistically with *The Hairy Ape*, but in the meantime O'Neill had another play in production. It is unfortunate that he did not have Arthur Hopkins, Pauline Lord, and Robert Edmond Jones to interpret *The Straw*. Had this been possible it is very likely that this much-underrated play would have reached the audience it never managed to find.

The Straw

Only two days after the successful opening of *Anna Christie*, the Lyceum Theatre in New London, Connecticut (the location of the James O'Neill home) presented a trial performance of *The Straw*. Under the direction of George C. Tyler with the staging assistance of John Westley,[101] O'Neill's quiet but depressing and sometimes sentimental depiction of life in a

94. Sergeant, *Fire*, p. 146.

95. Hammond, "Anna," p. 10.

96. Towse, "Play," Nov. 3, 1921, p. 9; Hammond, "Anna," p. 10; Hackett, "Anna," p. 154.

97. Woollcott did not use this phrase kindly. Woollcott, "Second," Nov. 13, 1921, p. 1.

98. See Seldes, "Theatre," Dec. 1921, p. 725.

99. Malcolm Cowley, "A Weekend with Eugene O'Neill," in Cargill, *O'Neill*, p. 46.

100. "Drab," *New York Herald*, Nov. 3, 1921, p. 15.

101. *The Straw* was first presented on Friday, Nov. 4, 1921. Lyceum Theatre *Straw* program, *Straw* folder, Theatre Collection, MCNY.

tuberculosis sanatorium and a very lonely female patient needed restrained direction, such as *Anna Christie* had received. Although treated with a quiet hand, the presentation of *The Straw* was effected with little imagination.

The Straw was scheduled to open in New York at the Greenwich Village Theatre on Monday, November 7, but production was postponed for three days. When the play opened on November 10, a new actor was in the leading male role and John Westley's staging credit was eliminated from the program.[102] What Parker described as Tyler's "uninspired production"[103] began as a collaboration of the producer-director and leading actor, but when Tyler removed Westley from the role of Stephen Murray, the director of *Chris* brought in a new uncredited assistant (one Mr. Ford), though officially he assumed all staging responsibility for *The Straw*.[104]

Westley was a competent performer in light comedy such as *Twin Beds* and *The Bridal Night*, but he had never before directed. Understandably disturbed at Westley's assignment, O'Neill feared that the actor's comic style and lack of directing experience would damage such a serious character and play. Tyler, however, who had planned on using Westley in *The Straw* since the spring of 1920, sent the forty-three-year-old actor to Provincetown to assuage O'Neill's anxiety, and the meeting convinced O'Neill of Westley's sincerity.

Although Tyler had this play scheduled for October rehearsals, he opened Westley in a very successful production of George S. Kaufman and Marc Connelly's comedy *Dulcy*, starring Lynn Fontanne, on August 13, 1921. In order to prepare *The Straw* Westley had to be removed from the popular production, which ran into the spring. Perhaps Tyler changed his mind for a while about Westley's acting in *The Straw*, because Woollcott announced after the play's publication that Charles Ellis was scheduled to play Stephen Murray.[105] Ironically, Westley, who had been discussing *The Straw* with Tyler for more than a year, did not satisfy Tyler as Stephen and was replaced by Otto Kruger, who prepared the role between Saturday

102. Greenwich Village Theatre *Straw* program, MCNY; advertisements, *New York Tribune*, Nov. 6, 1921, sec. 4, p. 3; *New York Times*, Nov. 6, 1921, sec. 6, p. 2; "The Stage Door," *New York Tribune*, Nov. 7, 1921, p. 8.

103. Parker, "American," p. 30.

104. The Greenwich Village program credits production and direction to Tyler only; advertisements, *New York Tribune*, Nov. 6, 1921, sec. 4, p. 3, and *New York Times*, Nov. 13, 1921, sec. 6, p. 2, credit direction to Tyler. O'Neill makes a passing reference to a Mr. Ford "who did wonders." O'Neill letter to Tyler, Dec. 2, 1921, Princeton.

105. Alexander Woollcott, "Second Thoughts on First Nights," *New York Times*, May 8, 1921, sec. 6, p. 1.

and Thursday's opening. This recasting obviously explains the opening-night-delay announced publicly on Monday, November 7.

Tyler's vicissitudes and eleventh-hour overhaul are astonishing when one considers how long he held and discussed *The Straw* in preparation for production. O'Neill had awaited production of this play since completing it in May of 1919. After John Williams, who had first option on O'Neill scripts at the time, dropped *The Straw*, O'Neill sent it to Tyler. Although he optioned it sometime that fall, and announced a tryout of the play in Boston with young Helen Hayes in 1920, Tyler did not produce it for two years.[106]

After another long battle of letters with Tyler throughout 1920, O'Neill grew weary of *The Straw*, just as he had of *Chris*. This struggle, like Tyler's infatuation with Westley, suggested another important problem with the 1921 production. In contrast to Hopkins' commitment to the scripts he selected, Tyler was fearful of the subject matter and wanted O'Neill to tone it down. O'Neill wisely refused throughout the preproduction period, but Tyler's reservations affected the production nonetheless.

O'Neill often lost interest in his plays which did not go into production within a year of composition. *The Straw* was no exception, as the long wait for production coupled with a rehearsal period running simultaneously with *Anna Christie* limited O'Neill's participation in production preparation. Sheaffer and Bowen state flatly that O'Neill did not attend at all,[107] but the O'Neill-Tyler correspondence verifies that O'Neill attended some early rehearsals. Furthermore, the Gelbs, using Margalo Gillmore as a source, suggest that the playwright at least attended some rehearsals. Gillmore, who played the central character Eileen Carmody, said that she remembered him sitting silently in the theater, never speaking to the actors.[108] It could be that Gillmore was recalling his presence at rehearsals for *Marco Millions*, in which she appeared in 1928. Whatever the case, O'Neill probably missed all rehearsals in the last week because he reportedly got roaring drunk after the opening of *Anna Christie* and remained so for many days.[109]

When delay in production also convinced O'Neill that publication might be the only way to secure an audience for his play, *The Straw* became his first play to be published before being performed.[110] In conse-

106. Bonte, "Chris," p. 9; O'Neill letter to Tyler, Mar. 26, 1920, Princeton.

107. Bowen, *Curse*, p. 134; Sheaffer, *Artist*, p. 69.

108. Gelbs, *O'Neill*, p. 483.

109. Sheaffer, *Artist*, pp. 69–70.

110. Published in April 1921. Jennifer McCabe Atkinson, *Eugene O'Neill: A Descriptive Bibliography* (Pittsburgh: University of Pittsburgh Press, 1974), p. 76.

quence, several critics attended the production with a prior knowledge of the play. Those who knew the text, such as Macgowan and Hornblow, tended to smile on the play and chastise Tyler's work with the production; those who attacked O'Neill's play but not the production rarely acknowledged previous familiarity with the published work. These and other reviews suggest or assert that Tyler was not very sympathetic to O'Neill's material.

Many people, including Tyler, found the subject sometimes moving but very dreary. Towse, for example, thought the play "persistently drab in color and depressing in tone,"[111] while in De Foe's view it was "the most lugubrious and depressing play that could possibly be encountered within theatre walls."[112] Such gloom was sounded by nearly all reports despite the narrow gleam of hope provided at the play's end. This time, unlike his nebulous conclusion of *Anna Christie*, O'Neill clearly conveyed his ironic "hopeless hope."[113] Tyler himself echoed De Foe when he wrote in his memoirs years later that *The Straw* "was a good play but its setting in a tuberculosis sanitarium just made it too lugubrious."[114] As early as 1920 O'Neill also referred to the play as "drastic in its subject matter,"[115] and after Tyler blamed the same for the play's failure just after the play closed ("people seemed to have the idea they would catch tuberculosis by going in the building"),[116] O'Neill somewhat reluctantly agreed that "the fault for the failure, if there is fault in it, is all mine."[117] This response seems unusually nice from O'Neill after the failure of material so near to him, but the dramatist had not worked closely with the production, nor had he yet decided to divorce himself from commercial producers. This decision still lay two years ahead.

At one time, however, O'Neill seemed prepared to contribute to rehearsals. He wrote to Tyler long before production suggesting that only he, the playwright, who had experienced the tuberculosis center, could properly instruct the actors regarding behavior. "'The Straw' can't go on without me," he insisted.[118] Although O'Neill reneged on this proposal, during preproduction he made arrangements with his old sanatorium to

111. J. Ranken Towse, "The Play," *New York Evening Post*, Nov. 11, 1921, p. 7.

112. Louis V. De Foe, "O'Neill's Triple Extract of Gloom," *World*, Nov. 12, 1921, p. 15.

113. Eugene O'Neill, *The Straw*, in O'Neill, *The Emperor Jones, Diff'rent, The Straw*, p. 140.

114. Tyler, *Whatever*, p. 273.

115. O'Neill letter to Tyler (c. Spring 1920), in Gelbs, *O'Neill*, p. 423.

116. Tyler letter to O'Neill, Nov. 29, 1921, Princeton.

117. O'Neill letter to Tyler, Dec. 2, 1921, Princeton.

118. O'Neill letter to Tyler, Mar. 26, 1920, Princeton.

provide a tour for John Westley in order to give him firsthand experience with the environment which inspired the play.[119] This field trip, however, must have been of little use to Westley, who was never able to handle the material as actor or director.[120]

Tyler, along with many reviewers, felt that, despite the "remarkably natural"[121] dialogue of the play, judicious pruning of some of the very long speeches (especially in act II) would have helped the production immensely. As usual O'Neill's "refusal to compromise" when the material touched him most personally made him balk at cutting this play.[122] Tyler, however, engaged in cutting of a different sort.

Whatever problems Westley and Tyler together may have had in directing the play ostensibly remained uncorrected after Westley's departure, for Woollcott among many critical attackers wrote that it was "ignorantly and helplessly directed."[123] Surprisingly, Hornblow and Macgowan, men of different generations who almost never agreed when reviewing production elements, found themselves taking similar admonitory points of view. The elder lamented that any "life-likeness and sincerity . . . were washed away by maladroit direction,"[124] while the younger was certain that "the directors . . . have done nothing at all to interpret"[125] the play.

Macgowan is not quite accurate, however, for Tyler, with or without Westley, consciously or otherwise, followed his impulse to soften the depressing material by undercutting the most uncomfortable elements of sanatorium life. As a result, O'Neill's hard-edged elements in conjunction with Tyler's evasions produced a vacillating effect as the production wavered and fell between interpretive stools. Parker claimed that the play was "almost conventionalized and sentimentalized into the familiar Broadway production."[126] A light touch, a mood somewhat akin to comedy, was used "in an obvious effort to be not too depressing."[127] Hammond agreed that the production did not approach the reality of the suffering in the play. "None of the harrowing symptoms of phthisis are employed to rack your

119. Gelbs, *O'Neill*, pp. 423, 483.
120. A field trip designed to acclimate the production personnel with one of O'Neill's unusual environments would be attempted again in 1929 for *Dynamo*, another failure.
121. "'The Straw' Is Play of Hopelessness Pain and Death," *New York Clipper*, Nov. 16, 1921, p. 20.
122. Arthur Hornblow, "Mr. Hornblow Goes to the Play," *Theatre Magazine*, Jan. 1922, pp. 31.
123. Alexander Woollcott, "Another O'Neill Play," *New York Times*, Nov. 11, 1921, p. 16.
124. Hornblow, Jan. 1922, p. 31.
125. Kenneth Macgowan, "Year's," Jan. 1922, p. 6.
126. Parker, "American," p. 30.
127. Hornblow, Jan. 1922, p. 31.

feelings, and, so far as outward appearances go, Eileen is not even asthmatic."[128] Rather than dramatizing austerely the pitiful demise of fragile commoner Eileen Carmody, Tyler endeavored to sustain a romantic mood. This is further verified by Tyler himself, who in written arguments with O'Neill stated that he found the weighing scene "was depressing and put an atmosphere that was unpleasant and unnecessary into the play." Likewise he thought that if the romance between Eileen and Stephen "was brought out in a more prominent way than the T.B. value, it would be better for the popular results."[129]

With the use of space Tyler betrayed an old-school practice which damaged the effectiveness of the production. In the first scene of act II a crowd of patients filled the room and took individual turns on the scales (an important emotional experience for each sufferer). The group (the script calls for about forty, but the number used is unknown) was meant to serve as something of a chorus as the mood shifted frequently in response to the fate of the patient being weighed. Instead of carefully orchestrating a crowd of actors, Tyler employed a "horde of supers" and staged them with little preparation or control. Thus, a large-scale emotional scene was at best "informative" and given over to poorly coordinated and under-rehearsed supernumeraries.[130]

Unfortunately, there are no available production photographs for *The Straw*,[131] and not a single review describes any of the play's five settings. Although uncredited in the program, the settings were arranged and built by one E. A. Morange, a scenic artist who based his work on pencil drawings which Tyler asked O'Neill to supply.[132] It is likely that most of the work was adapted from stock pieces. It would be especially interesting to know if Tyler attempted to present the split setting of the isolation room called for in the last act which would have allowed simultaneous staging, not unlike the barroom scene of *Anna Christie*. Such spatial possibilites continued to arise in many O'Neill scripts of the early 1920s.

Whatever was supplied scenically was mounted in the Greenwich Village Theatre, a selection which also reflected Tyler's reservations about the play. This moderately sized house, generously endowed when compared with its neighbor the Provincetown, was located downtown,

128. Percy Hammond, "Eugene O'Neill in 'The Straw' Depicts the Joys and Sorrows of the Tubercular," *New York Tribune*, Nov. 11, 1921, p. 8.

129. Tyler letter to O'Neill, June 4, 1920, Princeton.

130. Woollcott, "Another," p. 16; Hammond, "Eugene," Nov. 11, 1921, p. 8.

131. A collection of photos held by the Performing Arts Center of the New York Public Library is of an amateur production.

132. Tyler letters to O'Neill, Mar. 30 and Apr. 5, 1921, Princeton.

suggesting that Tyler feared that Broadway would not support *The Straw*. Open since 1917, and located at Fourth Street and Seventh Avenue near Washington Square, this theater, which would later house *Desire Under the Elms* and *The Great God Brown*, could accommodate complicated scenery, but production photographs of plays other than *The Straw* indicate that the stage was probably shallow.

Much easier to evaluate than the scenery, the acting company, led by Margalo Gillmore and Otto Kruger, clearly demonstrated Tyler's mistakes with interpretation. Among the fifteen performers credited with speaking roles (O'Neill created twenty), only one, Katherine Grey, had previously appeared in an O'Neill production. Although found dull and predictable as Captain Bartlett's wife in *Gold*, she was thought appropriately sympathetic as *The Straw*'s sanatorium superintendent, Miss Gilpin.[133] Grey was the only mentioned performer who did not come under critical fire.

If the five uncredited characters were cut or had their lines eliminated, only one exclusion would have damaged the play seriously. Two important scenes in I.1 and III which reveal much about Eileen's needs and priorities and the nature of her selfish family would be impaired and lightened in tone if Eileen's serious and youngest sister, Mary, were cut. This character, who is nowhere mentioned in criticism, stands apart from her family and mirrors much in Eileen before turning against her and siding with the family. Possibly Tyler felt compelled to cut the problematic eight-year-old character or at least remove important dialogue from the hands of a small child. It is clear from his letters that Tyler asked O'Neill to cut the child or make her older on account of problems with child labor under age sixteen. He probably used an undersized older child even though O'Neill begged him not to. Then again, he could have silently consolidated Mary's role with one of the three older children who were maintained in production. If he did not, he perpetrated irreparable injury to the emotional balance of the play.

Tyler's last-minute replacement for Westley proved a good decision tardily made. If the very experienced stock and commercial actor Otto Kruger had been granted more rehearsal time, perhaps he could have discovered ways to reveal the complicated, mixed feelings of Stephen Murray—selfishness alternating with altruism, cynicism with pathos, wit with brooding. Unfortunately, he brought to the role "an unnecessary suggestion of Broadway,"[134] for he had to rely almost solely on his stage

---

133. "Eugene O'Neill's 'The Straw' Is Gruesome Clinical Tale," *Sun*, Nov. 11, 1921, p. 12.

134. "Eugene O'Neill's 'The Straw' Profoundly Impressive Play," *New York Herald*, Nov. 11, 1921, p. 6.

experience, his knowledge of what would work, instead of careful character exploration.

Despite only five days of preparation,[135] the thirty-six-year-old actor's performance was thought by several critics the best of Kruger's career to date. Understandably, he encountered difficulty with some lines on opening night, but "managed to cover his difficulties with an appearance of spontaneity."[136] He was certainly able to arouse emotion, especially in the third act when, in Macgowan's words, "he sweeps the play up to the levels of pathos which are its natural domain."[137] It was in this scene that Stephen broke down and committed himself to the dying Eileen. Kruger reached this climax by presenting an appealing character who seemed to be blind to his own feelings and equally ignorant of Eileen's overwhelming love for him. Many critics described him as a "very nice," "frank, honest, kindly," "thoroughly agreeable and attractive"[138] young man whose principal fault lay in lack of observation. This is a far cry from the cynical and self-protective Stephen Murray of the play, who often deliberately suppresses his own feelings because he is afraid to allow himself to be vulnerable to others. Only Hornblow noted that important levels of Stephen's character were missing from this performance,[139] which remained primarily on one echelon, but in a key in keeping with the safe, sentimental direction of Tyler.

Reinforcing Tyler's approach even further, young Margalo Gillmore was cast in a demanding, emotional role before she had had the experience to present the character with authority. Since graduating from the American Academy of Dramatic Art in 1917, Gillmore had played several ingenues, but she had played nothing requiring emotional power.[140] In her early twenties but appearing even younger than her years, she was yet "roseate, ecstatic, tending to the over-sweet,"[141] qualities which softened Eileen's suffering. Found "beyond her depth,"[142] Gillmore was "unable to bend her personality and her present ability to the demands of the part."[143] She desperately needed strong guidance and creative direction to

135. Both Macgowan and Woollcott wrote that Kruger was given the part on Saturday, Nov. 5. Macgowan, "Year's," Jan. 1922, pp. 6–7; Woollcott, "Another," p. 18.

136. "The Straw," *Brooklyn Daily Eagle*, November 11, 1921, p. 8.

137. Macgowan, "Year's," Jan. 1922, p. 7.

138. Robert Benchley, "Drama," *Life* (New York), Dec. 8, 1921, p. 18; "Straw," *New York Clipper*, p. 20; De Foe, "O'Neill's," Nov. 12, 1921, p. 15.

139. Hornblow, Jan. 1922, p. 31.

140. See Margalo Gillmore, *Four Flights Up* (Boston: Houghton Mifflin, 1964), pp. 118–19, 152–53.

141. Sayler, *Our*, p. 145.

142. Woollcott, "Another," p. 18.

143. Macgowan, "Year's," Jan. 1922, p. 6.

help her avoid occasional mugging and "grotesquely abrupt transitions."[144] Unfortunately, such assistance was not forthcoming.

After criticizing Tyler for casting Gillmore before her time, and berating Woollcott for attacking the young actress' performance without mercy, actress Laurette Taylor in a letter to the *New York Times* admitted that Gillmore played unevenly and needed more experience. She also described, however, the contrast between Gillmore and the experienced actors around her: "To me, their experience made parts of her performance take on a divine quality, because it was all spirit. And I am not so sure, at such times, that her simplicity didn't make their experience seem very artificial."[145] Taylor, who saw both a dress rehearsal and the opening performance, detected in Gillmore a fear typical among neophytes. In anticipation of public presentation Gillmore sacrificed some of her honesty and simplicity for artifice and disorder.

Nonetheless, many found her endearing and captivating—herein probably lay the hope of Tyler. Benchley and Crawford especially succumbed to her attractiveness with aplomb and exaggeration. Crawford, for example, found her "so charming, one felt that any man who did not fall in love with her ought to be shot at sunrise."[146] Equally hyperbolic, Benchley exclaimed that "no one as appealing as Miss Gillmore is as she lies in her invalid's chair at the final curtain could be allowed to die. If necessary to save her life, I would have the show stopped by the police."[147] Kaufman, however, while recognizing her allure, realized the problem it created. "It was difficult to reconcile her charm and her beauty with the rest of the performance," he wrote. "She was too well. And by no means fragile."[148] Thus, by casting a lovely young actress, Tyler not only sidestepped the emotional development necessary to reach Eileen's suffering but also glamorized the tubercular condition and altered Eileen's somewhat plain countenance, which is described in the play complete with defects.

While O'Neill had lobbied Tyler for "the best dramatic actress in America"[149] to play the heroine opposite a cynical and brooding version of himself in "the best and truest thing I have done,"[150] what he got was an inexperienced ingenue playing opposite a slick leading man in a mawkish presentation which, while sometimes engaging the audience, managed in

144. Woollcott, "Another," p. 18.
145. Laurette Taylor, "In the Mail Bag," *New York Times*, Nov. 20, 1921, sec. 6, p. 1.
146. Jack Crawford, "Broadway Sheds Tears," *Drama* 12 (Feb. 1922): 152.
147. Benchley, "Drama," Dec. 8, 1921, p. 18.
148. S. Jay Kaufman, "The Straw," *Dramatic Mirror* 84 (Nov. 19, 1921): 737.
149. O'Neill in Bowen, *Curse*, p. 118.
150. O'Neill letter to Tyler (c. 1919), in Gelbs, *O'Neill*, p. 398.

many ways "to betray the author and befuddle the spectator."[151] Tyler later admitted that Gillmore "did not completely fulfill the requirements. The part really requires a girl of the experience of forty and the looks of eighteen—and there ain't no such animal."[152] The few critical references to staging indicate that Tyler's use of the space was sloppy, and apparently no unusual settings were designed or built for production. Furthermore, it was asserted that his "bad direction" had aided the actors in spoiling "several scenes that ought to be very effective."[153] Hampered by Tyler's last-minute changes in casting and direction and his second thoughts about the dramatic material, this interesting, intense play never received the production it deserved, although it may be that Gillmore and Kruger improved somewhat as the Tyler production ran its brief course. Describing the closing-night performance, Crawford wrote, "I saw no one in the audience who appeared to feel that there was any hope. . . . We were limp at the end—a silent crowd of tear-stained faces."[154] It was but the twentieth performance. After taking another big financial loss (more than nine thousand dollars),[155] Tyler sadly expressed to O'Neill that "nothing in the world would have given me greater pleasure than to have produced a successful play of yours."[156]

The regular failures of experienced Broadway producers with O'Neill's plays in the early 1920s signaled a lack of preparation for the new directions in which the young dramatist was trying to steer American drama and theater. Directors and producers like Tyler, Williams, Saint-Gaudens, and Kennedy represented the safe side of commercial New York production which was still at the center of the Great White Way even though important experimenters had been presenting exciting direction and design since 1915. It did not take O'Neill long to recognize that he could not realize his experimental devices, grand concepts and tragic themes with conservative producers unwilling to take great risks in Broadway houses, or succeed with eager but unsupported amateurs who would take gigantic chances in the Village but lacked the financial means or artistic vision to fulfill his dreams. There remained Arthur Hopkins, who could have made great progress with O'Neill. After *The Hairy Ape*, however, the two fell out over the worth of O'Neill's *The Fountain*. Unfortunately, the wound was never healed. O'Neill as it happened would have to

151. Hornblow, Jan. 1922, p. 31.
152. Tyler letter to O'Neill, Dec. 5, 1921, Princeton.
153. "Straw," *Brooklyn*, p. 8.
154. Crawford, "Broadway," p. 181.
155. *The Straw* account book, Princeton.
156. Tyler letter to O'Neill, Nov. 29, 1921, Princeton.

gather his own experimental company founded on very different principles from those of the Provincetown or uptown commercialism. Although
the playwright worked through two more productions under existing conditions (one of them quite splendid), he was beginning to dream of new
possibilities while gathering new theatrical friends. The resultant company would not only produce some of the finest O'Neill productions but
also help to redefine New York professional theater.

CHAPTER VI

Blood Sacrifice:
The First Man and *The Hairy Ape*

> Let us then first—oh sweet and lovely thought!—poison all the
> actors, then guillotine the managers, hang the playwrights—with
> one omission—feed the critics to the lions, . . . and as a final act
> of purification, call upon a good God to send a second flood to
> wipe out the audience, root and branch.[1]

For the first three seasons of the 1920s O'Neill seemed
fated to be tormented by overlapping production periods, as nine plays
were hurled at the public in quick succession with little time for reflec-
tion. In the first quarter of 1922 O'Neill once again had two productions
in rehearsal simultaneously. To complicate matters further, the plays
opened only five days apart, and just four days before opening night of the
first production O'Neill received news that his mother had died in California. On the day of the second premiere her body arrived in New York.

These two plays were brutal, strident dramas characterized by intense suffering, frustration, and agonizing death. Unlike the two comparatively quiet though emotional preceding productions, these noisy
plays focused on male protagonists who were, or were trying to be, part of a
much broader world than the narrow sphere of Eileen's and Anna's existence. Curtis Jayson and Yank Smith shared an angry intensity and personal despair; yet *The Hairy Ape* was a tremendous production success and
The First Man ended in dismal failure.

The First Man is one of the least convincing of the surviving full-
length plays in the enormously uneven oeuvre of O'Neill. As usual the
dramatist was unable to recognize this until after production, and he was
very excited when he learned that it would be directed by the talented
Augustin Duncan. One would expect the play, which opened on March 4,

1. Eugene G. O'Neill and Oliver Sayler, "The Artist of the Theatre," *Shadowland*, Apr.
1922, p. 77.

1922, at the Neighborhood Playhouse,[2] an organization and facility always noted for care and dedication in production, to have been mounted painstakingly and sensitively. If so, this production—despite the play's dubious events, doubtful characterization, and contrived conclusion—may have had moderate success in such an experimental house which had become an outlet for unusual plays not ordinarily seen in commercial theaters. Something, however, was strangely amiss.

Augustin Duncan at age forty-eight was widely praised in New York "as a director of taste and ambition"[3] who had brought to both America's art-theater movement and commercial theater a collection of productions which were not merely admirable and moving but important events in the development of American theater. He contributed to many productions a broad range of knowledge and talent from the fields of painting and music. Furthermore, as the brother of Isadora Duncan he assisted in her experiments in movement and dance, and as a student of acting he worked with masterful performers as disparate as Richard Mansfield, William Gillette, and Constantin Stanislavski. In fact, he was one of the first to bring some of the Moscow Art Theatre's practices to American theater after 1910.

As a director Duncan had mounted numerous Shakespearean plays, commercial realism like *Detour* by Owen Davis, and modern poetic work such as John Masefield's *The Faithful*. In addition, he helped to save the fledgling Theatre Guild in 1919 with his quiet, "direct simplicity,"[4] artfully managed in St. John Ervine's naturalistic play *John Ferguson*. O'Neill thus had every right to believe that *The First Man* would get a fair hearing.

On January 22 O'Neill wrote to Macgowan that "it is still a secret (I think) [but] there is a very great probability that the Duncan forces will do 'The First Man' . . . at the Belmont, rehearsals to start immediately."[5] This seems a late date indeed for "probability" for a production which opened only six weeks after this letter, and not in a commercial house as suggested here but in a small art theater. There is little doubt that the production was hurriedly prepared, as the criticism reveals, probably so as to occupy the Neighborhood Playhouse while its regular production team was busy elsewhere.

The conscientious guiding forces and production team of the Neighborhood Playhouse, Agnes Morgan and Alice Lewisohn, did not work with

2. "Theatrical Notes," *New York Times*, Mar. 4, 1922, p. 10. First reviews did not appear until Monday, Mar. 6, since the play opened on a Saturday.

3. Alexander Woollcott, "The New O'Neill Play," *New York Times*, Mar. 6, 1922, p. 9.

4. Philip Moeller, in Eaton, *Theatre Guild*, p. 161.

5. O'Neill letter to Macgowan, Jan. 22, 1922 in Bryer, *Letters*, p. 33.

"guest producer"[6] Duncan on this production. These talented women were already taxing their abilities and resources to the limit by coproducing and codirecting with Philip Moeller, Frank Reicher, and the Theatre Guild, G. B. Shaw's gigantic *Back to Methuselah*, which was presented in three long parts, the first opening on February 27, the second on March 5, and the third on March 12.[7] *The First Man* opened on March 4 without the Neighborhood's usual quality control.

First entitled *The Oldest Man*,[8] O'Neill's play had been completed in March 1921 and after revision dutifully submitted in the fall to Arthur Hopkins, who did not like it. Following another rejection, by the Theatre Guild (with which Duncan had been associated since its beginning) the play reached its director.[9] Duncan may have had it recommended to him by a dissenting Guild board member.[10]

With the beginning of simultaneous rehearsals O'Neill was apparently resigned to splitting his time. After mentioning Duncan's probable direction of *The First Man*, O'Neill told Macgowan that he would "again have the ghastly joy of attending two sets of rehearsals at the same time."[11] Once more he moved back to New York, but the excellence of the Hopkins and Light *Hairy Ape* compared to the ineptitude of Duncan's project, complicated by Ella O'Neill's death, persuaded the playwright to abandon *The First Man* and give what attention he could to the production at the Provincetown.

"Quite a distinguished little company of intellectual giants and gluttons for punishment journeyed last Saturday night to attend the opening performance,"[12] began the review of the *New York Clipper*. The punishment provided was almost uninterrupted agony and outrage on the part of the protagonist, Curtis Jayson, prolonged suffering for his wife, Martha, until she dies at the end of act III, and nonstop petty interference from Jayson's brood of meddling relatives drawn by O'Neill as near caricatures. Before play's end a polite and enduring audience became quite restless.[13]

Numerous production problems affecting acting interpretations

6. *The First Man* program, Theatre Collection, MCNY.

7. Kenneth Macgowan, "Broadway at the Spring," *Theatre Arts* 6 (July 1922): 181; Eaton, *Theatre Guild*, pp. 57–63.

8. Eugene O'Neill, *The Oldest Man*, typescript, Rare Book Collection, Library of Congress, 1921.

9. Tornqvist, *Drama*, p. 260; Miller, *Eugene*, p. 23; Gelbs, *O'Neill*, pp. 487–88.

10. The Theatre Guild's board of directors frequently bickered over play selections, which had to pass a committee of six.

11. O'Neill letter to Macgowan, Jan. 22, 1922, in Bryer, *Letters*, p. 33.

12. "'The First Man,' New O'Neil [sic] Play, at the Playhouse," *New York Clipper*, Mar. 15, 1922, p. 20.

13. A. S., "The New Play," New York *Globe*, Mar. 6, 1922, p. 8.

arose from textual difficulties which O'Neill left unresolved or unresolvable. Many critics, for example, correctly found the language of the play stilted and rhetorical and the situation artificial. The actors, led by Duncan, who unwisely added performing the leading role of Curtis Jayson to his producing and directing duties, were unable to plumb beneath "surface realism."[14] Their failure to provide depth in characterization was further complicated by Duncan's failure to exploit or at least acknowledge the obvious melodramatic form which governs most of *The First Man*. Gloom and agony, for example, continue unabated throughout most of the play (especially acts III and IV) until the forced resolution at the end when the protagonist makes a surprising, complete reversal resulting in a hopeful conclusion. In its serious subject matter, happy ending, mostly type characters, strength of situation, and rhetorical language, *The First Man* more closely resembles nineteenth-century melodrama than any other form. It does not, however, include comic relief, and the hopeful conclusion is not convincing because Jayson's reversal is not prepared for in either character or situation. O'Neill seemed to be more interested in shocking audience sensibilities than in reinforcing values as nineteenth-century melodrama was wont to do.

If Duncan recognized the melodramatic form as well as the emphatic and vigorous style of the play, he did not convey this perceptibly in his acting or direction. He and Margaret Mower "struggle[d] through the thing, making it appear slow and stuttering."[15] The climax of act II, for example, is a confrontation of Curtis and Martha. Their argument, which reflects their coincident love and disgust for one another, culminates in a fierce kiss followed by a stand-off boiling simultaneously with passion and revulsion.[16] Duncan, with Margaret Mower as Martha, approached this material with an easy naturalness which played against emotion with a level, controlled rhythm.[17] Much of the sudden, impulsive action and rhetorical language was rendered ridiculous or ineffective on stage, and the audience was never engrossed in the emotional onslaught.[18] Duncan killed the passion with control.

Numerous critics at the time, however, responded most negatively to Martha's offstage screams and groans as she gave birth to the son which

14. Macgowan, "Broadway," July 1922, p. 187; Louis V. De Foe, "Another Play by Eugene O'Neill," *World*, Mar. 6, 1922, p. 9; Alan Dale, "'The First Man,' Eugene O'Neill Play Staged," *New York American*, Mar. 6, 1922, in Miller, *Playwright's*, p. 13.

15. Arthur Pollock, "The First Man," *Brooklyn Daily Eagle*, Mar. 7, 1922, p. 10.

16. Eugene O'Neill, *The First Man*, in *The Hairy Ape, Anna Christie, The First Man* (New York: Boni and Liveright, 1922), p. 272.

17. Lawrence Reamer, "'First Man,' New O'Neill Play, Is a Gloomy Suburban Story," *New York Herald*, Mar. 6, 1922, p. 13; Dale, "First," p. 13.

18. Woollcott, "New," Mar. 6, 1922, p. 9; Macgowan, "Broadway," July 1922, p. 187.

killed her. With the opening curtain of act III the audience heard "a low, muffled moan of anguish"[19] which recurred periodically in various degrees of intensity until the end of the act. This brought the complaint that "the audience suffers as well as the mother"[20] in an ordeal which taxed the feelings. "It is a harrowing half hour and the sensibilities of an audience are assailed without any manner of justification,"[21] wrote the critic of the *Tribune* in a typical description. Only Quinn called the sound effects "a minor feature . . . not stressed in the production,"[22] but most critics emphasized the offstage sound which provided important counterpoint to the onstage action, a device used frequently by O'Neill in his plays with varying degrees of success.[23] Martha's audible suffering was one of the most dynamic achievements of Duncan's production: offstage labor pains so believable that theatergoers shared in the pain but unfortunately divorced themselves from the onstage action.

Scenically, *The First Man* was one of the least demanding of all of O'Neill's full-length plays. He called for only two settings for the four acts—two adjoining interiors (sitting room and study) of the Jayson home in Connecticut. No one is credited in the program or reviews with the designs, and, except for Woollcott's remark that "the whole third act [was] set in the twilight Bridgetown sitting room,"[24] the settings are not described or evaluated in detail outside the published play. De Foe, however, suggested generally that the settings were suitable.[25] With no available photographs one can only assume that the sets were probably stock pieces collected by Duncan rather than units designed specifically for this production. Also, the settings were not expansive, since the Neighborhood was a small, intimate proscenium theater which seated only about three hundred people.[26]

Duncan's biggest mistake with the actors was in miscasting the two leading roles. "It is one of the director's functions to select an appropriate cast," Woollcott glibly wrote, "and in casting himself for the central role

19. O'Neill, *The First Man*, p. 275.

20. "First," *New York Clipper*, Mar. 15, 1922, p. 20.

21. "Convocation of Woe in 'The First Man,' O'Neill's New Play," *New York Tribune*, Mar. 6, 1922, p. 6.

22. Arthur Hobson Quinn, *A History of the American Drama from the Civil War to the Present Day*, vol. 2 (New York: Harper, 1927), pp. 181–82.

23. Compare the offstage murder in act I of *Gold*, p. 25, and offstage joking and laughter while Emma suffers onstage in act I of *Diff'rent*, pp. 224–28.

24. Woollcott, "New," Mar. 6, 1922, p. 9.

25. De Foe, "Another," Mar. 6, 1922, p. 9.

26. Alice Lewisohn Crowley, *The Neighborhood Playhouse* (New York: Theatre Arts Books, 1959), pp. 56 ff.; Constance D'Arcy Mackay, *The Little Theatre in the United States* (New York: Henry Holt, 1917), pp. 54–57; Edward B. Kinsila, *Modern Theatre Construction* (New York: Chalmers, 1917), p. 42.

. . . Mr. Duncan did not do well by O'Neill."[27] Already ten years older than the character, Duncan's very mature appearance and voice and his deliberate, gentle manner undercut the vigor and energy of O'Neill's hero. Jayson "demanded more impetuosity and fervor than [Duncan] could impart."[28] More important, Towse and Macgowan realized the biggest danger in Duncan's inappropriateness as it affected the dynamics of the play. Towse noted that when the play suffered from "its trivialities and its indiscretions," Duncan's "somewhat indifferent performance" was unable to obscure them.[29] More to the point, Macgowan lamented that Duncan "failed to reach that tense and artificial dynamism which might have lifted the contrivances of the last acts into a deceptive sort of power."[30] It is unfortunate that Duncan did not call upon the lessons he learned under the dynamic Richard Mansfield in 1900.

Also miscast, but for somewhat different reasons, was the young Margaret Mower, who could not reach the maturity needed for thirty-nine-year-old Martha. "Too young and too exotic,"[31] the rather glamorous Mower supplied "the charm of a gentle and appealing personality"[32] but none of the agonizing torment which plagues the character. Alan Dale complained that she "played the suffering wife with such placidity that she got on one's nerves."[33] Thus, she also fell below the high level of energy and intensity necessary to animate the play's inflated passions.

Complicating this general dearth of stage ardor was an unmistakable lack of preparation. Duncan especially had numerous line problems, most notably in the first two acts.[34] The unfinished nature of the presentation was likely a consequence of Duncan's decision to direct himself in an unsuitable role while trying to coordinate all the logistics of production as the producer of the play. Also, the director's sudden decision to mount the play without preproduction with O'Neill resulted in a rehearsal period limited in part by the availability of the Neighborhood Playhouse, which was temporarily dark due to *Back to Methuselah*.

Because the playwright drew the minor characters rather superficially, the essence of each was not difficult to capture. In consequence, the supporting cast was found to be much more satisfactory than the

27. Woollcott, "New," Mar. 6, 1922, p. 9.
28. Reamer, "First," Mar. 6, 1922, p. 13.
29. J. Ranken Towse, "Eugene O'Neill's Lastest Play," *New York Evening Post*, Mar. 6, 1922, p. 6.
30. Macgowan, "Broadway," July 1922, p. 187.
31. "'First Man' Presented at Neighborhood Playhouse," *Sun*, Mar. 6, 1922, p. 16.
32. De Foe, "Another," Mar. 6, 1922, p. 9.
33. Dale, "First," p. 13.
34. Maida Castellun, "The First Man," *New York Call*, March 9, 1922, in Cargill, *O'Neill*, p. 158; "First," *Sun*, Mar. 6, 1922, p. 16; De Foe, "Another," Mar. 6, 1922, p. 9.

leads.[35] Jayson's sister Esther, for example (played by Duncan's wife, Margherita Sargent), is a conservative, unthinking, possessive woman easily given to jealousy. Her younger sister Lily is a bit more up-to-date and loves to shock her elder staid relations. They resemble the clearly drawn and quickly identifiable supporting characters of situation comedy and sensational melodrama. Not one of the supporting characters does anything that is startling or even surprising for the audience. These characters, adequately played, were both accessible and predictable. It was up to the leading actors to engage the audience.

The low-key approach of Duncan and Mower violated not only the temperamental needs of the play but the rhythmic ones as well. By mid-performance Castellun found the tempo dragging alarmingly,[36] a symptom of Duncan's deliberative methods more appropriate for a play like *John Ferguson* than for *The First Man*. Reamer noted monotony in Duncan's approach, "which does not always rise and fall with the emotion of the scene. The most slavish imitator of life would have to recognize an occasional change in rhythm under the impulse of emotion [which abounds in the play]. Mr. Duncan is likely to continue, however, at one tempo."[37]

Although it cannot be stated how the settings or Duncan's use of space contributed to the production, it is certain that many of the directorial decisions created additional problems for an already imperfect play. Miscalculations by the director in casting undermined audience belief in and sympathy for the leading characters. Obvious lack of preparation by Duncan, who tried to mount the play hurriedly as producer, director, and actor, resulted in slipshod work. Perhaps most damaging of all, through deliberate tempo and subdued delivery, Duncan reduced some of the aural and physical passion and intensity to an almost casual level in an attempt to naturalize and domesticate a play which demanded presentation, not just representation. As both director and actor, Duncan's inability to realize the demands of the drama certainly contributed to the play's hasty failure and departure from the stage after twenty-seven performances.[38] Perhaps the play, which O'Neill later dismissed as botched work,[39] would have miscarried even in more sympathetic hands, but Duncan's mistakes in attempting to naturalize and domesticate a play which was born of excess undoubtedly ensured the play's demise. *The First Man* represented O'Neill's last production of the 1920s with an unsuitable director.

35. Woollcott, "New," Mar. 6, 1922, p. 9; De Foe, "Another," Mar. 6, 1922, p. 9; "First," *New York Clipper*, Mar. 15, 1922, p. 20.

36. Castellun, "First," Mar. 9, 1922, p. 158.

37. Reamer, "First," Mar. 6, 1922, p. 13.

38. Advertisement, *New York Times*, Mar. 30, 1922, p. 20; Miller, *Eugene*, p. 55.

39. O'Neill, "Second," p. 118.

The Hairy Ape

Only five days after the disappointing premiere of *The First Man* a different O'Neill drama created a theatrical sensation. Opening on Thursday, March 9, 1922, at the Provincetown,[40] *The Hairy Ape* reflected O'Neill's continuing fascination with expressionistic techniques, discordant themes, suffering character, and ironic transformations. The experimental demands of this "bitter, brutal, wildly fantastic play of nightmare hue and nightmare distortion,"[41] however, exceeded all the requirements of previous work from O'Neill. Because the dramatist finished the quickly composed play in late December 1921,[42] the directors and designers took little time to ruminate before launching the production period.

O'Neill wanted Charles Kennedy to direct *The Hairy Ape* at the Provincetown and wrote him to this effect before production matters were settled with Provincetown and Hopkins.[43] Yet the director of *Anna Christie*, who owned the professional rights to *The Hairy Ape*, had other plans for Kennedy, who was still performing in *The Claw*.

Publicly the play was advertised, at both the Playwrights' and Hopkins' Plymouth Theatre, simply as a "Provincetown Players' production," with no credit given for direction.[44] Conflicting accounts of the early rehearsal period, however, credit George Cram Cook, James Light, Arthur Hopkins, and even O'Neill himself with directing the play. For example, Harry Kemp wrote that Cook was preparing to direct the play, assuming that he had O'Neill's authorization, when the playwright severed their relationship permanently by calling Cook "a rotten producer" and claiming that his plays now needed "more competent direction."[45] O'Neill's letters, however, do not indicate that Cook was ever part of the production plan. Nevertheless, Light told Sarlos in an interview of 1963 that he took over the production after Cook had started it.[46] Likewise, Sheaffer claims that Cook was the first director but proved inept.[47] The Gelbs, however, wrote that Cook was offended by the intrusion of

40. "The New Plays," *New York Times*, Mar. 5, 1922, sec. 6, p. 1; the first reviews appeared on Mar. 10, 1922.

41. Alexander Woollcott, "Eugene O'Neill at Full Tilt," *New York Times*, Mar. 10, 1922, p. 18.

42. Tornqvist, *Drama*, p. 261.

43. "Charles Kennedy," *New York Times*, Sept. 9, 1958, p. 35; O'Neill letter to Kennedy, in Gelbs, *O'Neill*, p. 489.

44. Advertisement, *New York Times*, Apr. 16, 1922, sec. 6, p. 2.

45. As noted in chapter III above, Kemp mistakenly attributed this argument over *The Hairy Ape* to *The Emperor Jones*. Kemp, "Out," p. 66.

46. Sarlos, *Jig*, p. 140; Sarlos, "Provincetown," vol. 2, p. 397.

47. Sheaffer, *Artist*, pp. 78–79.

Hopkins and refused to take part in production.[48] Whether Cook launched or only intended directing the production, it is clear that O'Neill was dissatisfied with Cook but willing to have Light at the helm so long as he was quietly guided by the experienced Hopkins.

Surprisingly, Sheaffer wrote that O'Neill actually directed with the assistance of Light and the advice of Hopkins.[49] This assertion is not documented by Sheaffer, however, and appears elsewhere only in a brief line in Macgowan's review, which refers to "the excellent direction of O'Neill himself."[50] In context this line can be interpreted as O'Neill's dramaturgy rather than actual stage direction. The possibility is essentially denied by O'Neill in a letter to Macgowan in the summer of 1923. Referring to future production work with Macgowan and Robert Edmond Jones, O'Neill wrote that he might be interested in taking a more active hand in mounting his play. "This would mean a good deal more active interest than I ever showed in the old P.P. except during their first [O'Neill's first, Provincetown's second] year [1916]—and even then my participation was alcoholically erratic."[51] Furthermore, it is very improbable that O'Neill helped direct the production, due to the simultaneous rehearsals of *The First Man*, the death of his mother, and the playwright's avoidance of direction throughout the rest of his professional career. Most of all, he probably could not direct due to his shyness with and resentment of actors.

Before *The Hairy Ape* opened Cook had not just absented himself from rehearsals but had left for Greece after effecting the temporary dissolution of the Provincetown Players, scheduled to commence at the end of the 1921–1922 season. Despite Cook's indisputable absence, however, the program carried the usual production credit, only noting ironically that the play was the work of the "Provincetown Players under the direction of George Cram Cook."[52]

When reviewing the production, Woollcott reported that "there is a rumor abroad that Arthur Hopkins, with a proprietary interest in the piece, has been lurking around its rehearsals."[53] Years afterward Hopkins gave the Provincetowners full credit for the production, explaining that "later I took the play over and brought it up to the Plymouth."[54] His involvement was almost certainly more extensive. Deutsch, for example,

48. Gelbs, *O'Neill*, p. 494.
49. Sheaffer, *Artist*, pp. 79, 81.
50. Macgowan, "Broadway," July 1922, p. 189.
51. O'Neill letter to Macgowan, summer 1923, in Bryer, *Letters*, p. 36.
52. *The Hairy Ape* program, Theatre Collection, MCNY.
53. Woollcott, "Eugene," Mar. 10, 1922, p. 18.
54. Hopkins, *Lonely*, p. 235.

called the direction a collaboration between Hopkins and Light.[55] Furthermore, O'Neill made several references in letters to minimal Provincetown control[56] and in one told Macgowan specifically that "Hopkins has offered to help in the directing gratis."[57] I shall proceed assuming that, under the watchful eye of Hopkins, Light actually staged *The Hairy Ape*.

Hopkins' level-headed, easy manner was an important controlling influence on the impulsive, sometimes out-of-control direction of James Light,[58] a twenty-seven-year-old actor and director who was struggling for leadership of the Provincetown. An intelligent but uncertain director "whose understanding often outruns his self-confidence,"[59] Light came to New York at age twenty-two to matriculate at Columbia after studying painting and architecture at Ohio State and Carnegie Tech. Also well versed in literature and philosophy, Light understood O'Neill's work and was excellent at analysis, but he often had difficulty communicating his ideas simply and directly to actors.[60] Also, his frequent prurience reportedly undermined his effectiveness with actresses.[61] Macgowan claimed that Light's direction was competent so long as he was carefully watched, but that when on his own, his work lacked "vitality and power and he's sloppy and irresponsible and incapable of inspiring confidence."[62] Although Light's direction was very erratic, he was pragmatic at stagecraft and understood the possibilities and limitations of the Provincetown stage. Light had directed plays at Provincetown since Cook's sabbatical season of 1919–1920 and had served steadily since 1917 as actor, stage manager, carpenter, and designer. The productions which he directed for O'Neill included some of the most effective as well as clumsiest moments among the playwright's work at Provincetown. Successful direction of *The Hairy Ape* required cynicism, a sneer and a smile within the anguish, characteristics close to the attitudes of James Light.

Although O'Neill told Barrett Clark in 1937 that *The Hairy Ape* "found its form as a direct descendent from *The Emperor Jones*,"[63] the younger play proved to be more distinctly expressionistic than *The Em-*

55. Deutsch, *Provincetown*, p. 86.

56. O'Neill letter to George Jean Nathan, Jan. 2, 1922 in Vilhauer, "History," p. 178; O'Neill letter to Mary Eleanor Fitzgerald, 1922, in Sarlos, *Jig*, p. 140.

57. O'Neill letter to Macgowan, Bryer, *Letters*, p. 32.

58. The year before his death Light admitted in an interview that his direction was often "impulsive and haphazard." Sarlos, "Provincetown," vol. 2, p. 278.

59. Sayler, *Our American*, p. 99.

60. Paul Robeson in *All God's Chillun Got Wings* was an exception who enjoyed and responded to Light's analytical method.

61. Wilson, *Twenties*, p. 400. Wilson was involved with Provincetown through his actress wife, Mary Blair, who performed under Light's direction.

62. Macgowan letter to O'Neill, Aug. 12, 1926, in Bryer, *Letters*, p. 129.

63. O'Neill letter to Clark, n.d., in Clark, *O'Neill*, p. 83.

peror Jones. What O'Neill himself subtitled "A Comedy of Ancient and Modern Life"[64] was treated by many reviewers as an allegory, a fantastic, symbolic, often inarticulate but detached abstraction which nonetheless approached tragedy because Yank struggled vehemently against the inevitable.

The task of the director with *The Hairy Ape* was to straddle differing styles of presentation which borrowed from the naturalistic as well as the abstract. O'Neill borrowed expressionistic techniques to distort and emphasize the emotional struggle of his stoker protagonist, Yank.[65] "It seems to run the whole gamut from extreme naturalism to extreme expressionism—with more of the latter than the former," he wrote to Macgowan in 1921.[66] This stylistic mixture was effectively managed by Light and Hopkins, who combined unusual staging with imaginative designs by Robert Edmond Jones and Cleon Throckmorton and a realistic and pathetic presentation of Yank in the hands of actor Louis Wolheim. This production team provided O'Neill with some of his most honestly as well as effectively produced scenes to date.

Light and Hopkins presented a series of eight "short, stabbing scenes so distorted and so fantastic that 'The Hairy Ape' takes on the bad dream accent and aspect of an ugly fable."[67] The obvious expressionistic devices, however, were not glaringly evident in the early scenes, due chiefly to the authentic characterization, "the emotional vigor and truth"[68] of Wolheim, and the suddenly intensified abstractions of the setting in scene 5 depicting Fifth Avenue.

Nevertheless, the four early scenes employed fragmented scenery, with lines askew, patterned movement and vocalization, and posed picturization. The four final scenes especially emphasized the production's stylization, employing masks (their first use in an O'Neill play), increased mechanical movement, and clearer use of choral chant. Stark Young proclaimed the production "a fine example of dramatic rhythm, of a pattern of movement."[69] Likewise, "the production," according to Lewisohn, "has a somber, imaginative glow, a visionary strangeness, a subtlety of tempo and modulation that make it a theatric achievement of a high

64. Eugene O'Neill, *The Hairy Ape*, in O'Neill, *The Hairy Ape, Anna Christie, The First Man* (New York: Boni and Liveright, 1922), p. v.

65. See Eugene O'Neill, "O'Neill Talks About His Plays," *New York Herald Tribune*, Mar. 16, 1924, in Cargill, *O'Neill*, p. 111.

66. O'Neill letter to Macgowan, Dec. 24, 1921, in Bryer, *Letters*, p. 31.

67. Alexander Woollcott, "Second Thoughts on First Nights," *New York Times*, Apr. 16, 1922, sec. 6, p. 1.

68. Macgowan, "Broadway," July 1922, p. 189.

69. Stark Young, "The Hairy Ape," *New Republic* 30 (Mar. 22, 1922), 112.

order."[70] The impetus for the production's choreographed, frequently mechanical elements came from the play itself, but the effective, ironic treatment was often well executed because (at least in part) of the rowdy, brusque nature of Wolheim and the studied cynicism of Light.

O'Neill was also experimenting with language, extending his rough jargon and profanity well beyond the slang and oaths which peppered *Anna Christie*. Woollcott adjudged the stokers' "speech more squalid than . . . heard before in an American theatre."[71] As a result, some critical objections were raised calling for circumspect editing, and the New York police made a serious though unsuccessful attempt to close the play for "obscene, indecent and impure" language.[72] Despite the objections, however, the profanity was only an approximation of sailors' lingo and much milder than genuine verbiage of the stokehold. O'Neill's public response to the brief incident was characteristic: "This stupidity was to be expected. Morons will be morons."[73] A free use of expletives on the public stage lay many years in the future, for New York witnessed many censorship struggles with sex farces, suggested nudity, and profanity from 1919 throughout the 1920s, reaching high points of conflict with citizen play juries and the Wales Padlock Law in 1922 and 1927, respectively.

For the first time Robert Edmond Jones worked with another designer also experienced in the dramatic world of O'Neill. Uniting the Hopkins camp with the Provincetowners, Jones and Cleon Throckmorton codesigned the settings along lines which emphasized the world surrounding Yank, which became steadily (except for scene 7) more alarming in its departures from normality. The older and more experienced Jones may very well have been in charge, but the resultant designs, though not alien to Throckmorton's work of the next few years, did not seem to be distinctly of either man's style. Especially the ethereal, dreamy quality of many of Jones' designs was not evident in *The Hairy Ape*.

As in the case of *The Emperor Jones* the Provincetowners were once again faced with a space problem. "The dingy little stage"[74] which graced the converted stable with horrible ventilation had slots cut in the floor to

70. Ludwig Lewisohn, "The Development of Eugene O'Neill," *Nation* 114 (Mar. 22, 1922): 350.

71. Woollcott, "Eugene," Mar. 10, 1922, p. 18.

72. See "Court Asked to Suppress 'Hairy Ape' as Indecent," *New York Tribune*, May 19, 1922, p. 1; "Object to 'The Hairy Ape,'" *New York Times*, May 19, 1922, p. 20; Oliver M. Sayler, "Our Theatre at Cross-Purposes," *Century Magazine* 104 (Sept. 1922): 755.

73. "O'Neill's 'Hairy Ape' Escapes Charge of Talking 'Indecently,'" *New York Tribune*, May 20, 1922, p. 18.

74. "'The Hairy Ape,' O'Neil [sic] Play, Is Dull and Tiresome," *New York Clipper*, Mar. 22, 1922, p. 22.

make accessible the cellar space beneath the stage. It was in this basement that the settings were stored, and the flats and set pieces were simply passed through the slots when both striking and raising. According to stagehand Greenberg, these slots were located on the apron of the stage,[75] which meant that scenery was moved either in full view of the audience or in the dark.

The scenery was changed seven times during the play; yet an intermission was taken only between scenes 4 and 5. A program note also indicates a brief dark change during scene 7. Since no internal change was needed, this note probably refers to the complicated scene change from the jail of scene 6 to the I.W.W. interior of the seventh scene. It is therefore likely that all sets for the first half were kept in the stage area until intermission (especially if scenes 1 and 4 used the same setting), when sets were shifted through the slots. The I.W.W. setting, however, was probably kept in the cellar until it was needed. The reasons for this are discussed below.

Once again the sky dome came to the rescue of the Provincetown. Ironically, on "one of the most cramped stages New York has ever known . . . the artists have created the illusion of vast spaces and endless perspectives."[76] Of course, the appearance of depth was countered by frequent depictions of compressed, constricted space, a condition which was actually exaggerated in the already restricted playhouse. Most reviewers appreciated or lauded the "well staged"[77] action within "quite wonderful"[78] settings that together created "scenic effects which," according to Benchley, made "those of uptown theatres appear like something you might do in a barn."[79] The Provincetown's tiny platform seemed to become an almost limitless protean field for the tragic journey of O'Neill's human ape.

Scenes 1 and 4 called for the same setting in the play, "the firemen's forecastle of a transatlantic liner,"[80] but photographic evidence[81] indicates that either two different settings were used, or that the same setting was significantly altered during the performance, or that the forecastle

75. By the time of Experimental Theatre, Inc., the stage also had a trap door for access to the cellar, but it is not clear if this was an addition of Robert Edmond Jones when he remodeled in 1924 or if it had been present all along. Mordecai Gorelik, "Life With Bobby," *Theatre Arts* 39 (April 1955): 95; Greenberg interview, in Vilhauer, "History," p. 283.

76. Woollcott, "Eugene," Mar. 10, 1922, p. 18.

77. "Hairy," *New York Clipper*, Mar. 22, 1922, p. 22.

78. Arthur Hornblow, "Mr. Hornblow Goes to the Play," *Theatre Magazine*, May 1922, p. 305.

79. Robert C. Benchley, "Drama," *Life* (New York), Mar. 30, 1922, p. 18.

80. O'Neill, *The Hairy Ape*, pp. 1, 37.

81. Sixteen photographs and proofsheet, Theatre Collection, Beinecke, Yale; fourteen photographs, Theatre Collection, MCNY.

was redesigned before being moved uptown for a commercial run at the Plymouth. A press release in April stated that "several of the scenes have been rebuilt . . . to take advantage of the larger stage"[82] of the Plymouth, but the scenes are not specified. The two different settings are the same size, however, (why not expanded for the much larger Plymouth?), evident both from photographs, which include actors, and Edna Kenton's report that the "little opening on the Plymouth stage of the firemen's forecastle, is—exactly—the proscenium opening of the Playwright's Theatre."[83] Also significant is the fact that photographs of both forecastle settings include the same stage floor.

In one photograph the walls, which are really cutouts of a pipe design and which surround the action, are regularized, a pattern of crisscrossing pipes which meet at right angles. The onstage action is from scene 1 because Yank is about to take a bottle from another stoker. All other photographs have pipes at rakish angles echoing the expressionistic motif evident in several other settings (see illustration 5). Some of the onstage action from these photographs is clearly from scene 4 which includes a physical struggle in which Yank is subdued by the gang. None of the action photographed in the angled setting is definitely from the first scene.

It is probable, thus, that scene 1 took place in the set with straight lines before Yank was disturbed by society's intrusion on his private world through the actions of Mildred Douglas in scene 3. Once he was disturbed, Yank's little world of the forecastle became more distorted, reflecting the protagonist's disturbance. It is likely, however, that instead of two sets, the photographs display the same scenic units and that the crossing pipes were movable, flat pieces of wood or pasteboard which were rearranged in their frames to effect the necessary distortion. Except for the angles of the crossing pipes, the sets are identical.

Within this "cramped, dim-lit, crowded"[84] setting director and actors combined realistic and stylized techniques which created surprising, hybrid results as though the product were "a mingling of Rembrandt and some sane cubist."[85] Significantly, O'Neill's stage directions for scene 1 read: "The treatment of this scene, or of any other scene in the play, should by no means be naturalistic."[86] To enhance the unreality and emotional confinement the already tiny playing space was further limited by four block-shaped benches which followed the lines of the cutout walls.

82. "O'Neill's 'The Hairy Ape Goes to Plymouth Theater," *New York Herald*, Apr. 16, 1922, sec. 3, p. 7.

83. Kenton, "Provincetown," *Billboard*, pp. 13–14.

84. Woollcott, "Second," Apr. 16, 1922, p. 1.

85. Macgowan, "Broadway," July 1922, p. 189.

86. O'Neill, *The Hairy Ape*, p. 1.

The only entrance was a small opening up center through which the stokers stumbled "from the furnaces, hot, sweaty, choked with coal dust, brutish,"[87] or exited en masse as an almost mechanized, conditioned unit. James Light used this space effectively by placing a character like Yank on his feet, dominating the visual focus, while surrounded by sitting, slouching stokers huddled closely on the benches and floor. Woollcott wrote that the forecastle was "packed with roaring sweating giants, glistening men stripped to the waists with mighty shoulders and low foreheads, motley men scooped up from all corners of the earth."[88] Yet Yank was often placed in visual relief against the mob, either standing in an attitude of protest or sitting in an obvious Rodin's *Thinker* pose downstage.

Following O'Neill's request for "a tumult of sound,"[89] Light and his company created a cacophony of human and mechanical noise which was often like a harsh chorus conflicting with or reverberating the singular, suffering, demanding voice and commanding physical presence of Wolheim as Yank. According to Quinn, "The first scene . . . crashed upon the auditor without apology. It was a carnival of force, expressed in terms of human beings, at first indistinguishable units in a chorus of international profanity."[90] This chorus of sound written in the text somewhat like disparate lines from crude poetry was delivered in what Atkinson called "group dialogue, like chants from an ominous underworld."[91] Singing sea chanteys, echoing Yank's cries of "Think," "Love," Law," "God" in voices "with a brazen metallic quality as if their throats were phonograph horns," shifting moods instantaneously from joviality to anger to threats to nostalgic melancholy lament, erupting suddenly with "a chorus of hard, barking laughter,"[92] the stokers worked effectively but stridently as a unit, disciplined in both voice and movement. Of scene 4 Eaton wrote that "the loud laughter of [Yank's] mates suddenly becomes rhythmic, like the fearful tattoo of a drum."[93] Most importantly, perhaps, the "coarse profanities, reechoed until almost a refrain, [took] on tragic dignity."[94] This choral activity culminated in the struggle at the end of this scene when the entire group of eleven captured Yank and with difficulty pinned the fiercely struggling actor to the floor while resuming its choric chants. A photograph captured strikingly the tension and constriction of this climactic

87. Woollcott, "Eugene," Mar. 10, 1922, p. 18.
88. Woollcott, "Second," Apr. 16, 1922, p. 1.
89. O'Neill, *The Hairy Ape*, p. 2.
90. Quinn, *History*, vol. 2, p. 183.
91. Atkinson, *Lively*, p. 14.
92. O'Neill, *The Hairy Ape*, p. 38.
93. Walter Prichard Eaton, "The Hairy Ape," *Freeman*, Apr. 26, 1922, in Miller, *Playwright's*, p. 34.
94. "The Hairy Ape," *New York Evening Post*, Mar. 22, 1922, p. 8.

action which occurred just before the intermission. No critic faulted Light's work with the stokers, and many had considerable praise for it.

The second scene of *The Hairy Ape* may have included little of the obvious abstraction evident in the forecastle, but artificiality abounded in the characters of anemic Mildred Douglas and her haughty, overweight aunt. The original setting has not survived in photographs, but the promenade deck was photographed after it had been mounted at the Plymouth. Naturally this outdoor scene, incorporating a cloth drop upstage at the Plymouth, lacked the Provincetown's plaster dome which provided "an incredibly blue sky"[95] and a field of sea and sky which was "apparently expansive,"[96] but the ship's bulkheads angling away from center to both right and left were hardly realistic representations of a ship.

This spare setting, with no adornments other than a side rail and two deck chairs set at a right angle head to head to facilitate conversation between the recumbent ladies, included at Provincetown (according to Woollcott) "a gayly painted smokestack . . . with no more smoke than just a ribbon of it to make an interesting composition"[97] against the glowing dome. This description is in keeping with O'Neill's direction: "black smoke swirls back against the sky."[98] If Woollcott's account is accurate, and if the Plymouth setting without the dome was otherwise identical to that at Provincetown, then the bulkhead which backed the deck chairs must have been the smokestack, the top of which was cut off in the photographs, which show no more than seven feet of that wall.

Scene 2 served also as a dynamic contrast to the first scene. O'Neill sought a calm, beautiful picture which reflected "the vivid life of the sea all about" in sharp opposition to the women—"two incongruous, artificial figures, inert and disharmonious."[99] The effect was staged precisely as requested, providing a spotless deck bathed in sunshine yet cool and breezy when compared to the forecastle. In the midst of this quietude lay "a foolish, bloodless girl . . . toying with some ideas."[100] Also following O'Neill's cue, pale-complexioned Mildred was dressed all in white. From shoes and hose to scarf and hat she presented at once a lovely yet ghostly picture which rudely violated the infernal world of scene 3.

Four photographs of scene 3's stokehold preserve some of the dynamics so enthusiastically described by reviewers. The shovelers, including Yank, were at work between four furnace doors which ran right to left

95. Woollcott, "Second," Apr. 16, 1922, p. 1.
96. "'The Hairy Ape' a Logical Tragedy," *World*, Mar. 10, 1922, p. 14.
97. Woollcott, "Second," Apr. 16, 1922, p. 1.
98. O'Neill, *The Hairy Ape*, p. 20.
99. O'Neill, *The Hairy Ape*, p. 19.
100. Woollcott, "Second," Apr. 16, 1922, p. 1.

upstage and two flat, parallel, knee-high ground rows placed downstage. The spatter-painted walls suggest that there should be much more to this dark, hellish room which one cannot see. Towse wrote that the Provincetowners "succeeded in giving a striking picture on a small scale"[101] in this scene, an achievement due in no slight part to the vigorous lighting.

The photographs reveal stark, selective illumination featuring shadows, bright streaks, patches of low-angle light, and brilliant flashes from the furnace openings—a discordant chiaroscuro effect. Many critics stressed the intense red lighting emanating from the furnaces, which appear to be lined with reflective material. Eaton, for example, enthusiastically wrote that "when the boiler-doors are open . . . red, searing searchlight-glares strike into the eyeballs of the audience like flashes from the Inferno."[102] O'Neill sought a similar bold effect with the slamming of the doors after the fires were fed, "one fiery eye after another being blotted out with a series of accompanying bangs."[103] Sound was effective throughout this scene, as it was in the first. Castellun described "the horrible noises of screws and boilers and engines mingling with the shoveling of coal and the raucous voices of the men."[104] This scene launched a brief visual, aural, and emotional attack on its usually spirited audiences.[105]

As most critics emphasized, the stokers' feeding of the fires was certainly a remarkable stage effect. Again O'Neill wanted (and received) tumultuous noise, "the grating, teeth-gritting grind of steel against steel"[106] as the men shoveled rhythmically, machinelike. Although "the stokers shovel AIR into the blazing fires,"[107] Patterson James wrote with surprise, the below-decks turbulence of curses, whistles, clangs, and engines accompanied the real but empty shovels which the stokers mechanically moved from dark flat ground rows to explosive furnace light.

Most dynamic of all in this compact but busy scene was the confrontation of sweaty, filthy, cursing Yank with spotless Mildred in diaphanous white. Quinn called it one of "the unforgettable stage pictures of our time. With true economy, the meeting is over almost at once, but there has been time to fix in the Yank's soul her look of horror, that sends him out seeking for revenge upon her and her kind."[108] Two photographs have preserved

101. J. Ranken Towse, "Eugene O'Neill's Latest Effort," *New York Evening Post*, Mar. 10, 1922, p. 7.

102. Eaton, "Hairy," p. 34.

103. O'Neill, *The Hairy Ape*, p. 31.

104. Maida Castellun, "The Plays that Pass," *New York Call*, Mar. 12, 1922, p. 4.

105. See Kenneth Andrews, "Broadway, Our Literary Signpost," *Bookman*, 55 (May 1922), 284.

106. O'Neill, *The Hairy Ape*, p. 29.

107. James, "Off," p. 36.

108. Quinn, "Significance," p. 100.

the visual contrast effected in an instant in perhaps O'Neill's most incongruous but intriguing image prior to his Triumvirate experiments.

Although the most frequently discussed of the play's eight scenes, the fifth is important most of all for an effect which was created for production rather than specified in O'Neill's text. In this scene set on a wealthy business row along Fifth Avenue representing "magnificence cheapened and made grotesque by commercialism," O'Neill called for a chorus of socialites, "a procession of gaudy marionettes" characterized by "detached, mechanical unawareness."[109] This was an abrupt escalation of expressionistic devices further emphasized by distorted fur- and jewelry-shop windows and absurdly large and overpriced tags in the windows.

The Jones and Throckmorton rendering beautifully captured the lines of marble for the buildings but distorted the rippling lines to approach the jagged line of typical expressionistic design. Although many angles were suggested in the painted walls and rakish windows, the constructed line of the set was a flat plane and like all preceding scenes ran parallel to the apron. While including the most obviously stylized setting by this point in the production, the scene's sudden use of masks and overtly stylized movement of actors was responsible for startling members of the audience, some of whom, according to Macgowan, did not earlier notice the "extreme exaggeration" but took the first half of the play "for grubby but terrific naturalism."[110] This seems odd in retrospect, and may be due not only to Wolheim's acting but also to audience expectations in a small, experimental theater with modest budget and means.

Masks for the socialite chorus came not from O'Neill but from costumer Blanche Hays in an effort to make O'Neill's desire for uniformity complete. Her thin masks were reportedly finished at the last moment,[111] suggesting that the use of masks may have been a late idea. The results were fascinating. In the photographs the masks are expressionless, ominous face masks, just slightly larger than life size, and seem to be fitted to the actors' hats, which are lodged tightly in place to allow the actors' jerky movements. More importantly, however, the masks significantly accentuated the mechanical, featureless crowd described by critics as "sinister dolls,"[112] "masked manikins,"[113] "denaturalized . . . promenaders [moving with] . . . mechanical gait,"[114] "who walk like automata

109. O'Neill, *The Hairy Ape*, pp. 49, 54.
110. Macgowan, "Broadway," July 1922, p. 189.
111. Gelbs, *O'Neill*, pp. 495–96.
112. Lewisohn, "Development," p. 350.
113. Eaton, "Hairy," p. 34.
114. Sayler, *Our American*, p. 212.

and prattle,"[115] "a social chaingang shuffling through life."[116] James, however, provided the most useful description of their stylized movement, "all," he observed, "mincing upstage-downstage-upstage-downstage."[117] Three matched couples hurried on as a unit, some with hands on one another's shoulders, oblivious to Yank and impervious to his attacks. Thus, Light and his actors found comic, "burlesque comment"[118] amid the harsh, bitter struggles of Yank within an alien dream world. The work of director, designers, and actors melded most perfectly here in capturing an unforgettable style which was not only emblematic but also established a stylistic staging model for American expressionism of the 1920s. Although German expressionism certainly predated and probably influenced O'Neill, it should be noted that *The Emperor Jones* and *The Hairy Ape* preceded on the American stage the importations of European expressionism (*From Morn to Midnight, R.U.R, Johannes Kreisler*—all in 1922, beginning in May) and the other American ventures into this style, such as *The Adding Machine, Roger Bloomer*, and *Beggar on Horseback*.

Scene 6 revealed Yank in a jail cell which resembled the gorilla's cage of the play's final scene. Yank's cell was clearly joined to another, and a bit of a third is discernible in the photographs; yet only Yank was visible, although a chorus of unseen prisoners chattered at the frustrated protagonist. Yank's cell was placed left center, and the adjoining cells, constructed like Yank's in forced perspective, receded on a slight angle into the darkness up right. This economical setting, though isolating Yank, suggested myriad other cells beyond. The only direct light splashed onto Yank and the bars of his cell. One photograph shows him in his *Thinker* pose bathed in a single spot from above, but a second photo includes strong side and low-angle light, perhaps from the floor, distorting his figure. Throughout the play Light and his designers worked to isolate Yank with both stage placement and selective lighting in order to enhance his loneliness and personal frustrations.

Again the use of choral sound (as in the stoker scenes), complicated by metal sounds from bar rattling, created an ominous, overwhelming, emotional fervor. In the words of Eaton, "a score of other voices, howling, jeering, cursing, groaning, [produced] the terrific strophe of the caged."[119] Unlike in the previous scenes, however, the strident vocal barrage arose mysteriously from the void.

115. Woollcott, "Eugene," Mar. 10, 1922, p. 18.
116. Castellun, "Plays," Mar. 12, 1922, p. 4.
117. James, "Off," p. 37.
118. Young, "Hairy," p. 112.
119. Eaton, "Hairy," p. 34.

For practical reasons the production had to depart from O'Neill's text for the conclusion of this scene. The script called for Yank to be subdued with a blast from a fire hose as he bent a bar in a burst of incredible outrage. In production he was "reduced to impotence by blackjacks and a strait jacket."[120] This substitution was less startling, but in keeping with the group attacks on Yank in scenes 4, 5, and 7.

The penultimate scene of *The Hairy Ape* would not be particularly noteworthy here for its setting or staging were it not for the "brief dark scene change"[121] which occurred probably just before this scene, although the program note which records it could indicate the setting change before the final scene if scene 7 proved less difficult to set than strike. Although the seventh scene's "cheap, banal"[122] I.W.W. local union headquarters and the street outside were stark, the setting included no distorted lines or images.

Scene 7 probably took considerable time to change due to the movement of much furniture, a logistical problem not present in the other scenes. Adding to the shift time were the moving of the large box set and door unit and the hanging of two practical lamps from above in a theater with no fly space. It is very likely that the limited wing space would not have accommodated all of this scenery and that some was stored under the stage until needed, thus requiring a dark delay but not an intermission.

Again a small crowd of actors was used to people the barren room. At least seven actors subdued Yank and threw him outdoors in a group fray which echoed the struggle at the close of the fourth scene. In the later scene, however, the union workers engaged in no vocal or physical choral activity.

The gorilla's cage of the eighth and final scene was very similar, but not identical, to the jail cell of scene 6. The basic shape was the same, with an equal number of bars, but the rakish angle of the top of the cell was more severe than the top of the gorilla cage, which had an additional panel at the base bearing the legend *gorilla*. The zoo's ape was played by an actor dressed in an outfit of goatskins and papier-mâché mask.[123] In the dim illumination of the "night-shrouded zoo,"[124] however, the animal's presence was malevolent. Stark Young was fascinated by the image of "the beast's figure looming up in the cage, more terrible and more beastly because half seen!"[125]

120. Towse, "Eugene," Mar. 10, 1922, p. 7.
121. *The Hairy Ape* program, MCNY.
122. O'Neill, *The Hairy Ape*, p. 71.
123. Gelbs, *O'Neill*, p. 495.
124. Woollcott, "Second," Apr. 16, 1922, p. 1.
125. Young, "Hairy," p. 113.

Punctuating such strong visual images was O'Neill's final chorus, a nonhuman, unseen "chorus of angry chattering and screeching"[126] zoo animals. These energetic and frightening sounds issued from the darkness, much as the prisoners' chorus accompanied the incarcerated Yank,[127] who once again returned to a cage and after a brotherly embrace replaced the animal in death.

In general, Jones, Throckmorton, Light, and Hopkins designed and used their space effectively and meaningfully regardless of the severe limitations of the Provincetown and various acting problems. Towse, for example, found that the director's "groupings were, as a rule, exceedingly animated and well managed."[128] Similarly, Woollcott felt that the production team's accomplishments with the space drove "one to the conclusion that when a stage seems pinched and little, it is the mind of the producer that is pinched and little."[129] Despite the tiny facility, Macgown found some of the stage pictures simply "staggering."[130] The Provincetown Players and their artistic guests avoided this constriction and "achieved a focus with their effects on this miniature stage,"[131] which surprisingly held up (many critics doubted the possibility) after the Broadway move.

In less than six weeks, between January 22 and March 9, the Provincetowners had gathered and rehearsed a cast of at least nineteen,[132] most of whom played multiple roles. Louis Wolheim of course garnered a wealth of accolades, but the cast as a whole was cheered for its commitment and enthusiasm, if not its talent. Only Mary Blair was singled out for ineptitude. The casting of Blair as the cold, distant Mildred Douglas was Light's biggest error, a mistake corrected by Hopkins when he moved the show to the Plymouth.[133] Macgowan told the Gelbs that Blair "was not enough of a personality for uptown—not luxurious enough,"[134] but this was not the only reason for recasting the role. It is clear that Blair's emotional methods (discussed in chapter IV) almost precluded her ability to approach such an artificial character. Woollcott especially found her inappropriate and incapable of playing Mildred with any sort of conviction.[135]

126. O'Neill, *The Hairy Ape*, p. 83.
127. Suggested by Young, "Hairy," p. 113.
128. Towse, "Eugene," Mar. 10, 1922, p. 7.
129. Woollcott, "Eugene," Mar. 10, 1922, p. 18.
130. Kenneth Macgowan, "The New Play," New York *Globe*, Mar. 10, 1922, p. 14.
131. Benchley, "Drama," Mar. 30, 1922, p. 18.
132. In a letter of Jan. 22 O'Neill indicated that the play was not yet cast. Bryer, *Letters*, p. 32.
133. Hopkins replaced Blair with Carlotta Monterey, who became O'Neill's third wife many years later.
134. Gelbs, *O'Neill*, p. 502.
135. Woollcott, "Eugene," Mar. 10, 1922, p. 18.

In other supporting roles, however, the critical verdict differed considerably. Most critics found the bulk of the cast competent—sometimes barely so—and occasionally exciting, thanks most of all to the actors' desire, which often made their performances "much more energetic than artistic."[136] Nevertheless, special praise was given to several performers who provided excitement or distinction independent of Light's composition and the rage and pain of Wolheim's Yank. An unknown player's impersonation of the gorilla, especially after Yank granted it freedom, demonstrated imagination and close observation of apes, not stage animals. Stark Young was intrigued, as the gorilla "came so fearfully out of the cage. It was fine, extraordinary, out of class with any animal motive I have ever known on the stage."[137] Also notable were "the sharp, strident Cockney keenness of Mr. Harold West [as Long, the social crusader] and the soft, misty, poetical resignation of Mr. Henry O'Neill's Irishman [Paddy, who nostalgically longed for the sailing ships]."[138] Their performances provided much-needed contrast and counterpoint for the sometimes relentless onslaught of Wolheim.

A forty-year-old but relatively inexperienced actor, Louis Wolheim came to O'Neill and the Provincetown from Hopkins' camp, probably at the suggestion of Charles Kennedy.[139] Wolheim was a brutish-looking man with a thick, muscular body, a twisted broken nose, and squat harsh physiognomy. Nonetheless, he was intelligent and known as "he of the forbidding face and fine mind."[140] He had appeared in *The Jest* with the Barrymores and would later cement his *Hairy Ape* notoriety with a brilliant portrayal in *What Price Glory?* for Hopkins. Naturally, his physical presence suited him perfectly for the role of Yank, so much so that some wondered if O'Neill might have written the role with Wolheim in mind. By creating "the illusion of brute force"[141] Wolheim engaged "animalistic acting"[142] to bellow and bully his way through much of the strident action. "He terrifies, he menaces,"[143] wrote De Casseres. "No actor we know," Mantle asserted, "could roar more effectively, swear with more freedom and give less offense, or suggest the pathetic groping of a primitive human better than [Wolheim]."[144] Although the actor transformed the play,

136. Towse, "Eugene," Mar. 10, 1922, p. 7.
137. Young, "Hairy," pp. 112–13.
138. Lewisohn, "Development," p. 350.
139. Sarlos, *Jig*, p. 139; Halverson, "Arthur," p. 103.
140. "Wolheim, 'Bad Man' of Movies," *New York Times*, Feb. 19, 1931, p. 25.
141. Macgowan, "Broadway," July 1922, p. 189.
142. Atkinson, *Lively*, p. 16.
143. Benjamin De Casseres, "Adrift in the Roaring Forties," *Theatre Magazine*, June 1922, p. 370.
144. Burns Mantle, in Deutsch, *Provincetown*, p. 88.

according to Atkinson, "into a savage hubbub with devastating philosophical and political overtones,"[145] Wolheim sometimes drove the character's violence near the point of monotony. [146]

Yet the audience could not but "loathe him and simultaneously feel a profound sympathy with him."[147] Herein lay the near magic of Wolheim's portrayal. He alternately engaged and alienated his audience, always returning to the empathic suffering in Yank's journey, arousing "profound pathos"[148] even in the most artificial of the production's environments. This was particularly obvious in Yank's final moments when "the wail of the dying man was echoed and prolonged through the house"[149] as Wolheim crumpled to the bottom of his cage. The casting of such an actor obviously relieved Light of many directorial struggles he would otherwise have suffered. As with *The Emperor Jones*, the Provincetown had once again mounted an expressionistic pilgrimage which featured a consummate performer in the midst of a beautifully stylized stage environment.

Light and Hopkins treated *The Hairy Ape* with remarkable sympathy and imagination. The direction ignited the production with a profusion of exciting moments and poignant images by mixing styles (especially visually), by drawing on expressionistic devices and scenery and realistic acting as well as choral chant and movement, and by experimenting with masks, mechanical movement, and sound. In Macgowan's words, "It leaps out at you from the future."[150] Both at the Provincetown and the Plymouth the play emotionally aroused audiences who often cheered and shouted after each highly charged scene. [151] Though blemished, the production was "so vital and interesting and teeming with life"[152] that the play stood apart as a leading theatrical event not just of the season, but the decade.

Nevertheless, as *The Hairy Ape* was soaring, the old Provincetown was dying. O'Neill found himself at a crossroads. He was very dissatisfied with all of his commercial productions (even Hopkins' *Anna Christie*, despite its obvious beauty and success), and his standby experimental outlet at the Provincetown would soon be no more. An obvious producer for his plays was the Theatre Guild, which at that time was becoming the

145. Atkinson, *Lively*, p. 16.

146. Percy Hammond, "'The Hairy Ape' Shows Eugene O'Neill in a Bitter and Interesting Humor," *New York Tribune*, Mar. 10, 1922, p. 8; Young, "Hairy," p. 112.

147. De Casseres, "Adrift," p. 370.

148. Sayler, "Our Theatre," p. 755.

149. "Hairy," *World*, p. 14.

150. Macgowan, "New," Mar. 10, 1922, p. 14.

151. Such audience responses were recorded even by critics who were not themselves ecstatic over the production, e.g., Towse and Andrews.

152. Woollcott, "Eugene," Mar. 10, 1922, p. 18.

foremost American producer of important new plays, albeit mostly ones of European extraction. The Guild was not yet interested, however, and it took six more years before the Guild and O'Neill finally united. The evident alternative seemed to be to found one's own company. This O'Neill did—though it was nearly two years in the making, and during this formation period the American public, after an onslaught of nine productions in just three years, saw no new O'Neill play until 1924. In that year, however, four new plays by America's leading dramatist appeared under the banner of Experimental Theatre, Incorporated. Never again in O'Neill's lifetime would a new play of his be presented by an independent producer.

When the Playwrights' Theatre closed in the spring of 1922, Cook was gone, and with him many of the Provincetown's original ideals. Part of the Provincetown would be revitalized in two seasons as the fully professional Experimental Theatre, under the direction of Macgowan, Jones, and O'Neill, but the Provincetown Players, who had served O'Neill's early experiments faithfully and often effectively, were gone—in the words of George Cram Cook, "Gone like a dream."[153]

---

153. George Cram Cook, "Though Stone Be Broken," in Cook, *Greek Coins*, p. 54.

CHAPTER VII

Hitching Pegasus:
Welded, The Ancient Mariner, and *All God's Chillun Got Wings*

. . . he rushes out of the door as if furies were pursuing him.[1]

Here Pegasus was hitched.[2]

In the two-year hiatus of O'Neill and the Provincetown following the spring closing of the Playwrights' Theatre, New York was graced with further important expressionistic experiments such as Elmer Rice's *The Adding Machine* and John Howard Lawson's *Roger Bloomer.* Perhaps more importantly for the future of the American theater, however, 1923 brought the first visit of the Moscow Art Theatre and the formation of Richard Boleslavski and Maria Ouspenskaya's American Laboratory Theatre, which would train Harold Clurman and Lee Strasberg, representatives of the next generation of major American theatrical leadership after O'Neill's tenure subsided in the 1930s.

As the old Provincetown company became a memory, O'Neill at first envisioned the Hopkins organization as his production center. Yet Hopkins decided against producing O'Neill's next play, *The Fountain,* after at first optioning the poetic but awkward drama, and O'Neill's expectations turned to gall. He pronounced that no hope lay with Hopkins[3] and began to look elsewhere. His search was not quickly resolved. He continued to write while waiting for production commitments, and when *Welded* opened on Monday, March 17, 1924, at the Thirty-ninth Street Theatre,[4] he had three other new plays prepared for the stage.

1. Eugene O'Neill, *Welded,* in *All God's Chillun Got Wings, Welded* (New York: Boni and Liveright, 1924), p. 119.
2. Painted on the wall above an old hitching ring in the Playwrights' Theatre of the Provincetown Players. Deutsch, *Provincetown,* p. 59.
3. O'Neill letter to George Jean Nathan, in Gelbs, *O'Neill,* p. 524.
4. Advertisement, *New York Times,* Mar. 17, 1924, p. 18. The first reviews appeared on Tuesday, Mar. 18, 1924.

During his respite from production O'Neill shifted his attention from unpredictable uptown producers to a replacement for his standby, the Provincetown Players. He sought a professionalized forum for his work, but also an ongoing organization upon which he could rely to accept all of his work as well as commit itself to theatrical experiment. Since what he envisioned did not exist in New York, he set about with Kenneth Macgowan and Robert Edmond Jones to fashion such a theater from the residue of the Provincetown. For the next three years O'Neill virtually abandoned the haphazard commercial struggle on Broadway for often important but frequently self-indulgent flights of fancy with Experimental Theatre, Incorporated.

Throughout most of 1923 O'Neill, Jones, and Macgowan made plans (and sometimes schemed to overcome the opposition of old Provincetowners) for the reorganization of the Provincetown Players and the reopening of their theater. Making stringent objections to any commercialization of Provincetown, Edna Kenton, George Cram Cook, and Susan Glaspell chorused: "We will let this theatre die . . . before we let it become another voice of mediocrity."[5] O'Neill, who now wanted professionalism, certainly not mediocrity, with his Village experiments, nonetheless advised Macgowan that the Provincetown name should be dropped in order to minimize difficulties.[6] The name was ultimately altered, but the public always associated the new organization with the old, not just because of the presence of O'Neill but because Experimental Theatre, Inc., performed in the newly christened Provincetown Playhouse, a name which still survives on a quite different little building on Macdougal Street. Furthermore, the Triumvirate sometimes exploited the old connection. For example, when opening for a tryout run of *Welded* in Baltimore, the first advertisement read in part: "Produced under the supervision of Kenneth Macgowan, Eugene O'Neill and Robert Edmond Jones, who are the directors of the famous Provincetown Playhouse in New York."[7]

At first O'Neill wanted Macgowan to be the all-controlling director of the entire project, with no production committees or group decision making. "You ought to be absolute head with an absolute veto," he wrote. "To hell with democracy!"[8] Macgowan, however, suggested a triumvirate of O'Neill and Jones with himself; when agreement was impossible, though, he consented to make executive decisions.[9] Such was the plan adopted, with Macgowan as company director but not stage director.

5. Kenton, "Provincetown," *Greek*, p. 19.
6. O'Neill letter to Macgowan, c. Sept. 1923, in Bryer, *Letters*, pp. 43–47.
7. Advertisement, *Baltimore News*, Mar. 3, 1924, p. 13.
8. O'Neill letter to Macgowan, c. summer 1923, in Bryer, *Letters*, p. 38.
9. Macgowan to Arthur Friedman, taped interview, in Vilhauer, "History," p. 313.

O'Neill was on hand to make production suggestions even for plays other than his own, and Jones not only designed five of the six O'Neill productions with the Triumvirate but also directed four of them. All three men were responsible for selecting each season of plays.

When the Provincetown reopened in January 1924, Macgowan was thirty-five years old, the same age as O'Neill and just one year younger than Jones. Although not experienced in production, Macgowan after graduating from Harvard had had fourteen years of experience in professional dramatic criticism; he had traveled to Europe with Jones to prepare *Continental Stagecraft*, a study of European theatrical innovation in direction and design; he had written *Theatre of To-morrow*, an important examination of experiment in the modern theater; and he had co-authored *Masks and Demons*, a book which in part pointed to the importance of masks in both ritual and theater. Like his new partners, Macgowan was a champion of theatrical experiment and new dramatic forms. Perhaps just as importantly, the three men were friends.

From the old organization the Triumvirate recruited Cleon Throckmorton as technical director and designer, along with Jones, James Light for direction and stage management, Harold McGee for stage management and acting, and a few others in business management. With one or two exceptions (like Charles Ellis), everyone in the acting company was new, and critic Stark Young joined the staff temporarily as a stage director for *Welded*.

This reorganization was directed toward production rather than American playwriting, which had been Provincetown's lifeblood since 1915. The *"emphasis* shall be upon *experiment in production,"* O'Neill wrote, "utilizing any play ancient or modern, foreign or native, to that end. . . . It is to be a directors' theatre."[10] The experimental urge expressed by O'Neill and welcomed by Macgowan and Jones was willingness to explore theatrical space, form, and methods together as well as individually. "A new and exciting spirit has arisen," Agnes Boulton wrote as *Welded* was opening. "Perhaps it comes from a unity in which each individual is allowed to be selfish in his own finest way."[11] The sentiment may appear noble, but in the Triumvirate's first venture with an O'Neill script the playwright's automania resulted in calamity.

After appropriately opening Experimental Theatre, Inc., in January with Strindberg's *Spook Sonata* performed in masks, the Triumvirate revived the nineteenth-century comedy of manners *Fashion* by Anna Cora Mowatt, which proved so popular that Macgowan was afraid to move it to

10. O'Neill letter to Harry Weinberger, c. Sept. 1923, in Bryer, *Letters*, p. 48.
11. Agnes Boulton, "An Experimental Theatre," *Theatre Arts* 7 (Mar. 1924): 188.

make way for the next production, *Welded*. In consequence, Macgowan temporarily joined forces with the established Broadway producers Selwyn and Company, presided over by Edgar Selwyn, who controlled a number of uptown theatres including the Thirty-ninth Street Theatre, a small commercial house used for O'Neill's premiere. Also, Macgowan wrote that actress "Doris Keane and the Selwyns were ready to place such services and resources at our command as we couldn't have had in our tiny theatre in Macdougal Street."[12] In addition, "the little houses in the village could never draw the gross required for salaries for such players as Doris Keane and Jacob Ben-Ami,"[13] who had been induced to star in *Welded*. Such a casting move seemed heretical after the preceding year of lip service to free theatrical experiment, but the Selwyns appear to have put little pressure on production decisions besides wanting stars for the two leading roles.

When Stark Young joined Experimental Theatre, Inc., he was known, as he still is, as an expressive critic of the theater and a skillful man of letters. After sixteen years of teaching English literature at several universities, this unlikely man from Mississippi joined the critical staffs of *New Republic* and *Theatre Arts*, positions which he maintained while working occasionally for the Theatre Guild and the Triumvirate. At forty-two Young was a man of taste and reserve, a sometime poet, translator, and playwright who had just directed *The Failures* by H. R. Lenormand in November for the Guild.[14] The Triumvirate would produce Young's play *The Saint* in the fall of 1924 under the direction of Richard Boleslavski.

Young was a gentle and often esoteric director. Like Robert Edmond Jones he was sometimes abstruse or at least too circular when dealing with actors. This difficulty arose in his work with Ben-Ami and Keane. Insisting on the importance of "the actor's own truth,"[15] Young granted his actors freedom to make personal discoveries and make the creations their own. Unfortunately, Keane and Ben-Ami never understood O'Neill's anxious characters, and the result was two ridiculous impersonations which Young could not control and return to the world of the play.

Young's usual approach to dramatic structure, however, was very appropriate for *Welded*. "A director can best study the layout of a play as if

---

12. Keane invested production money, and the Triumvirate did not yet control the Greenwich Village Theatre in addition to Provincetown. Kenneth Macgowan, "Eugene O'Neill as Realist," *New York Times*, Mar. 23, 1924, sec. 8, p. 2.

13. Ibee [Jack Pulaski], "Welded," *Variety*, Mar. 26, 1924, p. 16.

14. For a review of this dark and bitter production which featured outbursts of "desperate passion" see John Corbin, "The Right Word," *New York Times*, Nov. 23, 1923, p. 20.

15. Stark Young, "The Art of Directing," in Robert W. Corrigan and James L. Rosenberg, eds., *The Context and Craft of Drama* (San Francisco: Chandler, 1964), p. 379.

it were a musical composition," he wrote a year after production.[16] The mood shifts of O'Neill's characters lent this play easily to scoring. If Young followed his own advice with *Welded*, his analysis—which one should not doubt was sound—was never translated effectively to the means and language of the stage. His theater essays and reviews, for example, display careful study, insightful analysis, imaginative thinking, and a constant search for grace in the written word.[17] Young knew the principles of directing, but he experienced difficulty in executing his own lessons in *Welded*. His extraordinary discipline in criticism was not matched in his coordination of this production.

Young understood more fully than many others of his time the transformation a play must undergo in rehearsal. "When a drama emerges from the hands of the director it has undergone a restatement of itself," he reasoned.[18] Yet Macgowan[19] and Woollcott maintained that Young presented a "straight" production of the play without additional concept. "Stark Young seemed to leave it pretty much as it lay," observed Woollcott.[20] Macgowan, who had watched rehearsals, was more specific. "The method of *Welded* was dictated by the author's script, and so the part the director, Stark Young, plays in it is simply that of steering Doris Keane and Ben-Ami towards as perfect a performance as their talents and temperaments permit."[21] Although Young did much less than he could have in shaping the production, he contradicted Macgowan's evaluation as impossible. "There is no such thing as a play directed exactly as it is written any more than there is a landscape painted as it really is."[22] Young also wrote, however, that "the importance of the thing added will measure the importance of the director."[23] Thus, in the case of *Welded* at least, the director condemned himself out of his own mouth.

With *Welded* O'Neill stepped up his participation in the rehearsal process, but he always tried to avoid the performers. When describing his anticipated involvement in Triumvirate rehearsals, he first wrote that he had "ideas about the how & what of production & acting" but then deleted "& acting" before mailing the letter.[24] In later correspondence he wryly

16. Young, "Art," *Context*, p. 369.

17. See especially his *Immortal Shadows* and *The Flower in Drama*.

18. Young, "Art," *Context*, p. 366.

19. It is amusing but useful that Macgowan reviewed his own Triumvirate productions in *Theatre Arts*.

20. Alexander Woollcott, "The Stage," *New York Herald*, Mar. 18, 1924, p. 11.

21. Kenneth Macgowan, "Crying the Bounds of Broadway," *Theatre Arts* 8 (June 1924): 359.

22. Stark Young, "The Art of Directing," *Theatre Arts* 9 (Apr. 1925): 227.

23. Young, "Art," *Context*, p. 366.

24. O'Neill letter to Macgowan, c. summer 1923, in Bryer, *Letters*, p. 37.

characterized his production role as that of "consulting engineer"[25] to the director. When a rehearsal crisis involving actors arose, O'Neill would not get involved. Doris Keane, for example, wanted to drop out of the cast after only a week of rehearsals because she quite rightly felt unsuited for the role of Eleanor. Young, Macgowan, and Jones all harnessed their powers of persuasion to keep her in the show, but O'Neill pretended to be unaware of the difficulty.[26]

With this production O'Neill yielded to a practice he usually abhorred. *Welded* was given a week of tryouts in Baltimore beginning March 3. This is the only time that O'Neill appears to have made no objections to out-of-town previews. In fact, he is reported to have attended tryout performances for the purpose of revision;[27] the production team had many reasons to doubt the viability of the play.

At the opening performance at the Baltimore Auditorium an unusually large audience was surprised to find itself bored and disappointed by the acting and the lack of apparent action. Two reviewers claimed that the restless audience lost interest in the stage action and actually demonstrated its disdain openly with laughter and conversation both during and after the play.[28] "Time after time," the *Sun* reported, "the heavily emotional scenes between the two stars missed fire, evoking wide-spread titters."[29] Norman Clark complained of the play's form, which in his view avoided modern dramaturgy and failed "to build up dramatic intensity."[30] The result was found to be little more than emotional conversation.

Welded, which O'Neill completed nearly a year before production, represented the playwright's closest conscious attempt to approach a "Strindberg 'Dance of Death' formula."[31] Termed a "vulgar, stupid, dogfight play"[32] by Keane, who admitted to never having understood her character, and "a treatise on conjugal neurosis"[33] by Torres, *Welded* was

25. O'Neill letter to Macgowan, c. Sept. 1923, in Bryer, *Letters*, p. 45.

26. Stark Young, "Eugene O'Neill: Notes from a Critic's Diary," *Harper's Magazine*, June 1957, p. 70.

27. "Plays on the Road," *New York Times*, Mar. 9, 1924, sec. 8, p. 2; Sheaffer, *Artist*, p. 132.

28. "O'Neill Play Falls Far Short of Ideal Upon Its Premiere," *Baltimore Daily Post*, Mar. 4, 1924, p. 5.

29. T. M. C., "Eugene O'Neill's Drama, 'Welded,' at Auditorium," *Baltimore Sun*, Mar. 4, 1924, p. 9; T. M. C., "Retrospect Reveals 'Intellectual' Values in O'Neill's New Drama," *Baltimore Sun*, Mar. 9, 1924, part 2, p. 2.

30. Norman Clark, "New Play by O'Neill at Auditorium," *Baltimore News*, Mar. 4, 1924, p. 9.

31. O'Neill letter to Macgowan, Sept. 23, 1922, in Bryer, *Letters*, p. 34.

32. Doris Keane, in Gelbs, *O'Neill*, p. 543; Young, "Eugene," *Harpers*, p. 70.

33. H. Z. Torres, "'Welded' Displays Morbid Tendency," *New York Commercial*, Mar. 18, 1924, p. 4.

intended as a presentation of a married couple in an intense, emotional love-hate relationship who "enact their spiritual struggle to possess one the other."[34] The results on stage were a stream of hyperbolic words and flamboyant physical action which caused confusion and anxiety for the director and actors. Young, for example, felt "that the words were a misplaced travesty of some genuine feeling, the results of an uncertain taste and an uncertain sense of the banal."[35]

Nathan complained that the characters were intensified "to the point where they are no longer human beings, or symbols of human beings, but just actors."[36] Nevertheless, Young and the actors occasionally overcame the play's synthetic limitations and uncovered "the torment that underlay the lines."[37] This was especially true in the prostitute's room of II.2. The honest, simple presentation of this scene, however, only pointed up as "so much surplusage"[38] the artificiality of the following act. Much of what O'Neill thought would be a presentation of spiritual passion became in the theater emotional agitation and carping.

O'Neill set his field of emotional upheaval in relief with an experimental use of pauses, which may be said to anticipate playwrights like Pinter and Shepard. "It's what . . . men and women do not say," he suggested, "that usually is most interesting."[39] The text called for many pauses and silences, which Young maintained, but the actors did not understand the usage, the implied subtextual meanings which O'Neill said he wanted yet could not satisfactorily explain. O'Neill told Clark that "the actors . . . did about as well as they could, but the whole point of the play was lost in the production. The most significant thing in the last act was the silences between the speeches. What was actually spoken should have served to a great extent just to punctuate the meaningful pauses. The actors didn't get that."[40] Unfortunately, O'Neill was of little help to Young or the actors in interpreting what seemed obvious to him. The result for the audience was a very slow pace which retarded the progress of the play, sometimes comically so. Benchley glibly described the effect on opening night: "As if to accentuate the repetitious and obvious monotony of the dialogue, the play has been directed much as slow-motion pictures must be directed. In order to acquire the extraordinary tempo at which the piece now creeps along, it must have been necessary for the players at

34. O'Neill, in Louis Kantor, "O'Neill Defends His Play of Negro," *New York Times*, May 11, 1924, sec. 9, p. 5.

35. Young, "Eugene," *Harpers*, p. 70.

36. George Jean Nathan, "The Theatre," *American Mercury* 2 (May 1924): 115.

37. Young, "Eugene," *Harpers*, p. 70.

38. A. K. [Allen Kelcey], "The New Plays," *World*, Mar. 18, 1924, p. 11.

39. O'Neill to Kantor, "O'Neill," p. 5.

40. O'Neill to Clark, in Clark, *O'Neill*, p. 91.

rehearsals to stop after each line and touch the floor ten times without bending their knees before going on with the next."[41] Obviously, the pauses were not being filled with mimetic action or subtextual implication. In some of his future work O'Neill would leave less to chance by spelling out both text and subtext.

In keeping with this liberal use of silence O'Neill and Young used a dynamic effect in act I which anticipated the interior monologues of *Strange Interlude* and *Dynamo,*[42] and which may suggest to later theatergoers the dramatic experiments of Samuel Beckett. The *Welded* script described Michael and Eleanor Cape taking seated positions. "Their chairs are side by side, each facing front, . . . they stare straight ahead and remain motionless. They speak, ostensibly to the other, but showing by their tone it is a thinking aloud to oneself, and neither appears to hear what the other has said."[43] Although Young gave them stools rather than chairs, he followed this direction closely. Macgowan recalled the characters in production as "side by side talking out to the audience in parallels of expression that seemed never to touch."[44] A few days after *Welded* opened Macgowan described the couple "facing the audience and speak[ing] what are practically their inner thoughts directly at the spectators. It is like two streams of emotion flowing parallel, each a comment on the other."[45] The Triumvirate leader much later remembered that O'Neill in rehearsals stressed the characters' lack of communication and internal revelation.[46]

Although O'Neill's strangest experimental device in *Welded* (the use of follow spots for the two major characters and no other stage lighting) was never incorporated by Young into the staging, the director did recreate most of O'Neill's suggested directions. This device ("auras of egoism") appears in all major editions of the play except the first, which describes the lighting in realistic terms. It is not likely that O'Neill intended the spotlights from the beginning, since the typescript of 1923 also calls for normal lighting with onstage practicals.[47] It is probable, then, that O'Neill got the idea of "auras of egoism" after the play failed when staged with realistic trappings.[48]

41. Robert C. Benchley, "Drama," *Life* (New York), Apr. 3, 1924, p. 26.

42. In a review of *Dynamo* Macgowan called *Welded* an early *Strange Interlude* experiment. Kenneth Macgowan, "Eugene O'Neill's New Play," *Vanity Fair*, Feb. 1929, p. 94.

43. O'Neill, *Welded*, p. 106.

44. Macgowan, "Eugene," *Vanity*, p. 94.

45. Macgowan, "Eugene," Mar. 23, 1924, p. 2.

46. Macgowan, "Eugene," *Vanity*, p. 94.

47. Eugene O'Neill, *Welded*, typescript, Rare Book Collection, Library of Congress, 1923, act I, p. 1.

48. See O'Neill, *Welded*, p. 89; Eugene O'Neill, *Welded*, in *Six Short Plays of Eugene O'Neill* (New York: Vintage Books, 1965), p. 257.

Young was quite adept at preparing stage pictures. Reviews generally praised his staging while attacking the play or the acting. In addition to faithfully mounting the side-by-side monologues of act I, Young recreated the crucifixion symbol described at the end of the play. As the characters ascended the stairs they formed a cross by stretching out their hands together. Now reunited in love and indivisible, the characters were nonetheless destined to continue suffering. Young had the actors deliberately but briefly touch their extended hands on the staircase, "making for a moment the sign of the cross,"[49] an image which anticipated the final picture of *Days Without End.*[50]

Despite occasional stylization like the human cross and the interior monologues, the production was essentially a realistic presentation which eventually seemed a mistake to both O'Neill and his producers. At the time of production, for example, Macgowan wrote that the play struck "a curious compromise between the realistic surface and the deep inner emotions which realism seldom can express."[51] By June he realized that the concept was wrong, that the action should have been removed from a realistic setting.[52] Sergeant likewise agreed that the play's failure was related to its too realistic presentation: "Its verisimilitude was over-logical, photographic."[53] O'Neill himself recognized this failing. "The principal reason why my 'Welded' was misunderstood by some," he wrote, "was that I erred when I conceived the dialogue against a naturalistic setting."[54]

The play's three authentic New York interiors were designed by Robert Edmond Jones, whose designs in this period almost always transcended the mundane world. None of the biographical and critical accounts of Jones and his work discusses the play, and most even fail to mention his *Welded* designs, which have all but disappeared.

In the fourteen-year-old Thirty-ninth Street Theatre, an intimate house by Broadway standards, seating between five hundred and eight hundred, Jones had more space than at the Provincetown, but was cramped nonetheless. The thirty-foot-wide proscenium opened onto a stage only twenty-six feet deep, with eleven and one-half feet of wing space on each side.[55] The offstage area must have been crowded with the play's three stage sets complete with two staircases.

49. Young, "Eugene," *Harpers*, p. 70; O'Neill, *Welded*, pp. 169–70.
50. Tiusanen, *O'Neill's*, p. 209.
51. Macgowan, "Eugene," Mar. 23, 1924, p. 2.
52. Macgowan, "Crying," p. 360.
53. Sergeant, *Fire*, p. 98.
54. O'Neill, in Kantor, "O'Neill," p. 5.
55. Pichel includes a ground plan of the stage and main floor of the house. Irving Pichel, *Modern Theatres* (New York: Harcourt, Brace, 1925), p. 27; Henderson, *City*, p. 276.

Jones designed realistic, contemporary interiors, two fashionable and one drab, with all features "carefully worked out in detail."[56] The studio apartment of the Capes (I and III) and John's library (II.1) were full-stage designs filling the proscenium opening, while the prostitute's bedroom (II.2) was considerably smaller.

Only one production photograph is available.[57] This shot, which captures the climactic action of act I just after Cape has attempted to strangle his wife and has broken away, does not display the entire setting, but it does provide a good view of the wide wooden central staircase with a heavy cloth runner set perpendicular to the proscenium line. What can be seen of the apartment seems spare and free of clutter, an observation reinforced by Whittaker's description of this set as "a neat studio."[58] Due to its size and central position the staircase dominated the setting and undoubtedly dictated much blocking, especially since the most important emotional events utilized its myriad levels. Its use may in fact have been inspired by the German expressionist director Leopold Jessner's *Jessnertreppen.*[59] Nathan referred to the staircase and center stage in this setting as "the battle ground of the actors."[60] Here again, both in text and production, the play incorporated theatricality which seemed at the time inappropriate in a realistic environment.

Several reviewers were engaged by the small, wretched quarters in "a Sixth Avenue bed house"[61] of the young woman of the evening. O'Neill described it as a "dingy bedroom" with "a filthy threadbare carpet" and "ugly wallpaper, dirty, stained, criss-crossed with match-strokes."[62] Pulaski found the design a literal rendering of a low-caste rooming house,[63] while Corbin ventured further. "The atmosphere of the street-walker's drab and squalid lodgings," he wrote, "is like a breath from the gutter."[64] Unlike his work with *Anna Christie*, Jones' designs reportedly captured sordidness without charm.

The lighting design was either done sloppily and haphazardly, per-

56. Ibee, "Welded," p. 16.

57. Theatre Collection, MCNY.

58. James Whittaker, "Eugene O'Neill's Play Shown at 39th Street," *New York American,* Mar. 18, 1924, in Miller, *Playwright's,* p. 14.

59. Jones and Macgowan saw his *Richard III* in Germany in 1922 and were profoundly affected. Kenneth Macgowan and Robert Edmond Jones, *Continental Stagecraft* (New York: Harcourt, Brace, 1922), pp. 137–43.

60. Nathan, "Theatre," May 1924, p. 116.

61. O'Neill, *Welded* typescript, II.2, p. 1.

62. O'Neill, *Welded,* p. 139.

63. Ibee, "Welded," p. 16.

64. John Corbin, "Romantic Marriage," *New York Times,* Mar. 18, 1924, p. 24.

haps tardily, or Jones and Young[65] were actually experimenting with stylization with results which only confused the audience. Whatever the problem may have been, it is clear that the production team as well as critics were dissatisfied with the results. Nathan graphically enumerated some of the lighting difficulties:

> Unless my eyes deceived me on the opening night, it was high noon outside the window of the room in Act II [the prostitute's room] although the time was two o'clock in the morning. Again, the dawn of the last act was of a peculiar pea-green shade, as of Maeterlinck full of chartreuse. Still again, although the room of Act I was illuminated only by a small and arty table lamp at the extreme left of the stage, the center of the stage . . . was whimsically bathed in a dazzling radiance by a powerful balcony spotlight.[66]

Such messy work was uncharacteristic of Jones with his usual attention to the effects of illumination. It is therefore possible that the "dazzling radiance" of stage center was deliberate, to accentuate the severe agitation of the Capes.

Nevertheless, the lighting decisions made or mistakes allowed added to the stylistic inconsistencies and excesses of both play and production. Macgowan later told O'Neill that if *Welded* had not closed so quickly "we could have fixed up the production and the lights and pulled the acting into better shape."[67] This was probably true of lighting, but it would have been almost impossible to adjust the acting problems effectively without recasting.

O'Neill once wrote that his chief difficulty in theater-going was that "the actor is ever present to me and the character is lost."[68] In *Welded* the actor's presence was too evident for nearly everyone. Keane and Ben-Ami were cast in roles for which they were unsuitable and which they failed to understand. Macgowan understated the difficulty when he wrote that the two stars were cast "in parts decidedly difficult for them to compass."[69] The actors were lost and resorted to flamboyant physical and vocal methods which felt familiar and comfortable, but which were clearly inappropriate—sometimes comically so.

At forty-two Doris Keane was twelve years older than her character, and even further removed from Eleanor Cape's personality and temperament. Keane was at her best in sentimental, dreamy characters of a bygone age, such as the opera diva Cavallini in Edward Sheldon's *Romance*,

65. At this time the lighting was usually the joint responsibility of director and stage designer. Kenneth Macgowan, "Enter the Artist—As Director," *Theatre Magazine*, Nov. 1922, p. 289.
66. Nathan, "Theatre," May 1924, p. 116.
67. Macgowan letter to O'Neill, Aug. 12, 1926, in Bryer, *Letters*, p. 129.
68. O'Neill letter to Macgowan, Mar. 18, 1921, in Bryer, *Letters*, p. 20.
69. Macgowan, "Crying," p. 359

which even in 1913 was a throwback to an earlier theatrical era.[70] "She could not have been farther than she was from the heroine of 'Welded' as written,"[71] Young later recalled. In the constantly shifting, almost schizophrenic behavior of Eleanor, the elegant and polished Broadway performer was all at sea. Young described her as having "an almost painful tenderness toward any suffering in human beings, but these two people in 'Welded,' with their wrangling violence and what she would have taken as squabbling, belonged to another world from hers. She had a physical horror of a row and almost as much of bad taste in one's conduct."[72] Matching such tenderness was Keane's graceful, "sylph-like"[73] presence, physical beauty "which cannot be blighted,"[74] and a "lovely and melodious"[75] voice which sometimes leaned too much to the musical. The "fineness and delicacy" which arose in her work was "cursed by an incantation delivery,"[76] Woollcott mourned. She was in many ways "eternally the prima donna,"[77] in vain search of another vehicle like *Romance*.

Two years earlier Keane explained to an interviewer, "It is impossible to play any role without having an understanding of the soul of the person portrayed. . . . You must know the character from the inside."[78] Nevertheless, having little or no understanding of Eleanor's psychology, Keane attempted to approach from the outside what she saw as a "modern" woman. She bobbed her hair for the first time in the popular twenties style and tinted it with red; she bravely struggled physically and vocally with Ben-Ami, but without internal commitment, without encouraging belief.

When Keane recognized that her efforts were probably hopeless, she attempted to bow out by claiming that she thought O'Neill's play which she initially read in manuscript was a scenario, not the finished play.[79] Her uncertainty doubtless persisted beyond rehearsals to performance, provoking Quinn to write that the prostitute scene was the best of the production probably because Keane, "who was playing Eleanor without any apparent understanding of the part, was not on the stage."[80] Likewise,

70. For an account of Keane in *Romance* see Eric Wollencott Barnes, *The Man Who Lived Twice: The Biography of Edward Sheldon* (New York: Charles Scribner's Sons, 1956), pp. 77–97.

71. Young, "Eugene," *Harpers*, p. 69.

72. Young, "Eugene," *Harpers*, p. 69.

73. Arthur Hornblow, "Mr. Hornblow Goes to the Play," *Theatre Magazine*, May 1924, p. 16.

74. Whittaker, "Eugene," p. 15.

75. Benchley, "Drama," Apr. 3, 1924, p. 26.

76. Woollcott, "Stage," Mar. 18, 1924, p. 11.

77. Young, "Eugene," *Harpers*, p. 69.

78. Doris Keane, in "You Fail If Bored Says Doris Keane," New York *Daily News*, Mar. 5, 1922, p. 21.

79. Young, "Eugene," *Harper's*, p. 70.

80. Quinn, *History*, vol. 2, p. 185.

Metcalfe assumed that "Keane evidently despaired of making anything human of her character and took refuge in making it as artificial as possible."[81] Eventually Young was mortified at what happened to one of his closest friends, and lamented Keane's having been allowed to perform as Eleanor.[82]

"The electric Jacob Ben-Ami"[83] was at thirty-three certainly more suitable physically for his role of Michael Cape, but this handsome, Russian-born actor, who had been working exclusively in Yiddish theaters since 1914, had first appeared on the English-speaking stage only four years before *Welded*. Also a good friend of the director, he had just finished a short run under Young's guidance in *The Failures* for the Theatre Guild.

Ben-Ami's Russian-Yiddish dialect was troublesome for many who witnessed *Welded*, but theatergoers of the 1920s often seemed to enjoy encountering a variety of "exotic" European dialects in the production of American plays, especially when Alla Nazimova was in the cast. Nevertheless, Ben-Ami's delivery came under attack. "His accents and pronunciation are disheveled," wrote Hammond, "and he is given to grunting. The word 'suffering,' for instance, is full of sympathetic possibilities, but when it is called 'soffering' it lacks the pathetic note."[84] Hornblow complained that the actor played, "as usual, with much unnecessary gesture and a thick-voiced oratory that renders half his words unintelligible."[85] On the other hand, his delivery was sometimes childishly explosive, "like the rapid firing of a cap pistol."[86] Ben-Ami, who took pleasure in his ranting and grand gesturing, reveled "in his oratorical soliloquies, beating the air with disconsolate philosophies."[87] Woollcott reported that he played with "continuous vehemence."[88] Such an actor had no difficulty arousing stage emotion, but it was deemed inappropriate, artificial, and monotonous for the swiftly altering moods of Michael Cape. Before the evening had ended, Burns Mantle claimed that he was eager to hurl his orchestra chair at Ben-Ami.[89]

Although chagrined by the play and production (but obviously enjoy-

81. Metcalfe, "The Theatre," *Wall Street Journal*, Mar. 19, 1924, p. 3.

82. John Pilkington, ed., *Stark Young: A Life in the Arts, Letters, 1900–1962*, vol. 1 (Baton Rouge: Louisiana State University Press, 1975), p. 161; Gelbs, *O'Neill*, p. 544.

83. Corbin, "Romantic," p. 24.

84. Percy Hammond, "Eugene O'Neill's 'Welded,'" *New York Tribune*, Mar. 18, 1924, p. 12.

85. Hornblow, May 1924, p. 16.

86. David Carb, "To See or Not to See," *Bookman* 59 (May 1924): 332.

87. Hammond, "Eugene," Mar. 18, 1924, p. 12.

88. Woollcott, "Stage," Mar. 18, 1924, p. 11.

89. Burns Mantle, "'Welded' Intense but Monotonous," New York *Daily News*, Mar. 18, 1924, p. 26.

ing writing his review), Benchley referred to Ben-Ami's rendering of Cape's frequent mechanical, preoccupied delivery and movement as "behaving as if he had just been hit on the head by what the police call 'some blunt instrument.'"[90] Likewise delighting in his attack, Nathan called Ben-Ami in his artificiality "an actor who would play Huckleberry Finn in the manner of Ermete Novelli making a gala address at a Lambs' Club banquet in honor of Robert B. Mantell. . . . This Ben-Ami, an actor intensified to such a degree that he seems always in danger of biting himself, brought to the already highly actorized role an artillery of histrionic nonsense that made it doubly unreal and absurd."[91] Accordingly, any important confrontations between suffering husband and wife sounded like bombastic bickering and neither principal "discovered any way to break the monotony"[92] produced by relentless, unfelt, misunderstood, emotional upheaval. The audiences of *Welded* found little respite from the artificial "trancelike spell which seemed to afflict the troupe,"[93] the rootless *Sturm und Drang* of Ben-Ami, Keane, and O'Neill's rocky marriage to Agnes Boulton, which was the real subject of this play.

Welded was another play which O'Neill later rejected with good reason as unworthy of revision. Although he was present and active during the rehearsal process, he chose to blame the production for failure as though he were not part of it. The play, which Benchley claimed had "one hundred and eleven different readings of the lines, 'I love you,' 'I hate you,' and 'Can you ever forgive me?'"[94] closed after only three weeks.[95]

In a statement inaugurating Experimental Theatre, Inc., written only two months before the opening of *Welded*, O'Neill's rebellion against stage realism seemed to be in fine form: "We have taken too many snapshots of each other in every graceless position; we have endured too much from the banality of surfaces."[96] Nevertheless, O'Neill and Young failed to commit *Welded* deeply to the stylization which seemed to be necessary; the playwright, Young, and the Triumvirate made great mistakes and compromises, some of which would not be repeated. Because it took place in a Broadway house, under partial commercial auspices and with mainstream Broadway stars, this production was not a proper trial of

90. Benchley, "Drama," Apr. 3, 1924, p. 26.

91. Novelli was an Italian tragic actor with a big voice and romantic style who died in 1919. Mantell was an aging Scotish-American romantic Shakespearean touring star. Nathan, "Theatre," May 1924, pp. 115–16.

92. Woollcott, "Stage," Mar. 18, 1924, p. 11.

93. Woollcott, "Stage," Mar. 18, 1924, p. 11.

94. Benchley, Apr. 3, 1924, p. 26.

95. Newspaper ads ceased after April 5, 1924.

96. Eugene O'Neill, "Strindberg and Our Theatre," in Horst Frenz, ed. *American Playwrights on Drama* (New York: Hill and Wang, 1965), p. 2.

the Triumvirate's organization and principles. Despite erratic lighting, Young created effective stage pictures, yet his serious errors in casting led to disconnected, emotional upheaval and to unfilled pauses and silences. Realistic scenery and staging were incongruous with the occasional stylized moments of the play and were ultimately seen to be a great mistake. At the time, the results of the production's hyperbole were discouraging if not alarming. In the words of Eleanor Cape in act I, "It would be funny—if it weren't so exasperating."[97]

Although it was not influential either as play or production on other theater artists, O'Neill's *Welded* helped his development as he experimented with important devices which would surface powerfully later. It was obvious that half-measures in stylization would not be effective: O'Neill and his collaborators would have to go much further with theatricalism to be successful. The next O'Neill experiment exhibited excesses in this very direction.

The Ancient Mariner

Less than one month after the appearance of *Welded* the Triumvirate ventured into murky theatrical waters with an experiment quite unlike anything else seen in New York with the exception of some of the poetic presentations at the Neighborhood Playhouse.[98] Under the codirection of Robert Edmond Jones and James Light, the Provincetown Playhouse mounted *The Ancient Mariner*, "a dramatic arrangement" by O'Neill of the romantic poem by Samuel Taylor Coleridge,[99] O'Neill's only adaptation of another literary work. Appearing on the same bill with Stark Young's production of *George Dandin* by Molière, *The Ancient Mariner* opened on April 6, 1924, and ran for only thirty-three performances.[100]

When describing the spirit of the times which spawned or at least encouraged such free-wheeling experiments as the Triumvirate pursued with *The Ancient Mariner*, Gassner wrote, "It was high time to make life more abundant with esthetic gratifications. The old forms had to be discarded, new forms had to be created, and the sons of Zenith returned to convert Philistia into Paradise."[101] Heywood Broun, who often lauded Provincetown efforts, could not endorse their attempt with *The Ancient*

97. O'Neill, *Welded*, p. 110.
98. The Neighborhood often produced difficult poetic plays by playwrights such as Yeats and festival dramatizations of long poems such as "Hiawatha" by Henry Wadsworth Longfellow.
99. *The Ancient Mariner* program, Provincetown Players folder, Theatre Collection, MCNY.
100. "The Week's Events," *New York Times*, Apr. 6, 1924, sec. 8, p. 1; Mantle, *Best Plays, 1923–24*, p. 444. The first reviews appeared on Monday, Apr. 7, 1924.
101. John Gassner, *Masters of the Drama*, 3d ed. (New York: Dover, 1954), p. 638.

Mariner. "A cracked test tube in the Provincetown laboratory"[102] characterized his evaluation of this serious and imaginative, but too self-conscious and artistically precious, dramatization. Karl Decker called it "pure melodrama masquerading as high brow stuff."[103] Nevertheless, O'Neill and his compatriots made important progress in their explorations of theatrical space, light, the chorus, and the dynamics of masks.

Late in 1922 Macgowan began to look forward to a new force in the theater, an artist-director who came to the process of direction via the field of design. "If the director cannot acquire the talents of the artist," he asked while lamenting the obtuse eye of many stage directors, "why cannot the artist acquire the talents of the director?"[104] As if in response, Lee Simonson described the need of the designers of his time to create not only the setting and costumes but the production's interpretation as well. "We became architects of a third dimension rather than painters," he wrote, "projectors of a plastic stage picture. . . . It is symptomatic that Jones and Geddes . . . have again and again felt that design, in itself, left their intentions truncated, and undertaken the job of directing a play."[105] From 1924 to 1926 Jones pursued this enlarged production role in a series of plays which he both directed and designed. His first direction of O'Neill, however, incorporated only some of the director's responsibilities.

In sharing the directing duties with James Light, Jones had both an ally who understood the limitations and intricacies of the Provincetown facility, and a director who shared an admiration and understanding of O'Neill's approach to experiment and dramaturgy. O'Neill was usually happy to have Light directing his plays. "Jimmy Light . . . is certainly 'aces' compared to any [directors] I know. . . . And I know he is fine for me to work with,"[106] he wrote to Macgowan after Experimental Theatre, Inc., ceased activity.

Despite Light's predilection for analytical discussion, he was much more adept at communicating effectively with actors than was Jones, and in their directorial collaboration, both in *The Ancient Mariner* and a few months earlier in *Spook Sonata*, the two directors shared design decisions (Light created the masks for both) as well as staging duties. Several brief accounts of their partnership, however, suggest that Jones was more concerned with physical staging and composition, while Light con-

102. Heywood Broun, "The New Play," *World*, Apr. 7, 1924, p. 9.

103. Karl Decker, "'Mariner' Thrills Fail to Register," New York *Morning Telegraph*, Apr. 8, 1924, p. 7.

104. Macgowan, "Enter," p. 289.

105. Lee Simonson, in Theodore Komisarjevsky and Lee Simonson, *Settings and Costumes of the Modern Stage* (New York: Benjamin Blom, 1966), p. 96.

106. O'Neill letter to Macgowan, July 15, 1926, in Bryer, *Letters*, p. 118.

centrated on acting problems and the mundane logistics of rehearsal.[107] Light was usually pragmatic and efficient, but Jones sought the special, the unusual, the extraordinary elements of the world of the play.

Although Jones had directed his first play as early as 1917,[108] he did not begin an active directing career until 1924. This student of George Pierce Baker's 47 Workshop at Harvard was an almost indefatigable worker, who during the spring of 1924 was suffering from some kind of cancerous condition in one leg, which was fortunately relieved after an operation in May. As a result, Jones was lame throughout the rehearsals of *The Ancient Mariner*, but apparently unfazed so far as productivity was concerned. Nevertheless, this period in Jones' career was "a very happy one" because he "now had the freedom to carry out some of his dramatic theories,"[109] Mordecai Gorelik later recalled. It was true that Jones had much more freedom to experiment with space and devices than he ever had while only designing for Arthur Hopkins. With his newfound liberty Jones quickly discovered a way to define his dual contributions in terms of design. "The director of today thinks in terms of sculpture," he wrote in the *Ancient Mariner* program, "and arranges his actors in powerfully expressive groups as a sculptor might wish to arrange them. . . . The scene-designer models with light."[110] Jones enjoyed considerable success in both areas with this play, yet the production failed.

O'Neill, who apparently completed his dramatic arrangement some time in 1923,[111] made few alterations in the text of the Coleridge poem but reassigned many lyrical, descriptive lines to stage directions. O'Neill's working text used for production was simply a published copy of the poem with handwritten marginal notes and directions and two inserted pages of opening stage directions.[112]

Barrett Clark wrote that "O'Neill seems . . . to have been driven by some inner necessity to devise a whole new set of tools every time he planned a new work."[113] With *The Ancient Mariner*, however, he strayed further afield than at any other time, living up to his promise to Macgowan

107. See 1968 interview with Guy Gillespie in Hicks, "Robert," p. 85; 1960 interview with Walter Abel in Vilhaur, "History," p. 426.

108. Jones directed and designed *Three Plays for a Negro Theatre* by Ridgely Torrence with an all-black cast (Apr. 5, 1917). See "The Negro in American Drama," *Theatre*, June 1917, pp. 350, 352; Zona Gale, "The Colored Players and Their Plays," *Theatre Arts* 1 (May 1917): 138–40.

109. Gorelik was an assistant to Jones for a season with the Triumvirate. Mordecai Gorelik, "Life With Bobby," *Theatre Arts* 39 (Apr. 1955): 95.

110. *The Ancient Mariner* program, Theatre Collection, MCNY.

111. Donald Gallup, "Eugene O'Neill's 'The Ancient Mariner,'" *Yale University Library Gazette* 35 (Oct. 1960): 61.

112. Eugene O'Neill, "The Rime of the Ancient Mariner," *Yale University Library Gazette* 35 (Oct. 1960): 63–86.

113. Clark, *O'Neill*, p. 82.

made in the Triumvirate's organizational year. He stated that he was interested not just in his "original writing . . . [but in] many things outside of my own stuff that I have a creative theatre hunch about as being possibilities for experiment."[114] This production was not merely a dramatization or reenactment of the poem but an expressionistic experiment which emerged as a series of "subjective projections."[115]

The Ancient Mariner, something of a "semi-pantomimic recital,"[116] was the only O'Neill production which included a narrator. Although the Mariner, played by E. J. Ballantine, addressed his story in a rhetorical manner to the Wedding Guest instead of the audience throughout the play, in the final moments "he turn[ed] to audience as a prophet proclaiming truth"[117] and delivered the final speech, after which he returned to the world of the play. Furthermore, Macgowan wrote that as the production progressed Jones and Light had the Mariner "gradually drawn into the action he describes,"[118] so that the audience sometimes did not know if they were watching dramatic narration or narrative drama. One critic declared that the change was not gradual but sudden. "At such times when the Mariner steps from his part as story teller into that of actor there is a transition which halts the whole thing."[119]

The mixed style of the Mariner's presentation may have been disconcerting to some, but it was overwhelmed by the dynamics of the Triumvirate's "new preoccupation with masks."[120] O'Neill's stage directions called for a chorus of "six old sailors" to wear "masks of drowned men" when they first appear, masks of "holy spirits" after they die, to revert later to original masks, to conclude with the angelic vizards. In addition, a female death figure appears in "the mask of a black skull" nearly midway through the play.[121]

Jones and Light were anxious to use masks in order to project emotion and character through movement and to suppress the clichés of facial expression.[122] In designing and building the masks Light maintained a serious and spiritual purpose. "We do not use the mask to imitate life," he wrote, "but to intensify the quality of the theme. The mask cannot represent life, because it always has a life of its own. . . . But it can be used, as we are trying to show it, to show the eyes of tragedy and the face of

114. O'Neill letter to Macgowan, c. summer 1923, in Bryer, *Letters,* p. 37.
115. Valgemae, *Accelerated,* p. 43.
116. "Molière Satire at Village Playhouse," *Journal of Commerce,* Apr. 8, 1924, p. 7.
117. O'Neill, "Rime," p. 85.
118. Macgowan, "Crying," p. 358.
119. "The Ancient Mariner," *New York Evening Post,* Apr. 7, 1924, p. 13.
120. Deutsch, *Provincetown,* p. 105.
121. O'Neill, "Rime," pp. 64, 71, 76, 79, 81.
122. Robert Edmond Jones, "Fashions in the Theatre," *Theatre Arts* 3 (Apr. 1919): 115.

exaltation."[123] The production team therefore hoped to cover the human face not only so as to accentuate movement but to reveal part of what lay hidden beneath the face.

More specifically, Light attempted to capture the possibility for variety in the masks. Inspired by the enigmatic Japanese Noh masks, Light tried to build masks which seemed to alter expression when the angle of lighting was changed. Whatever the success with alterability, the masks were clearly grotesque: "dank hair hung clammily over sea-green mouldy visages."[124] The "gangrenous," "cadaverous" masks, which fitted over the face rather than the whole head, were "plaintively ominous" until an actor turned his back to reveal the "incongruity of modern tonsures" or until the light caught the exposed pink necks and ears which "give a ready lie to the imagination."[125] Although Lewisohn admired the fantastic masks, he found "the little theatre of mere human voices . . . utterly inadequate"[126] for the majesty conjured up by the images of horror. The masks in this case clashed with the miniature scale dictated by the Provincetown space.

Although O'Neill and Light had achieved choral effects before, in *The Hairy Ape*, *The Ancient Mariner* marked their first use of a declared chorus. The six-man chorus, dressed simply in light open shirts and baggy trousers, represented the Mariner's crew which in production mimed the action described by the narrative and often sang, hummed, chanted, and moved rhythmically. The script, for example, called for them to "sway to the roll of the ship," "sing a hymn to a sort of chanty rhythm," and "after one staccato scream of horror, fall on their faces."[127] Jones and Light kept the chorus busy with often dancelike "pantomimic accompaniment" as they "acted with macabre postures" the Mariner's tale.[128] Deutsch reported that the chorus "grouped and regrouped about the tall mast of the phantom ship,"[129] supplying, in Vreeland's words, "much of the half-world undercurrent of the piece."[130] Hornblow found "much beauty of

123. James Light, "The Mask," *The Ancient Mariner* program, MCNY, p. 5.

124. Frank Vreeland, "'Ancient Mariner' Made Vivid Even for Schoolboys," *New York Herald Tribune*, Apr. 7, 1924, p. 8.

125. John Corbin, "What Boys Will Be," *New York Times*, Apr. 13, 1924, sec. 8, p. 1; John Corbin, "A New Provincetown Playbill," *New York Times*, Apr. 7, 1924, p. 15; Mary Cass Canfield, *Grotesques and Other Reflections on Art and the Theatre* (Port Washington, New York: Kennikat, 1968), p. 187; John Anderson, *The American Theatre* (New York: Dial, 1938), p. 73.

126. Ludwig Lewisohn, "Diversions," *Nation* 118 (Apr. 23, 1924): 486.

127. O'Neill, "Rime," pp. 64, 66, 67.

128. George Jean Nathan, "The Rime of the Ancient Mariner," *American Mercury*, June 1924, in Cargill, *O'Neill*, p. 166; Vreeland, "Ancient," p. 8.

129. Deutsch, *Provincetown*, p. 104.

130. Vreeland, "Ancient," p. 8.

motion in the rhythmic movements,"[131] but some critics like Broun were disturbed by the too exacting correlation of description and action. Nonetheless, Light asserted that the chorus was intended to "indicate a flow of emotion, not at all to represent action. . . . what they do," he said, "affects the audience much as music does."[132] Often the effects were simple but haunting. When the ship was struck with blight, for example, the chorus lay flat on the floor; after the blight had passed the chorus slowly rose to its feet. The overall effect, enhanced of course by the masks, was one of "poetized robots."[133] As a press release described them, the members of the chorus were meant to be "assistants in a ritual, celebrants in a ceremony."[134]

From the inception of his work on this material O'Neill had planned a significant use of music accompanied by recitative. The play text is sprinkled with musical references, which in production became "old country dances, celestial chords, sailors' chanteys [which] provide[d] an almost constant accompaniment to the verse."[135] *Theatre Arts* in fact described the music when joined with "lights and the movement and voices of the chorus . . . [as] a symphonic accompaniment,"[136] a tribute to the variform production which reflected the dedication of Jones and Light to theatrical experiment which transcended the expected boundaries of American theater.

The effect of the presentation both in intent and perceived result was unmistakably related to oriental forms. Light reported that the directors sought an emotional effect more akin to music than dramatized representation.[137] Furthermore, Macgowan called the production "an attempt to formalize the stage almost to the point of the Japanese No drama."[138] Something of this goal was discernible to Vreeland, who acknowledged "an almost Chinese simplicity and transparency"[139] in the production's presentation and style.

Upon taking charge of the Provincetown Playhouse Jones imme-

---

131. Arthur Hornblow, "Mr. Hornblow Goes to the Play," *Theatre Magazine,* June 1924, p. 19.

132. James Light in "The Chorus as Used in 'The Ancient Mariner,'" *Sun,* Apr. 23, 1924, p. 24.

133. Vreeland, "Ancient," p. 8; Nathan, "Rime," p. 166.

134. "Chorus," *Sun,* p. 24.

135. Macgowan, "Crying," p. 360.

136. Caption for illustration in *Theatre Arts* 8 (June 1924): 366.

137. James Light (1924), in Bogard, *Contour,* p. 231.

138. Macgowan, "Crying," p. 357.

139. Vreeland, "Ancient," p. 8.

diately changed the interior design, an alteration which had an important effect on the performance space and an immediate influence on the staging of *The Ancient Mariner*. Jones enlarged the downstage playing area a few feet by extending the apron as far as possible toward the seats. In addition, he added curtained proscenium doors to each side of the stage, a device which he put to full use, especially in *Fashion* and *The Ancient Mariner*.[140]

Since at least 1922 Macgowan had looked forward to a return to an open-platform stage for acting, a breakout from what he saw as an inhibiting proscenium picture frame. "In such a house," he wrote, "an actor will be all but forced to desert . . . the retreative, the purely representational style of today, and to present himself and his emotions in an open, assertive . . . manner as objects of art and of emotion."[141] Indeed Jones and Light were partially successful in their restoration of the open platform.

There are no useful photographs for this production, but a dynamic rendering by Jones survives along with helpful and consistent critical descriptions of the open space, which was dominated by the dome and numerous lighting effects, most notably projections. A screen was mounted stage right next to the proscenium door to signify the entrance to the wedding party. Shadows occasionally appeared on the screen to indicate activity within.[142] According to Macgowan, when the Mariner began his tale for the Wedding Guest, "the screen fade[d] and [the chorus] carr[ied] on the prow, the stern, and the mast of the boat."[143] This small vessel, "no larger than a rowboat," recalled Gorelik, enhanced the legendary, epic flavor of the poem.[144] The piecemeal ship was actually "a few bits of canvas and cardboard" which were held together by the chorus when at sea, but at the beginning all "was quite openly carried on the stage by the ghostly crew without subterfuge."[145] Few properties were used, and those which appeared were emblematic, such as the albatross which resembled a flat Christmas-tree ornament.[146] Stage pictures had a deliberate two-dimensional effect without attempts at perspective, though they were enhanced by distortions in light and shade. The directors made no attempt to maintain a sense of dramatic action with the arrival of the disassembled ship but sought to expose all of the presentational elements of the performance.

140. Boulton, "Experimental," p. 187; Gorelik, "Life," p. 95.
141. Macgowan, "Enter," p. 292.
142. Rendering in Robert Edmond Jones, *Drawings for the Theatre* (New York: Theatre Arts Books, 1970), plate 33.
143. Macgowan, "Crying," p. 358.
144. Mordecai Gorelik, letter to Waldo, Apr. 9, 1968, in Waldo, "Production," p. 234.
145. Vreeland, "Ancient," p. 8.
146. Decker, "Mariner," p. 7.

Placing the actors on a nearly bare stage in front of the plaster dome used as a surface for great splashes of color and projected images, Jones "was exploring the subtle relationship of actor and scenery."[147] The Mariner and his chorus were set against a seemingly endless, luminous ocean vista as "the dome called up the wide sea and made possible a quality of brooding immensity."[148] Together the human figures swayed in rough seas when appropriate, moving the fragmented ship with their own motion. Canfield recalled "darkly solid figures against a pale green cyclorama." The chorus, she continued, "was handled as sculpture, its black silhouettes posed with bleak meaningful effect against the sky."[149] Jones' rendering reflects this description very effectively. The dark ghost ship seems dead in the water stage left on an empty stage backed by an intensely lit dome which prominently features the projection of a skeletal figure in the sky. If the rendering and critical descriptions are accurate, some of the choral activity must have been dark, hazy figures moving against a brightly illuminated field with front lighting of low intensity. Thus, the aforementioned incongruity of mask and skin would not always be evident. Full, shadowless illumination was also used, however.

As usual Jones devoted considerable time to his lighting design. When free to experiment as he was here he often sought light which would surround the actors "in a luminous, shadowless aether," an environment in which the characters might sometimes seem "self-luminous and radiant—important, heroic."[150] He therefore worked for lighting effects which enhanced character as well as created mood. In fact *The Ancient Mariner* was one of Jones' most obvious attempts to render general illumination obsolete. Never settling for "ordinary light," his "moonlight [became] the visible wake of ghosts."[151] The changeable sea and sun were created by much movement in light and shifting colors, especially various greens and reds which frequently changed to follow the descriptive narration. The results, while not always intense enough for some viewers, were usually considered eerie and mysterious.[152]

The play was divided into seven parts, each indicating a time shift. All shifts were achieved through use of lighting instead of the curtain, with slow-count blackouts "fading out each episode like a movie."[153] Al-

147. Donald Oenslager, in Jones, *Drawings* (1970), p. 17.

148. Deutsch, *Provincetown*, pp. 104–05.

149. Canfield, *Grotesques*, p. 187.

150. Jones, in Sayler, *Our American*, p. 158.

151. Marya Mannes, "Robert Edmond Jones," *Theatre Guild Magazine* 8 (Nov. 1930): 15.

152. Nathan, "Rime," p. 166; Broun, "New," Apr. 7, 1924, p. 9; Vreeland, "Ancient," p. 8; Macgowan, "Crying," p. 358.

153. Vreeland, "Ancient," p. 8.

though not an innovation, this device was unusual at that time on the American stage,[154] and had never before been used in an O'Neill play.

While the use of the chorus was often dynamic, the Mariner as played by E. J. Ballantine, a thirty-six-year-old serviceable British actor, fell short of the needs of the "irregularly sonorous ballad rhythms"[155] of Coleridge's masterpiece. O'Neill believed his friend Ballantine to have "a presence & a touch of mad quality,"[156] and the actor too often resorted to declamation and intoned the lines instead of finding the passion and terror of the piece. Ballantine clearly understood the language, but he failed to discover "the grisly, spectral horror of the poem."[157] "With a voice full of cramps and a face full of whiskers,"[158] the wide-eyed Ballantine carefully recited and often mimed action as accompaniment to his own narration. He may have looked appropriately weathered and wild,[159] but he failed to match his physical presence with a believable emotional portrayal.

Although O'Neill was on hand for many rehearsals and reportedly shared much of his knowledge of sea-going life with the actors,[160] the stylization of the production divorced the performers, especially Ballantine, from applying what lessons they learned from the playwright. Nevertheless, Light and Jones devised a presentation which approached but failed to secure significant artistic success. Inconsistency and excess in stage effects and conceptualization seem chiefly responsible for failure. "Some moments were effectively startling and briefly but memorably thrilling," reported the *Evening Post*. "The weird imagery of the thing came through time and again, but was not sustained."[161] Although the production avoided realistic interpretation, the directors zealously tried to literalize much of the fantasy in the poem, to present events verbatim rather than through suggestion. Unfortunately, many viewers had the impression that the directors and O'Neill were "playing at theatre"[162] rather than being creative.

Incongruously, the production also suffered from unrelieved tension; the playwright and directors created a brittle world marked by excess, but

154. The American production of *Johannes Kreisler*, an expressionistic "fantastic melodrama" by Carl Meinhard and Rudolph Bernauer under the direction of Frank Reicher in Dec. 1922, had used lighting and levels to divide and differentiate the play's forty-one scenes. Ludwig Lewisohn, "Drama," *Nation* 116 (Jan. 10, 1923): 48.

155. Corbin, "New," Apr. 7, 1924, p. 15.

156. O'Neill letter to Macgowan, Jan. 21, 1927, in Bryer, *Letters*, p. 147.

157. Corbin, "New," Apr. 7, 1924, p. 15.

158. Nathan, "Rime," p. 166.

159. Photographs of Ballantine as the Mariner in *Theatre Arts* 8 (June 1924): 365, and *Theatre Magazine*, July 1924, p. 5.

160. Quinn, *History*, vol. 2, pp. 185–86.

161. "Ancient," *New York Evening Post*, p. 13.

162. Metcalfe, "Playing Theatre," *Wall Street Journal*, Apr. 8, 1924, p. 3.

entrapped in a small theater where the Mariner's visions seemed to shrink almost to pettiness. "Mr. O'Neill and his associates have taken art and made it arty,"[163] Broun complained. Despite disappointment, however, *The Ancient Mariner* was a significant trial with masks, music, chorus, lighting, oriental simplicity, and the open space, all of which would be used successfully in future O'Neill productions. Although Jones and Light together created interesting stage effects, both would create much more effective work when staging O'Neill's plays without directorial collaboration.

It was now clear with this production that O'Neill and his associates were becoming very eclectic and free-spirited in their experimentation. They were willing to explore any avenue from the most disparate fields of theater and graphic arts so long as they might serve the immediate purposes of the production. Such a point of view would continue throughout the existence of Experimental Theatre, Inc., and for O'Neill far beyond until his first retirement from the stage in 1934. By 1924 O'Neill was clearly recognized as America's leading dramatist (as many had claimed already in 1920), but during his tenure with the Triumvirate he also became the impetus for America's most significant production experiments in the theater. This position remained secure for some ten years until the rise of the Group Theatre.

All God's Chillun Got Wings

James Light, finally on his own, found himself in the midst of public controversy with O'Neill's next play. When *All God's Chillun Got Wings* premiered on May 15, 1924, at the Provincetown,[164] it had attracted far more preopening publicity (including furor) than any previous O'Neill production[165] and vied with notorious American productions such as *Mrs. Warren's Profession, Sapho,* and *The Demi-Virgin.* The play's controversial subject matter of miscegenation, and Light's willingness to cast a black actor opposite a white actress, aroused the best and worst sentiments in many critics as well as numerous citizens who normally paid little or no attention to the theater, especially to a modestly budgeted production mounted in the tiny Provincetown Playhouse.

While the sympathetic treatment of miscegenation may have been

163. Broun, "New," Apr. 7, 1924, p. 9.
164. "Theatrical Notes," *New York Times,* May 15, 1924, p. 22. Reviews first appeared on Friday, May 16, 1924.
165. Deutsch reported that "the press-clipping bill exceeded the cost of the scenery." This hyperbole probably grew out of a casual statement by Macgowan: "I wish I knew how many clippings we paid for. . . . I shouldn't be at all surprised to find that they cost us more than the scenery." Deutsch, *Provincetown,* p. 108; Macgowan in Gelbs, *O'Neill,* p. 551.

enough to provoke huffy editorials and outraged sermons, the decision to cast a black actor-playing opposite a white actress in the play's troubled marriage provoked threats of violence and murder. Furthermore, the mayor's office complicated Light's problems by denying work permits to the eight interracial child actors who performed all of the action of the first scene of the play. Officially the press release stated that Mayor John Hylan deemed the children "too young to plays the parts," despite the fact that he had not read the play.[166] Since this government opposition arose on the day of the premiere, James Light came before the first-night audience and read the prohibitive announcement issued by the mayor's office.[167] "When he asked the audience if he should read the prologue [I.1], cries of 'Read, Read' came from all parts of the house."[168] For subsequent performances the opening scene was routinely read by stage manager Harold McGee, and the dramatized performance commenced with act I, scene 2.

This stormy production was Light's only solo direction of an O'Neill play. Teaming with Cleon Throckmorton as designer, the slender but heavy-drinking Light attacked his material with relish, and he apparently remained in control throughout the rehearsal period. Macgowan, however, once emphatically asserted that Light was only efficient when he was carefully watched. A strong producer or playwright could "boss the life out of him."[169] If Light was indeed so docile with O'Neill it is not surprising that the strong-willed dramatist liked to use him.

Whatever Light's shortcomings may have been, Paul Robeson, who played the leading role of Jim Harris, found the acting lessons and suggestions of the director a tremendous lift to his development of the part and his self-assurance as a performer. "I couldn't have had a better start than the direction of James Light," Robeson told an interviewer.[170] "I'm sure even he thought I was rather hopeless at first. . . . But he was patient and painstaking, and any success I may have achieved I owe in great measure to Mr. Light."[171] With Robeson Light excelled as a confidence builder who helped the fledgling but vocally powerful actor to feel free emotionally and physically despite his lack of experience, the constrictions of the Provincetown Playhouse, and the sensitive nature of the play.[172]

166. "O'Neill Play Theme Unknown to Mayor," *Sun*, May 16, 1924, p. 3.

167. "New O'Neill Play," *New York Evening Post*, May 16, 1924, p. 13.

168. "Prologue of 'All God's Chillun' Is Read," *World*, May 16, 1924, p. 13.

169. Macgowan letter to O'Neill, Aug. 12, 1926, in Bryer, *Letters*, p. 129.

170. Paul Robeson, in Philip S. Foner, ed. *Paul Robeson Speaks: Writings, Speeches, Interviews, 1918–1974* (New York: Brunner/Mazel, 1978), p. 67.

171. Paul Robeson, "Reflections on O'Neill's Plays," *Opportunity* 2 (Dec. 1924): 370.

172. See Dorothy Butler Gilliam, *Paul Robeson: All-American* (Washington, D.C.: New Republic, 1976), p. 36; Shirley Graham, *Paul Robeson: Citizen of the World* (New York: Julian Messner, 1946), p. 141.

Robeson's wife recalled in detail some of Light's work with the actor:

> He never told Paul what to do nor showed him how to do it . . . he merely sat
> quietly in the auditorium and let him feel his way; he often helped him, of
> course. When Paul had trouble with a speech Jimmy would sit down on a
> soap-box beside him on the empty stage, and they would analyze the speech
> thought by thought, word by word. "I think Gene means so and so," Jimmy
> would say, and they would argue and discuss. . . . "I can't tell you what to
> do," said Jimmy, "but I can help you find what's best for you."[173]

Light was clearly a guide, a director who revered the text and tried to help
his actors make discoveries without insisting on his own strict interpretations.

"America's poet laureate of gloom"[174] had completed the text of *All
God's Chillun* in the fall of 1923,[175] and the rehearsal period began soon
after it was published in *American Mercury* in February. By March 3 at
least six rehearsals had been held, but Mary Blair, who was cast as Ella
opposite Robeson, fell ill and production was postponed until she recovered. Blair's husband was certain that her attack of pleurisy was the
result of the barrage of threatening letters which she, Robeson, and
O'Neill began receiving soon after the casting was announced.[176]

O'Neill was on hand for much of the rehearsal period. The playwright told Langner that he was actively involved with *All God's
Chillun,*[177] and Eslanda Robeson wrote that O'Neill sometimes assisted
her husband and Light with interpretation in rehearsal.[178] O'Neill's presence was undoubtedly a boost to Light, who reportedly needed strong
support and encouragement when directing new and difficult material.[179]

All God's Chillun underwent few changes from the *American Mercury*
publication to production.[180] In fact the only significant alterations were
in the production's set design. The surviving experiments remained intact, although only one, O'Neill's venture into the subject of racial bigo-
try, received significant attention in the press. Indeed, Macgowan found
himself promising the press that the Triumvirate would never attempt to
move the production to a commercial theater uptown.[181] Absurdly,

173. Eslanda Goode Robeson, *Paul Robeson, Negro* (New York: Harper & Brothers, 1930),
pp. 80–81.

174. Kantor, "O'Neill," p. 5.

175. Tornqvist, *Drama,* p. 261.

176. "Public Protests Ignored," *World,* Mar. 3, 1924, p. 1; Wilson, *Twenties,* p. 112.

177. O'Neill letter to Langner, n.d., in Langer, "Eugene," p. 89.

178. Eslanda Robeson, *Paul,* p. 80.

179. Macgowan letter to O'Neill, Aug. 12, 1926, in Bryer, *Letters,* p. 129.

180. "Public," *World,* p. 1.

181. "O'Neill Appeals for His 'Chillun,'" New York *Morning Telegraph,* Mar. 17, 1924,
p. 1.

O'Neill had to defend his position against ridiculous interview questions such as, "Isn't the white race superior to the black?"[182] The play's use of music, chorus, mask, and schizophrenic monologues paled in the face of envisioned race riots all but promised by the daily scandal sheets.[183]

Although a few days before *All God's Chillun* opened O'Neill tried to steer an interviewer toward his need to experiment and asserted that "the purely naturalistic play doesn't interest me any more, never did interest me much,"[184] the reporter, like most of the critics who reviewed the show, concentrated on the race issue. In response to sensational public rhetoric Light could have underplayed the physical contact of his interracial couple, but he remained loyal to the text and had Ella kiss her black husband's hand as she told him in a childlike way that she loved him. Several reliable critics reported that the kiss occurred in a "mingling of genuine affection and demented fancy."[185]

The environment for the first act of O'Neill's sensitive story was a street "corner in lower New York" which the playwright wanted treated symbolically with an all-black street meeting an all-white one.[186] This environment which Throckmorton and Light provided helped to emphasize the use of chorus so important to milieu and mood in the play. O'Neill wrote, "The secondary figures are part and parcel of the Expressionistic background of the play, a world at first indifferent, then cruelly hostile, against which the tragedy of Jim Harris is outlined."[187] Two groups of white and black actors moved about, talked, laughed, sang, and created street noises to contrast the discriminate cultures living side by side but segregated. When Ella and Jim married in I.4, blacks and whites lined up on each side of the church, creating a symbolic gauntlet through which the couple had to pass to leave the ceremony.[188]

O'Neill wanted the choral noises sometimes "rhythmically mechanical" or "dulled with a quality of fatigue,"[189] but most often musical. Responsive and solo singing voices onstage and off contrasted the tastes

182. Kantor, "O'Neill," p. 5.

183. The public uproar was not unlike the arousal of conservative elements of American society when *Hair* was mounted with nudity in 1967–1968. See Sheaffer, *Artist*, pp. 134–43, for an account of the public struggle.

184. O'Neill, in Kantor, "O'Neill," p. 5.

185. John Corbin, "A Sensation Manque," *New York Times*, May 16, 1924, p. 22. See also Percy Hammond, "The Theaters," *New York Herald-Tribune*, May 16, 1924, p. 10. Nevertheless, one reviewer emphatically denied the deed, claiming that Robeson's "hand is still unkissed, unless he kissed it himself." "New O'Neill," *New York Evening Post*, May 16, 1924, p. 13.

186. Eugene O'Neill, *All God's Chillun Got Wings, Welded* (New York: Boni and Liveright, 1924), p. 15.

187. O'Neill, "Second," p. 119.

188. Hammond, "Theaters," May 16, 1924, p. 10; O'Neill, *All God's Chillun*, p. 42.

189. O'Neill, *All God's Chillun*, pp. 22, 32.

and styles of the two cultures, and a blind organ grinder frequently strolled on playing music like "Annie Laurie" and "Bon Bon Buddie the Chocolate Drop," which added mood or served as ironic counterpoint.[190] Sometimes, however, the irony was too obvious and did not serve the serious action well. The organ grinder played "Old Black Joe," for example, just after the wedding.[191]

Throughout much of the second act Ella carried on disturbing, schizophrenic conversations with herself. Alternately racist and loving, terrified and threatening, haughty and beaten, the character was among O'Neill's most haunted creations. She was prepared for in such plays as *Gold* and *Diff'rent* and pointed forward to *Strange Interlude* and *Mourning Becomes Electra,* but Ella's sudden emotional and persona shifts in both speed and intensity mark a peak in O'Neill's work. The device created great acting problems for Mary Blair, who was emotionally equipped for such a character but lacked the polished technique to make Ella's monologues consistently effective.

Once again O'Neill turned to the mask, but for very different purposes. In the second act the domestic interior setting included a "negro primitive mask from the Congo . . . conceived in a true religious spirit. . . . It dominates by a diabolical quality that contrast imposes upon it."[192] Macgowan's description of Congo masks almost certainly inspired O'Neill here. The producer described "emotional freedom" created by the mask maker, who was trying to imitate not people but God.[193] The design of the mask is preserved in a poster created by Hugo Gellert for the play when it moved from the Provincetown to the larger Greenwich Village Theatre.[194] Although exaggerated somewhat for the poster, the mask features close-set eyes and an intense stare. The Congo masks photographed for Macgowan's book also have close-set eyes.

Unfortunately, the mask in production was not so effective as one would expect. "Though this symbol of jungle ancestry was spot-lighted more or less subtly," wrote Hammond, "it lacked the hypnotic lure that it has in the printed version."[195] A chief difficulty here was probably the size of the mask. In a photograph from the final scene of the play[196] the mask can be glimpsed lying on the table where Ella left it after stabbing it both

190. Heywood Broun, "The New Play," *World,* May 16, 1924, p. 13.
191. Hammond, "Theaters," May 16, 1924, p. 10.
192. O'Neill, *All God's Chillun,* p. 47.
193. Macgowan, *Masks,* p. 43.
194. Reproduction of poster in *Theatre Arts* 9 (Jan. 1925): 51.
195. Hammond, "Theaters," May 16, 1924, p. 10.
196. Photograph of II.3, one of three photographs, Theatre Collection, Beinecke Library, Yale University; also three photographs, Theatre Collection, MCNY.

viciously and gleefully. The dark mask is much too small to be effective from any distance from the stage, even in the little Provincetown.

Only one experiment suggested by O'Neill was not incorporated in production. As the situation of Jim and Ella became more oppressive in act II, O'Neill wanted the walls and ceiling actually to contract, physically to oppress the characters. The shrinking room was never attempted, however, and no other device was substituted. It was left to the actors to convey growing isolation and agony.

This, the last new O'Neill production staged at the Provincetown Playhouse, was the fourth and final design of Throckmorton for O'Neill. Although the dramatist would present three more plays with the Triumvirate, all would be designed by Jones and staged at the Greenwich Village Theatre, which Experimental Theatre, Inc., secured for its second season. Light and Throckmorton remained part of the organization, but they staged productions only at the smaller Provincetown.

Although O'Neill had sought an expressionistic scenic style, the three settings of *All God's Chillun* reflected a combination of expressionistic and realistic approaches. For the first three scenes, which Lewisohn found to be an excellent presentation of the "slum scene,"[197] Throckmorton recreated O'Neill's convergence of "three narrow streets," dominated by a centrally placed "triangular building."[198] Three photographs reveal that the playing space was very shallow and restricted, but Throckmorton's leaning buildings—painted in forced, angular perspective backed by the dome—suggested considerable distance down each segregated street running up left and up right, with the cross street following the stage apron. The designer echoed the distorted buildings with a narrow sidewalk made of platforms which were virtually low ramps raked up right and up left. The setting signified the presence of many people crammed tightly together. Nevertheless, when peopled with only one or two actors, the corner looked lonely and desolate. With five actors the setting seemed to be teeming with activity.

The second setting (which appeared only in I.4) was an old brick church from which Jim and Ella emerged after the marriage ceremony. Photographs have not survived, but critics recalled that it was the most expressionistic of the settings. A set of steps led down from the elevated church door, and the church building itself was distorted somewhat like an hourglass "with a waist like a human being's and flying buttresses of brick that seem to be streaming away in the wind."[199] Hammond wrote

197. Ludwig Lewisohn, "Drama," *Nation* 118 (June 4, 1924): 664.

198. O'Neill, *All God's Chillun*, p. 15.

199. Edmund Wilson, "Eugene O'Neill and the Naturalists," in Edmund Wilson, *Shores of Light* (New York: Farrar, Straus and Giroux, 1952), p. 103.

that the newlyweds "emerged theatrically from the church . . . and [Jim] stood spectacularly upon the top step, like Oedipus, while theatrical groups of blacks and whites gathered on each side of him."[200] Light handled this crowd scene effectively, utilizing levels, and contrasting the mass with individuals, but the steps probably numbered no more than three to avoid keeping the six-foot-three-inch Robeson well below the top of the low proscenium arch.

All three scenes of the final act took place in the parlor of the Harris apartment in the black district. Although there is no full stage shot of this interior, the extant photograph reveals cheap furnishings and a draped doorway upstage within a box set dressed sparsely but realistically. Only the crude wall painting of the Harris patriarch suggests stylization. The quality of the painting, however, was probably more a product of exigency than aesthetic choice. If Light and Throckmorton had attempted to reduce the size of the room with each scene in act II, the use of space for the play's second half would have been more consistent with the visual style of act I. Therefore, opting for a realistic interior seems a poor choice.

For the final moment of the play Light attempted to create a strong stage picture with a "tableau showing the negro on his knees praying for a happiness he does not seem likely to get."[201] Some reviewers found the conclusion weak and disappointing, a final whimper after the play dealt so explosively with much of its conflict. Light's picturization could not overcome the anticlimactic nature of the play's finish, but the production enjoyed popularity because many theatergoers were nevertheless moved by the story and its sensitive presentation. Mantle, for example, who had misgivings before he saw the show, wrote that "there can be no offense in a play as sincerely and intelligently done as this one is, whatever one may think of the taste prompting its production."[202] Once *All God's Chillun* had premiered the public storm passed away, almost as quickly as it had arrived. This would not be the case with the next O'Neill script: *Desire Under the Elms.*

Quite rightly Stark Young realized with his review of *All God's Chillun* that by failing to be wholly realistic or expressionistic O'Neill had for some time been demanding an acting style which was not practiced in America. O'Neill's characters were frequently given to sudden emotional shifts within a context which was alternately realistic and theatrical, expressionistic and surreal. Young thought the actors in *All God's Chillun* understood their characters as people but ultimately worked too hard at

200. Hammond, "Theaters," May 16, 1924, p. 10.
201. Metcalfe, "The Theatre," *Wall Street Journal,* May 17, 1924, p. 3.
202. Burns Mantle, "'All God's Chillun' With One Scene Cut," New York *Daily News,* May 16, 1924, p. 24.

acting, that is, in an effort to straddle acting styles they failed to mask their labor on the stage.[203]

As usual Mary Blair's "intense sincerity"[204] revealed her total commitment to her very emotional character. Yet some of her old problems were once again obvious. In the first act, before Ella broke down and yielded to her emotional disturbance, Blair "was a little halting" and unsure of her way, but in act II, as Ella plummeted almost headlong into insanity, "she rose to the occasion and was literally thrilling at moments."[205] Especially in her scenes of schizophrenic dialogue and vehement struggle with the African mask, Blair, with her "flaming hair and . . . hectic pink complexion,"[206] was at her freest and most believable. It was easy for Light to exploit positively the actress' flair for instability on stage, but it was difficult for the director to bring her under control.

Paul Robeson, on the other hand, was a very controlled if unsure actor. Recruited by Jones and Macgowan, who had first seen him perform in an amateur production at the Harlem YMCA, twenty-six-year-old Robeson was a very intelligent and ambitious performer who was a graduate of Rutgers and Columbia Law School. Not eager to struggle as a black in the world of law, he opted for a professional career in acting and singing. "Extraordinarily sincere and eloquent"[207] as well as humble in his approach to humanity, acting, and O'Neill's play, Robeson was frequently characterized as bearing both publicly and privately "considerable dignity of presence."[208] He was appreciated and admired by many in both the black and white communities of the time; "he was the Negro typical of what white America thought of as the 'noble' Negro."[209] In consequence, he was a much safer actor to use in a play about miscegenation than an outspoken, heavy-drinking performer like Charles Gilpin.[210]

His effectiveness as Jim Harris was due in part to his physical power. His sheer bulk and apparent strength coupled with directness and emotional force complicated by "strong repression" rendered him "entirely equal to the emotional displays"[211] required of the character. Ironically, however, he was very self-conscious about his size and thus was ungraceful. In the first act Pollock found him essentially "a big awkward boy."[212]

203. Stark Young, "The Prompt Book," *New York Times*, Aug. 24, 1924, sec. 7, p. 1.
204. "New O'Neill," *New York Evening Post*, May 16, 1924, p. 13.
205. Lewisohn, "Drama," June 4, 1924, p. 664.
206. Corbin, "Sensation," p. 22.
207. Lewisohn, "Drama," Jun. 4, 1924, p. 664.
208. Metcalfe, "Theatre," May 17, 1924, p. 3.
209. Edwin P. Hoyt, *Paul Robeson: The American Othello* (Cleveland: World, 1967), p. 40.
210. Robeson's political difficulties arose many years later.
211. Metcalfe, "Theatre," May 17, 1924, p. 3.
212. Arthur Pollock, "All God's Chillun," *Brooklyn Daily Eagle*, May 16, 1924, in Miller, *Playwright's*, p. 38.

Metcalfe agreed that he was often "uncouth in movement,"[213] but what the critics saw on stage was significant progress since Robeson's arrival at Provincetown. Light spent considerable time with the actor trying to help him feel free in the small space. Since Robeson was often afraid to move, the director would frequently talk him through physical action, attempting to break down inhibitions and inviting him to make the blocking his own. "You must have complete freedom and control over your body, and your voice," Light asserted, "if you are to control your audience."[214] Actually Robeson was much freer in the second half of the play and, according to Pollock, "loses his self-consciousness, . . . lets himself go and gives a good performance."[215]

As an aid to Robeson's self-assurance and a stopgap for the postponed production during Blair's illness in March, the Triumvirate revived *The Emperor Jones* starring Robeson. This was a great boost to his morale and helped to settle him down for the much ballyhooed opening of *All God's Chillun.*

Perhaps the most significant quality of Robeson's acting, however, was his deep, mellifluous voice, which Light exploited to the fullest. Robeson was not only encouraged to fill the space with his "sonorous and agreeable speaking voice"[216] but was also given a song to sing offstage. Due to his beautiful and distinctive singing style, the song contributed less to mood than it served to call attention to Robeson's talents and essentially stop the show.[217] The song which came during act I, scene 4 was "Sometimes I Feel Like a Mourning Dove," which preceded the appearance of Ella and Jim at the church door.

Light's directorial success with *All God's Chillun* was clearly uneven. He demonstrated bravery in his interracial casting and commitment to the theme of miscegenation. His guidance of Robeson produced moving results, but he was no more successful with controlling Blair's inconsistency than was Charles Kennedy. Most significant of all, the visual style of the production was inconsistent and especially weak with the interior of act II.

In the final analysis critics found numerous problems with the play and production. Wilson, for example, called it "an attempt to impose subjective fancies upon an idea objectively conceived."[218] The *Evening Post* found much of the presentation arbitrary, "dull and irrelevant."[219]

213. Metcalfe, "Theatre," May 17, 1924, p. 3.
214. Eslanda Robeson, *Paul,* pp. 80–81.
215. Pollock, "All," p. 38.
216. Metcalfe, "Theatre," May 17, 1924, p. 3.
217. Broun, "New," May 16, 1924, p. 13.
218. Edmund Wilson, "All God's Chillun and Others," *New Republic,* May 28, 1924, p. 22.
219. "New O'Neill," *New York Evening Post,* May 16, 1924, p. 13.

Nevertheless, the production touched its audience. Many people flocked to the "sensational tragedy of racial intermarriage"[220] in search of thrills, "determined to be shocked."[221] Instead, many viewers found themselves caught up in the plight of Jim and Ella. Even the critic who found much of the evening dull admitted that "at the climax of the second act the sheer conflict of it seizes you by the throat and forces from you a reluctant cheer." O'Neill, Light, and the actors left "the landscape a wreckage, but it is breathtaking."[222]

Thus, the critical and popular response to *All God's Chillun* was mixed. O'Neill had not produced a commercial hit since *The Hairy Ape* but had forged ahead with his commitment to sometimes fanciful, occasionally silly, though often important and interesting experiments. In his next play O'Neill, allied with Jones, would engender and explore an exciting new direction.

220. Caption for photograph of Mary Blair in *Theatre Magazine*, Aug. 1924, p. 42.
221. Lewisohn, "Drama," June 4, 1924, p. 664.
222. "New," *New York Evening Post*, May 16, 1924, p. 13.

ILLUSTRATION 1: *Beyond the Horizon* (1920), act I, scene 1, and act III, scene 2 (road exterior), Morosco Theatre.

ILLUSTRATION 2: *The Emperor Jones* (1920), scene 4 (chain gang), Playwrights' Theatre of Provincetown Players.

ILLUSTRATION 3: *Diff'rent* (1920), act II, Playwrights' Theatre of Province-town Players, stage right to left: Mary Blair as Emma, Charles Ellis as Benny, Elizabeth Brown as Harriet.

ILLUSTRATION 4: *Anna Christie* (1921), publicity photo of Pauline Lord as Anna.

ILLUSTRATION 5: *The Hairy Ape* (1922), scene 4 (fireman's forecastle), Playwrights' Theatre of Provincetown Players, Louis Wolheim as Yank standing at center.

ILLUSTRATION 6: *Desire Under the Elms* (1924), part II, scene 2 (bedrooms), Greenwich Village Theatre, stage right to left: Charles Ellis as Eben, Mary Morris as Abbie, Walter Huston as Ephraim.

ILLUSTRATION 7: *The Fountain* (1925), scene 7 (Florida beach), Greenwich Village Theatre, stage right to left: (squatting) John Taylor as the Medicine Man, (standing) Ray Corning as the Chief, (held) Curtis Cooksey as Nano.

ILLUSTRATION 8: *The Fountain* (1925), scene 2 (flagship), Greenwich Village Theatre, (pointing from up right platform) Walter Huston as Ponce de Leon, (up center) Henry O'Neill as Columbus, (far stage left) Crane Wilbur as Menendez.

ILLUSTRATION 9: *The Great God Brown* (1926), prologue (the pier), Greenwich Village Theatre, Robert Keith as Dion kissing Leona Hogarth as Margaret.

ILLUSTRATION 10: *The Great God Brown* (1926), act II, scene 2 (drafting room), Greenwich Village Theatre, (standing stage right) Robert Keith as Dion, (sitting in chair stage left) Leona Hogarth as Margaret, surrounded by her three sons.

ILLUSTRATION 11: *Marco Millions* (1928), act III, scene 2 (grand throne room), Guild Theatre, (standing downstage in pit) Alfred Lunt as Marco, (sitting on throne up center) Baliol Holloway as Kublai Kaan.

ILLUSTRATION 12: *Strange Interlude* (1928), act VII (Park Avenue sitting room), John Golden Theatre, Lynn Fontanne as Nina.

ILLUSTRATION 13: *Strange Interlude* (1928), act VIII (yacht afterdeck), John Golden Theatre, stage right to left: Earle Larimore as Evans, Ethel Westley as Madeleine, Glenn Anders as Darrell, Lynn Fontanne as Nina, Tom Powers as Marsden.

ILLUSTRATION 14: *Dynamo* (1929), act I (Light and Fife houses), Martin Beck Theatre, stage right to left: George Gaul as Reverend Light, Dudley Digges as Ramsay Fife.

ILLUSTRATION 15: *Dynamo* (1929), act III (powerhouse), Martin Beck Theatre, stage right to left: Catherine Doucet as May Fife, Glenn Anders as Reuben Light.

ILLUSTRATION 16: *Mourning Becomes Electra* (1931), "The Homecoming," act II (study), Guild Theatre.

ILLUSTRATION 17: *Mourning Becomes Electra* (1931), "The Homecoming," act IV (bedroom), Guild Theatre.

ILLUSTRATION 18: *Mourning Becomes Electra* (1931), "The Hunted," act IV (clipper ship), Guild Theatre.

ILLUSTRATION 19: *Mourning Becomes Electra* (1931), (Mannon mansion), Guild Theatre, (standing) Alla Nazimova as Christine, (sitting) Alice Brady as Lavinia.

ILLUSTRATION 20: *Days Without End* (1934), act II, scene 2 (Loving's living room), Henry Miller Theatre, stage right to left: Robert Loraine as the priest, Selena Royle as Elsa, Earle Larimore as John, Stanley Ridges as Loving.

ILLUSTRATION 21: *Days Without End* (1934), act III, scene 2 (the church),
Henry Miller Theatre, (lying) Stanley Ridges as Loving, (standing) Earle
Larimore as John.

CHAPTER VIII

Eleusinian Mysteries:
Desire Under the Elms

I'm not writing any more "Anna Christies."[1]

Great drama does not deal with cautious people.[2]

In his direction and design of O'Neill's *Desire Under the Elms* Robert Edmond Jones demonstrated quite clearly his dynamic use of space and facility of design, as well as a strong pictorial approach in his use of actors—methods which at once point to his strengths and weaknesses as a director yet reinforce his appropriateness for the plays of O'Neill at that time. This is especially true of his staging of O'Neill's "stark, morbid, thrilling tragedy of New England life and character"[3] which opened on Tuesday, November 11, 1924, at the Greenwich Village Theatre,[4] a larger house rented by the Triumvirate for its second season. Although Experimental Theatre, Inc., maintained the Provincetown just four blocks away for numerous experiments (eight productions in the second season), the Greenwich Village was reserved for its large-scale efforts or productions which promised popular success. The intent was to use a nucleus of repertory actors in both theaters and eventually rotate productions as well as regularly revive successful or important plays. Because actors and staff were frequently shuffling back and forth from theater to theater, rehearsal to performance, directing to advisement, confusion and

1. Eugene O'Neill (1924), in Kantor, "O'Neill," p. 5.
2. Robert Edmond Jones, "Art in the Theatre," in Kendall B. Tafts et al., eds., *Contemporary Attitudes* (Boston: Houghton Mifflin, 1929), p. 467.
3. Mantle, *Best Plays, 1924–25*, p. 98.
4. Advertisement, *New York Times*, Nov. 11, 1924, p. 20. The first reviews appeared on Wednesday, Nov. 12, 1924.

lost time were often the order of the day. With *Desire Under the Elms*, however, Jones and most of the company had considerable time to prepare.

Mounted with a modest budget of only six thousand dollars—about half the cost of a nonmusical production at the time[5]—*Desire Under the Elms* enjoyed a successful downtown run before moving uptown on January 12, 1925, to the Earl Carroll Theatre,[6] where it fell victim to tasteless commercial advertising and scurrilous official attack for public indecency. After being earmarked as an exhibition of morbid, cheap, "naked nastiness,"[7] a play in which "infanticide, ugliness, sin and appalling freedom of speech are frankly illustrated,"[8] the play was attacked by the district attorney, the Actors' Association for Clean Plays, and the Society for the Suppression of Vice, but a citizens' play jury unanimously acquitted the production.[9]

For Jones, however, *Desire Under the Elms* was an important achievement with which he presented some of his most notable creative and recreative work. With this production Jones made his first lasting simultaneous contribution to direction and design. Although as director-designer he had always had some of the shortcomings which Macgowan feared any sensitive designer would have upon attempting directing with its managerial, executive, and organizational obligations, he was tireless in his efforts to explore the possibilities of the stage and the dramatic literature assigned to him. "We have to experiment endlessly," Jones wrote, "until our work is as nearly perfect as we can make it, until we are, so to speak, released from it."[10] This "most practical of all dreamers"[11] was eager to assume the multitude of artistic and managerial responsibilities incumbent upon his dual role, and he was also willing to "adopt any fashion, any convention"[12] in service to the text of the play which he greatly revered. Yet, as always, he sought to elevate the presentation, especially visually, to capture mood through his use of space and coax the play to an echelon which transcended realism and bespoke the theatrical event.

Jones' advance preparation with *Desire Under the Elms* was especially

5. Kenneth Macgowan, *Footlights Across America* (New York: Harcourt, Brace, 1929), p. 63.

6. Advertisement, *New York Times*, Jan. 12, 1925, p. 10.

7. Fred Niblo, Jr., "New O'Neill Play Sinks to Depths," New York *Morning Telegraph*, Nov. 13, 1924, p. 3.

8. Burns Mantle, "O'Neill's New Play is Lustful and Tragic," New York *Daily News*, Nov. 14, 1924, p. 30.

9. "Banton Would Stop Two Plays as Unfit," *New York Times*, Feb. 17, 1925, pp. 1, 13; "Play Juries Acquit 2 Shows as Clean," *New York Times*, Mar. 14, 1925, p. 15.

10. Jones, *Dramatic*, p. 87.

11. Jo Mielziner, in Jones, *Dramatic*, pp. 10–11.

12. Jones, "Fashions," p. 115.

extensive. He is said to have habitually planned a production with deliberation and to have entered the rehearsal period with numerous stage pictures in mind. Nevertheless, Jones relied heavily upon his own emotional reactions, his intuitive and often romantic response to the play, actors, and the rehearsal process.[13] As a result, he often achieved very spontaneous moments with a well-conceived framework of dynamic picturization—so long as he cast actors who did not need extensive directorial assistance, most notably acting coaching.

Because Jones was insecure with the acting process, he relied heavily on the actors to solve most of their major problems. He was very good at discussing themes, images, and symbols as they affected the characters, but reticent to suggest specific solutions to many acting problems which lay outside the play's big ideas and mood and the visual world of movement, position, and composition. In consequence, he preferred to concentrate on picturization (both static and moving), visual and aural motifs, and thematic interpretation. He acknowledged the actors' needs for directorial assistance but preferred, like his former associate Arthur Hopkins, to cast independent actors whom he knew well from previous productions, and who could work creatively with minimal guidance. In short, he needed to collaborate openly with actors.

As rehearsals were about to commence in October, Jones and O'Neill prepared much of the production together, especially the plans for the setting. They shared personal anxieties and a fascination with their New England backgrounds and "produced with almost classical severity"[14] their interpretation of a tragic experience in the bleak landscape of a rocky New England farm. The rehearsal period was an amicable one for director and playwright. After extensive preproduction preparations at various times throughout the summer, O'Neill attended a number of rehearsals as well. *Desire Under the Elms* was rehearsed for four weeks, but as late as October 12 (with a November 11 opening date) O'Neill was still inquiring about the casting of Ephraim Cabot.[15] Either Walter Huston was cast at the last moment or rehearsals began without him. This practice, which also occurred in *Mourning Becomes Electra*, was not unusual.

Jones' approach to the text of *Desire Under the Elms* was typical both

13. Interviews and letters of the 1960s stress this information about Jones' work but provide no detail. Unfortunately, the promptbook which survives at Lincoln Center is not Jones' personal copy. Hicks, "Robert," p. 118; Waldo, "Production," p. 186; Gilbert Seldes, "Profiles: The Emperor Jones," *New Yorker*, May 9, 1931, pp. 26–27; Lee Simonson, in Pendleton, *Jones*, p. 17.

14. Gilbert Seldes, "The Theatre," *Dial* 78 (Jan. 1925): 82.

15. Sweeney, "Back," p. M-5; O'Neill, in Langner, "Eugene," p. 89; O'Neill letters to Macgowan, Sept. 6 and Oct. 12, 1924, in Bryer, *Letters*, pp. 60, 64; Mary Morris, in Vilhauer, "History," p. 418.

of his acceptance of the playwright's creation and his reverence for the domain of the dramatist. O'Neill's script, which was essentially completed in July and August, 1924, underwent few textual changes during production. The surviving promptbook,[16] dated November 11, 1924, contains only minor line cuts, word alterations, and occasional contractions throughout. The single serious line cutting occurs in part III where a long speech by the Fiddler at the close of scene 1 is reduced to two brief sentences. The text as emended by hand is almost identical to the text of the first publication of the play in January 1925. Jones trusted O'Neill's language and structure and devoted most of his efforts to realizing rather than modifying O'Neill's vision.

As an experiment for O'Neill and Jones *Desire Under the Elms* combined poetic imagery with stark realism, innovative staging with familiar techniques, and sensitive subject matter with traditional classical tragedy. Certainly the characters seemed to be authentically drawn creatures whose rustic dialects created a localized and flat sound which emphasized the earthbound nature of the characters. Nonetheless, their relentless passions and desires which are literally for the earth as well as the flesh lend the story and language an almost mystical quality. "Such writing as this," remarked Young, "employs realistic instances and realistic details for ends that are in the end poetic."[17] The plainsong of the New England speech and environment provided mordant contrast for the ornamental mood of reverie which enveloped so much of the action.

Ritualized and stylized activity, however, was also a significant aspect of play and production. This was most notable in O'Neill's use of a chorus in part III. For a kitchen dance celebrating the birth of Abbie's son, O'Neill introduced a small crowd led by a fiddler. Their general noise and laughter were reminiscent of the racial chorus work of *All God's Chillun Got Wings*. Most importantly, however, the chorus created an undercurrent of *sotto voce* gossiping: "Their voices die to an intensive whispering. Their faces are concentrated on this gossip. A noise as of dead leaves in the wind." The sound of the chorus continued into the next scene although the crowd was unseen.[18]

Robert Garland's review of the production suggested that O'Neill was returning "to the style of *Beyond the Horizon*."[19] Garland was referring to vacillating indoor and outdoor scenes which caused enormous set-shift-

16. Eugene O'Neill, *Desire Under the Elms*, bound promptbook, Theatre Collection, Performing Arts Center, New York Public Library, copyrighted 1924 by Yale University.

17. Stark Young, "The Prompt Book," *New York Times*, Dec. 7, 1924, sec. 8, p. 5.

18. Eugene O'Neill, *Desire Under the Elms* (New York: Boni & Liveright, 1925), pp. 128–31; Leon Whipple, "Two Plays by O'Neill," *Survey* 53 (Jan. 1, 1925): 422.

19. Robert Garland, "Eugene O'Neill and This Big Business of Broadway," *Theatre Arts* 9 (Jan. 1925): 3.

ing difficulties in the older play. For *Desire Under the Elms* the problem was solved by O'Neill himself, who provided a solution before Jones produced his design. The playwright's scheme was to present a unit set which could reveal both the interior rooms and the exterior of the house as well as the overshadowing elm trees. Downer noted that as a result the production's "multiple playing areas permit O'Neill to create visual ironies and reveal psychological relationships."[20] This capability of the unit setting was ultimately more significant than rapid scene shifting.

O'Neill actually made small sketches[21] and shared these with Jones, who maintained the basic shape of the house and the position of the four rooms but created a more attractive stage picture, yet a more severe homestead, by softening the angle of the roof, adding shutters, enlarging the windows, and eliminating the porch, the absence of which denied invitation to outsiders. His design was at once more engaging to the eye but forbidding to entrance. Naturally, the critics assumed that the design was primarily the work of Jones, yet O'Neill was very distressed by the public's identification of "Bobby's house,"[22] which in all fairness was born in O'Neill's mind but given artistic expression and completion through the graceful eye of Jones.

In the Greenwich Village Theatre, which was considerably larger than the Provincetown yet seated only about three hundred,[23] Jones mounted a simultaneous setting dominated by one end of a mid-nineteenth-century farmhouse flanked by elm trees whose overhanging branches functioned as a teaser across the top of the stage picture. The drooping leaves were unusually large, rendering the picture a bit primitive in appearance.[24] Despite the fact that the "malevolently brooding elms"[25] are impressive as a stage composition, O'Neill was disappointed. "There have never been the elm trees of my play, characters, almost," he complained in 1926.[26] O'Neill probably would have agreed with Whipple, who felt that each "elm persists in resembling a banana tree."[27] These elms nonetheless watched over the house in a protective manner not unfaithful to the text.

20. Alan S. Downer, "Eugene O'Neill as Poet of the Theatre," in Cargill, *O'Neill*, p. 471.

21. An early crude sketch of the house appears in Tornqvist, *Drama*, p. 60. Four later sketches showing the house with different rooms revealed appear in George Altman et al., *Theater Pictorial* (Berkeley: University of California Press, 1953), plate #460.

22. O'Neill letter to Macgowan, Jan. 21, 1927, in Bryer, *Letters*, p. 146.

23. Edba, "Desire Under the Elms," *Variety*, Nov. 19, 1924, p. 19.

24. Seven extant photographs display the exterior and the four rooms of the farmhouse. MCNY and Yale.

25. Gagey, *Revolution*, p. 53.

26. O'Neill letter to Macgowan, August 1926, in Bryer, *Letters*, p. 132.

27. Whipple, "Two," p. 422.

O'Neill requested a stone wall be placed between the house and the audience, with a wooden gate which Cabot's oldest sons removed when abandoning the farm. Instead of building and painting a scenic unit, Jones erected an actual low fence of large, heavy stones which he placed very close to the audience in a line parallel to the curtain. The irregular pile not only provided weight and visually anchored the scenery but also supplied a severe, prohibitive barrier between most of the stage action and the audience. The presence and nature of the wall reinforced the unwelcome feeling one received from this use of space as well as enhanced the sense of voyeurism, of peeping in on the sordid lives of this New England family.

Despite the wall, however, or perhaps because of it, O'Neill and Jones wanted the farmhouse very close to the audience. The playwright's working notes indicated that he wanted the downstage edge of the house "as near to the proscenium line as possible."[28] Indeed, Jones placed the house so close to the edge of the stage that the *Post* critic complained that the director presented "the action almost too near the audience for perfect comfort."[29] There is little doubt that Jones wished to maintain an uneasy distance.

The house itself was a small-scale, "somewhat doll-like"[30] structure which if built to a realistic scale would have required the actors to be perhaps two-thirds their normal height.[31] This reduction both allowed Jones to place an entire house in his limited space and accentuated the cramped, confined feeling which the play demanded. Parallel to the stone wall and curtain line, the wall of the house was actually divided into four panels which could be removed separately to reveal four interiors. Painted an off-white,[32] virtually nondescript color in keeping with the text's "sickly-grayish"[33] walls in need of paint, the exterior of the house featured four green-shuttered windows with "dilapidated green blinds"[34] which indicated the four cramped rooms. The supporting removable panels must have been sturdy, since the two upstairs bedroom windows were functional and the downstairs parlor window was broken with rocks by the drinking brothers in I.4.

28. O'Neill in Floyd, *Eugene Work*, p. 54.

29. "Mr. O'Neill Runs Aground on a Bleak New England Farm," *New York Post*, Nov. 12, 1924, p. 14.

30. Garland, "Eugene," Jan. 1925, p. 5.

31. R. M. L., "Desire Under the Elms," *New Republic* 41 (Dec. 3, 1924): 44.

32. Two doctoral dissertations on Jones report that the designer painted the house pumpkin yellow like the New Hampshire house of his youth. If this is true he changed the color after the play had opened, perhaps for the move uptown for the commercial run. Opening-night reviews describe the house in whites and grayish whites.

33. O'Neill, *Desire Under the Elms*, p. 11.

34. R. M. L., "Desire," p. 44.

Whatever Jones' design owed to O'Neill's directions, designer Donald Oenslager, a production assistant to Jones and onstage crowd member during *Desire Under the Elms*, asserted that part of the final design was based on the house in which Jones grew up.[35] These details most likely appeared in the four stark interiors.

The "mean and circumscribed"[36] recesses of the house were topped by two bedrooms of equal size which divided the gable half of the building (see illustration 6). Only a thin wall separated the two bedrooms, whose sharply raked ceilings severely limited mobility. O'Neill wanted bedrooms in which the actors "can stand upright only close to the center dividing wall,"[37] and this is precisely what Jones provided. These tiny rooms, furnished only with indispensable set properties, not only accentuated the confinement of the characters but also sometimes heightened ironically comic moments, such as the three brothers all plotting in the bed of one room in I.3.[38]

Beneath the bedrooms were the kitchen stage right and the smaller parlor stage left. The parlor was the most completely furnished of all the rooms and occupied approximately 40 percent of the downstairs area.[39] Despite its diminutive dimensions, the parlor's importance to production was paramount. Seen only by candlelight, it conjured up visions of rites, libations, and classical as well as New England sacrifice. The room was a center of ceremony of both death and lust, "a grim, repressed room like a tomb in which the family has been interred alive."[40] This room, the site of the seduction scene (II.3), remained mysteriously closed to the audience throughout the entire play except for this one brief scene; yet the exterior wall of the much mentioned room was always present.

Although Jones departed from O'Neill's scheme by making the kitchen the largest room of the setting (his intention must have been to accommodate the crowd scene of III.1), it still appears small and confining in photographs which include actors. The furnishings were simple, austere in the stark room which had an unusually low ceiling only about seven feet from the floor, since the top of the normal door frame upstage was flush with the ceiling. The low ceiling, which had to be repeated in the parlor, was the result of a low proscenium arch and Jones' attempt to keep all of the house visible below the arch while remaining shaded by a border of elm

35. Donald Oenslager, in Jones, *Drawings* (1970), p. 10.
36. R. M. L., "Desire," p. 44.
37. O'Neill, *Desire Under the Elms*, p. 34.
38. R. M. L., "Desire," p. 44.
39. This is another departure by Jones. O'Neill's four drawings divide the house into four quarters, with each room extending to the center line.
40. O'Neill, *Desire Under the Elms*, p. 104.

branches. As a consequence, when Ephraim Cabot was standing in the kitchen he seemed gigantic. Jones' use of the kitchen in III.1 was "a marvel of economy of space": he effectively mounted a square dance with twelve to fifteen actors,[41] who danced, stamped, clapped, and created a strange stage picture with sudden inactivity when Ephraim began to dance wildly to "Pop Goes the Weasel." The staging of this scene was so effective and surprising that audiences frequently "burst into spontaneous applause for the dance number just as they would have done at the Palace vaudeville."[42]

O'Neill wanted to move quickly from room to room, inside to outside, with a minimum of scene shifting. In early working notes he wrote, "The front wall of each of the four rooms must be in a separate removable section so that the interior may be shown separately or in any desired combination."[43] Although this is precisely what Jones provided (four portable clapboard wall units, each containing a shuttered window), O'Neill was dissatisfied with the results and complained that he did not get the scene shifts he had requested. "My acts were chopped into four distinct scenes through lack of time to get the changes perfected in blackouts," he wrote in 1926, "the flow of life from room to room of the house, the house as character, the acts as smooth developing wholes have never existed."[44] This seems an odd charge, especially since several reviewers specifically praised the "extreme ingenuity"[45] of the shifting device, and one particularly noted that "the action of the play slips easily from room to room without delay for changes of scene."[46] It is also significant that O'Neill's text for the promptbook was divided into four scenes per act by the playwright himself in the typed preproduction manuscript, not in added directions.

Perhaps O'Neill was chagrined by the accolades which went to Jones alone for the effective design. It is likely of course that the shifting of the panels never occurred as quickly or smoothly as O'Neill desired, but one should note that the next time O'Neill required shifting and simultaneous indoor-outdoor scenes (in *Dynamo*), his designer, Lee Simonson, eliminated walls altogether, allowing instantaneous shifts with lights alone.

The setting for *Desire Under the Elms* with its various levels and numerous possibilities for hiding and revealing enabled O'Neill and Jones

41. The actual number included in this scene is not clear from the program or promptbook, but at least twelve of the actors were onstage. A review reads: "a dozen or more." R. M. L., "Desire," p. 44; program, *Desire* folder, MCNY.

42. Whipple, "Two," p. 422.

43. O'Neill in Floyd, *Eugene Work*, p. 54.

44. O'Neill letter to Macgowan, 1926, in Bryer, *Letters*, p. 132.

45. For example, Metcalfe, "The Theatre," *Wall Street Journal*, Nov. 15, 1924, p. 3.

46. R. M. L., "Desire," p. 44.

to create dynamic, powerful stage pictures with action occurring simultaneously in different locations. In III.1, for example, Ephraim stood outside staring up at the sky while Abbie and Eben stood in an upstairs bedroom staring into the cradle of their bastard child. At the same time the chorus of gossipers in the kitchen commented ironically on the suspicious birth. Important speeches were delivered from all three locations before the scene culminated in an outburst of music, dancing, and merriment. With its "qualities of poetry, terror and at the same time unflinching realism,"[47] this staging was found by Young to be especially electrifying.

Perhaps even more memorable was a comparatively quiet monologue by Ephraim in his bed "drooling about his past"[48] while his wife, Abbie, stared at the wall, beyond which her lover Eben stared back. "Her eyes fasten on the intervening wall with concentrated attention. . . . Their hot glances seem to meet through the wall. Unconsciously he stretches out his arms for her and she half rises."[49] This scene reportedly gave "a poignant revelation of simultaneous life which counteracts the narrowing effect of the crowding walls."[50] Hammond was ecstatic over the effect of this staging. "I have seen few pictures in a theater so stark as that," he wrote, "few women's profiles so brooding with tragedy."[51] This production's concurrent staging at once enhanced the play's tragic elements and the environment's apparent reality.

Nearly all critics, even those who despised the play, admired the staging and design of the production, insisting that Jones "used his perpendicular stage with great skill, to minimize its difficulties and enhance its possibilities."[52] The design and its use illuminated Jones' penchant for displaying simultaneously realistic and theatrically heightened effects. With *Desire Under the Elms* as much as with any other design of his career, Jones revealed "his selective capacity as an artist for distilling in a stage setting the essence of a realistic background"[53] while maintaining elements of stylization which reinforced the ethereal vision of O'Neill.

"Bobby's house" became so inextricably associated with the play that it made its way into publicity. A promotional flyer circulated for the commercial run was shaped, drawn, and colored like the farmhouse, and it boldly announced: "*Desire Under the Elms* strips away the fourth wall of

47. Stark Young, "Eugene O'Neill's Latest Play," *New York Times*, Nov. 12, 1924, p. 20.
48. Percy Hammond, "The Theaters," *New York Herald-Tribune*, Nov. 12, 1924, p. 14.
49. O'Neill, *Desire Under the Elms*, p. 93.
50. R. M. L., "Desire," p. 44.
51. Hammond, "Theaters," Nov. 12, 1924, p. 14.
52. R. M. L., "Desire," p. 44; see also Louis Bromfield, "The New Yorker," *Bookman* 60 (Jan. 1925): 621.
53. Donald Oenslager, in Jones, *Drawings* (1970), p. 18.

life."[54] The card could then be opened up for publicity information just as the setting opened to reveal the dark secrets of the Cabot family.

With an austerity at once classical and rustic the Cabot farmhouse, created with utter simplicity in line and detail, loomed close to the audience, suggesting confinement, hidden secrets, and burgeoning tragedy, as if Jones and O'Neill were carrying out a mysterious clan ceremony of blood and passion, harnessing ancient gods of vengeance and sensuous yearnings of the flesh. Krutch described the impact of the direction and design of Jones meeting the dramatic material of O'Neill: "This method of staging is admirably calculated to draw attention to the controlling circumstances of the play. It is a story of human relationships become intolerably tense because intolerably close and limited, of the possessive instinct grown inhumanly powerful because the opportunities for its gratification are so small."[55] Here at one time the frustrations of the imprisoned characters found dramatic expression in milieu, picturization, restricted movement, and ultimately in an acting style which attempted to embrace simplistic naturalism, carefully planned movement and composition, and controlled tragic rhetoric disguised with a New England country dialect.

Just as the setting attempted to bridge different theatrical worlds, the actors had to be convincing in a realistic sense yet transcend realism with abbreviated movement in the tiny spaces, with carefully wrought stage pictures which demanded specific, unvarying placement to work successfully and with sudden shifts to self-revealing monologues which burst out of the naturalistic fabric of the dialogue. The monologues of course were colored by a heavy dialect and a sense of the poetic within a linguistic style which imitated the almost inexpressible limitations of the rustic characters' evasive speech. Broun found that "the eloquence of the inarticulate is achieved with rare skill and beauty,"[56] that this constraining but passionate agitation in speech was maintained superbly by the major performers. The individual New England dialects, however, were less accurate and consistent. Jones spent little time with dialects and left the problem up to the actors, who according to Benchley presented "eight different varieties of the New England dialect (all wrong but one)."[57] Likewise, Woollcott found the dialects "as implausible as a bad [stage] beard."[58] The exception was Walter Huston, whom the *New Republic*

54. Promotional flyer, *Desire* folder, MCNY.

55. Joseph Wood Krutch, "Desire Under the Elms," *Nation*, Nov. 26, 1924, in Hewitt, *Theatre USA*, pp. 361–62.

56. Heywood Broun, "The New Plays," *World*, Nov. 12, 1924, p. 15.

57. Robert Benchley, "Drama," *Life* (New York), Dec. 11, 1924, p. 18.

58. Alexander Woollcott, "Through Darkest New England," *Sun*, Nov. 12, 1924, p. 28.

found to be "the only member of the company whose mastery of his [dialectal] tongue is easy and assured."[59] The failure of Jones here is symptomatic of his limitations when working with actors.

Jones was very protective of his actors' feelings, however, as well as their freedom to create as individual artists. He would not try to impose his own ideas upon his actors and never raised his voice with them. He insisted upon a spirit of collaboration.[60] Although he could inspire actors with his imagination and emotional support, it was exceedingly important to Jones to cast experienced, independent actors who could respond to his often abstract concepts and yet take very specific blocking directions as Jones painted unforgettable pictures not only behind the actors but with them.

Despite his inclination to rely heavily upon actors he knew, like the old Provincetown standby Charles Ellis in the role of Eben, Jones occasionally took adventurous casting risks which amazed everyone around him. His long shots usually either succeeded famously or failed miserably. Whereas he would blunder with the casting of *The Fountain*, his selection of Walter Huston, a barely known veteran of vaudeville, for the pivotal role of the hardened father Ephraim Cabot resulted in one of the most memorable performances of the 1920s. At age forty, this Canadian variety performer had fifteen years of experience singing and dancing in vaudeville (with occasional acting) to his credit. He was a controlled craftsman who understood the demands of O'Neill's style and adapted easily to the methods of Jones. Young found him a perfect exponent of O'Neill's brand of realism,[61] and even O'Neill, who rarely praised an actor's performance, was very pleased with Huston's portrayal.[62] Onstage Huston seemed to become O'Neill's almost impossibly hardened stony-faced patriarch who thrived on adversity. Atkinson called his rendering "a self-confident, pitiless, heroic performance of evil and piety."[63] Vocally he rose to moving but rhetorical austerity as his powerful delivery reverentially conveyed "the dignity of scripture quotation."[64] Yet underlying this magnanimous, overwhelming, trenchant facade Huston revealed a contradictory emotional life. Young wrote that "beneath the surface . . . he glows with his own hungry, bitter passion; he is, in his own fashion, an unheard poet, dumb even to his own ears, inarticulate, unrelenting."[65] In a word, Huston's

59. R. M. L., "Desire," p. 44.
60. Seldes, "Profiles," pp. 26–27; Jones, *Dramatic*, p. 37.
61. Young, "Prompt," Dec. 7, 1924, p. 5.
62. Gelbs, *O'Neill*, p. 569.
63. Atkinson, *Lively*, p. 41.
64. R. M. L., "Desire," p. 44.
65. Young, "Prompt," Dec. 7, 1924, p. 5.

performance was mesmerizing. Even critics who railed against the immorality of the play ecstatically acclaimed Walter Huston's Ephraim Cabot.

Huston's preparation required little assistance from Jones, who was undoubtedly pleased with the actor's minimal needs. Indeed, the director's most significant accomplishment with the acting was his willingness to risk casting the vaudevillian. Perhaps Jones had Huston, soon one of his favorite actors, in mind when several years later he asserted that an actor's most important task was not to exhibit but to reveal.[66]

Although Mary Morris grew up in Massachusetts, the Radcliff-educated actress had difficulties with the homespun dialect of O'Neill's Abbie Putnam. At twenty-nine, she had considerable experience in stock companies but had only begun a New York career with the Triumvirate's *Spook Sonata* in January. A very dependable, consistent performer, Morris was an excellent choice for Abbie due to her fiery, passionate displays, intense physical brooding, and smoldering longing which sometimes matched, but more frequently served as counterpoint to, Huston's stoic presentation. In a photograph in which the two are confronting one another in the kitchen (probably the final scene), both are strong and unyielding, yet Huston's body is an erect, rigid pole, while that of Morris is curving backward like a serpent about to strike.

In performance Morris conveyed a sense of the exotic; she seemed a destructive tigress[67] whose open, passionate display was a moving manifestation of Abbie's "horribly frank mixture of lust and mother love"[68] which at once intrigued and alarmed theatergoers. One review asserted that she was so moving and poignant in her physicalization that her speeches were almost superfluous. "The look of her is all sufficient, especially in part III where her blighted face and ravaged eyes make a portrait not easily forgotten."[69] Morris was a nearly perfect actress and advocate for the visual directing style of Jones.

Jones was said to have treated the production of *Desire Under the Elms* much like a benevolent conductor with much reverence for his music. He controlled the stage and its pictures and unified the production with a carefully evoked atmosphere. The hand of the director was obvious, but in the American theater of 1924 such manipulation was welcome. Jones believed it was his duty as director to energize and animate the stage action while enshrining the pain of the human condition. "We are all so maimed and scarred,"[70] he said, and when directing *Desire Under the Elms* he cast

66. Jones, "Art," *Contemporary*, p. 461.
67. Whipple, "Two," p. 422; Atkinson, *Lively*, p. 41.
68. O'Neill, *Desire Under the Elms*, p. 108.
69. R. M. L., "Desire," p. 44.
70. Jones, in Sergeant, *Fire*, p. 47.

actors who seemed part and parcel of the often tragic, sometimes sadistic world of O'Neill. With Huston and Morris, Jones had actors whose characters seemed irrevocably burdened by emotional wounds. As they moved within the stark environment the actors did not seem so much realistic as "possessed by the real,"[71] a description which Jones reserved for the most satisfying and stirring of his actors' performances. The result of the bombardment of the actors' portrayals, O'Neill's text, and Jones' design and direction was an "incessant, cumulative portrayal of moral and spiritual death,"[72] an experience "so real and tragical," in Bromfield's words, "that one leaves the theatre in a state bordering upon exhaustion."[73]

Despite the obvious achievements with this production, O'Neill remained dissatisfied with the results—although he grudgingly admitted it was "well done, as things go."[74] His disappointment may have been as much disgust with the censorship problems and crass commercial advertising which accompanied the show to Broadway[75] as with anything Jones may have failed to do with the play. The production nevertheless stands as one of the most significant theatrical achievements of the 1920s due to its design, staging, and treatment of modern tragedy.

With *Desire Under the Elms* the *Morning Telegraph*, displaying typical hyperbole, proclaimed that "Greenwich Village is now completely under the dramatic dominance of Eugene O'Neill."[76] Jones and O'Neill had, however, successfully explored a dark, earthy world replete with personal memories and frustrations for both. The next two O'Neill plays would also be directed and designed by Jones, and these plays were flights of fancy with which the Triumvirate at first believed it was embarking on the theater of the future. As it turned out, although Jones contributed beautiful designs and staging, the continuing artistic journey of Jones and O'Neill after *Desire Under the Elms* more closely resembled the flight of Icarus.

71. Jones, "Art," *Contemporary*, p. 461.

72. R. Dana Skinner, "Decay and Flowing Sap," *Independent* 114 (Jan. 10, 1925): 51.

73. Bromfield, "New," p. 621.

74. O'Neill letter to Macgowan, 1926, in Bryer, *Letters*, p. 132.

75. After the play moved to the Earl Carrol Theatre under the production wing of A. L. Jones and Morris Green, who normally produced projects such as *The Greenwich Village Follies*, advertisements like the flyer described earlier began to appear. Unfortunately, no other commercial producers were willing to risk financing such a controversial play. The following advertisement appeared in the *New York Times*, Feb. 11, 1925, p. 18: "U.S. Cast Iron Pipe may be the big buy in the market—but Eugene O'Neill's greatest play *Desire Under the Elms* is the real bargain of Broadway."

76. "New O'Neill Play Opens Downtown," New York *Morning Telegraph*, Nov. 12, 1924, p. 5.

CHAPTER IX

Icarus Aloft:
The Fountain and *The Great God Brown*

> High above this world hovers a mythical horse, the Thibetan
> Pegasus, bearing on his back the figure of the Artist. Horse and
> rider are bound to one another by heavy chains. With one hand
> the Artist brandishes aloft his staff of power; in the other he
> holds his own heart, torn from his body, bleeding and burning.[1]

> Naturalism is too easy.[2]

For his last two adventures with the Triumvirate
O'Neill's fanciful flights carried him into a poetic, romantic past and a
stark, ironic present (or perhaps future). Despite a remarkable effort by
Robert Edmond Jones, the romantic play, *The Fountain*, failed miserably,
while *The Great God Brown*, although confusing to audiences, enjoyed
considerable notoriety. Nonetheless, after directing and designing these
productions Jones parted ways with the Triumvirate, and O'Neill abandoned the downtown experimental arena as well.

In *The Fountain* O'Neill's fanciful flights with legend, ritual, and
mysterious dreams carried him into a poetic, romantic past of sixteenth-
century Spain, crude conquistadors, the Catholic faith, the American
noble savage, and the conquest of the unknown, verdant New World.
Central to the play is the quest for renewal, the recapture of lost youth, of
rebirth of the body and the spirit by discovering and drinking from the
mythical Fountain of Youth.

Most of the critics who hammered away at *The Fountain* laid the
greatest blame at the feet of O'Neill. While nearly all reviewers praised
and appreciated much of the work of Jones, it was evident that the play
failed to measure up to O'Neill's usual proficiency. More than a disap-

1. Jones, *Drawing* (1925), p. 15.
2. O'Neill, in Kantor, "O'Neill," p. 5.

pointment, *The Fountain* was awkward in language, predictable in structure, unexciting in character. In short, much of the dramatic material was dull and lifeless. In this vein Metcalfe wrote that O'Neill had "lately rediscovered Mr. Ponce de Leon and embalmed him."[3] O'Neill had indeed written a play without the sense of urgency which dominated so many of his plays. "Desire Under the Palms,"[4] as Anderson labeled *The Fountain*, offered few dynamic confrontations and characters such as those which abound in the script of *Desire Under the Elms*. In consequence, Jones set about trying to fabricate dynamic moments for the production—and he succeeded.

Jones, however, was not the first choice for production. In fact, this play was written in 1921 and optioned in 1922 by Arthur Hopkins.[5] After attempting unsuccessfully to secure John or Lionel Barrymore for the leading role, Hopkins hired Fritz Leiber for Ponce de Leon, but rehearsals never began.[6] Hopkins finally rejected *The Fountain* entirely, and the play passed to the Theatre Guild, which planned a production for the 1924–1925 season and hired Jones to design it, but the play was again dropped.[7] It is not surprising, then, that O'Neill began to lose interest; by the time the Triumvirate planned production for the fall of 1925 *The Fountain* was old work for the playwright. Even Macgowan tried to postpone production in the early fall pending further revision and to stage *The Great God Brown* first, but O'Neill overruled this suggestion emphatically. The play had been revised so frequently since 1921 that O'Neill feared with cause that the play would only get worse with additional rewriting.[8] Therefore, with Jones at the helm, *The Fountain* opened at the Greenwich Village Theatre on December 10, 1925, and closed within three weeks.[9] As with *Desire Under the Elms*, the Triumvirate had planned to move the production uptown to the Forty-eighth Street Theatre in a month,[10] but only the subscription audience kept the production on the boards past opening night.

3. Metcalfe, "The Theatre," *Wall Street Journal*, Dec. 12, 1925, p. 3.

4. John Anderson, "O'Neill Writes a Romance About Ponce de Leon," *New York Evening Post*, Dec. 11, 1925, p. 12.

5. Sisk, "The Fountain," *Variety*, Dec. 16, 1925, p. 27.

6. Flora Merrill, "Fierce Oaths and Blushing Complexes Find No Place in Eugene O'Neill's Talk," *World*, July 19, 1925, p. M-4; O'Neill letter to Macgowan, Sept. 23, 1922 in Bryer, *Letters*, p. 34.

7. O'Neill letters to Macgowan, Mar. 18 and May 1, (1925), in Bryer, *Letters*, pp. 90, 93.

8. Nathan's review lamented that the play he saw at the Greenwich Village was a poor shadow of the original text (due apparently to "endless rewriting") which O'Neill let him read in 1922. George Jean Nathan, "Eugene O'Neill," in Downer, *American*, p. 86.

9. "Theatrical Notes" and advertisement, *New York Times*, Dec. 10, 1925, pp. 28–29; Miller, *Eugene*, p. 60. Reviews first appeared on Dec. 11, 1925.

10. Sisk, "Fountain," p. 27.

In the 1925–1926 season O'Neill, Jones, and Macgowan mounted all of their productions at the Greenwich Village, leaving James Light and Cleon Throckmorton to operate the Provincetown under the Triumvirate's banner. O'Neill was obviously weary of his old little theater with its cramped space and poor ventilation. "Imagine writing of the cosmic tides of Being," he told Macgowan, "when you're thinking of how nobody in the audience will be able to draw their own breath after Scene One!"[11] Unfortunately, it was a too self-conscious approach to cosmic tides which helped to undermine the impact of *The Fountain*.

Opening night was the conclusion of a busy year of directing and designing for Jones, who worked with both the Triumvirate and Arthur Hopkins. Jones was so busy with other productions that both Macgowan and O'Neill feared he might not have time to direct *The Fountain* unless it were postponed until the new year. Therefore, Lionel Atwill was approached, but Jones finally decided to mount the production as soon as he finished the designs for Hopkins' production of Philip Barry's *In a Garden* at the Plymouth (November 16).[12]

The overworked Jones came very close to resigning from Experimental Theatre, Inc., after its second season, but O'Neill and Macgowan persuaded him to remain for another year, after which Jones, in an emotional shambles, fled to Carl Jung in Zurich for help.[13] Despite his obvious talents, his skittish temperament was perhaps unsuited to full-time direction, because he was never able to project the kind of authority and toughness necessary to survive as a director in New York.[14]

Jones' production of *The Fountain* was found to be visually beautiful but too compromising in its ultimate style. Seldes, for example, wrote that "the direction . . . seemed to waver a little between a stylistic presentation and a matter-of-fact representation; but this, too, was in spots in keeping with the uncertainty of the text."[15] Once again Jones insisted upon fidelity to the play as written, a commitment which always resulted in a fascinating and engaging production when the play was well written, like *Desire Under the Elms*. For the failure of *The Fountain*, however, "the fault lies not with the producers," Sisk insisted, but with O'Neill.[16]

The accounts of O'Neill's assistance at rehearsals beginning in November are mixed. Reports indicate that the playwright was present for

11. O'Neill letter to Macgowan, Mar. 14 (1925) in Bryer, *Letters*, p. 89.

12. O'Neill telegram and letter to Macgowan, Aug. 1 and Sept. 2, 1925, in Bryer, *Letters*, pp. 95, 96; Mantle, *Best Plays 1925–26*, p. 495.

13. Bryer, *Letters*, p. 80.

14. See Simonson, in Komisarjevsky, *Settings*, p. 97, and Macgowan, "Enter," p. 292.

15. Gilbert Seldes, "The Theatre," *Dial* 80 (Feb. 1926): 168.

16. Sisk, "Fountain," p. 27.

some early rehearsals, probably available when necessary, but not enthusiastic about this production.[17] Significantly, he omitted this play from his Langner list of productions for which he was on the job. He met with Jones and Macgowan in Bermuda during the summer of 1925 to go over the text for a final revision, and by September 28 he had the script ready for production.[18] Although this version pleased O'Neill, the text was very long and underwent considerable cutting and minor alteration during rehearsals, as the promptbook clearly demonstrates.[19] These revisions, however, made no changes in themes, style, plot, or character. The production was essentially a shortened version of the written play.

While the amount of cutting and alteration of dialogue varies from scene to scene, a fairly uniform approach to streamlining is evident. None of the eleven scenes was entirely eliminated, but two complete pages of scene 2 (the gambling sequence) were cut. This, the longest omission, was restored in publication.[20] Another significant cut was a lengthy speech by Beatriz at the conclusion of scene 4 in which she rationalized her decision to help the villain Menendez for De Leon's sake. The speech was not published.[21] Additional emendations included cuts of single lines and words, minor word changes, word contractions, occasional short additions, reassigned lines, and pauses replacing single-word replies. None of the changes affected very important lines or moments, and roughly half of them were retained in the published text. Several major speeches, however, were marked for possible cuts, though the cuts were never approved.

One further major change was made to the play's final speech. This speech by Luis, which was rewritten for production, included a request for offstage chanting by unseen monks, a musical strain which finished the produced play. In the published play O'Neill altered Luis' speech to

17. In a notable exception, Paul Waldo claims that O'Neill attended all rehearsals but provides no source for this information. Waldo, "Production," p. 324. See also Hicks, "Robert," pp. 146, 152; Sheaffer, *Artist*, p. 187.

18. O'Neill letters to Macgowan, May 1, (1925) and Sept. 28, 1925, in Bryer, *Letters*, pp. 93, 100.

19. The promptbook is considerably different from the play published in Mar. 1926. Pagination of the promptbook is highly irregular. It seems to be a compilation of several different manuscript copies, although one hand kept notes and changes throughout (except for scene 10). While the text is complete, many different pages bear identical page numbers. Therefore, all references to this promptbook will be by scene number and page number of that scene. Eugene O'Neill, *The Fountain*, bound promptbook, Theatre Collection, Performing Arts Center, New York Public Library, copyrighted 1925 by Yale University.

20. O'Neill, *Fountain* promptbook, scene 2, pp. 3–4; Eugene O'Neill, *The Fountain*, in *The Great God Brown, The Fountain, The Moon of the Caribbees, and Other Plays*, (New York: Boni and Liveright, 1926), pp. 120–21.

21. O'Neill, *Fountain* promptbook, scene 4, p. 11; O'Neill, *Fountain*, p. 147.

eliminate the reference, but the playwright added a stage direction to include "deep and vibrant" chanting.[22] More than any other alteration to the text, this one suggests the influence of Jones, who loved to create mysterious sound effects as well as unusual stage pictures.

Despite considerable cutting, the play was still found by critics to be tiresome, overlong, and verbose. Barretto complained that while the play was staged beautifully, the text "needs a knife. . . . Under the wordy speeches . . . the characters became wooden without a semblance of life, and along about scene ten . . . the monotony became positively painful."[23] Little did the critics imagine that O'Neill's loquaciousness would accelerate in subsequent productions. Their complaints were well grounded with *The Fountain*.

The promptbook contains playing times for the first nine scenes; together they total 108 minutes. Using these times and their corresponding number of pages as a guide, a reasonable length for the final two scenes is twenty-seven minutes. After adding two fifteen-minute intermissions and only three minutes for each scene change, the time of production is three hours and fifteen minutes. Reviewers, however, complained of very slow scene changes, so that the audience was probably in the theatre for three and one-half hours or more.

Yet it was not length alone which retarded the effectiveness of the play in the theater; it was O'Neill's insistence on experiment sometimes for its own sake. "Instead of trimming his play of nonessentials," Atkinson observed, "Mr. O'Neill has rather filled it with a profusion of irrelevant ornaments that clog the action and imprison the meaning."[24] Some of his experiments worked in *The Fountain*, but by and large most were misplaced. Perhaps he learned important lessons with this production, because he did not produce another incongruous experiment until 1929.

The overlong sojourn of the audience was accentuated by one of the play's most striking departures from O'Neill's previous work, a major production problem which was never satisfactorily solved. The dramatist reportedly cast the language in verse but typed the dialogue as though it were prose.[25] Although the 1921 typescript maintained none of the original meter except in the songs,[26] the heightened, romantic sound of the

22. O'Neill, *Fountain* promptbook, scene 11, p. 9; B. D., "Second Thoughts on 'The Fountain,'" New York *Morning Telegraph*, Dec. 13, 1925, sec. 2, p. 8.

23. Larry Barretto, "The New Yorker," *Bookman* 62 (Feb. 1926): 704.

24. J. Brooks Atkinson, "New O'Neill Aspects," *New York Times*, Dec. 20, 1925, sec. 7, p. 3.

25. Gelbs, *O'Neill*, p. 468.

26. Eugene O'Neill, *The Fountain* typescript, Rare Book Collection, Library of Congress, 1921.

language remained and survived numerous structural and language revisions over the years, leading one critic of performance to label the play "a tone poem."[27] Most of the reactions to the language, however, were negative, likening the often stilted dialogue and grandiloquent monologues to "sublimated Percy MacKaye."[28] The lyricism and artificiality created formidable difficulties for the actors and Jones.

The director could not overcome O'Neill's preoccupation with language in the play. The word, far more than action, was important here, and O'Neill's language edged toward philosophical and self-conscious symbolism. Both Woollcott and Sisk complained that the play, not the production, was almost lifeless and destructive to dramatic movement.[29] With a dearth of action, Jones relied on stage pictures, mood, and music. O'Neill wrote in 1928 that Jones found most of his plays "had the definite quality of a musical composition."[30] With *The Fountain* an O'Neill production incorporated more actual music than ever before. Macklin Morrow was engaged to write incidental music for the play, which included songs, chants, dances, and anthems. Unfortunately, the dark, moody music was said to have "weighted oppressively"[31] most of the scenes in which it was used. An exception was the use of music in Ponce de Leon's vision in scene 10. Filled with music, song, and dance in a rapidly shifting cacophony of sight and sound, the scene suggested a modern-day masque. While the promptbook does not elucidate the specific nature of the music here, reviews are generous in praise of the visual and aural splendor of this scene.

Other scenes included a chanting Moorish minstrel, Indian dances, offstage drumming, a Te Deum sung aboard ship, a hymn of thanksgiving upon landing in the New World, chanting Christian monks, and an intriguing use of a seafaring chanty song initiated by a sailor and picked up by the mob "in mighty chorus, dancing wildly, waving their torches"[32] as the mood of the scene shifted in a moment from menacing strife to euphonious elation. Most of this chanting and singing was done by large groups (requiring considerable crowd manipulation by Jones), as once again O'Neill incorporated a strong choral element with the dramatic action. In six of the eleven scenes O'Neill used a chorus of Indians (Jones cast six

27. "Mr. O'Neill Seeking Romance," *New York Times*, Dec. 11, 1925, p. 26.

28. H. J. M., "Critique," *New Yorker*, Dec. 19, 1925, p. 17.

29. Alexander Woollcott, "The Stage," *World*, Dec. 11, 1925, p. 16; Sisk, "Fountain," p. 27.

30. O'Neill, in Sheaffer, *Artist*, p. 306.

31. Louis Kalonyme, "Delectable Mountains of Current Drama," *Arts & Decoration* 24 (Feb. 1926): 84.

32. O'Neill, *Fountain* promptbook, scene 6, p. 13.

plus a chief and medicine man), rioters, conquistadors, and offstage monks.[33]

O'Neill's most dynamic experiment with this play was Ponce de Leon's vision, an extravagant dream sequence in which the dark forest came to life with emblems of the hero's quest, hopes, and delusions. Images appeared, transformed, and vanished as the Spaniard lay wounded but entranced. As Travis Bogard suggests, this scene recalled the dramatic experiment of *The Emperor Jones* whereby the mysterious forest provided a field of hallucinations for the protagonist.[34] Jones staged the scene magnificently, perhaps prompting O'Neill to use undisguised visions again in *Marco Millions* and *Lazarus Laughed*. The sequence of apparitions facilitated once again the use of masks, especially for transforming the figure of Beatriz from a stony-faced automaton to an old Indian woman and back to the real Beatriz. This was O'Neill's fourth major use of masks before his most important venture with them in his next production, *The Great God Brown*.

With *The Fountain* O'Neill called for eight different scenic locations, more than ever before. Unlike *The Emperor Jones*, however, in which six of the seven locations could be variations of a unit design, *The Fountain* required a large study, a dungeon, three different courtyards, a beach, a dark forest (which transformed), and the flagship of Christopher Columbus. Although Jones created stunning designs, he did not satisfactorily solve the problems posed by this "badly proportioned"[35] arrangement of scenes. Referring to the production team, a *New York Times* review said: "As usual, Mr. O'Neill has made their task none too easy."[36]

Jones labored with the design problems of *The Fountain* for about a year before mounting it at the Greenwich Village. Perhaps his original designs for the much larger Guild Theatre were scrapped, though it is likely that they were reworked for the shallow stage downtown. The final product was visually stunning and stylistically appropriate, but was too cramped by the limited facility and much too cumbersome to shift quickly.

"It is Mr. Jones, by the way, who furnishes most of the excitement in the play,"[37] Benchley nonetheless asserted in his review. He was reacting, as did many others, to the enchanting pictures adorning the limited stage. "The settings are uncommonly beautiful," wrote Woollcott.[38] "If you can

33. Neither promptbook nor program clarifies the number of actors in these groups, but in production photographs twenty people are visible on the ship of explorers (scene 2) and twenty-three in the riot (scene 6).

34. Bogard, *Contour*, p. 237.

35. Atkinson, "New," Dec. 20, 1925, p. 3.

36. "Mr. O'Neill," Dec. 11, 1925, p. 26.

37. Robert Benchley, "Drama," *Life* (New York), Dec. 31, 1925, p. 18.

38. Woollcott, "Stage," Dec. 11, 1925, p. 16.

withdraw all the tawdry and tricky associations from the word," added Seldes, "you may call [the settings] magical."[39] Such enthusiasm for the visual grandeur was common in the critical response.

With *The Fountain* Jones was at his best in following his own rules of design, striving for splendor in simplicity but refusing to settle for creating "just a beautiful thing." He sought to capture "a presence, a mood," to provide stage environments which were "not descriptive, but evocative" of the prevailing atmosphere of the play, primarily through careful selection and subordination of detail.[40] When looking at the production photographs,[41] one is reminded of the Throckmorton designs for *The Emperor Jones* with the broad expanses of color, the strong contrast of darks and lights, the large brushstrokes creating the dark forests so like the effect of some fauvist paintings. *The Fountain* designs, however, create a flatter effect, without the three-dimensional nature of Throckmorton's forest. The stage world of Jones is more akin to the jungles of Henri Rosseau's primitive renderings. On stage the environment "seemed composed for ideal actors, for heroic gestures;"[42] it was a place where the poetic word and romantic spirit could not be stifled by authentic surroundings.

Set in striking relief against his rather simply drawn designs were a host of elaborate fifteenth- and sixteenth-century Spanish costumes meant to serve the unavoidable pageantry of the play. Many costumes, especially the women's, were large and generously laced with glittery braiding, jewels, satins, and—occasionally—stiff material which resembles taffeta. Several costumes appear garish in close-ups, and the brightest were splashed with "hot vermilion, the color of blood in sunlight," but these were balanced by a collection of grays and blacks ("the black of the robes of Spanish madonnas")[43] on the clerical characters who were onstage in nearly every scene.

Jones, who was faced with what Stark Young called "the most difficult problem of this season in the theatre,"[44] chose to be as frugal as possible when dressing his central performance space, which he kept bare in five scenes and decorated only with a fountain in the remaining six. As a result, the stage floor was generally an acting platform, an open space which was meant to focus attention on the actors. In this respect the

39. Seldes, "Theatre," Feb. 1926, p. 169.

40. Jones, *Dramatic*, pp. 26, 81; Macgowan, *Continental*, p. 43.

41. Ten photographs, Theatre Collection, Beinecke Library, Yale; five photographs, Theatre Collection, MCNY.

42. Sergeant was generalizing here about many of Jones' settings, but the description is most apt for *The Fountain*. Sergeant, *Fire*, p. 51.

43. Mannes, "Robert," p. 15.

44. Stark Young, "The Fountain," in Cargill, *O'Neill*, pp. 173–74.

"scenic investiture [was] economical and practical to the extreme,"[45] but many scenes were so crowded with actors that the open space frequently seemed very restricted.

Although Jones was praised for his beautiful and effective composition of the stage groupings, the actual stage size was paltry for such pageantry and the final effect seemed "earnestly elaborate in a small way."[46] Hammond found that O'Neill's "spacious romance . . . suffered from lack of elbow room."[47] These descriptions are pointedly supported by the production photographs, which sometimes reveal actors at or slightly below the proscenium frame in order to avoid crowding other actors. When the stage bears more than about twelve actors, it appears to be a crowded box rather than a governor's courtyard or a Florida beach. Fortunately, however, with careful placement Jones created the effect of large mobs with only twenty actors.

The most disappointing feature of the settings was the inability to change them quickly. There was a delay with every shift, long waits which Barrett Clark could hardly believe that Americans still tolerated. "These only served to accentuate the slowness of the performance," he lamented.[48] The intervals were said to be "of such length as definitely . . . break the thin threads of O'Neill's illusion and poetry."[49] Therefore, because it was "cramped by stage machinery,"[50] forward movement was undermined both by a sometimes lethargic script and many undesirable "intermissions between scenes that insufficiently reward one for waiting."[51] The result was a production which did not end until 11:40 P.M.[52]

With limited shifting space and storage room at his disposal, Jones decided—he probably had no other option—to design all settings with a shallow distance between the upstage boundary and the proscenium line. Thus, all scenes were staged close to the audience. Hammond remarked that "those in the good, or critics' seats, could almost reach out and touch Ponce de Leon."[53] Jones appears to have attempted to mollify this proximity by framing all scenes with an ornate inner proscenium. The effects

45. H. J. M., "Critique," p. 17.

46. Gilbert W. Gabriel, "De Leon in Search of His Spring," *Sun*, Dec. 11, 1925, in Miller, *Playwright's*, p. 15.

47. Percy Hammond, "The Theaters," *New York Herald-Tribune*, Dec. 11, 1925, p. 22.

48. Clark, "New," Feb. 1926, p. 175.

49. H. J. M., "Critique," p. 17.

50. Kalonyme, "Delectable," p. 84.

51. A note in the promptbook indicates that there was particular difficulty in shifting from the dungeon (scene 5) to the governor's palace (scene 6). Scene 6 was then followed by a regular intermission. O'Neill, *Fountain* promptbook, scene 6, p. 1. Arthur Pollock, "Plays and Things," *Brooklyn Daily Eagle*, Dec. 11, 1925, p. 18.

52. "Ponce de Leon a la Mr. O'Neill," New York *Morning Telegraph*, Dec. 12, 1925, p. 5.

53. Hammond, "Theaters," Dec. 11, 1925, p. 22.

of this device were unfortunately minimized, since the proscenium further reduced the stage size, emphasized the lack of space, and sometimes forced the actors to move out of the framework.

All eight settings have survived in photographs, and all are unified by the repeated motif of a crucifix which appears in every setting and in many costumes. If a setting was not decorated with a cross, a character introduced one by wearing or carrying it prominently. These settings fall into six types: courtyard, dungeon, beach, sailing ship, forest, and monastic interior (the only set using flats, and the only one without dynamic staging problems). Each type created specific problems and effects, and the results in production were widely different.

Scenes 1, 3, 6, and 11 were all walled Spanish courtyards of a house, palace, or monastery. For both monastery and palace Jones erected walls and a central door unit extending across the stage parallel to the curtain line. Both "sunny bits of architecture"[54] disappeared in the wings offstage. The monastery was much softer in line, however, because the walls, decorated with greenery as well as pink and scarlet flowers,[55] were gently raked upward toward a thin cross mounted at the peak of a small arched central building. The palace walls by contrast were parallel to the floor and intersected by a much higher and wider flat-roofed building at center. The Granadan house courtyard also had a back wall and central door unit, but the walls were arranged in something of a semicircle, arcing away from the audience. The walls here were much lower, at most only three feet in height.

All of these settings had a fountain center stage. The monastery's fountain was low and unimposing, but the fountains of the palace and house were very large, two-tiered constructions which dominated the stage picture and emphasized the lack of playable space. These were functioning fountains with running water, an effect which went awry because of the "ridiculously thin trickle of water"[56] in the middle of the large fountain, which measured approximately eight to ten feet in diameter.

The promptbook demonstrates that Jones used the fountains as sittable-standable units. He staged some scenes with a few characters in circular patterns around a fountain, but only rarely did Jones move the actors together far left or right of a fountain to create new playing areas. For example, when De Leon met Maria in scene 1, the fountain was usually between them, and Jones never moved them to either side of the

54. Gabriel, "De Leon," p. 16.
55. The promptbook includes a hand-drawn setting (which corresponds to a photograph) with the flowers drawn in and labeled by color. O'Neill, *Fountain* promptbook, scene 11, p. 9.
56. Kalonyme, "Delectable," p. 86.

stage. In a few cases when there were five to eight characters on the stage, Jones spread the actors almost in a lineup, with little attempt to stagger them in order to gain a stronger sense of depth. In scene 1, however, when Menendez murdered the Moor, the staging exploded, scattering the eight actors to all parts of the stage. In moments of crisis or large crowds Jones would give very careful attention to placement and compositional use of actors.

The most important use of a courtyard was the mob riot of scene 6. For this and other crowd scenes Jones enlisted the aid of an assistant, Perry Ivins, who also played the small role of Oviedo, to help him control and arrange the twenty or more actors involved.[57] The effect of the crowd "swinging clubs, brandishing swords and crying for their victim"[58] was appropriately dynamic and replete with considerable movement and shifting of compositional arrangements. In the one photograph of this scene the crowd members are in various attitudes, occupying several different planes and levels (some are crouched and bent), and all areas of the stage are utilized except one important space of a few feet between Ponce de Leon and Nano, the Indian he is protecting in the downright corner of the stage. In consequence, this empty space became the most dynamic compositional element of the scene.

For the torture sequence in the dungeon of scene 5, Jones designed a wide expanse of stone wall which was painted on a drop; when lit it had an almost metallic effect. In the center of the wall he placed the Indian Nano, chained to a wooden panel with arms spread, creating another crucifix. Most of the light fell on the tortured Indian, and much of the surrounding emptiness was left in semidarkness. Although the drop extended out of view in all directions, Jones' design as a drawing[59] is much more impressive than the finished setting because the Greenwich Village did not have the height necessary to make the image as grand as it appears on paper. Nonetheless, Ponce de Leon had much room in the suitably dank setting to roam about below Nano as he questioned the stubborn Indian, occasionally retiring down left to a small bench, the only furniture on an otherwise bare stage.

Scenes 7 and 8 took place on a Florida beach which Jones suggested with his most Rosseau-like design (see illustration 7). Flat, stylized vegetation appeared on each side of the stage like old wing pieces extending into the flies on stage right and to a height of no more than seven feet stage left. Low ground rows some two feet high ran parallel to the curtain line upstage. Beyond the ground rows was only a cyclorama. The entire playing

57. *The Fountain* program, Theatre Collection, MCNY.
58. "Mr. O'Neill," Dec. 11, 1925, p. 26.
59. Jones, *Drawings* (1970), plate #27.

space was bare in scene 7 and contained only a rock altar near center stage in the following scene.

The secretive nighttime action of scene 7 was dimly lit, save for a strong pool of light center stage into which the three principal Indians moved while the six supporting Indians remained on the edges of illumination. Woollcott recalled the impressive picture of "shadowy Indians seen dimly like a cluster of beech trees in the Florida moonlight."[60] For his staging of the Indian scenes with their primitive movement and dance, Jones used another assistant, William Stahl, who in addition played the small role of Pedro.[61]

The same setting used in scene 8 provided dynamic contrast to the quiet nocturnal scene. Here under bright sunshine, around their makeshift "Christian" altar with a large inverted cross which stood five feet tall, the Indians impressively danced and chanted to the accompaniment of drums, "invoking the mercy of the Great Spirit at the approach of white men."[62] After Ponce de Leon's party landed and the Indian medicine man was stupidly killed for performing a "black mass," Jones created one of his most impressive stage pictures. Woollcott called this one of the play's "electric moments . . . when, with the unfurled banners of Castille and Aragon drooping in the noonday sun, Ponce de Leon kneels to name the new land Florida."[63] All of the Spanish company of some twenty actors were kneeling across the stage in three major groups arranged around the altar with flags freestanding in holes bored into the stage floor. Jones flooded the stage with light, even using footlights, which he often avoided, as the company sang a religious hymn of thanksgiving. Although he liked the scene, Gabriel (always the cynic) suggested that this moment had the "bliss of grouping and coloration which used to characterize such tableaux on the sides of the old time moving vans."[64] The stage picture nonetheless was an effectively mounted, if obviously unspontaneous, composition.

Virtually all reviewers were impressed by the design and staging of scene 2, the main deck of the flagship on the second voyage of Columbus (see illustration 8). Here Jones produced several "haunting visual effects"[65] as "individual moments blaze with dramatic beauty."[66] Using the stage floor as the main deck and backing it with a stern created by platforms, bulkhead railing, and two rope ladders, the ship seemed to be

60. Woollcott, "Stage," Dec. 11, 1925, p. 16.
61. *The Fountain* program, MCNY.
62. "Mr. O'Neill," Dec. 11, 1925, p. 26.
63. Woollcott, "Stage," Dec. 11, 1925, p. 16.
64. Gabriel, "De Leon," p. 16.
65. John Mason Brown, "The Director Takes a Hand," *Theatre Arts* 10 (Feb. 1926): 77.
66. Kalonyme, "Delectable," p. 84.

headed down right. Since the action took place just before and at dawn, Jones surrounded these scenic elements with darkness and never filled in the edges of the ship. Up center, just above the stern deck, Jones hung a huge lantern topped by a cross which dominated the composition at first when "drenched in the dim light before dawn."[67] When Columbus came on deck beneath the lantern, Jones created an "unforgettable picture . . . with the figure of Columbus standing silhouetted beside his helmsman,"[68] both men outlined by "the after-light against the background of the sky."[69] This somber beauty was followed by a sudden, dynamic, visual shift.

Near the end of scene 2, as Columbus and Ponce de Leon were vehemently arguing, land was sighted down right. This moment was coincident with the dawn, so with "the devout fervor of a 'Te Deum,'" the company fell to its knees "straining their eyes toward the new land," as "the sun suddenly and inexplicably [rose] from the west."[70] Jones, of course, violated natural law in order to heighten the effect of the moment by flooding the stage with intense light emanating from the direction of the New World. With the sudden explosion of light, however, Jones worked selectively, focusing almost all of the light downstage on the crowd while isolating as secondary focus the separated figures of Ponce de Leon and his future nemesis, Menendez, who were elevated up center and stage left, respectively. According to Benchley, "most of the thrill" of this scene "comes from the setting and direction,"[71] a tribute to Jones' success with visual imagery and the handling of crowds who attacked the scene vigorously and, according to the *Telegraph*, "hurl[ed] it over the footlights like a hand grenade."[72]

The most taxing scenic effect occurred in scene 10 when Ponce de Leon experienced his glorious vision. He lay wounded beside a spring surrounded by a forest which was also used in the preceding scene. Painted foliage appeared right and left as in the beach scenes, but the upstage treatment is impossible to discern in the photograph. Young described the setting as "all black and somber green. In form it is harsh and severe, clawing, hard edges, simple, strict forms."[73] While Ponce de Leon drank from the spring at center in scene 9, the Indians encircled him and ambushed him with a shower of arrows. Woollcott and stage directions suggest that the effect was achieved with sound.[74]

67. "Mr. O'Neill," Dec. 11, 1925, p. 26.
68. Woollcott, "Stage," Dec. 11, 1925, p. 16.
69. Metcalfe, "Theatre," Dec. 12, 1925, p. 3.
70. Gabriel, "De Leon," p. 16; "Mr. O'Neill," Dec. 11, 1925, p. 26.
71. Benchley, "Drama," Dec. 31, 1925, p. 18.
72. B. D., "Second," p. 8.
73. Young, "Fountain," p. 174.
74. Woollcott, "Stage," Dec. 11, 1925, p. 16; O'Neill, *Fountain* promptbook, scene 9, p. 3.

In the illusionary masque of scene 10 a scrim was lowered between Ponce de Leon and the audience. The spring, above the scrim, was transformed to a magical fountain from which all of the ghosts and images were meant to emerge. A tall female death figure draped in deep blue appeared to De Leon in a pale face mask almost devoid of features. As she sang the spring was replaced by a fountain in which a youthful Beatriz danced, before giving way to a dumb show of Chinese poet, Moorish minstrel, American Indian, and Spanish soldier, all sharing myths of the fountain of renewal. Four figures representing the world's major religions also appeared and merged in the fountain. Eventually the death figure and youthful Beatriz became one and the vision faded away.

The only photograph of this scene is very hazy, primarily due to the filmy scrim which appears to be accented by many hanging, gleaming strings. In the center of the stage stood a masked Beatriz figure, above whom glitter fell from the flies, drifting down toward her.

The light cues for scene 10 in the promptbook indicate many rapidly changing pictures with "sudden bursts" and "shimmering" effects coming from the proscenium and from low angles, presumably for the fountain. Lighting areas seem to be indicated on each side of the scrim for special effects.[75] Although the critical reactions to this scene varied markedly, the descriptions are consistent in recreating the essence of the mystical display. The scene was called a magnificently staged "ghastly dream,"[76] in which Jones eerily "blended lighting and screening in a luminous stage picture"[77] while "a procession of shades file past to tease the dying explorer."[78] Several reviewers noted that the scrim created a "mist-en-shrouded"[79] stage dominated by a "dreamy blueness,"[80] behind which "the dream fountain of Christmas tinsel, dimmed in a palely luminous light, was surpassingly lovely."[81] As "gleaming jets"[82] issued from the fountain the mute figures "appeared and reappeared at intervals in a show of gold,"[83] with Macklin's music and the singing of Beatriz underscoring the mysterious reverie.

While the spectacle was interesting, the effectiveness ultimately was less than desirable, since the pageantry seemed to serve little purpose and could not make up for so much tedium which preceded it. "The audience

75. O'Neill, *Fountain* promptbook, scene 10, pp. 1–6.
76. Sisk, "Fountain," p. 27.
77. Atkinson, "New," Dec. 20, 1925, p. 3.
78. Benchley, "Drama," Dec. 31, 1925, p. 18.
79. M. W. [Michael Williams], "The Play," *Commonweal* 3 (Dec. 23, 1925): 189.
80. Gabriel, "De Leon," p. 16.
81. Anderson, "O'Neill," Dec. 11, 1925, p. 12.
82. Gabriel, "De Leon," p. 16.
83. Barretto, "New," Feb. 1926, p. 705.

grew restive"[84] with the beautiful and well-intended "hallucinations and symbols by means of which," Williams wrote, "the playwright seeks to express the inner meanings of his conception, but which have little more than the arbitrary significance of a conventional, pantheistic pageant."[85] The visual display was impressive, but, as Atkinson observed, "'The Fountain' rarely stirs the emotions."[86] After sitting in the theater for more than three hours, the highlights of which had been imaginative picturization, the audience was not likely to be overwhelmed by yet more spectacle.

The Triumvirate spent eighteen thousand dollars on this production,[87] considerably more than any other, and it remained a mechanical leviathan, an unmanageable "trial by scenery."[88] Although Jones created an admirable if slow-moving panorama of sights for *The Fountain*, he could not "quicken it into theatrical life."[89] Nowhere was this more apparent than in the acting.

The director's biggest problems with the acting grew from the large size of the cast in a small theater, language and stylistic uncertainties, and the play's lack of action, which resulted in severe tempo difficulties. Even with considerable double-casting Jones employed some thirty actors, seventeen of whom took the twenty-three speaking roles. The remaining performers filled in as Indians, monks, sailors, soldiers, nobles, and rioters.

Only one reviewer, Woollcott, mentioned the cast with favor. Others attacked the acting along stylistic lines which were usually related to the handling of the language. Echoing a previous lament by Stark Young during *Desire Under the Elms*, Barrett Clark wrote that "*The Fountain* requires acting of a kind that is practically non-existent in this country . . . a certain mixture of tradition [contemporary realism] and untrammeled ecstasy."[90] It was in this pursuit of flamboyant, romantic glorying in the spoken word and emphatic gesture that the actors failed. Some of the actors when faced with this language seemed "dry, sapless and inarticulate,"[91] even lethargic. Occasional odd pronunciations apparently inserted for authenticity, such as "Floreeda" for "Florida,"[92] only accentuated those actors who were unsuited to ornamental dialogue.

Walter Huston, so impressive in *Desire Under the Elms*, was inap-

84. Baretto, "New," Feb. 1926, p. 706.
85. Williams, "Play," Dec. 23, 1925, p. 189.
86. Atkinson, "New," Dec. 20, 1925, p. 3.
87. O'Neill letter to Macgowan (1926), in Bryer, *Letters*, p. 134.
88. Gabriel, "De Leon," p. 15.
89. Nathan, "Eugene," *American*, p. 87.
90. Clark, "New," Feb. 1926, p. 175.
91. Kalonyme, "Delectable," p. 84.
92. Sisk, "Fountain," p. 27.

propriate for the swashbuckling hero, Ponce de Leon. He never managed to convey the charm and charisma necessary for the frustrated conquistador, who instead remained a bit "crude and unmagnetic."[93] As early as August O'Neill was concerned that "Huston would need long intensive work with Bobby and Carrington" and might not be ready by December.[94] O'Neill's fears were justified. In October Stark Young warned O'Neill that Huston might have difficulty achieving "lyric force and eloquence. . . . Eloquence," he explained, "implies . . . a rush and impulse of feeling, as if the lines were speaking themselves."[95] When Young reviewed the performance in December, he reported that Huston was too prosaic and could not capture the romance.[96]

Although Huston attacked the role vigorously, he was never a moving presence. As the photographs bear out, he looked physically attractive and "made a fairly glamorous picture . . . but his dry voice and brittle gestures [more suitable to Ephraim Cabot] were ruinous to the part."[97] O'Neill believed, probably correctly, that the only actor in America capable of carrying off such a role on the stage was John Barrymore.[98]

Jones was in the habit of discussing with each actor early in rehearsal "the problem of movement and attitude and style imposed by the modes and manners of the period"[99] of the play, but something went awry with *The Fountain*. Brown suggested that as a director with this material Jones "dived beyond his depth. . . . Jones," he continued, "naturally sees more in the theatre than he hears . . . [and] when the director must manage tempo and take care of the pacing . . . there is little continuity."[100] Whether or not Brown's assessment is accurate, it is certain that aurally the performance was often tedious.

"There is a note of Episcopalian delivery about the whole thing," Benchley complained.[101] Each scene, Anderson agreed, "is played on a somber, sustained level without relief, depriving the action of cumulative interest along with its incidental color."[102] As a consequence, the play vocally seemed "languorously delivered,"[103] resulting in a slow, sluggish

93. Metcalfe, "Theatre," Dec. 12, 1925, p. 3.
94. Margaret Carrington was a vocal coach and Huston's sister, who often worked with and later married Jones. O'Neill telegram to Macgowan, Aug. 1, 1925, in Bryer, *Letters*, p. 95.
95. Young, "Eugene," *Harper's*, p. 68.
96. Young, "Fountain," p. 174.
97. Kalonyme, "Delectable," p. 86.
98. O'Neill, in Merrill, "Fierce," p. M-4.
99. Jo Mielziner, in Pendelton, *Jones*, p. 25.
100. Brown, "Director," Feb. 1926, p. 77.
101. Benchley, "Drama," Dec. 31, 1925, p. 18.
102. Anderson, "O'Neill," Dec. 11, 1925, p. 12.
103. Barretto, "New," p. 704.

performance which was not aided by the words the actors were given to deliver.

Jones was struggling to do justice to a play which probably could not have been successful even with more appropriate actors and faster scene changes. Earlier in the year Jones had written, "As he works [the artist] may be all too aware of the outward limitations of the play . . . and the actors. . . . But in his mind's eye he must see the high original intention of the dramatist, and follow it."[104] O'Neill's intention, however, was not clear. He was "at war with shadows,"[105] trying to produce a play which no longer meant much to him but did represent yet further experiment in a theater of ferment. Some of his extravagant experiments were bound to fail. O'Neill certainly recognized the failure as his own and refused to return to the play after the first production.

Despite the vocal difficulties of the actors and the scene shifting problems, Jones' chief failure with *The Fountain* appeared to be an inability to meet some of the demands of O'Neill's play—but no one seemed able to explicate what those needs were or how they might be met. Regarding the effort of Jones, Seldes wrote, "there was no indecision; there was only a groping for clairvoyance."[106]

The Great God Brown

Only six weeks after the disappointing opening of *The Fountain* O'Neill and Jones stunned reviewers and audiences with the mysterious and fascinating production of *The Great God Brown*, O'Neill's most significant experiment with masks and one of his greatest departures from realistic acting. Opening *The Great God Brown* in the same week as the American premiere of Strindberg's *A Dream Play*, directed by James Light at the Provincetown,[107] the Triumvirate organization mounted an impressive panegyric for stylized theater.

It should not be surprising that as production time approached the Triumvirate began to fear that *The Great God Brown* might be met with confusion. Accordingly, on Saturday, January 23, 1926, when the critics gathered at the Greenwich Village Theatre,[108] they received copies of the

104. Jones, *Drawings* (1925), p. 16.
105. Atkinson, "New," Dec. 20, 1925, p. 3.
106. Seldes, "Theatre," Feb. 1926, p. 168.
107. *A Dream Play* opened on Jan. 20, 1926. See "'The Dream Play' Not in a Key of Reality," *New York Times*, Jan. 21, 1926, p. 18.
108. Advertisement, *New York Times*, Jan. 23, 1926, p. 19. Reviews first appeared on Monday, Jan. 25, 1926.

play.[109] Although much argument ensued regarding the meaning and merit of O'Neill's latest offering, and while many audiences remained perplexed by the proceedings, "there was in it the intangible something that holds the interest of even a mystified following."[110] *The Great God Brown* played downtown for over a month before moving to Broadway in the Theatre Guild's Garrick and the Klaw Theatre, where it ran until fall.

Although this was O'Neill's second-greatest success with Jones and Experimental Theatre, Inc.,[111] it was their final effort with downtown production and the last direction by Jones of an O'Neill script.[112] Jones was weary of the pressure as well as unsure of himself as a director, and O'Neill was periodically disgusted with what he considered the Triumvirate's compromise of artistic principles. "What the hell are we, anyway?" he wrote just before *The Fountain* went into production. "It seems to me we're nothing but another New York theatre."[113] The Triumvirate frequently gave into the lure of possible long commercial runs, and its original dream of a repertory company never materialized.

Despite the disintegrating producing organization and the personal anxieties of Jones, *The Great God Brown* was one of the director's most effective and lasting directorial efforts. "Jones has never directed a piece with greater intuitive understanding, nor, perhaps, had finer actor material at his disposal," Skinner wrote enthusiastically.[114] When Jones was at his best "he possessed both the vision of an artist and the imagination of a militant visionary,"[115] a description appropriate for his success with this play due to his excellent design and his sensitivity to the dramatic material and its interpretation. Nonetheless, Pollock astutely predicted that this play was "one of those dramas destined to be done all over Europe and to please theatregoers there more completely than it can please here."[116] Ironically, O'Neill's experimental work was always more welcome on the other side of the Atlantic.

The experimental devices of *The Great God Brown* required a strong interpretive voice as well as an authoritative guiding hand. As a result,

109. Brooks Atkinson, "Ibsen and O'Neill," *New York Times*, Jan. 31, 1926, sec. 7, p. 1; Sheaffer, *Artist*, pp. 192–93.

110. Mantle, *Best Plays 1925–26*, p. 79.

111. Their most successful production, both financially and critically, was *Desire Under the Elms*.

112. Jones would be called upon to design O'Neill plays for the Theatre Guild in 1931, 1933, and 1946.

113. O'Neill letter to Macgowan, Sept. 28, 1925, in Bryer, *Letters*, p. 100.

114. R. Dana Skinner, "The Play," *Commonweal* 3 (Feb. 10, 1926): 384.

115. Lee Simonson, in Pendleton, *Jones*, p. 14.

116. Arthur Pollock, "Plays and Things," *Brooklyn Daily Eagle*, Jan. 25, 1926, p. 10A.

this production, more than any O'Neill play before it, was by necessity a concentrated collaboration of director and playwright. O'Neill was aware early on that his presence at rehearsals would be very important. He told Macgowan that *The Great God Brown* would need much more careful preparation than *The Fountain*. "To me it is worth a dozen 'Fountains.'"[117] (Of course he had said the same thing to Tyler in 1920 when comparing *The Straw* to *Chris*.) This time, however, O'Neill followed through and was present for nearly all rehearsals, frequently discussing production problems—but only with the director; he religiously avoided the actors.[118] Though O'Neill was pointedly concerned about interpretations of lines, he (as noted earlier) had little faith in American actors. He and Jones would confer quietly, and, according to Jones, when O'Neill was working at rehearsals, "time and again, he would provide the exact clew to readings."[119] This indirect method of conveying suggestions from playwright to actor was probably the best possible way for the reclusive dramatist to serve the performers.

O'Neill did not have to wait long for production of this play, which he began in 1924 and completed in late spring of 1925. It was ready for the Triumvirate by June, and since he wanted *The Great God Brown* to follow *The Fountain* on stage,[120] a January production was about the earliest possible production date.

The promptbook of *The Great God Brown*[121] which survives from production is not as detailed as that for *The Fountain*. Lacking stage manager's markings, the script was probably held by an assistant to O'Neill rather than Jones, but it is a useful copy of the manuscript with numerous penciled emendations, about half of which were added to the published text. The remaining changes were obviously necessary for this particular production, and all refer to the use of masks. These additional directions are very important, however, and help to clarify and verify comments in reviews which are at variance with the published play. This manuscript indicates no cuts in dialogue at all, and only a few minor additions. This seems likely for production since O'Neill was almost always present and the play, unlike *The Fountain*, was not overlong.

As an experiment *The Great God Brown* was yet another play steeped in considerable autobiographical material. It is not known if Jones was

117. O'Neill letter to Macgowan, Sept. 2, 1925, in Bryer, *Letters*, p. 96.

118. This became the usual procedure for O'Neill with most productions until 1934. O'Neill letter to Lawrence Langner, in Langner, "Eugene," p. 89; Sheaffer, *Artist*, p. 192.

119. Rhodes, "Robert," p. 4.

120. O'Neill letter to Macgowan, Sept. 2, 1925, in Bryer, *Letters*, p. 96.

121. Eugene O'Neill, *The Great God Brown*, bound promptbook, Theatre Collection, Performing Arts Center, New York Public Library, copyrighted 1926 by Yale University.

privy to O'Neill's personal connection, which would have been of use to him in analyzing and preparing the play, but even if the director was not, he certainly demonstrated an unusual sensitivity to the material.

Once again O'Neill used music significantly, though not nearly to the extent evident in *The Fountain*. Jones incorporated the music which was called for in four scenes. Opening and closing the play in the prologue and epilogue were offstage waltzes and a barber-shop quartet rendering of "Sweet Adeline," which were meant to be coming from the unseen casino attached to the seaside pier of the setting. The use of music helped to establish a nostalgic mood and then reestablish it at the conclusion of the play, thus framing the drama with a memory device which invited the characters and audience to indulge in the past.

More intriguing was a second use of nostalgic music in I. 3 and II. 1— the quiet scenes in Cybel's parlor. Cybel turned on her old player-piano, which emitted the same sentimental "Mother-Mammy" tunes over and over. The music had a calming effect on Dion Anthony and reinforced through reiteration the role of mother which the whore Cybel played in Dion's troubled life. Jones recognized the rhythmic uses of such repetition, which was important to O'Neill, who treated repetition like a choral refrain and called it "significant recurrences of theme."[122]

The play's expressionistic devices provided Jones with interesting challenges. Although not such a conscious attempt at expressionistic form as had been achieved in *The Hairy Ape* and *The Emperor Jones*, the new play used "retrospective, reverie, and psychoanalytic confusion" in the manner of Strindberg and Kaiser.[123] More important for the director, however, was O'Neill's "splitting of the protagonist . . . into two separate characters."[124] Valgemae calls this use of Brown and Dion "an expressionistic objectification of a multiple personality,"[125] a notion reinforced by O'Neill's early idea to use one actor to play Dion until his death in II. 3, and Brown through the remainder of the play.[126] This would have been an interesting experiment, but after John Barrymore and Alfred Lunt showed no interest in assuming both roles, the idea was dropped.[127]

The play's most obvious experiment was of course the unusual use of masks. O'Neill and Jones used masks as they never had before. In the program notes Macgowan wrote, "O'Neill's play is the first in which masks have ever been used to dramatize changes and conflicts in charac-

122. O'Neill letter to Theatre Guild, Sept. 10, 1928, in Sheaffer, *Artist*, p. 306.

123. Broussard, *American*, p. 15.

124. Mardi Valgemai, "Eugene O'Neill's Preface to *The Great God Brown*," *Yale University Library Gazette* 43 (July 1968): 28.

125. Valgemae, *Accelerated*, p. 37.

126. O'Neill telegram to John Barrymore, July 6, 1925, in Floyd, *Eugene Work*, p. 46.

127. O'Neill telegram to Macgowan, Sept. 5, 1925, in Bryer, *Letters*, p. 97.

ter."[128] The novelty here was not in changing masks but in using the actor's face in conjunction with the mask, removing or donning the mask in order to protect or reveal the vulnerable human being beneath it.

Jones and his actors were faced with an unusual acting and staging problem with the masks which "dramatized," according to Sievers, "the discrepancy between the private *animus* of the individual and the social personality which he must put forth for others to see."[129] O'Neill himself believed that the mask was probably the best device by which a play "can express those profound hidden conflicts of the mind which the probings of psychology continue to disclose to us." Furthermore, the dramatist asserted, the unmasking of psychological exploration had "impressed the idea of mask as a symbol of inner reality."[130] Effective and novel presentation of hidden character and struggle had been a recurring project of O'Neill's at least since *The Emperor Jones*, but this was the first major experiment of this sort for Robert Edmond Jones as director.

While O'Neill and Jones were fervently pursuing psychological revelation, they were also interested in the mystical aspects of the mask, ideas shared with their coworkers James Light, who designed the masks for *The Great God Brown*, and Kenneth Macgowan. "For the end of the mask is Drama," Macgowan wrote. "When a man puts on a mask he experiences a kind of release from his inhibited and bashful and circumscribed soul. He can say and do strange and terrible things, and he likes it."[131] Not only could the mask on stage promote a new kind of freedom, it could convey things inexpressible by the face. "No human brow can come bearing the thunder of divine anger," Light offered. "The human is too inconstant, too petty, too individual, too much itself. The mask alone is constantly true, the sublimation of the attributes of the god in a face that human eyes can bear."[132] The production team for *The Great God Brown* was clearly dedicated to the conceptual necessity of experimenting with masks.

Jones, however, had to explore many uses and purposes of the masks because for O'Neill the masks were not merely a dynamic experiment in character exploration—they were at the heart of the play's dramatic conflict. As a review noted, "The action turns on the use of masks."[133] Although only four of the play's eighteen speaking characters[134] wore

128. Macgowan, in *The Great God Brown* program, Theatre Collection, MCNY.
129. Sievers, *Freud*, p. 108.
130. O'Neill, "Memoranda," pp. 116–17.
131. Macgowan, *Masks*, p. xii.
132. Light, "Mask," p. 1.
133. Geddes Smith, "Three Mirrors," *Survey* 56 (Apr. 1, 1926): 43.
134. The dramatis personae of the published play omits three committeemen, the police captain, and a squad of policemen, but it includes a stenographer who does not appear in either the text of the play or the production. Eugene O'Neill, *The Great God Brown*, in *The Great God*

masks, the stage was never without a mask except momentarily, and every scene included at least one special use of a mask which affected the action of the scene and the development of characters.

The director followed most of O'Neill's instructions for the use of masks in production, but some departures as well as some faithful adherence led to difficulties for the audience and playwright. Several interesting uses of the masks, however, caused no problems and were accepted by the audience. In II.3, for example, Margaret threw her mask away, believing she no longer needed it; Brown's real face in III.1 was shown to be ravaged by wearing Dion's mask; but surprising in its acceptance was Dion's and Brown's removal of their masks which they commenced to address and even kiss in II.2 and III.2, as though they were objectifying and externalizing the activity of subconscious conversation and flattery.

O'Neill intended some of the masks to change in appearance as the play progressed. For example, Dion would get a new, more diabolical mask as he grew older. For production, however, each actor was given only one mask. This was probably due to the limited time which James Light, who was directing *A Dream Play* at the time, could devote to mask-making.[135] Since neither Jones nor O'Neill was satisfied with the first set of masks and adjustments were made several times,[136] Light had to drop the project in the final week. O'Neill foresaw this possible difficulty as early as September when he wrote, "Jimmy would have to come back and make the masks, just at the time when the most important thing in his mind, rightly, will be his opening bill."[137]

It is clear from photographs, the promptbook, and reviews that multiple masks were not used. In all extant photographs no difference in the masks of any players can be discerned.[138] Furthermore, cut from the promptbook were stage directions which call for changes in the masks, such as Dion's mask growing younger in III.2 and IV.1. Finally, Atkinson wrote: "We cannot observe the subtle transformations in Dion's mask indicated in the script."[139]

In keeping with the text, however, Brown assumed the mask of Dion,

Brown, The Fountain, The Moon of the Caribbees, and Other Plays (New York: Boni and Liveright, 1926), p. 9; *The Great God Brown* program, MCNY.

135. Although Light was assisted by William Stahl (who also played the minor role of a committeeman), it was Light who was experienced with mask making and who bore the responsibility for the product. *The Great God Brown* program, MCNY; R. W., Jr. [Richard Watts, Jr.], "'The Great God Brown' Is Fascinating Enigma," *New York Herald-Tribune*, Jan. 25, 1926, p. 13.

136. Guy Gillespie, in Hicks, "Robert," p. 153.

137. O'Neill letter to Macgowan, Sept. 2, 1925, in Bryer, *Letters*, p. 96.

138. Fourteen photographs, Theatre Collection, MCNY.

139. Atkinson, "Ibsen," p. 1.

resulting in confusion for many theatergoers. The difficulty began in II.3, when Brown put on Dion's mask and clothes and convinced Margaret, Dion's wife, of his new identity. This psychic confusion was multiplied by Brown assuming a mask for himself in order to play himself as well as Dion beginning in III.1. Furthermore, when Brown wore Dion's mask he could design like the more talented Dion. Most confusing of all, when Brown as Dion abandoned the mask of Brown, other characters treated the discarded mask as an entire corpse. O'Neill seemed to be changing the ground rules of the play without explaining them.

Macgowan anticipated this problem in September, but O'Neill dismissed it. "Naturally anything so arbitrary may confuse an audience for a second," the playwright wrote, "but by the end of the scene they will have accepted it."[140] He was mistaken. The mask changing led not only "to the confusion of the spectator," Smith observed, but "frequently to the blurring of the theatric fiction."[141] Skinner called the exchange "a technical bewilderment for the audience, no matter how clear its intention and meaning may remain."[142] Young and Atkinson, however, specifically looked to this moment as a turning point, asserting that the masks were never confusing until Brown put on Dion's mask.[143] Despite such complaints, bewilderment in the audience never seemed to disturb O'Neill.

But the playwright *was* troubled by one aspect of the masks which he originally requested. He at first wanted masks very close in appearance to the actors' faces. Dion's, for example, was called in the script "a fixed forcing of his own face," while Margaret's was an "almost transparent reproduction of her own features."[144] Although the masks maintained the slightly abstract quality which O'Neill wanted, they were "excellent likenesses of the individual players."[145] Ultimately, O'Neill decided the masks "were too realistic . . . and sitting way back in the theater you couldn't be sure if the actors had on masks or not."[146] This is curious, since the masks when held by the actors were obviously of a markedly darker shade than the actors' made-up faces. Furthermore, Atkinson pointed up the difference in actor and mask by noting that Leona Hogarth as Margaret had a "personal radiance . . . [which] contrasts wonderfully with the phlegmatic countenance of her mask."[147] It is also interesting

140. O'Neill letter to Macgowan, Sept. 28, 1925, in Bryer, *Letters*, p. 102.
141. Smith, "Three," p. 43.
142. Skinner, "Play," Feb. 10, 1926, p. 384.
143. Young, *Immortal*, p. 60; Atkinson, "Ibsen," p. 1.
144. O'Neill, *The Great God Brown*, pp. 14, 17.
145. Sisk, "Great God Brown," *Variety*, Jan. 27, 1926, p. 26.
146. O'Neill, in Clark, *Eugene*, p. 116.
147. Brooks Atkinson, "Symbolism in an O'Neill Tragedy," *New York Times*, Jan. 25, 1926, p. 26.

that O'Neill blamed production despite his own instructions. Such behavior was typical of the playwright when he was at all troubled by theatrical interpretation, leaving one to wonder at times why O'Neill continued to write for the theater but complain without ceasing.

The masks were not head pieces fitting over the entire head but pliable, full-face designs from chin to hairline which "slipped over the face."[148] Since they were not inflexible, the actor had to use two hands effectively to remove and don the mask. Accordingly, Cybel's action of removing and returning Dion's mask to his face in II.1 was altered to Dion at her gesture executing the action himself.[149] Precisely how the masks were made to stay in place is not evident, but they were clearly molded from casts of the actors' faces.

Although most reviewers found the masks effective and economical in appearance, and expressive of the characters in ways impossible to reveal by any other method, a few critics were troubled by the use of masks. Benchley, for example, found that they "faintly suggest children at Halloween."[150] Corbin, however, though overreacting negatively to their extensive use, verified the pliant nature of the masks: "While the actor was speaking, his chin worked up and down against the rubber, with the result that the lips of the mask moved with precisely the expression of a goldfish gaping against its bowl of glass."[151] This unfortunate effect from a critic's close seat is not unlikely, since close-up photographs show that the mouths are only slightly open, not agape as in representations of Greek tragic masks. Because the mouths were not wide open, the actors' voices were sometimes muffled, resulting in difficulties with articulation, projection, and vocal quality. The unfortunate result was an occasional "queer voice distortion" which sometimes undercut serious moments in the play.[152] Nonetheless, many critics praised the actors for overcoming these difficulties most of the time.

O'Neill kept urging Macgowan and Jones to cast the play early in order to experiment with masks, but this was not done—although Jones and possibly Light did do some kind of unspecified experimenting in August or September without actors.[153] After production O'Neill com-

148. Mantle, *Best Plays, 1925–26*, p. 79.

149. O'Neill, *The Great God Brown* promptbook, II.1, p. 5.

150. Robert Benchley, "Drama," *Life* (New York), Feb. 11, 1926, p. 20.

151. Corbin was not completely against masks, because he found them effective in *The Hairy Ape*. John Corbin, "O'Neill and Aeschylus," in Erich A. Walter, ed., *Essay Annual, 1933* (Chicago: Scott, Foresman, 1933), p. 163.

152. Metcalfe, "The Theatre," *Wall Street Journal*, Jan. 25, 1926, p. 3; Gilbert W. Gabriel, "The Great God Brown," *Sun*, Jan. 25, 1926, in Cargill, *O'Neill*, p. 177; Benchley, "Drama," Feb. 11, 1926, p. 20.

153. O'Neill letters and telegram to Macgowan, Sept. 2, 5 and 10, 1925, in Bryer, *Letters*, pp. 96, 97, 99.

plained that the masks "only get across personal resemblance of a blurry meaninglessness," that the project had been too hurriedly done.[154] He ultimately decided that the masks should have been larger and more abstract. He would get such masks in *Lazarus Laughed*.

Although to some viewers the mask scheme seemed primarily a technical novelty, most critics and audience members quickly accepted the convention, and continued to accept it even when confused by the esoteric action in the last half of the play. Yet the masks always remained, even if to a minor degree, "a thorn in your imagination," Gabriel complained in a review which had high praise for the production.[155] Uncertainty in the minds of the audience regarding the meanings of the masks never allowed the intriguing device to be completely successful despite "the extraordinary refinement of emotion achieved by"[156] the shifting, concealing, sometimes character-stifling masks. Anita Block, though she did not applaud the use of masks here, nonetheless found it "a necessary experiment that resulted in the clear technique of the *utterance* of hidden thoughts and emotions"[157] which O'Neill made manifest in *Strange Interlude*.

Despite O'Neill's attempt to clarify publicly the mysteries of the play, he presented little in his analysis that was not evident in reading or seeing the play.[158] He probably enjoyed waving "a decisive farewell to the most remote outposts of reality"[159] and puzzling his audience, which was "quite virgin to the author's secret intentions."[160] In a preface to the play, unpublished until 1968, O'Neill sounds like Jones explaining that the theatrical experience can stand alone as a meaningful but mysterious journey at the level of dreams: "We have had quite enough of life invading the theatre. . . . It is time the theatre invaded life. . . . The theatre should be a refuge from the facts of life which we all feel, if we do not think, have nothing to do with the truth. . . . [The theatre] should return to the spirit of its Greek grandeur. And if we have no gods, or heroes to portray we have the subconscious the mother of all Gods and heroes."[161] This was the kind of theatrical world in which the visions and fancies of Jones perpetually thrived, and it was almost certainly close to his approach to the play.

154. O'Neill letter to Macgowan (after Aug. 12, 1926) in Bryer, *Letters*, p. 131; O'Neill letter to Benjamen de Casseres in Sheaffer, *Artist*, p. 194.

155. Gabriel, "Great," p. 177.

156. Atkinson, "Ibsen," p. 1.

157. Anita Block, *The Changing World in Plays and Theatre* (Boston: Little, Brown, 1939), p. 160.

158. Eugene O'Neill, "The Playwright Explains," *New York Times*, Feb. 14, 1926, sec. 8, p. 2.

159. Atkinson, "Ibsen," p. 1.

160. Benchley, "Drama," Feb. 11, 1926, p. 20.

161. O'Neill in Valgemae, "Eugene," p. 29.

The last production of Jones and O'Neill at the Greenwich Village indicates that once again the shallow depth of the stage notably influenced the design. Knowing as he wrote it that *The Great God Brown* would probably open in this theater, O'Neill seemed to suggest the flat, shallow pattern of scenes, although Jones did make a few significant departures from the scenery described in the text.

For the eight settings of the play Jones created some of his most obvious New Stagecraft designs. Unobtrusive simplicity was the key. His pictures were decorative and colorful without being busy, suggestive rather than literal. Each setting was deliberately incomplete, like one of Jones' ideal designs which "contains the promise of a completion, a promise which the actor later fulfills."[162] For this kind of scenery, Jones wrote, "everything that is actual must undergo a strange metamorphosis, a kind of sea-change, before it can become truth in the theatre."[163] Thus, his settings were suggestive of specific locales but stripped nearly bare save for occasional detail which emblemized a wealth of detail.

Jones received no negative criticism for his designs, and considerable praise for his skill and effectiveness in executing them. Most of this approval, however, was sweeping in nature, without specificity. Skinner, for example, said, "The stage settings and the direction . . . have achieved a perfect harmony with O'Neill's ideas and feeling."[164] Likewise, Watts praised the sets and staging for "aiding in partially clarifying the O'Neill mysteries,"[165] and to Kalonyme "the sets . . . illustrate[d] the lives of the characters, and their growth with interpretive precision."[166] Most critics were more concerned with discussing the masks, but a few scenic and staging details survive in reviews, and luckily full-stage photographs of all eight settings are extant.

Jones reportedly spent only four thousand dollars in preparing this production,[167] a paltry sum compared to the eighteen thousand for *The Fountain*, but the effort yielded results eminently more satisfying. With oriental simplicity Jones produced obvious, painted surfaces, all parallel to the curtain line, like "flat symbols,"[168] in front of which he placed only as much three-dimensional furniture or set properties as necessary for the actors to function. All settings included three or four set pieces, except the most complex (III.1 and IV.1), which included six.

162. Jones, *Drawings* (1970), p. 18.
163. Jones, *Dramatic*, p. 25.
164. R. Dana Skinner, "Blossoms in the Arid Desert," *Independent* 116 (Mar. 6, 1926): 275.
165. Watts, "Great," p. 13.
166. Louis Kalonyme, "Dramatica Dionysiana," *Arts & Decoration* 24 (Mar. 1926): 98.
167. Sheaffer provides no source for this figure. Sheaffer, *Artist*, p. 192.
168. Smith, "Three," p. 43.

Within this long, shallow field created for each setting, Jones' use of space through movement and picturization with actors was also lauded, but again with little detailed clarification. Young wrote that even though the actors themselves were not necessarily compelling, "the layout of the stage movement, of the positions, of the emphasis of individuals and groups is distinct and telling."[169] The photographs fortunately record a number of specific, interesting stage pictures. Although Jones created a less varied acting area than in *Desire Under the Elms*, his use of this space was once again memorable.

The eight settings of the production represented six locations, since Cybel's parlor of I.3 was redecorated (a new backdrop) for II.1 to indicate that Brown was keeping her. Also, Brown's office of I.2 and the drafting room which was meant to be adjacent to it in II.2 were combined to show both spaces in III.1 and IV.2. The combined setting was actually a new scenic unit, although it used most of the same furniture from the two earlier scenes. Each location appeared in the play either two or three times, but four of the settings were used only once.

All scenic backgrounds were painted drops, except the romantic casino pier of the prologue and epilogue (see illustration 9). Jones constructed a railing approximately three and one-half to four feet high which extended right to left upstage, and at the extremities the railing broke gently in down-left and down-right lines. This four-tiered railing was surmounted by two practical lamp posts which seemed to cast eerie pools of light on the pier below. Beyond the railing was only darkness, and in the playing space Jones placed three benches. O'Neill wanted the railing and benches to create a rectangular space which suggested a courtroom, but Jones softened the effect and raked both the side benches and side railing to open up the action. Later courtroom references in other scenes were also modified by Jones, who always raked the side pieces of furniture. Except for the pier, all scenery was stark and severe without creating rigid lines with the furniture.

For Margaret's sitting room of I.1 and III.3, in a standardized housing complex, Jones painted a garish backdrop with an obvious, ugly, cheap-looking wallpaper design broken by a three-tiered window with tasteless curtains (all painted). Before the drop, in the center of the playing space, stood a wooden table, two chairs, and a small sofa, all inexpensive and uncomfortable. Like most of the settings in the play, this was an island set in emptiness, accentuated by a pool of light which was surrounded by darkness, both on the floor and on the drop. As in all eight settings, actors could enter and exit only through the wings. There were no doors except in the combined office set.

169. Young, *Immortal*, pp. 58–59.

Brown's office (I.2) was very austere and symmetrical in design. A large expanse of bare wall was broken by nothing other than an "overwhelming panel of the filing cabinet" painted on the drop to a height of at least twelve feet. This obvious symbol of "Brown's profitable and laborious office,"[170] which was two oversize drawers wide, stood like a monolith before which Brown worked mechanically at his desk. Outside Brown's office lay the drafting room, seen only in II.2 (see illustration 10). This was the simplest set of the production, a bare backdrop with a large blueprint of a complex building's floor plan painted at center. Directly beneath the blueprint was a drafting table with two stools, behind which Dion could work while facing the audience. Like Brown's office, the drafting room was another isolated island of activity.

The sets of III.1 and IV.1 were an odd combination of office and drafting room. The objective was to show simultaneous activity in the two adjoining spaces, but the result was Jones' least satisfactory design in the production. With the drafting room at stage right and the office left, Jones split the drop in half with a new blueprint right and the filing cabinet repeated left, but he erected an actual door unit at center next to the drop to divide the rooms. Since all other doors were assumed to be offstage, the addition of a door here, especially so late in the play, was an intrusion. The setting filled the stage, was too cramped and literal compared to the others, and seemed stylistically out of place.

Brown's library of II.3, III.2 and IV.2, however, was at once lush, aristocratic, and spare. Creating another island of activity with furniture and light, Jones painted a dark backdrop dominated by a low bookcase, mirror, and urns. Before the drop stood the most ornate furniture of the production; placed symmetrically, it was surrounded by a void. In this setting occurred some of the most intense action of the play—Dion's death, Brown's first assumption of Dion's mask, Margaret's discarding of her mask, Brown's monologue to Dion's mask, and Brown's death. Jones made one major departure here from the script. In IV.2 Brown was supposed to appear dressed only in a white cloth around his loins after denuding himself of Dion's mask and clothing. In production, however, Brown remained dressed in shirt and trousers. It was also in this scene that Jones created a dynamic stage picture of Cybel cradling Brown in a pietà, the first of many such poses seen throughout the O'Neill plays which lay ahead.[171]

Perhaps the most interesting scenic investiture was the parlor of the

170. Young, *Immortal*, p. 58.

171. Although there are suggestions of this in the texts of *Anna Christie* and *Desire Under the Elms*, there is no visual evidence of this pose until *The Great God Brown*. It would appear again notably in *Strange Interlude*, *Dynamo*, *Mourning Becomes Electra*, and several of the late plays.

prostitute Cybel (I. 3 and II. 1). The room appeared to undergo a dynamic metamorphosis between the two adjacent scenes as a new backdrop was flown in for II. 1. In the first encounter O'Neill called for a wall of "dull yellow-brown,"[172] described in production as a "drab, odorously colored wall,"[173] upon which Jones painted the sole decoration, a primitive picture of cats. In the following scene O'Neill's request for "crimson and purple flowers"[174] appeared on walls which seemed to be "bursting into red blossoms"[175] thanks to "a rich flowery design, as though the room has a luscious bodily bloom."[176] The transformation of course signaled the financial protection of Cybel assumed by Brown in his attempt to control everything touched by Dion.

For both scenes all furniture was isolated in the center and dominated by a real, functioning player-piano upstage against the painted drop. Only in these scenes was an object which was located along the drop line practical rather than painted. This piano, of course, was an important symbol of nostalgia in the play as well as a live source of music.

While the designs were not uncharacteristic of Jones' work, the casting choices were rather surprising, since none of the leading actors came from the director's stable of regulars. The previous work of all four major performers was barely known, and *The Great God Brown* marked their first important theatrical roles. Although the actors were generally praised for good, serviceable work, O'Neill was somewhat distressed by the casting of this production, which meant so much to him. Most of all, however, he was afraid that the actors, no matter who was cast, would not have enough rehearsal time with the masks. Surprisingly, the actors acquitted themselves well with the masks, handling them with ease and assurance.[177] Before the masks were constructed Jones had the actors mime the action of removing and donning them. They were without them, for example, during a run-through and simply mimed the required action,[178] but they ultimately mastered the manual manipulation. While the women were said to fare better with the masks vocally,[179] all the actors made an important physical transformation. Jones stressed the need to make up for the absence of changing facial expression, and, as O'Neill wrote, in late rehearsals as the actors grew accustomed to the masks, their bodies became more "alive and expressive," a condition he believed nor-

172. O'Neill, *The Great God Brown*, p. 39.
173. Kalonyme, "Dramatica," p. 98.
174. O'Neill, *The Great God Brown*, p. 46.
175. Young, *Immortal*, p. 58.
176. Kalonyme, "Dramatica," p. 98.
177. Alexander Woollcott, "The Stage," *World*, Jan. 25, 1926, p. 15.
178. Albert Lewis, in Gelbs, *O'Neill*, p. 592.
179. Metcalfe, "Theatre," Jan. 25, 1926, p. 3.

mally occurred only with actors' faces.[180] Reviews clearly support this observation, saying that the actors made important broadening adjustments in gesture and movement to overcome limitations created by the masks.[181]

Contrasts in the performances of Brown and Dion provide the most important commentary on Jones' approach to acting interpretation. At age twenty-eight, Robert Keith (father of Brian Keith) handled the pathetic nature of Dion's struggles very well. Although he sometimes overprojected to attempt to make up for the mask's restrictions, he seemed to catch the spirit of O'Neill's troubled artist without making him effete. Trying to create the artistic struggle as subtly as one can in a mask, Keith imbued "his acting of the real man," wrote Atkinson, "with an interior distress that sets off the surface mockery of his mask."[182] O'Neill was satisfied with Keith's work, since the actor was cast as Robert Mayo in an important revival of *Beyond the Horizon* in the fall.

William Harrigan as Brown, however, was a bit more heavy handed in his approach to the role. The thirty-one-year-old actor was nonetheless found to be appropriate and effective as the unartistic business mind. Although often blunt and not very subtle during Brown's self-satisfied, ecstatic period in act II, Harrigan demonstrated considerable power on the stage and was most successful at "broadening his gestures to compensate for the loss of facial play and achieving thereby a consistent and complete effect."[183] Perhaps this son of Ned Harrigan not only responded to Jones' appeal for dynamic movement but also utilized much of his theatrical family's physical comic training in assuming the role of William Brown.

It was evident in production that the actors and director were not ignorant of the intentions of the playwright. They demonstrated "a remarkably complete grasp of the possibilities which the script affords."[184] It seemed that Jones had a special sensitivity to the play and "managed to cast its spell completely upon the players, and they act[ed] it with high inspiration and an almost religious fervor."[185] To this end, Clark felt that in performance, although presented skillfully, "there was too much self-consciousness and 'pointing' . . . [because] the director and players were too familiar with the author's intentions."[186] This seems an odd charge,

180. Eugene O'Neill, "A Dramatist's Notebook," in Cargill, *O'Neill*, pp. 120–21.

181. John Anderson, "O'Neill's Newest Play Opens at the Greenwich Village," in Miller, *Playwright's*, p. 52; John Mason Brown, "Doldrums of Midwinter," *Theatre Arts* 10 (Mar. 1926): 146.

182. Atkinson, "Symbolism," p. 26.

183. Anderson, "O'Neill's," Jan. 25, 1926 p. 52.

184. Joseph Wood Krutch, "The Tragedy of Masks," *Nation* 122 (Feb. 10, 1926): 165.

185. Anderson, "O'Neill's," Jan. 26, 1926, p. 52.

186. Clark, *Eugene*, p. 107.

but the production may have been guilty of belaboring some business for fear of losing the audience. When considering the unusual production demands, and given the confused popular reaction to presentation, director and actors were probably justified in their choices.

With this "bold and exhilarating attack on the inexpressible,"[187] Jones and O'Neill ended their journey with the Triumvirate and Greenwich Village. Ironically, the dissolution came at a time when many critical voices were noticing important growth in the directors of Experimental Theatre, Inc. Jones had staged *The Great God Brown* beautifully, if starkly, by accentuating the strange psychological world of the O'Neill play. The director's and playwright's work with masks remains one of the most significant experiments of the modern theater and an abstract evocation of some of the psychological exploration used by realistic actors in the generation which followed O'Neill. The playwright's last downtown effort, in Atkinson's words, broke "through old barriers and penetrated a little into the next chamber where human values are more sensitive; and if he has not made them entirely actual this time, he has made them possible."[188] Much that was begun here would be continued in *Strange Interlude* and *Days Without End* as O'Neill persisted in exploring the furies of humankind.

The dramatist's theatrical exploration would continue under different direction, however. Some of the reverence and magic with which Jones endowed his productions would be missing, for Jones always approached each play as though it might change the way people looked at the world. His statement "It is evident that this play we are about to see is no common play"[189] could have prefaced all of his productions with O'Neill. Both men, however, needed a change. Jones fled to Europe, and O'Neill soon left his wife and many of his old theatrical friends (including collaboration with Macgowan) for Carlotta Monterey. O'Neill did not, though, abandon experiment. In 1927 he joined forces with the Theatre Guild, which became his theatrical home until 1934. After leaving the Triumvirate, he fittingly wrote to Macgowan: "What I need for my new voyage is fresh fair winds and new ports of call."[190]

187. Smith, "Three," p. 44.
188. Atkinson, "Ibsen," p. 1.
189. Jones, *Drawings* (1925), p. 16.
190. O'Neill letter to Macgowan, Apr. 4 (1926), in Bryer, *Letters*, p. 107.

CHAPTER X

Dithyrambs:
Marco Millions and *Lazarus Laughed*

> Write a dance . . . a poem to bring back the dreams of the Mys-
> teries with visible beauty and hypnotic music.[1]
>
> It simply can't be done "economically," you know that.[2]

For nearly two years after the premiere of *The Great God Brown* no new play of O'Neill's reached the boards. The playwright released two new plays for publication in 1927, however; these poetic works, which called for extravagant scenery and composition, were produced in 1928. Although important and interesting experiments in staging, *Marco Millions* and *Lazarus Laughed* now seem like musical and beautiful (if somewhat pretentious) interludes which preceded a new wave of painful experiment from O'Neill in league with the Theatre Guild, the most prestigious permanent theater company in the United States during the 1920s and early 1930s.

Between the productions of *The Great God Brown* and *Marco Millions* the American theater continued to enjoy important experiments such as Jacques Copeau's staging of *The Brothers Karamazov* for the Theatre Guild and Max Reinhardt's German repertory, including his celebrated *A Midsummer Night's Dream*. Most significant for our purposes, however, was the sensational New York debut of the director of *Marco Millions*, Rouben Mamoulian, with *Porgy*, a folk drama which stunned theatergoers through Mamoulian's fluent orchestration of crowds and stage composition, integration of music, and contributions to the emergence of black theater in America.[3]

1. George Cram Cook, in Cook, *My Road*, p. 49.
2. O'Neill letter to Macgowan regarding *Lazarus Laughed*, July 9 (1926), in Bryer, *Letters*, p. 116.
3. *Porgy* by Dorothy and DuBose Heyward opened Oct. 10, 1927. For an excellent review see John Mason Brown, "Sermons in Plays," *Theatre Arts* 11 (Dec. 1927): 904.

Before Mamoulian and the Theatre Guild began preparations for *Marco Millions*, O'Neill's play lingered under the option of David Belasco. Although O'Neill, like other experimenters, usually belittled the dramatic products of this old-line manager-director, the playwright believed Belasco was one of the few producers capable of giving *Marco Millions* the sumptuous production it required.[4] Accepted by the Guild in the spring of 1927 and published in April, *Marco Millions* finally reached the stage in a modified form on Monday, January 9, 1928, at the Guild Theatre.[5]

Reorganized after the demise of the Washington Square Players, the Theatre Guild had been producing important new plays since 1919. Before enlisting O'Neill the Guild staged several memorable American experiments like *The Adding Machine* and *Processional*, and, more significantly, many American premieres of European experimental drama such as *Back to Methuselah*, *From Morn to Midnight* and *R. U. R.* Throughout the 1920s and beyond, the self-supporting Guild rebelled against usual Broadway methods and dedicated itself to the careful staging of serious but usually commercially viable experimental plays. Direction and design were deemed just as important as dramaturgy in this company, which had no artistic director but presented plays, in Lawrence Langner's words, as "strictly a group expression."[6]

The most conspicuous manifestation of group expression culminated in the activities of the Guild's board of directors, "six people of fiery temperament"[7] who in their individual capacities served the Guild as actress, director, designer, producer, administrator, and treasurer. As a collective they selected the season and made important administrative decisions, but the board's most unusual function was superintending productions of all plays. While most productions were directed by people outside the board of directors, this committee watched some rehearsals as a group and reserved the right to guide the work of the director or even overrule his decisions.

According to Lee Simonson, the designer of the board, "no director who staged a play for the Guild worked alone. He was under continual crossfire of suggestion and criticism from every member of the Guild board."[8] This volatile group always attended two late run-throughs on

4. Belasco at one time planned to spend $250,000 and send Robert Edmond Jones to China to do research. "O'Neill and His Plays," *New York Times*, Jan. 8, 1928, sec. 8, p. 2; O'Neill letter to Macgowan, Mar. 18 (1925), in Bryer, *Letters*, p. 90; Burns Mantle, *American Playwrights of Today* (New York: Dodd, Mead, 1929), p. 17.

5. Advertisement, *New York Times*, Jan. 9, 1928, p. 21. Reviews first appeared on Tuesday, Jan. 10, 1928.

6. Lawrence Langner, *The Magic Curtain* (New York: E. P. Dutton, 1951), p. 158.

7. Atkinson, *Broadway*, p. 210.

8. Lee Simonson, *Part of a Lifetime: Drawings and Designs, 1919–1940* (New York: Duell, Sloan and Pearce, 1943), p. 84.

Sunday nights before the final dress rehearsal. Nicknamed "the death watch," these rehearsals were followed by a meeting with the director and sometimes the playwright to solve problems. The administrator, Theresa Helburn, recorded that in these sessions "our convictions are so intense that when opinions disagree the battle often becomes violent."[9] Luckily for O'Neill, all of his Guild productions before World War II except one were directed by Philip Moeller, the stage director on the board who was thoroughly acclimated and amenable to the ordeal. While Mamoulian was something of a maverick, he knew how to work with and usually satisfy the board while maintaining his strong personal stamp on the finished production.

At twenty-nine or thirty,[10] Rouben Mamoulian was one of the youngest directors with whom O'Neill had worked since his early Provincetown days.[11] This Russian-born director, who was educated in Paris and Moscow and trained under Vakhtangov, made his way to New York via theatrical work in London and the Eastman Theatre in Rochester, where he staged numerous operas and operettas. Joining the Theatre Guild as a teacher in their school in Scarborough in 1926, Mamoulian was not long in securing a major New York production, *Porgy*, which brought him instant attention and notoriety for his unusual staging techniques.[12]

Usually very specific in his instructions to actors, this tall director could be imposing, if not prohibitive, but he was normally very patient, especially with inexperienced performers. His style of giving directions is preserved in an article of 1928: "To demonstrate a point he frequently stalks about the stage, his long arms waving as he carries on the thread of the story, elaborating and extemporizing, indicating the positions and desired movements."[13] Naturally his flamboyant but strict methods elicited a variety of responses from his fellow artists.

Like Jones, Mamoulian had a keen visual sense, and his most successful results with actors occurred in group scenes, most notably crowds, for which he had an unusual proclivity. Time and again reviewers note his picturization, manipulation of crowds, and attention to detail. Most significant, however, is the frequent appearance of the word "rhythmic" in assessments of Mamoulian's work. Sayler, for example, praised the "aristocratic, not garish, munificence" of *Marco Millions* as well as "the wealth of rhythmic variety, of skill in the handling of grouped players . . . on the

9. Theresa Helburn, in Eaton, *Theatre Guild*, p. 136.

10. The year of Mamoulian's birth is variously reported as 1897 and 1898.

11. Only James Light was younger with *The Hairy Ape*.

12. See Tom Milne, *Rouben Mamoulian* (Bloomington: Indiana University Press, 1969), pp. 174–75.

13. "Men and Their Shadows, Mamoulian Deals in Both," *New York Herald-Tribune*, Dec. 16, 1928, sec. 7, p. 6.

part of the stage director."[14] With significant success Mamoulian melded dynamic stage pictures with music, choral activity, poetry, chanting, and Simonson's unforgettable color. As Hammond succinctly remarked, "Nothing is left undone by Mr. Mamoulian."[15]

The choice of Mamoulian for *Marco Millions* was a wise one. Philip Moeller probably could have directed it if he so chose, but he preferred to stage *Strange Interlude*, which was in rehearsal for much of the same time. The special needs of *Marco Millions* were more suited to Mamoulian's abilities, an opinion to which O'Neill acceded after he saw *Porgy* in early November.[16]

The rehearsal period, which began in early December,[17] lasted for five weeks because Actors' Equity agreed with the Guild that the play presented special production problems and needed an extra week of rehearsal.[18] As a result, Mamoulian had a comfortable period of time for preparation. The director, however, was often working without the assistance of O'Neill, who divided what time he devoted to rehearsal between both *Marco Millions* and *Strange Interlude*. Burns Mantle reported that O'Neill attended few Guild rehearsals before *Mourning Becomes Electra*,[19] and Mary Arbenz, who played walk-ons in *Marco Millions*, recalled that the playwright was usually not in attendance.[20] As was his practice with Jones, O'Neill usually remained quiet at rehearsals and communicated nearly all of his responses to the director.

Like *The Fountain, Marco Millions* had been long in reaching production. Begun by O'Neill in 1923, it was completed as two full-length plays in 1924 and revised and condensed the following year as one long play.[21] *Marco Millions* remained lengthy nevertheless, and Mamoulian as well as the board wanted O'Neill to make some severe cuts. Although O'Neill agreed, sometimes reluctantly, to make major alterations,[22] some critics still found the production overlong for the material it was trying to support.

Production reviews indicate that an entire scene and the epilogue in the published play were eliminated from the production. These cuts are

14. Oliver M. Sayler, "The Play of the Week," *Saturday Review* 4 (Feb. 11, 1928): 590.

15. Percy Hammond, "The Theatres," *New York Herald-Tribune*, Jan. 10, 1928, p. 28.

16. "O'Neill," *New York Times*, Jan. 8, 1928, p. 2.

17. The Gelbs report that rehearsals began on Nov. 22, 1927, while Sheaffer lists Dec. 5. Five weeks before the opening date of Jan. 9 was Dec. 4. Gelbs, *O'Neill*, p. 645; Sheaffer, *Artist*, p. 272.

18. "O'Neill," *New York Times*, Jan. 8, 1928, p. 2.

19. Mantle, *American*, p. 18.

20. Arbenz, "Plays," p. 91.

21. Floyd, *Eugene Work*, pp. 57, 63; Tornqvist, *Drama*, p. 261.

22. Theresa Helburn, "O'Neill: An Impression," *Saturday Review*, Nov. 21, 1936, p. 10; Mamoulian, in Oberstein, "Broadway," p. 63.

verified by the two extant promptbooks.[23] Exclusion of the epilogue had little effect on the play, since it was not intended as a staged scene. In the written play Marco appears in the audience after the final curtain and exits with it to his limousine. Mamoulian and the Guild chose not to violate the space of the audience. By cutting the fifth scene of the first act, however, Mamoulian eliminated a complete setting and the entrance of the Polos through the Great Wall of China from the poor Mongolian peasant side to the majestic court of Kublai Kaan.[24] This unfortunate alteration did not occur until a dress rehearsal, because the setting proved too cumbersome to shift.[25] Since Lee Simonson had the setting photographed,[26] one can discern some of the difficulties caused by this design, which did not follow the scheme used for the rest of the production.[27]

Although numerous major and minor cuts of dialogue and action were also made, few speeches were rewritten. The major purposes of revision were economy in casting and costuming and simplification of the play for smooth and efficient presentation. The most significant cuts occurred in scenes 3 and 4 of act I to eliminate a host of nonspeaking characters who symbolize the human life cycle of the Middle East and India,[28] and many dialogue cuts were made in act III, especially in the funeral scene (III.2) which closed the production.

As with so many of his plays, with *Marco Millions* "Mr. O'Neill has not made the director's lot a happy one," Atkinson wrote. Yet this reviewer found that Mamoulian met the challenge and commanded the complicated production, summoning "the image of a satiric idea through all the cloth of gold, rococo investiture of the play."[29] Sayler found that the play leaned "heavily on producer, player, and designer. Fortunately," he observed, "the anchorages are secure."[30] Most of O'Neill's experiments in *Marco*

23. The texts and stage directions of the promptbooks are not contradictory, but the promptbook at Lincoln Center includes more cue sheets, production plots, and inventories, while the promptbook at Yale has additional cues and directions within the script. Eugene O'Neill, *Marco Millions*, bound promptbook, Theatre Guild Collection, Beinecke, Yale; Eugene O'Neill, *Marco Millions*, bound promptbook, Theatre Collection, Performing Arts Center, New York Public Library (NYPL), copyrighted 1928 by Yale University.

24. Act I, scene 6 of the published play became I.5 in the promptbooks. Eugene O'Neill, *Marco Millions* (New York: Boni & Liveright, 1927), pp. 34–42, 183.

25. Arbenz, "Plays," pp. 66–67.

26. Nine photographs, MCNY, and twelve photographs, Yale.

27. The wall of the setting was placed much farther downstage than in other scenes and did not fit into the permanent framework which held all other scenic units except the prologue.

28. Twenty-seven characters, who would have been played by nine actors, were cut. O'Neill, *Marco Millions* promptbook, Yale, act I, pp. 14–27; Lee Simonson, *The Stage Is Set* (New York: Dover, 1946), p. 116.

29. Brooks Atkinson, "Eugene O'Neill's Gorgeous Satire," *New York Times*, Jan. 10, 1928, p. 28.

30. Sayler, "Play," Feb. 11, 1928, p. 590.

Millions were handled efficiently and imaginatively by Mamoulian and his designer, Simonson, despite their personal squabbling.

O'Neill attempted to unite poetry and satire in a play that was alternately romantic and cynical. As he began the play he wrote, "Satiric or not remains to be seen—but Beauty must be the word."[31] Both remained, and the result was stylistic problems for Mamoulian, whose direction more frequently sided with the romantic. Nonetheless, some critics were troubled by the inconsistency, at times blaming the play, at others the director. For the most part, however, Mamoulian's attempt at combining enchantment with "Menckenese"[32] met with approval.

Both in O'Neill's scheme and in the production, sound and music played a prominent role in the shape and style of the play. Mamoulian had to coordinate a vast score of not only incidental music for every scene but bells, gongs, drums, chanting, keening and singing voices, unison speech, a martial band, and several special sound effects. Emerson Whithorne and Rudolf Friml supplied the score for the offstage music.[33] Frequent composers of music for the theater and operetta, they contributed orchestral and percussive pieces in imitative Venetian, Middle Eastern, Indian, and Chinese styles, ranging from sentimental love songs to oriental dances to military marches to funeral dirges.[34] The music was performed by a live eighteen-piece orchestra offstage.[35]

Either this music or a special effect like the tolling of church and temple bells or trumpet calls was used to open and close all scenes.[36] Transitions from one scene to another were often made by shifting from one kind of sound to another. For example, at the close of the papal announcement at Acre in I.2 the bells rang madly but soon gave way to the orchestra playing Middle Eastern music through the setting shift to the Islam scene (I.3). Of course, music was often played under most of an entire scene, such as II.1, in the Little Throne Room, where offstage flute music played softly in the quiet beginning, but the lyrical sound was overpowered by martial music when Marco arrived.

31. O'Neill letter to Macgowan (Spring 1923), in Bryer, *Letters*, p. 37.

32. Robert Littell, "Mr. O'Neill Pillories a Venetian Babbitt," *New York Evening Post*, Jan. 10, 1928, p. 20.

33. Friml's "Chinese Suite" was composed in 1923, but all of Whithorne's *Marco* music was composed specifically for this production. *Marco Millions* program, Theatre Collection, MCNY; Stanley Sadie, *The New Grove Dictionary of Music and Musicians* (London: Macmillan, 1980), Vol. 6, p. 854; vol. 20, pp. 388–89.

34. "*Marco Millions* Entre Act Music," typescript, Theatre Guild Collection, Beinecke, Yale.

35. Since the orchestra pit was prominent in the staging, the orchestra had to be backstage. "Music Plot," in O'Neill, *Marco Millions* promptbook, NYPL; [Jack Pulaski] Ibee, "Marco Millions," *Variety*, Jan. 11, 1928, p. 50.

36. The promptbook gives specific sound instructions for each scene until the conclusion.

Two special sound effects were especially memorable and required imaginative preparation and careful rehearsal. In the prologue the body of Princess Kukachin suddenly came to life and spoke. O'Neill provided a detailed description of her sound which was meant to be unearthly, "more musical than a human voice" and laughter of a "supernatural gaiety, comes from her lips and is taken up in chorus."[37] Although the promptbook gives no clues about how this was managed, oriental "wind-bells"[38] were added to human sounds. Woollcott acknowledged the moment and was clearly enchanted by the unusual sound as well as the "wraithlike and moonlit"[39] voice of Kukachin (Margalo Gillmore) in this scene. Perhaps some kind of amplification, sounding board, or distortion was used.

The most well-orchestrated sound effects occurred in the loading of the junk flagship in II.2. As a line of men carried cargo aboard ship, the foreman beat out a rhythm with a gong and drum and chanted all the while. This continued strongly at first, then more softly under the scene until Marco's arrival (once again with his martial music) overpowered the working rhythm.[40]

Again incorporating a chorus for singing, chant, dance, and rhythmic movement, O'Neill gave Mamoulian the opportunity to experiment with stylized movement and composition (something of a trademark with Mamoulian). The choral activity was especially prominent and effective in II.3 with a chorus of court women and sailors in "mysterious declamation"[41] on the ship and a chorus of mourners with its "fury of wild voices"[42] added to tolling bells in the funeral of the final scene. If the directions of the promptbooks are complete the play ended in silence—a dynamic choice after bombarding the audience with sound and movement.

In addition to rhythmic choruses and large court groupings, O'Neill wanted four major crowd scenes, another source of staging delight for Mamoulian. In each instance he created interesting stage pictures well integrated with movement, music, and sound. Although the director reduced the number of people indicated in the published play, he realized much of O'Neill's vision by creating pomp and pageantry—often martial, sometimes bizarre[43]—which resulted in "a brilliant procession of rich

37. O'Neill, *Marco* promptbook, Yale, prologue, pp. 8–9.
38. "Prop Plot," *Marco Millions*, Theatre Collection, MCNY.
39. Alexander Woollcott, "The Stage," *World*, Jan. 10, 1928, p. 15.
40. See Vandamm, "Master of Stage Illusion—Mr. Simonson," *Theatre Magazine*, Feb. 1931, p. 43.
41. Brooks Atkinson, "After the Battle," *New York Times*, Jan. 22, 1928, sec. 8, p. 1.
42. Atkinson, "Eugene," Jan. 10, 1928, p. 28.
43. This was the only O'Neill play and production which called for and used a live animal on stage: "Chow puppy with pink bow." "Prop Plot," O'Neill, *Marco Millions* promptbook, NYPL, p. 2.

pictures."[44] Mamoulian not only filled the stage but also extended the pageantry below the proscenium arch onto the apron and down into the orchestra pit.[45]

Some of the biggest difficulties O'Neill caused for Mamoulian and Simonson sprang from the play's espisodic structure, which took the action from place to place across many years as in *The Fountain*, but demanding much more extravagance than the De Leon play. In a review of the published edition of *Marco Millions* Firkins foresaw this difficulty: "Travel, which rejects concentration, is unfriendly to drama, and 'Marco Millions' is migratory and saltatory to an extent that would have dismayed Shakespeare."[46] The published play called for ten locations and eleven settings. The production reduced the number of each by only one, and the frequent shifting led Woollcott to call the play and its production "a mosaic of stencils"[47] which presented pieces of a portrait of Marco Polo.

The design requirements of *Marco Millions* were not excessive for the very experienced Simonson, who at age thirty-nine had been the principal designer for the Guild since its inception. As an experimentalist he had helped to found not only the Guild but also the Washington Square Players, and his most successful unusual designs included *From Morn to Midnight* and *The Adding Machine*, excellent designs which reflected his penchant for European theater. Also fond of the exotic, Simonson felt very comfortable with challenges like *Marco Millions*, but his approach was very different from that of the visionary Jones. Although inventive, Simonson was more of a craftsman than a dreamer. His watchwords were pragmatism and (when appropriate) splendor.

Nowhere were his practicality and love of grandeur more evident than in his intentions and execution of the designs for *Marco Millions*. Prepared for the three-year-old Guild Theatre, the settings could not take up considerable wing space, for the Guild had little to spare for large productions. On the other hand, this ornate building with an interior of Italianate arches and tapestries made it an ideal setting for the play. A standard house which seated just over nine hundred, the Guild had generous fly space, extensive trapping, and a deeper stage than was usual in New York (nearly fifty feet), though it was problematic for shifting voluminous scenery which was not flown.[48] Simonson found that the scenic "demands of 'Marco' . . . continue the stimulating struggle with the

44. Hammond, "Theatres," Jan. 10, 1928, p. 28.
45. Ground plan, O'Neill, *Marco Millions* promptbook, Yale; ground plan, elevation, and rendering, Simonson, *Art*, pp. 140–41.
46. O. W. Firkins, "O'Neill and Other Playwrights," *Yale Review* 17 (Oct. 1927): 173.
47. Woollcott, "Stage," Jan. 10, 1928, p. 15.
48. See Pichel, *Modern*, pp. 43–45; Henderson, *City*, pp. 204–05; Eaton, *Theatre Guild*, p. 86; Malcolm Goldstein, *The Political Stage* (New York: Oxford University Press, 1974), p. 104.

limitations of space and time,"[49] a situation symptomatic of most of his New York career.

Mamoulian and Simonson were both headstrong craftsmen who had very clear and personal approaches to the use of space. Simonson believed the director's job was to specify "rhythm, tone, tempo, and pattern of movement," while the designer's set and lights determined "how a play can be performed."[50] Mamoulian, on the other hand, needed complete freedom of picturization with both the performers and their illumination. Obviously, Simonson considered lighting the province of the set designer alone, a belief which led to a volatile confrontation which Simonson lost (the board supported Mamoulian).[51] Ultimately, the director designed the lighting for Simonson's ten settings, but both men made lighting decisions in technical rehearsals.[52]

Despite their artistic quarrels, director and designer produced a stunning, "entrancing"[53] pictorial display which was hailed by many as opulent, "magnificent exoticism"[54] which bombarded the audience in a "cataract of color."[55] Wyatt described it as "the visual unfolding of a poem,"[56] while Brackett, who did not care for the play, found the "spectacle so enchanting to the eye that what it's about doesn't matter."[57] Even if critics were not universal in such affirmation, an overwhelming majority praised the spectacular pageantry and effective staging.

Simonson's intention was to capture much of the majesty of the Orient with its "grandiose architectural forms covered with a mesh of ornament."[58] Yet he worked selectively, presenting carefully chosen non-Western emblems and decor to suggest, as Krutch insisted, "that Chinese art through which we inevitably see all things Chinese."[59] Although the results were colorful and ornate, Allen found "they [were] never over-gaudy to the point of flamboyance, never splotchy or variegated, but always harmonious both in costume and in background."[60] It was an ex-

49. Simonson, in Eaton, *Theatre Guild*, p. 201.

50. Simonson, *Art*, pp. 30–31.

51. For an interesting account of Mamoulian's version of the conflict see Oberstein, "Broadway," pp. 66–67.

52. *Marco Millions* program, MCNY; Lee Simonson, "Moving 'Marco,'" *New York Times*, Jan. 22, 1928, sec. 8, p. 2

53. Barrett H. Clark, "Eugene O'Neill and the Guild," *Drama* 18 (Mar. 1928): 170.

54. Joseph Wood Krutch, "Marco Millions," *Nation* 126 (Jan. 25, 1928): 105.

55. Kelcey Allen, "Marco Millions Is Poignant O'Neill Satire," *Women's Wear Daily*, Jan. 10, 1928, in Miller, *Playwright's*, p. 56.

56. Euphemia Van Rensselaer Wyatt, "The Drama," *Catholic World* 126 (Mar. 1928): 820.

57. Charles Brackett, "The Theatre," *New Yorker*, Jan. 21, 1928, p. 25.

58. Simonson, "Moving," p. 2.

59. Krutch, "Marco," p. 105.

60. Allen, "Marco," p. 56.

pansive "flaring production" kept under control nonetheless by the organization and orchestration of Mamoulian.

As with *Desire Under the Elms* O'Neill made preliminary drawings and plans for the settings which Simonson described as "a series of backdrops formally typifying each country let down like the pages of a book."[61] The designer, however, rejected this scheme because it lacked the depth and plasticity which Simonson found necessary to suggest the mystery of the Orient. Simonson's problem was not only to create an elaborate yet efficient scenic solution which could be shifted easily through many locations, but also to devise scenery which would adapt to the Guild's experiment with repertory. The final design of *Marco Millions* had a basic scenic frame which also served the Guild productions of *Volpone* and *Faust* which entered the repertory in the same season.[62]

Building a large "decorative framework"[63] of gray-colored pillasters with three openings like doorways, Simonson placed this tripartite unit above a set of platforms and wide steps which always remained on stage along with the frame. The basic unit became the play's various locations by adding flown drops and arches, additional platforms, and inserts for the three openings. Simonson further set off the stage picture and for some scenes reduced its size with two flown inner prosceniums, one black and one blue.[64] Above all of this scenery was a large sky drop, seen in many scenes and frequently used to create strong silhouettes. Brown found that the permanent construction lent needed unity to the play's globe-trotting.[65]

The three high openings of the frame were quite wide, measuring fourteen feet at center and five feet for each doorway stage right and left. The central opening was parallel to the curtain line, while each side frame and opening was raked at a forty-five-degree angle down left and right. Also permanent was a platform one step below stage level which extended over part of the orchestra pit like a small apron with stairs right and left receding into the pit.[66]

Shifting the various scenic inserts and additions to the permanent unit seemed efficient in concept. Yet significant difficulties were created by the logistics of moving some ten platform pieces, two drops, twenty-one inserts for the openings, and numerous large set properties such as a

---

61. Simonson, "Moving," p. 2.

62. *Marco Millions* was at first performed in repertory with *The Doctor's Dilemma*, each play running for a week at a time in the Guild Theatre with many of the same actors.

63. Lee Simonson, "Scenic Designs in the U.S.A.," *Studio* 127 (June 1944): 200.

64. "Setting Inventory," in O'Neill, *Marco Millions* promptbook, NYPL; ground plan in promptbook, Yale.

65. John Mason Brown, "New York Goes Native," *Theatre Arts*, Mar. 1928, p. 165

66. Elevation in Simonson, *Art*, p. 140.

funeral bier, a huge banquet table, five thrones, and a giant Buddha.[67] Although two critics were impressed enough by the frame device to be satisfied that the changes were not uncomfortably long,[68] many others complained that delays were inordinate, unnecessary, and destructive to the effectiveness of the production. Hammond specifically noted eight delaying intermissions,[69] while Clark complained of "thirty or forty minutes' intermissions" for a production which ran approximately two and one-half hours.[70] In answer to such reproof Simonson insisted that "in this age of mechanical marvels, there is not a device which can solve problems of this sort."[71] He remained convinced that his scenic solution was the best one.

The most notable feature of Simonson's design which affected Mamoulian's direction was a large open space between the platforming and the apron—an unadorned area in which the director could, with or without the five available levels above the stage floor, compose dynamic stage pictures, easily isolate actors from groups, or flood the stage with pageantry. His results, along with his lighting, were called the "Mamoulian symphony,"[72] a carefully wrought array of compositional effects resulting from a strong controlling hand directing "with a big gesture."[73]

Helburn wrote that Mamoulian had "an exquisite sense of design"[74] which was especially useful since he responded most strongly to a play pictorially. In *Marco Millions* specifically Brown found the director "with a fine unerring eye for pictorial imagery."[75] Wyatt's assessment was less prosaic: "The stage pictures blend and melt into each other as in a poet's fancy."[76] Such was the effect which Mamoulian sought and frequently achieved, especially in his crowd scenes.

Although Mamoulian used Simonson's three openings for dynamic solo effects like isolated silhouettes of characters framed against the sky, his most sensational stage pictures utilized most of his thirty-five actors.[77]

67. "Prop Plot" and "Setting Inventory," in O'Neill, *Marco Millions* promptbook, NYPL.

68. R. H., "The Theatre," *Wall Street Journal*, Jan. 11, 1928, p. 4; Pulaski, "Marco," p. 51.

69. Hammond, "Theatres," Jan. 10, 1928, p. 28.

70. Clark, "Eugene," Mar. 1928, p. 170.

71. Simonson, in Eaton, *Theatre Guild*, p. 200.

72. "Men," *New York Herald-Tribune*, p. 6.

73. David Carb, "Seen on the Stage," *Vogue*, Mar. 1, 1928, p. 83.

74. Theresa Helburn, *A Wayward Quest* (Boston: Little, Brown, 1960), p. 195.

75. Brown, "Marco," p. 182.

76. Wyatt, "Drama," Mar. 1928, p. 820.

77. The program is not clear about the number of extras, but the most populous production photograph includes thirty-three actors. Twenty-one actors played all the speaking roles, and an additional six women were used for the chorus and banquet. At least eight male extras were used as slaves in the prologue, yielding a minimum of thirty-five actors.

His work in composing and moving crowds was called an unusual gift and praised for continuity, pleasing patterns, and masterful orchestration. Atkinson noted "brilliantly composed groupings,"[78] while the *Literary Digest* nominated Mamoulian as "a fair candidate for Reinhardt honors in designing his mob scenes."[79] Yet his crowds were usually created by suggestion, using smaller numbers than seemed to be on stage by frequently incorporating much movement and a variety of levels and planes for the placement of actors. Littell alone complained of Mamoulian's group work, but this critic's grievance was a response to extensive variety among the crowd members, which called attention to individuality within the mass.[80] Others found this a virtue, and Arbenz testified to Mamoulian's intention to create such distinction in character within carefully coordinated groups.[81] The promptbooks reinforce Mamoulian's painstaking compositional design. The directions are very specific for movement as well as stage position in both small-scale and crowd scenes.

In lighting the stage Mamoulian made the most of his own compositions as well as Simonson's settings and multicolored silk, satin, and velvet costumes.[82] Alternately manipulating stark light and shadow in chiaroscuro effects with sudden bursts of rich, brilliant light flooding the stage, Mamoulian created radical mood shifts while maintaining an overall sense of glamour.[83] The gray framework and platforms were actually spattered and speckled with many different colors which were brought out dynamically when the lights changed sharply, but the frame could always return to a neutral tone.

Although the settings were united by this common framework, four distinct scenic and spatial uses were made of this device.[84] Only in the prologue was the frame unseen, because it was masked by a drop on which was painted a large sacred tree of Persia. The position of this drop left just a shallow strip of playing space plus the small apron. The funeral cart was slowly pulled on from stage left by a long double line of at least twenty half-clothed slaves which disappeared into the wings stage right as the white palled coffin reached the playing area.[85] In this opening scene Mamoulian

78. Atkinson, "After," p. 1.

79. "Marco Polo Masquerading as 'Babbit,'" *Literary Digest*, Feb. 4, 1928, p. 26.

80. Robert Littell, "Mr. O'Neill Pillories a Venetian Babbitt," *New York Evening Post*, Jan. 10, 1928, p. 20.

81. Arbenz, "Plays," p. 89.

82. "Costume List," O'Neill, *Marco Millions* promptbook, NPYL.

83. *Marco Millions* "Light Cue Sheet," MCNY.

84. The descriptions and usages of the settings which follow are based on photographs, ground plans, promptbooks, production plots, and cue sheets. When reviews are used to support these sources they will be noted.

85. Charles Brackett, "The Theatre," *New Yorker*, Jan. 21, 1928, p. 25.

established important conventions of the production by manipulating a crowd and using the pit and apron for the entrance of the three travelers.[86] By keeping the three outsiders on the apron through much of the scene the director was able to maintain a sense of depth despite the shallow stage space and lineup of slaves.

The presence of the frame was most obvious in the travel scenes (1–4) of the first act as the action moved from Venice to Syria to Persia to India. These settings had few additions other than the three inserts for the frame openings. All used an inner proscenium and the central stair unit, and three scenes incorporated the sky drop. The chief differences were achieved through color alteration as well as culturally distinct decorative motifs based on the artistic conventions of each country.[87]

For the Venetian nocturnal scene (I.1) only the central opening was an entrance, with a tall, narrow archway at the top of the stairs beyond which appeared part of a gondola and posts silhouetted against the sky. The stage-left opening became a latticed window behind which Donata flirted with the serenading Marco. A decorative insert closed off the stage-right opening. Although different in detail, all three inserts repeated the same tall, narrow, arching outline. Mamoulian flooded the setting with blue light but included a few pools and shafts of bright illumination. Marco had the entire stage to himself, creating a marked contrast to the prologue as well as I.2.

When the scene shifted to the papal legate's palace at Acre in Syria (I.2), Mamoulian shifted the mood severely with a churchlike feeling created with much amber light surrounded by deep shadows. Simonson hung heavy tapestried archways in the central and stage-left openings, while at right he placed a relief wall dominated by an altar with burning candles. Mamoulian usually kept Tedaldo, the legate, on the highest platform at center, with Marco and the elder Polos on the lower steps, often kneeling. Again a crowd scene was used when the legate was elected pope. The director created a stunning stage picture with the suppliant, kneeling mass appealing to the new pope. Their outstretched hands and bodies extended from the darkness stage right, rising up the stairs to Tedaldo at the pinnacle raising his right hand in a blessing.

The Mohammedan mosque of Islam (I.3) used both the right opening and the left as doorways spilling onto a courtyard. Through a doubled archway at center a pale mosque ground row could be seen against the sky. The effect was of a picture matted and framed. Decoration was very detailed and ornate, yet the overall representation was one of sparseness and simplicity. This setting was brighter than those in previous scenes,

86. Pulaski, "Marco," p. 50.
87. Krutch, "Marco," p. 105.

giving an impression of heat, but prominent shadows still remained on selected portions of the walls and platforming. The space was very open and uncrowded by performers and provided the scene's whirling dervish with sufficient room in which to perform.

Very similar in spatial effect and scenic arrangement was the court temple of India (I.4). Considerably different, however, was the use of color in this scene. Again doorways appeared right and left and a large three-dimensional Buddha replaced the mosque at center. The performance space was still quite open, but the lighting was very cool (many blues and greens), lending the scene a calm, detached mood.

This low-key atmosphere of India was overwhelmed by the resplendent Chinese court of Kublai Kaan which followed it. Although both the Grand Throne Room and the Little Throne Room used the permanent frame and its three openings as well as an inner proscenium, the inserts and additional adornments made the neutral unit seem virtually nonexistent. The first appearance of the Grand Throne Room (I.5) was intended to startle and delight the audience (see illustration 11). The curtain rose in black as Chinese drums and music began to build. The music stopped abruptly. Three loud crashes of a gong followed, and on the last a blaze of light flashed up to full on a panoply of bright, colorful costumes adorning flamboyant courtiers, burly guards, and delicate women surrounding the great Kaan on his ceremonial throne up center. The inserts created three gold-and-silver archways, and the Kaan was set majestically against the sky drop. Littell found this picture "particularly lovely" and decoratively composed,[88] and even Simonson called his own setting spectacular.[89]

Mamoulian used every part of the stage, including the pit steps and apron for this scene. He gave Marco strong visual focus despite the Kaan's powerful stage position by placing Marco on the pit steps on a diagonal down right of the throne. Mamoulian left the stage bare only along this line, connecting the two men with space.

The most interesting use of the Grand Throne Room occurred in III.1. With the stage blanketed in darkness, the Kaan squatted on his throne as a bright light hit him from the floor. In this illumination he stared into a crystal ball to see what had become of Marco after his return to Europe. The vision was played below the throne. A long banquet table piled with food and greenery was rolled out just a few feet from the footlights. Fourteen actors crowded behind the garish table, while the Kaan's throne remained prominently in the background. Having witnessed the awful truth, the Kaan dropped and shattered the crystal,

88. Littell, "Mr. O'Neill," Jan. 10, 1928, p. 20.
89. Simonson, Stage, p. 458.

causing the underlighting and vision to disappear. Although De Casseres despised most of the production as too much like slick Great White Way escapist fare, he found this scene perfect in its eerie execution.[90]

Princess Kukachin's funeral, also staged in the Grand Throne Room (III.2), received mixed reactions. Again most of the actors were used for processions, mourning, and dances, but Young reported that the women did not execute very well here with dance and rhythmic movement.[91] Nonetheless, Mamoulian's stage pictures were once more interesting, with the chorus of women chanting while encircling the body of the princess stage center as the Kaan looked on morosely from his throne silhouetted against the drop. Supported by smoking censors, rattling chains, and tolling bells, this song and dance of lament was the penultimate image of the production. The final picture was of the Kaan at the bier, grieving over the body of his granddaughter.

In sharp contrast to the Grand Throne Room, especially in mood, was the Little Throne Room (summer palace) used only in II.1. This cool scenery painted with greens and blues captured the simplicity of oriental painting with subtle, simple, gentle brush strokes. The central opening featured a beautiful grilled frame of "filigreed jade"[92] which enclosed a painting of a mountainous landscape. The painting was done on a translucent muslin drop which had the shadows of bamboo painted on the upstage side. By means of lighting from behind as well as onstage the setting captured some of the effect of shadow-puppet screens, while Mamoulian could use onstage actors to create strong silhouettes when they were placed near the drop. The extraordinary beauty of this setting was used ironically in the last half of the scene by introducing Marco and the two elder Polos in their grandiose, tasteless, gaudy and ill-fitting costumes of the "Mystic Knights of Confucius."

The most complex scene changes of the production occurred in II.2 and II.3, in a scheme which did not so strictly follow the insert system of other scenes. The junk flagship of Princess Kukachin was created by adding temporary platforms below the permanent stair unit which extended the platforming as a unit downstage almost to the curtain line. In addition, new platforms were inserted at the central opening to allow the platforming to continue upstage to a higher level, thus suggesting a ship's stern and poop deck. The side openings were used in II.2, when this setting represented the wharf and ship, but traveler curtains masked the sides for II.3 (the shipboard scene). The pit was also used in II.3 to allow

90. Benjamin De Casseres, "Broadway to Date," *Arts & Decoration*, March 1928, p. 96.
91. Stark Young, "Dilations," *New Republic* 53 (Jan. 25, 1928): 273.
92. Krutch, "Marco," p. 105.

the women's chorus to come on deck from below. For the wharf scene only a "sail ground row" was added to the central opening to suggest that the downstage platforms led to the ship at dockside. Working diagonally across these platforms from down left to up right, Mamoulian created a line of men in rhythmic movement keeping time to the drum, gong, and chant of the foreman.[93]

The loveliest stage picture which survives from production was that of Princess Kukachin in a golden robe on a silver throne in II.3 being greeted by her women's chorus ascending from the pit while the boatswain chanted high atop the stern railing—a solitary silhouette against the sky. Finding this scene with its off- and onstage chanting and its final painful moment of the princess waving farewell to an unfeeling Marco "rarely beautiful,"[94] David Carb expressed the reaction of many, including Simonson, who believed that in this scene the poetic values rather than the satiric reached a climax[95] and engaged the audience as nowhere else in the production.

Mamoulian's results with group composition, lighting, and the use of space were much more consistent and successful than his direction of the three leading actors. The performances of Holloway, Gillmore, and Lunt reflected stylistic inconsistencies which weakened some of Mamoulian's otherwise impressive direction. Mamoulian was often more successful with young, untried actors than with seasoned professionals, who in this production seemed less than eager to acclimate themselves to his methods.

Unfortunately for the director, the Guild board cast the principals of this play with little aid from O'Neill or Mamoulian,[96] primarily because the Guild was attempting to operate as a repertory company. The principal performers in the Theatre Guild Acting Company of the 1927–1928 season appeared in either *Marco Millions* or *Strange Interlude*.[97] Although the experienced actors were found by most to be efficient and often moving, the accounts of the portrayals of Marco, Princess Kukachin, and the Great Kaan strongly suggest markedly different, if not confusing, acting styles.

Baliol Holloway's rendering of Kublai Kaan, for example, captured much of the distant, objective detachment and majestic dignity necessary to distinguish the wisdom of the Orient from the impulsive gaucheness of

93. Vandamm, "Master," pp. 42–43.

94. Carb, "Seen," Mar. 1, 1928, p. 83.

95. Simonson, *Stage*, p. 458.

96. Mamoulian was not assigned until nine weeks before opening, when many actors from *The Doctor's Dilemma* were already cast. "O'Neill," *New York Times*, Jan. 8, 1928, p. 2.

97. This experiment by the Guild began in the fall of 1926 and ended after the second season. Sayler, "Play," Feb. 11, 1928, p. 590; Eaton, *Theatre Guild*, pp. 102, 222.

the Italian merchants.[98] In movement and presence his characterization was graceful, yet he frequently fell into oratorical patterns which represented an antiquated style of delivery and partially undermined the pathos which the character needed, especially in the funeral scene (III.2).[99] Holloway's failure to move the audience here with the final speech of the play over the body of the princess was damaging to the ultimate emotional response to the play.

Margalo Gillmore, who had starred six years earlier in the ill-fated production of *The Straw*, was an excellent choice for the emotional and pathetic aspects of Princess Kukachin, but her lack of elegant method and graceful style belied her kinship to Holloway's Kaan and weakened the character's royal dignity, which was meant to alienate her from Marco despite her unrequited love for him. De Casseres, for example, wrote that she was "no more Oriental than a movie queen of China."[100] Most reviewers responded positively, however, to her fragility, physical beauty, and fervent suffering. She was filled with "plaintive, hurt, wide-eyed wonder,"[101] according to Woollcott, yet, as Young summarily observed, "her performance had no style and by no means achieved the beautiful, . . . but it at least carried over the footlights the needed human pathos."[102] Though Gillmore was an asset to the role, she struck a dissonant note when onstage with Holloway.

A mainstay of the Guild since 1924, Alfred Lunt as Marco made one of his rare stage appearances without his wife Lynn Fontanne, who was cast in *Strange Interlude*. At thirty-four Lunt was one of the few genuine acting stars to grace an O'Neill production in the experimental era, yet this master of comedy was never at ease with Marco. A chronic worrier and an actor who approached a role primarily through intellectual analysis, Lunt failed to appreciate the role. Complicated by his distrust of directors in making acting decisions, his independent approach to rehearsal kept him wary of Mamoulian and the director's pictorial, rhythmic style.[103]

Although the critical reaction to Lunt was mixed, most reviewers

98. Wyatt, "Drama," Mar. 1928, pp. 820–21; De Casseres, "Broadway," Mar. 1928, p. 96.

99. Atkinson, "Eugene," Jan. 10, 1928; Brackett, "Theatre," Jan. 21, 1928, pp. 25–26; Young, "Dilations," p. 273.

100. De Casseres, "Broadway," Mar. 1928, p. 62.

101. Woollcott, "Stage," Jan. 10, 1928, p. 15.

102. Young, "Dilations," p. 273.

103. Brooks Atkinson, "Alfred Lunt, 1893–1977, Joy Was His Gift to the Stage," *New York Times*, Aug. 14, 1977, sec. 2, p. 3; Morton Eustis, *Players at Work* (New York: Theatre Arts, 1937), p. 43; Zolotow, *Stagestruck*, p. 155.

expressed disappointment with the actor, who seemed to be physically weary or unenthusiastic when the production opened. In fact, rumors of Lunt's inappropriateness circulated prior to opening. [104] One of his biographers claimed that the actor could not empathize with the crass character, [105] but De Casseres was probably more to the point in calling Lunt miscast. [106] Brown found that it was Lunt "who blurs the script most," [107] not only with a lack of performance energy but with the presentation of caricature rather than character. Lunt's work was at once broad in conception and low-key in execution, with results which were in part artificial and lethargic. On the other hand, Lunt displayed his usual technical expertise by subtly aging Marco through the twenty-three years of the play. [108] While he managed to capture some sympathy and agreeable responses to his characterization, few critics found his performance more than competent. His somewhat sluggish presentation lacked the zeal and unconscious density required to create the necessary contrast to Holloway and Gillmore.

Even though, as Woollcott wrote, the premiere "was a little groggy with fatigue," [109] no theater was likely to have granted *Marco Millions* such stage beauty as the Guild and Mamoulian provided. Yet the production's appeal was limited, and the moderate run of the play supported Hammond's pronouncement that *Marco Millions* was "entertainment for the upper class of drama-lovers." [110]

Nonetheless, Mamoulian's achievements in picturization and crowd staging were splendid, even if the director allowed some stylistic inconsistency and occasionally failed to realize completely the majesty of some of his conceptions. The director's visual results, according to Brown, displayed "a virtuosity seldom rivalled in our theatre." [111] Mamoulian would have been an appropriate, perhaps brilliant director for O'Neill's *Lazarus Laughed* had the Theatre Guild been willing to produce it.

Lazarus Laughed

Although *Lazarus Laughed* was not produced professionally, its special pageantry (which exceeded the ostentation of *Marco Millions*) and its unusual staging at the Pasadena Playhouse in 1928 deserve reconstruc-

104. Hammond, "Theatres," Jan. 10, 1928, p. 28.
105. Zolotow, *Stagestruck*, p. 155.
106. De Casseres, "Broadway," Mar. 1928, p. 62.
107. Brown, "Marco," p. 182.
108. Brackett, "Theatre," Jan. 21, 1928, p. 25.
109. Woollcott, "Stage," Jan. 10, 1928, p. 15.
110. Hammond, "Theatres," Jan. 10, 1928, p. 28.
111. Brown, "Marco," p. 182.

tion. O'Neill attempted for two years before, and some months after, the Pasadena production to get a professional production. When *Marco Millions* opened, the Guild was still considering producing *Lazarus Laughed*, but their interest was short-lived. The extravagant production needs of the play were prohibitive. With a tremendous community effort and hundreds of volunteers Gilmor Brown's production still cost $17,000.[112] Macgowan, who tried to interest backers in New York, estimated that a full professional production would have cost at least $50,000, perhaps much more.[113]

O'Neill's mystical "play for an imaginative theatre"[114] which opened in Pasadena on April 9, 1928,[115] was evidently the realization of two important theatrical influences on O'Neill. Sarlos and Alexander note George Cram Cook's desire for O'Neill to create "the Dithyramb of the Western hemisphere,"[116] the ritualized "theater that would be a 'Living Church.'"[117] Also, Macgowan's examination of masks pointed to "the greatest legend of all, the legend of death and resurrection, [which] carries man on into the greatest drama."[118] These were the obvious goals of O'Neill with *Lazarus Laughed*, and for Gilmor Brown the play was the perfect dramatic material for a grand expression of his artistic principles and virtuosity.[119]

Gilmor Brown's credo for production at Pasadena was to present unusual plays of importance and stature which were "not readily available for the professional theatre."[120] By 1928 the forty-two-year-old director had staged hundreds of plays, usually on a tiny budget, most of which were important historically or as dramatic literature. With a strong interest in the classics and dramatic verse forms as well as stylized production experiments, Brown brought to *Lazarus Laughed* an enthusiasm and energy which not only animated the community but also did justice to the spatial problems of the play.

Most of the difficulties which kept this play from the professional stage were the incredible demands of the music, crowds, choruses, masks, and stylized use of laughter. After beginning composition in 1925 O'Neill

112. Macgowan, *Footlights*, p. 241.

113. Macgowan letter to O'Neill, Aug. 12, 1926, in Bryer, *Letters*, p. 127.

114. Eugene O'Neill, *Lazarus Laughed* (New York: Boni & Liveright, 1927), p. 4.

115. George C. Warren, "'Lazarus Laughed' Produced on Coast," *New York Times*, Apr. 10, 1928, p. 33.

116. Sarlos, *Jig*, p. 52.

117. Doris Alexander, *The Tempering of Eugene O'Neill* (New York: Harcourt, Brace and World, 1962), p. 224.

118. Macgowan, *Masks*, p. xii.

119. Gilmor Brown, "A Dream on a Dime," in Stevens, *Ten Talents*, p. 170.

120. *Current Biography* (1944), p. 74.

increasingly complicated the pageantry of the play with each subsequent draft. Although completed by mid-1926, *Lazarus Laughed* lay unproduced for nearly two years.[121] Brown's solutions to the problems were uneven, but his effort was appreciated and admired in the limited critical response.

O'Neill's script called for music in six of the eight scenes, and while he did not ask for specific pieces of music, he frequently described the appropriate kind of music. O'Neill, for example, requested "festive dance," "pulsing rhythm," "exultant music," and "music in a strained theme."[122] The need for music was so strong, in fact, that Nathan called *Lazarus Laughed* an "operatic Biblical fantasy. Less a theatre play than a libretto."[123] Although O'Neill would not have agreed with Nathan's assessment, he expressed the need for "good incidental music" as early as 1926.[124] Brown likewise recognized the musical demands and commissioned Arthur Alexander, who wrote a score for twenty-two musicians to be played throughout most of the production. The presentation was said to capture the ideal of opera without becoming opera. Much vocal delivery became recitative as the music followed "every inflection in speech intensifying the mood and meaning."[125] Alexander's music lifted the play emotionally, especially at moments when it "might otherwise have been rather tedious."[126] In addition, some of the music had a rhythmic sense of laughter which underscored the difficult demands of prolonged laughter from the actors.[127]

Never before had O'Neill requested such crowds as occurred in every scene of the play. Creating well over four hundred roles, the playwright provided a scheme based on the number seven, often calling for two or three onstage groups of forty-nine actors each, for example. Large mob fights and struggles between companies of soldiers and pressing crowds appeared repeatedly, as did marching troops and processions. O'Neill said that the crowds had "to have size and volume or be absurd"[128] because he wanted the audience to experience "the voice of Crowd mind, Crowd emotion."[129] The crowds were indeed vital for production, since their vocal and physical duties were extensive, and the play made little sense without them.

121. Miller, *Eugene*, p. 20; Tornqvist, *Drama*, pp. 261–62.
122. O'Neill, *Lazarus Laughed*, pp. 20, 25, 62, 99.
123. George Jean Nathan, "The Theatre," *American Mercury* 63 (Dec. 1946): 717.
124. O'Neill letter to Macgowan, May 28 (1926), in Bryer, *Letters*, p. 113.
125. "American Music Enters the Theatre," *American Review of Reviews* 78 (Oct. 1928): 440.
126. H. O. Stechan, "Lazarus Laughed," *Billboard* 40 (Apr. 21, 1928): 11.
127. "American," *American*, p. 440.
128. O'Neill letter to Macgowan, July 9 (1926), in Bryer, *Letters*, p. 117.
129. O'Neill, "Dramatist's," p. 120.

Although for production Brown scaled down the crowd numbers, he still cast 159 performers in addition to fifteen actors with significant speaking roles.[130] Naturally the costume requirements were forbidding, so the scheme was simplified to hold the number at four hundred.[131] With such an unwieldy mass of performers, Brown, who also played Tiberius, employed two associate directors (Lenore Shanewise and Maurice Wells, also in the cast) primarily for crowd control.[132]

Once again O'Neill used the choral device, but for the first time he made a distinction in the choruses and the crowds, giving them separate functions, often having the chorus chant with the crowd, lead the crowd, or work in opposition to the crowd. He also wanted the choruses visually separated from the crowd, but sometimes providing "a strange & unreal intensification of the crowd."[133] The choruses engaged in much chanting, unison speech and movement, rhythmic laughter, dance, singing, and tableaux. Desirous of effective poetic and symbolic uses of the choruses, O'Neill called for them to dance with abandon, or suddenly freeze "in a distorted posture," or "weave in and out . . . moving mechanically in jerky steps to the music in a grotesque sort of marionettes' dance."[134] Not only the choruses but sometimes the crowds as well were called upon to present such action, and Brown realized that proper execution required extensive preparation and outside assistance. Accordingly, Brown procured a movement director, Katharane Edson, to train the choruses and crowds. The entire cast rehearsed for six weeks.[135]

In *Lazarus Laughed* O'Neill's experimentation with masks reached its peak (at least quantitatively). All characters except Lazarus wore masks,[136] resulting in a total of three hundred masks for staging the play at Pasadena.[137] The scheme of the playwright for mask typing was basically followed, but simplified. O'Neill charted the masks according to seven age groups (childhood to old age) and seven personality types (such as happy and loving, strong and proud, senile and envious).[138] In addition, three racial strains (Jewish, Roman, Greek) were distinguished. With seven types for each of seven age groups, forty-nine different masks for each of three races resulted in 147 distinct masks. Brown used fifty-four.[139]

130. Bogard, *Contour*, pp. 467–68.
131. Warren, "Lazarus," p. 178.
132. F. W. Hersey, "Lazarus Laughed," *Drama* 18 (May 1928): 245.
133. O'Neill letter to Macgowan, Jan. 23 (1927), in Bryer, *Letters*, p. 148.
134. O'Neill, *Lazarus Laughed*, pp. 25, 35, 37.
135. Hersey, "Lazarus," pp. 244–45.
136. Ten photographs, MCNY and Yale.
137. Warren, "Lazarus," p. 178.
138. O'Neill's chart in Floyd, *Eugene Work*, p. 100.
139. Hersey, "Lazarus," p. 245.

O'Neill was intent upon using masks as never before, yet recapturing elements of the masks of the classical Greek theater. It was very important that the masks of chorus and crowd suggest "impersonal, collective mob psychology" which suppressed the individual and stressed the crowd as "entity."[140] The Greek Dionysian chorus, for example, had "masks daubed and stained with wine lees."[141] In a photograph these devotees of Dionysus stand out from the crowd but, although slightly differentiated, seem all of a piece. For the audience the effects of the masks were often stunning. Called "hideous, grotesque, horrifying and disgusting,"[142] the masks bespoke the decadence and bizarre fantasy so plentiful in the text.

Brown followed closely O'Neill's plan for the size of the masks. The playwright wanted many masks, especially in the choruses, to be over-size—twice human size in fact—to distinguish strongly some groups and to suggest Greek masks. Photographs reveal that some large masks in II.1 and III.2 look almost African in design. Most crowd masks were human in size, while the masks of major characters like Miriam, Caligula, Pompeia, and Tiberius were half-masks with the mouths exposed, a scheme followed in both play and production. Fortunately for the director and designer, a stagecraft class at UCLA helped construct the masks.[143]

One of the most interesting production problems of *Lazarus Laughed* was the use and nature of laughter. The laughter of Lazarus was meant to be contagious, causing uncontrollable laughter in the crowds, choruses, and major characters even as they fought it. Crowds laughed in "rhythmic cadence" and frenzied abandon, while characters like Caligula and Tiberius killed, grieved, or writhed as they openly laughed. Brown blended music with much of this laughter to underscore and highlight the sound. This method was reasonably successful and worked especially well with the crowds.[144]

For the character of Lazarus, however, the problem was not so easily solved. The laughter posed extraordinary demands on the actor (Irving Pichel), who not only had to present the dignity of a god-like figure but had to laugh for extended periods of time both softly and majestically. At its fullest the laughter was meant to be "proud and powerful, infectious with love, casting on the listener an enthralling spell," yet it was also supposed to become a "blood stirring call."[145] O'Neill was afraid that he had posed an impossible task, but Pichel, who may not have escaped an exaggerated

140. O'Neill, "Dramatist's," p. 120.
141. O'Neill, *Lazarus Laughed*, p. 53.
142. Hersey, "Lazarus," p. 245.
143. Hersey, "Lazarus," p. 244.
144. "American," *American*, p. 440.
145. O'Neill, *Lazarus Laughed*, pp. 22, 84.

reverence for the role, nonetheless delivered elongated waves of continuous laughter with "absolute repose and poise" in a "splendid and resonant voice."[146]

Although O'Neill did not believe that *Lazarus Laughed* posed serious scenic problems, Brown realized that creating a space which could accommodate such vast crowds as well as serve the moods and style of the play was no simple task. The designs of James Hyde appeared to be uncomplicated, but they used virtually all of the available space and maintained a unit-set concept while allowing severe shifting of the onstage elements to suggest the play's seven locations.

The stage of the three-year-old Pasadena Community Playhouse was of generous size for most productions, but its thirty-six-foot depth and thirty-one-foot proscenium opening were taxed for *Lazarus Laughed* and its huge cast. While the stage was untrapped, it had reasonable wing areas and plenty of fly space.[147] Nonetheless, Hyde and Brown elected to fill much of the stage with a permanent platform unit and modify it with separate movable pieces like building blocks which could be shifted freely. Most of these scenic pieces remained onstage throughout all of the performance. Director and designer rejected O'Neill's scenic suggestions which were specific in the text and resembled in a representational, if simple, way the actual locations indicated. O'Neill had once again made drawings for the settings,[148] but it is not likely that Brown ever saw these, since O'Neill did not travel west for either rehearsals or performance. Simplicity and austerity, however, the scenic qualities most desired by O'Neill, were important aspects of the Pasadena design.

The set pieces when grouped together created "geometric, architectural"[149] forms which gave the impression of "dignity and massiveness,"[150] primarily because they were unadorned with decoration and filled the stage space both vertically and horizontally. Central to this collection was a huge sixty-foot-long platform which never moved and extended left to right across the stage and disappeared far into the wings. The downstage edge of this unit, which stood seven feet high, was cut in a broad zig-zagging line leaving deep recesses for movement, since portions of this unit almost reached the curtain line. The variable pieces of this setting included four two-fold screens which could be placed on top of or just behind the big platform; two tall monolithic columns which stood

146. "The Tributary Theatre," *Theatre Arts* 12 (June 1928): 447.

147. Frederick Arden Pawley, "Theatre Types: A Comparative Study," in Edith J. R. Isaacs, ed., *Architecture for the New Theatre* (New York: Theatre Arts, 1935), pp. 63–66; Pichel, *Modern*, pp. 36–37, plate facing p. 49.

148. Drawings reproduced in Floyd, *Eugene Work*, pp. 105–10.

149. Warren, "Lazarus," p. 178.

150. Hersey, "Lazarus," p. 246.

more than twelve feet higher than the platform and always remained upstage of it; four step units which were moved freely and provided access from stage floor to platform; and several small platform and step units to change the stage picture and provide alternate routes to the large stair units.[151]

Nearly all of the depth of the stage was used as the screens and columns upstage were placed just in front of the theater's back wall, which was white plaster and functioned as a permanent cyclorama (not unlike at the Provincetown). The stage was so full that photographs suggest the set had very little depth despite the fact that the upstage wall was thirty-six feet from the curtain line.[152] Also, for some viewers in the balcony the upper portions of the columns were certainly cut off visually by the top of the twenty-foot-high proscenium.[153] The reviews acknowledge that though the space was burdened, the setting nonetheless remained commanding.

All of these scenic units were painted various shades of gray to provide a neutral field for very colorful costumes. In a manner similar to the frame painting of *Marco Millions*, however, the platform and screens were spattered with gold and silver to heighten many lighting effects.[154] It is clear from photographs that deep shadows were often contrasted with great intensity and almost glaring pools of light. The angular, three-dimensional nature of the setting accentuated the play of light and shadow on nearly all parts of the stage.

Because of the very shallow downstage strip of stage space created by the platform, Brown had to manipulate most of his crowds and choruses on the platforms and stairs. He was very successful with his group compositions, which were almost always shifting throughout the play. Using Edson to help the actors (most of them very young) execute dynamic, rhythmic movements in unison as well as counterpoint, Brown created the compositions by usually leading a large group movement to a tableau. The movement was never intended to be realistic or natural, but orchestrated, stylized, sometimes synchronized with music, or performed in slow motion. Warren reported that the crowds and choruses were "trained to the minute to give effects to the mobs that are a continual procession before the audience."[155] All scenes suggest simultaneous activity all over the stage, extensive choreography, and variety in posture and levels, but never

151. Hersey, "Lazarus," p. 246; Warren, "Lazarus," p. 178.

152. Pawley, "Theatre," pp. 64, 65.

153. Theatre cross sections in Pawly, "Theatre," pp. 63, 66, and Pichel, *Modern*, p. 37.

154. "Irving Pichel as Lazarus in 'Lazarus Laughed,'" caption note, *Drama* 18 (May 1928): 243; Hersey, "Lazarus," p. 246.

155. Warren, "Lazarus," p. 33.

for the sake of naturalness, rather for the sake of composition. Photographs reveal that many poses and attitudes in the groups were clearly exaggerated. Even O'Neill acknowledged that *Lazarus Laughed* "is a play for a director, for sets composed of people arranged by that director."[156]

The development of the set changes was something of a progression, since some of the scenic pieces were masked by others and some were not yet on stage when the play began. By II.1 all major pieces were visible, although a few set properties arrived and departed throughout the production as the scenery was shifted six times after the opening scene.[157]

For the exterior of the house of Lazarus (I.2), the "House of Laughter," two major levels were created. The downstage portion of the big platform was exposed by moving the screens further upstage. On this level the disciples of Lazarus celebrated, danced, and sang, while the Christians and Jews fought at stage level. Two of the stair units and a small platform were added center stage to provide access to the upper level. From his high vantage point Lazarus could dynamically control the crowd below.

A public square in Athens (II.1) was represented by bringing all step units into the space facing off left, the direction of the much-awaited arrival of Lazarus. The screens were moved behind the platforms to clear all of the upper level. Columns and screens were also moved left and right, leaving a large expanse of white plaster at center and left center. At least fifty-two performers appeared in the crowd and choruses, which were placed on all levels and stairs except those just in front of the white plaster space. This open space was reserved for Lazarus after he entered in a hand-pulled chariot at stage level and thus was set apart visually from the crowds. Although the use of space was interesting and carefully orchestrated, the chariot itself was garlanded with paper flowers and unfortunately resembled a tissue-paper parade float more appropriate for Pasadena streets on New Year's Day.

Set just inside the walls of Rome, the next scene (II.2) was the most open of all on the upper level. The screens and columns were moved to extreme left and right positions, and a temporary low balustrade seemed to connect them along the upstage line of the major platform. The four large step units faced center to create the sense of a small arena as the crowd of senators gathered on these steps (along with the separate Senate chorus on a central platform), to await the appearance of Lazarus. Brown weighted

156. He also called it a play for the playwright and leading actor, but he listed director first. O'Neill letter to Macgowan, Jan. 21 (1927), in Bryer, *Letters*, p. 146.

157. All shifts followed the needs and locations of the published play. Fortunately, all settings are briefly described by Hersey, and Warren specifically describes two. Unfortunately, the photographs record but four of the seven arrangements.

the playing area with all performers positioned below the upper level. The effect was diametrically opposed to Brown's use of the platforming for the amphitheater in IV.2.

The absence of photographs for III.1, the entrance to the palace of Tiberius, is especially distressing, since this was the only scene in which unusual stage dressing was added to the architectural forms. Up center on the platform was a very large cross with a crucified lion marking the entrance to the palace. All steps were pulled away from the platform to create a wall and leave the only access to the platform at center stage at the position of the crucifix (a recurring scenic motif in O'Neill's plays since *Welded*).

The banquet hall of Tiberius (III.2 and IV.1), the most frequently reproduced scenic arrangement from this production, incorporated more set properties than other scenes. Central low platforming was turned around with steps facing upstage to create a banquet table at center for Tiberius and his chorus of deviates. Two more tables appeared right at stage level and up right on the major platform for the banquet crowd. Other crowd members had seating up left, and guards were scattered about the stage. The two columns were placed center only a few feet apart, with two standing lamps in front to create a grand entrance to the hall. Two large step units led directly to the central platform from the upper level, and the remaining two stair units were removed. At least thirty people appeared in these banquet-hall scenes, in which the down left area was kept clear of set properties to provide an open space for the first confrontation of Tiberius and Lazarus, and, more important, for the death of Miriam. In marked contrast to all preceding scenes, much of IV.1 seemed virtually bare, since the choruses and crowds were absent until the conclusion of the scene. The space suddenly seemed vast as only four actors stalked about the array of steps and platforms.

Some of the most dynamic compositional shifts of the production occurred in the final scene (IV.2) in which a Roman amphitheater was suggested. All four step units faced off left as in II.1. In this scene, however, Tiberius and every member of a huge crowd (Hersey says the entire cast) were on the upper platform facing off left, where Lazarus was supposedly burning at the stake. For the first time the stage level and stairs were devoid of people. The effect was quite stark, especially since light representing the flames burning Lazarus flickered against the crowd. Pompeia finally violated the vast space as she rushed alone down the steps and offstage to throw herself on the pyre. This was soon followed by the crowd swarming down all the steps and filling the arena with a frenzied dance and cacophonous chant. Just as suddenly, the crowd vanished, leaving the psychotic Caligula alone on stage.

Although much of Brown's work with the crowds and choruses was clearly stunning, the performances of the principal actors came under little scrutiny. Young Victor Jory's bizarre portrayal of Caligula was very impressive as he physicalized the mad, bratty Caesar-to-be as "half animal, with dangling arms and bended knees, and . . . snarling speech."[158] The grotesque creation of Jory suited the visual style of the production and stood in marked contrast to the "Christ-like" portrayal in both appearance and manner of Pichel as Lazarus.[159] In general the acting company was found to be competent and enthusiastic but limited, perhaps most of all by its youth.[160] Fortunately, the masks helped to allay inexperience.

Brown's effort was an admirable foray into the mysticism and pageantry of O'Neill's experimental world. As a theatrical exploration of space, crowds, chorus and music, the effort was worthwhile, but as dramatic material much of the language and action of the play was static, stilted, and self-consciously esoteric. Too demanding technically to expect professional production, *Lazarus Laughed*, Clark suggested, was written for an *imaginary* rather than what O'Neill called an *imaginative* theatre.[161] It was "as a pageant, perhaps, more than as a play"[162] that *Lazarus Laughed* was said to succeed at Pasadena.

158. Warren, "Lazarus," p. 33.

159. Stechan, "Lazarus," p. 11; "Tributary," p. 448.

160. One rehearsal photograph shows much of the crowd in costume but without masks; the effect is incongruous and suggests a school production in which all roles are taken by very young performers.

161. Clark, *Eugene*, p. 117.

162. Warren, "Lazarus," p. 33.

CHAPTER XI

Harnessing Furies:
Strange Interlude, Dynamo, and *Mourning Becomes Electra*

> As everyone knows, the audience will stand a performance lasting
> four or five hours only if it be presented by the Guild and the au-
> thor be Eugene O'Neill.[1]

> *Dynamo* doesn't count.[2]

The premiere of *Strange Interlude* on the afternoon of
Monday, January 30, 1928, at the John Golden Theatre[3] was a remarkable
experience for the some nine hundred people in attendance.[4] It was not
only an important and novel experiment in length and stage speech but
also the realization of a critical suggestion of 1915: "Suppose you had
written a play with scenes in which the things your characters thought
were more significant than the things they said?"[5] Attempting precisely
this, O'Neill presented a long, "torturous drama"[6] which was the first of
three plays in which the playwright's emotional intensity and exploration
of psychological furies reached an almost unbridled frenzy.

The subject of extensive critical analysis and boundless praise,

1. Eva Le Gallienne, *At 33* (New York: Longmans, Green, 1934), p. 240.
2. O'Neill (May 1929), in Frenz, *Eugene*, p. 65.
3. Advertisement, *New York Times*, Jan. 30, 1928, p. 19. Reviews first appeared on
Tuesday, Jan. 31, 1928.
4. Dudley Nichols, "The New Play," *World*, Jan. 31, 1928, p. 11.
5. This reviewer was responding to Alice Gerstenberg's experimental one-act *Overtones*,
in which two characters were stalked by their alter egos, who spoke the characters' real thoughts
and intentions, or subtext. "After the Play," *New Republic*, Nov. 20, 1915, p. 74. Hammond also
noticed the similarity to *Overtones* in his first-night review of *Strange Interlude*. Percy Hammond,
"The Theaters," *New York Herald-Tribune*, Jan. 31, 1928, p. 18.
6. Brooks Atkinson, "Pauline Lord in 'Strange Interlude,'" *New York Times*, Dec. 18,
1928, p. 37. In this review Atkinson compares a replacement cast with the original.

Strange Interlude won a Pulitzer Prize and proved to be the greatest popular success of all of O'Neill's plays produced before World War II. Yet it was also the recipient of critical jeers, parodies, and jokes. The Marx Brothers, for example, included *Strange Interlude* asides in their routines, and even Alfred Lunt called it a "six day bisexual race."[7] Extreme variance in the public response reflected the difficulties the Guild board encountered when debating acceptance of the play. It appears that Lawrence Langner fought diligently to add *Strange Interlude* to the season, and one of his opponents was the man who would ultimately direct it, Philip Moeller.[8]

At forty-seven the talkative, inordinately sensitive but sophisticated, somewhat mannered and romantic director had been staging productions for the Guild and Washington Square Players since their inception. Before beginning with O'Neill, Moeller was associated primarily with comedy such as *The Guardsman, Mr. Pim Passes By,* and *Arms and the Man.* He had, however, also staged important experiments in *The Adding Machine, Processional,* and *Right You Are If You Think You Are.* Educated at New York University and Columbia, the articulate Moeller was a sometime playwright[9] who displayed a strong interest in all the fine arts, which attracted him to European plays and methods and led him to an eclectic directing style.

"There are no excuses in the theatre,"[10] Moeller was fond of saying, always willing to accept the responsibility for failure but adamant in striving for just the right approach to a play. Yet he set about each directorial task rather casually and romantically, as if the assigned play were a sweeping piece of music which could be best appreciated and produced if interpreted intuitively rather than analytically.[11] "I consider myself the orchestra leader," he said, "who must blend all the tones so that they become parts of one composition."[12]

He did not see his role as maestro, however. Always a collaborator with actors, designers, and Guild board members, Moeller invited suggestions from all comers once he had taken charge of production. Although very imaginative, he preferred to start rehearsals before making many significant decisions. "He comes to his first rehearsal strangely and delib-

7. Zolotow, *Stagestruck,* p. 155.

8. Langner, "Eugene," p. 88; O'Neill letter to Macgowan, Mar. 24 (1927), in Bryer, *Letters,* p. 154; Wiley, "Philip," p. 479.

9. For example, Moeller wrote *Molière* (1919) and *Sophie* (1919).

10. Moeller, in Simonson, *Part,* p. 83.

11. Moeller, in Elizabeth Borton, "Philip Moeller Discusses Bridge and the Staging of Plays," *Boston Herald,* Dec. 31, 1933, p. 28.

12. Moeller, in Helen Ormsbee, "Philip Moeller, Director, Hollywood and Here," *New York Herald-Tribune,* Sept. 9, 1934, sec. 5, p. 3.

erately unprepared," Helburn wrote of him.[13] In agreement Moeller said, "I never start rehearsals with my mind made up about a play."[14] His method was to respond to the material intuitively, to be inspired by it, and shape the production only after the actors began attacking their roles. Moeller delighted in treating artistic expression and imagination as a "great mystery" which emanated "from secret, subconscious sources."[15] He summarized such an approach to creativity as "controlled insanity."[16]

Although Moeller brought very catholic tastes and interests to the theater from his voracious reading and European touring (eclecticism which he considered "essential to contemporary stage directing"),[17] he always maintained a strict belief in fidelity to the playwright's text. While he frequently requested cuts, he rarely asked for serious rewriting. Nor did he attempt to redesign the playwright's probable conception. "A director, he said, 'should only attempt to explore what the author has written, not what he, the director, gets out of a script.'"[18] It need hardly be said that such a directing philosophy was near and dear to the mind of O'Neill.

Nevertheless, Moeller was always looking for patterns—both visual and figurative—as he worked with the script and the actors. He awaited clues from the discoveries and accidents of actors and frequently arrived at his most effective ideas in response to rehearsal discoveries. Such a method left him reliant upon the actors to work imaginatively and with reasonable independence while the director acted as liberal guide. Like Arthur Hopkins, Moeller was at his best with independent, experienced actors such as the Lunts, who not only responded well to his often stimulating and unrestrained guidance but also provided him with a plethora of interesting options. With inexperienced actors, however, Moeller seemed almost resourceless. Not an actor himself, and not a teacher, he would rarely give specific, detailed directions. As much as possible, therefore, he sought intelligent performers who were already physically and emotionally appropriate for the roles.[19]

All of these directorial practices were evident to varying degrees in the preparation of *Strange Interlude*, and the critical reception to Moeller's work was overwhelmingly positive. At least ten reviewers displayed great

13. Theresa Helburn, "Staged by Philip Moeller," *Theatre Guild Magazine*, May 1929, p. 29.

14. Moeller, in Ormsbee, "Philip," p. 3.

15. Moeller, in Ormsbee, "Philip," p. 3; Simonson, *Part*, p. 83.

16. Moeller, in Borton, "Philip," p. 28.

17. Howard Barnes, "Moeller of the Theater Guild," *New York Herald-Tribune*, Feb. 10, 1929, sec. 7, p. 2.

18. "Philip Moeller, Director, Is Dead," *New York Times*, Apr. 27, 1958, sec. 1, p. 86.

19. "Direction by Moeller," *New York Times*, May 7, 1933, sec. 9, p. 2; Borton, "Philip," p. 28; Helburn, *Wayward*, pp. 184–85; Ormsbee, "Philip," p. 3.

regard for the direction specifically—including Seldes, who usually found fault with Moeller's work.[20] Described as admirable, beautiful, intelligent, decisive, skillful, expert, and imaginative, Moeller's labor was summed up by Hammond as "a miracle of stage direction."[21] Moeller was credited particularly with meeting the play's special experimental difficulties and solving them efficiently and with complete comprehension and stylistic consistency. Seldes and Littell, for example, were amazed that the almost "insuperable" production demands did not overwhelm the presentation and lapse into uncertainty and confusion.[22] Likewise, Clark believed that Moeller had never before directed anything which "required greater intelligence and a more sympathetic understanding. . . . His direction brought into relief as much as was humanly possible in a work that has so little of the theatrically conventional."[23] Stylistically the production was found to be not only consistent and appropriate but clever without being tricky, tasteful yet unmannered.[24]

Moeller's fellow board members in retrospect remembered *Strange Interlude* as this director's "finest serious production," as well as "the subtlest and most powerful piece of work" in Moeller's career.[25] When interviewed more than five years later, Moeller himself pointed to *Strange Interlude* as his "most thrilling experience and the most satisfying."[26]

Begun in 1925 and completed by mid-1927, the script of *Strange Interlude* steadily grew in length until it was virtually unmanageable. It was obvious to both playwright and director that extensive cutting was necessary, so they had numerous sessions together for several months.[27] This kind of preproduction work was unusual for Moeller, but it was vital in order to reduce the script to a playable length. In February Moeller referred to "conferences with O'Neill" in which severe reductions were made,[28] but he continued with "quiet insistence"[29] throughout rehearsal to convince O'Neill to cut more. When the text was finally prepared, some forty pages of the manuscript had been excised.[30] Cuts came from both

20. Gilbert Seldes, "The Theatre," *Dial* 84 (Apr. 1928): 350.

21. Hamond, "Theaters," Jan. 31, 1928, p. 18.

22. Robert Littell, "O'Neill's Strange Interlude," *New York Evening Post*, Jan. 31, 1928, p. 18; Seldes, "Theatre," Apr. 1928, p. 350.

23. Clark, "Eugene," Mar. 1928, p. 170.

24. For example, David Carb, "Seen on the Stage," *Vogue*, Apr. 1, 1928, p. 140.

25. Helburn, *Wayward*, p. 259; Simonson, *Part*, p. 83.

26. "Direction," May 7, 1933, p. 2.

27. Philip Moeller, "Silences Out Loud," *New York Times*, Feb. 26, 1928, sec. 8, p. 4.

28. Philip Moeller, "Some Notes on the Production of O'Neill's Strange Interlude," *Theatre Guild Quarterly*, Feb. 1928, p. 26.

29. Helburn, "Staged," p. 58.

30. O'Neill, in Richard Watts, Jr., "Realism Doomed, O'Neill Believes," *New York Herald-Tribune*, Feb. 5, 1928, sec. 7, p. 2; Langner, "Eugene," p. 88.

dialogue and asides, but no significant events or background information were removed (although a few were rearranged).[31] While the several months of cutting work forced Moeller to do much more preproduction work than he liked to do, he tried to avoid decisions about characterization and production details so that he could still rely on the intuition of his actors and his own inspiration during rehearsals.

As he had with *Marco Millions*, O'Neill attended rehearsals of *Strange Interlude* sporadically and communicated solely through the director. Moeller did not adjust quickly to O'Neill's personality and called him "an outsider,"[32] but eventually the two learned to work together smoothly. "He is a silent man," Moeller said; "he saves his communications for the play form. He almost never makes suggestions about how to stage or act his plays."[33]

Again receiving Equity permission for extra rehearsal time, the cast and Moeller had seven weeks to prepare for opening.[34] Unaccustomed to a rehearsal period almost twice the normal length, the cast was nearly exhausted when the play finally opened. Fatigue led to uncertainty, and in the final week many of the actors began to fear openly that the production would prove to be "torture to even the most patient audiences."[35] Fortunately, Moeller's almost interminable patience with the actors and his enthusiastic but unrushed speech which conveyed a sense of ease helped to maintain rehearsal discipline and prevent panic.

Moeller did, however, encounter a special problem with O'Neill. Occasional lines which O'Neill never intended as humorous tended to play comically when acted. The playwright always wanted to cut these from this production, but Moeller found them refreshing and struggled to retain them. Yet when O'Neill insisted, Moeller always yielded to the dramatist.[36]

As an experimental work with special directorial challenge *Strange Interlude* had few of the typical logistical difficulties so plentiful in the previous work of O'Neill. Without pageantry, chorus, crowds, masks, music, poetry, or exotic settings, *Strange Interlude* seemed stark and intimate. Yet O'Neill, as he told Langner in 1927, was still "experimenting

31. Eugene O'Neill, *Strange Interlude*, bound promptbook, Theatre Guild Collection, Beinecke, Yale; Eugene O'Neill, *Strange Interlude*, bound promptbook, Theatre Collection, Performing Arts Center, NYPL, copyrighted 1928 by Yale University.

32. Moeller, in Gelbs, *O'Neill*, p. 647.

33. Moeller, in Borton, "Philip," p. 28.

34. [Jack Pulaski] Ibee, "Strange Interlude," *Variety*, Feb. 1, 1928, p. 52.

35. Gilbert Gabriel, "The Newer O'Neill," *Vanity Fair*, Apr. 1928, p. 52.

36. Langner and Helburn report such incidents but provide no specific examples. Langner, *Magic*, p. 236; Helburn, "Staged," p. 28.

with ways and means to break down 'realism' in the theatre."[37] Seven of the nine acts were played in domestic interiors, and only rarely did more than three characters appear on stage at once. The play was nevertheless particularly problematic in its spatial demands due to difficulties which arose from the most obvious experiments in the play—inordinate length and extensive asides.

At a time when a typical Broadway nonmusical production ran from two to two and one-half hours,[38] a four and one-half hour performance broken midway by a dinner intermission was startling. Beginning in the late afternoon at 5:15 and finishing after 11:00 P.M., the nine-act play was interrupted after Act V for seventy-five minutes at about 7:30 (playing length varied slightly from night to night).[39]

This scheme of course precluded matinees and helped to eliminate the Guild repertory system. Such performance length was nevertheless tiring for both actors and audience. While some imaginative audience members delighted in changing into evening clothes during the dinner break,[40] most were enthralled, if not spell-bound, by the performance as they were "gradually caught up by the sweep of the thing."[41] Yet even the most profoundly moved or fascinated theatergoers found themselves physically weary and drained, even relieved that the performance had concluded.[42] Despite the fact that the extended intermission abetted audience fatigue, Moeller insisted that the actors needed the break and that, just as important, the audience needed it for "discussion and digestion of Part 1 and a preparation, physical, mental and emotional, for Part 2."[43] The "Bayreuth"[44] intermission was not altered.

The unusual protraction of the play was the result of a surprising amount of repetition, which fascinated Moeller. The director likened *Strange Interlude* to a musical composition which needed delicate shaping and faithful rendering on the part of himself and the actors. O'Neill, he

37. Langner, "Eugene," p. 88.

38. N. Bryllion Fagin, "Eugene O'Neill," *Antioch Review*, Spring 1954, p. 22; Le Gallienne, *At* 33, p. 240.

39. Running times vary in different reviews and reports by as much as fifteen minutes. The play premiered at 5:15 P.M., but in the second week the time was changed to 5:30. *Strange Interlude* program, MCNY; advertisements, *New York Times*, Jan. 30, 1928, p. 19, and Feb. 9, 1928, p. 29.

40. Otto Kahn and Max Reinhardt initiated this game on opening afternoon/night. John Anderson, "'Strange Interlude' Profound Drama of Subconscious," *New York Evening Journal*, Jan. 31, 1928, in Miller, *Playwright's*, p. 57.

41. Robert Benchley, "Drama," *Life* (New York), Feb. 16, 1928, p. 21.

42. For example, Charles Brackett, "The Theatre," *New Yorker*, Feb. 11, 1928, p. 24.

43. Moeller, "Silences," p. 4.

44. Smyser, "Temporary," p. 1.

said, "takes a theme, devises its answer; and plays around with it, in different keys, building up complexities of counterpoint until the whole is resolved in a magnificent climax."[45] The solution to making the repetition and refrains effective in the theater lay, Moeller believed, in the execution of O'Neill's asides.

Labeled by many as spoken thoughts, inner monologues, thought asides, double dialogue, poetry of the unconscious, Freudian chorus, and silences out loud, the asides were thoughts (conscious and unconscious), subtext, motivations, emotional responses, and comments on normal spoken dialogue. Although some critics believed that such passages were better left to the actors to perform than speak,[46] nearly all reviewers were at least intrigued by the novel device.

Moeller interpreted most of the asides as "conscious thought,"[47] even "spoken commentary which . . . is a kind of autobiographical criticism and analysis . . . of thoughts which either intensify or contradict or comment upon the speech or speeches which are being heard."[48] This is in keeping with O'Neill's working notes during composition in which he stressed aloud conscious thinking as being more important and dynamic than speech.[49] Although the playwright devised the aside scheme, he had no suggestion for how it should be executed in the theater. The problem became Moeller's exclusively.

More than any other device in an O'Neill play, the asides seemed to Simonson "a director's problem."[50] Moeller, however, also found it "the most subtle problem."[51] The difficulty was finding a performance method whereby spoken dialogue could be clearly distinguished from the asides without confusing the audience or resorting to a multitude of acting tricks. Not only did asides appear throughout, often alternating with speeches, but many appeared vis-à-vis asides of different characters. Moeller wanted the play "to seem suddenly to stop and, at the same time, not to stop;"[52] he was seeking lucid isolation of asides, but without such obtrusive execution that the action seemed to halt. "The problem here," he said, "was to make an extremely complex situation as simple as possible."[53] He did not find the answer quickly.

45. Moeller, in Borton, "Philip," p. 28.
46. For example, Brooks Atkinson, "Strange Interlude," *New York Times*, Feb. 5, 1928, sec. 8, p. 1.
47. Moeller, in John K. Hutchens, "Miss Fontanne on How It Feels to Play Nine Acts," *New York Evening Post*, Mar. 3, 1928, sec. 3, p. 8.
48. Moeller, "Some Notes," p. 9.
49. O'Neill, in Floyd, *Eugene Work*, p. 74.
50. Simonson, *Part*, pp. 83–84.
51. Moeller, "Silences," p. 4.
52. Moeller, "Silences," p. 4.
53. Moeller, in Hutchens, "Miss," p. 8.

Moeller experimented with special designated areas of the stage for asides, a method which retarded the stage action; unrealistic lighting shifts, a distracting and tiresome device; and vocal changes for the actors which sometimes proved confusing or too subtle when used alone. Finally, he was inspired by an incident outside the theater. While riding on a train and pondering this problem, Moeller was suddenly frozen into position along with his fellow passengers as the train made an emergency stop. The immobile but living humanity suggested another possibility for asides.[54]

Moeller instructed all performers except the speaking actor to freeze during asides. Describing these stops as "arrested motion" and "physical quiet,"[55] Moeller tried to avoid severe, dynamic halts which would call attention to themselves in their abruptness. He thought of them as momentary lulls in which the secret thoughts could unobtrusively emerge. Moeller was successful in maintaining a sense of life in the static pictures which Helburn described as "suspended animation."[56] Although the actors remained "absolutely stationary,"[57] they halted their action "almost imperceptibly"[58] and held "their pose to give the impression of instantaneous and continuous expression."[59] Moeller furthermore heightened the sense of arrested motion by sometimes interrupting small movements and gestures, which were completed when normal dialogue resumed.[60] On the whole, however, the freezes were executed as subtly as possible.

While all others were immobile, the speaking actor was completely free to gesture and move. This helped to maintain forward movement of the play and avoid monotony. Most of the time, however, the actors faced downstage when delivering asides, except when the frequent occurrences of contiguous asides would have rendered the moment ludicrous.

Although Moeller reported that he abandoned vocal changes for the asides, they clearly made their way into performance. All of the actors were said by many critics to alter volume, vocal inflection, tone, and speed when delivering the asides. Atkinson, for example, wrote that the asides sometimes resembled "chants or prayers,"[61] and *Vanity Fair* referred to

54. Moeller, "Silences," p. 4; George Freedley, *The Lunts* (New York; Macmillan, 1957), p. 53.

55. Moeller, in Barnes, "Moeller," p. 2; Hutchens, "Miss," p. 8; Moeller, "Some Notes," p. 9.

56. Helburn, "Staged," p. 59.

57. Richard Dana Skinner, "The Play," *Commonweal*, Feb. 22, 1928, in Hewitt, *Theatre USA*, p. 373.

58. Block, *Changing*, p. 163.

59. Euphemia Van Rensselaer Wyatt, "The Drama," *Catholic World*, Apr. 1928, p. 78.

60. This interrupted activity was most evident in the mutual seduction of Nina and Darrell at the end of act IV, a situation which Fontanne found comic.

61. Brooks Atkinson, "Strange Interlude Plays Five Hours," *New York Times*, Jan. 31, 1928, p. 28.

Fontanne's "clamorous anguish and *sotto voce* asides."[62] Seldes even assumed that Moeller had "created a style of utterance for these monologues,"[63] so consistent was the actors' approach to delivery. It was likely that early vocal experiments remained with the actors, or that the arrested motion caused unconscious vocal shifts.

Moeller was surprised at the actors' ease in adjusting to the device, but the theatergoers, after a few puzzling moments, also accepted the new conventions quickly.[64] As O'Neill was fond of telling the Guild, "the audience will stand for anything provided we do it well enough."[65] The director reported that the audiences adjusted with such facility that no important postopening changes in the performance were necessary.[66]

Although some critics complained of O'Neill's pretentiousness, too literary and analytical style, over-articulate characters and repetition of asides ad infinitum, nearly all praised Moeller for his effective handling of the experiment. Moeller's work was most of all lauded for finesse, clarity, and honesty in melding the abstract and realistic worlds of the play and producing a surprisingly "actable" excursion into modern psychology.

Because of the limited size of the cast, the domestic nature of the locations, and the extensive use of the aside device which encouraged reduced physical activities, the director's challenges with the performance space were subtle. Perhaps most important of all was procuring a serviceable design which could solve the logistics of the quarter-century journey of the play.

Moeller was teamed with Jo Mielziner, a twenty-six-year-old designer who had not yet made his reputation with *Street Scene* (1929) and the score of memorable designs which would follow. Trained in America in easel painting and in Europe in stage design, Mielziner came under the influence of Jones and Simonson in the early 1920s and began designing professionally in 1924 with Moeller's production of *The Guardsman*. By Mielziner's own assessment, at the time of *Strange Interlude* he did not give considerable attention to the needs of scene changing, was not good at collaboration with directors, and had a weak understanding of theater space.[67] Most significantly, however, his now familiar method of reducing the commonplace to its essentials, which were in turn magnified and given a subtle beauty, had not yet appeared. In consequence, his designs for the nine-hundred-seat John Golden Theatre with its restricted space were

---

62. "Three Strange Interludes," *Vanity Fair*, Feb. 1929, p. 63.
63. Seldes, "Theatre," Apr. 1928, p. 350.
64. "Strange Interlude," *Saturday Review* 4 (Mar. 3, 1928): 641.
65. O'Neill, in Helburn, "O'Neill," p. 10.
66. Moeller, in Hutchens, "Miss," p. 8.
67. Jo Mielziner, *Designing for the Theatre* (New York: Atheneum, 1965), pp. 3–10.

adequate but rather dull and lifeless, save one imaginative environment—
the yacht of act VIII. Few critics seemed even to notice the six settings or
took "time to consider them, so engrossing was the action."[68] The designs
received occasional nods of mild approval for being atmospheric, appropriate, or "quietly rich,"[69] but Young found them very uneven in their suit-
ability to the play,[70] an observation supported by the production photographs.[71]

In general the settings were rather stark and bare, although essentially representational. They did not, however, emphasize selective detail,
which may have given the settings power or poignancy and stronger support for the dramatic material. The lack of specificity usually contributed
little more to the play than simplicity.

Probably inspired by Simonson's designs and the desire of the Guild
to keep the scenic expenditures economical due to the excesses of *Marco
Millions,* Mielziner attempted with reasonable success to design a permanent scenic framework which would accommodate most of the settings.
The first four settings (acts I-VII) and the sixth setting (act IX) all utilized
the large frame. Only the yacht of act VIII was erected independently.
The six ground plans[72] reveal that the frame was actually four separate
permanent pilasters with slots (Mielziner uses the word *portal*) placed at
the four corners of the primary performance space (two pilasters downstage just inside the proscenium arch and two pilasters directly upstage).
Rooms of the settings were created by connecting the pilasters with "flat
back and side walls slipping into permanent slots at the corners."[73] The
resultant rectangle of these rooms was of course uniform in size and rather
shallow. The long upstage walls were battened together to allow them to
be inserted as a unit and effect rapid set changes. Several reviews attest to
efficient and swift scene changes of "Mielziner's utilitarian sets,"[74] and
no critics complained of delays.

Within the rectangular playing space Moeller and Mielziner placed
little furniture or stage dressing. With few characters in most scenes—
almost always one to three at any one time—the space seemed open and
nearly empty. Moeller accentuated this openness by usually spreading out
the few pieces of furniture across the stage with no attempt to create

68. Nichols, "New," Jan. 31, 1928, p. 12.
69. Pulaski, "Strange," p. 52.
70. Stark Young, "The New O'Neill Play," *New Republic* 53 (Feb. 15, 1928): 350.
71. Five photographs, MCNY; twenty photographs, Yale.
72. Six ground plans, O'Neill, *Strange Interlude* promptbook, NYPL. The Yale
promptbook also has reproductions of the ground plans, but they are very pale.
73. R. S., "The Theatre," *Wall Street Journal,* Feb. 2, 1928, p. 4.
74. Atkinson, "Strange," Jan. 31, 1928, p. 28.

conversational units. As a result, he heightened the isolation of the characters and enhanced the play's dual presentational and representational acting styles created by the asides.

Furthermore, Moeller incorporated little movement throughout the play. The promptbooks indicate only occasional blocking (characters frequently sat or stood in one location for extended periods of time), and most of this movement was individual crosses, rarely multiple character movements. Helburn verified this in 1929 when she wrote that "Moeller permitted no unnecessary movement to intrude into the production, there was no deliberate breaking up of groupings in a conscious striving for variety. He stripped the action to its essentials."[75] While there is no reason to doubt this, the extraordinary amount of arrested motion followed by normal activity must have had the effect of copious movement.

Although most of the lighting for these settings was rather ordinary in color, angle, and location (Atkinson found it "indifferent"),[76] a few special effects were attempted, and one was especially memorable. The use of footlights throughout created grotesque shadows and an unnatural cast on faces as the full-stage photographs reveal, but the footlights were useful for highlighting asides.[77] Most significant, however, was a special amber spotlight which came up on Nina when she knocked on the wooden table at the conclusion of a long series of asides while surrounded by her three men. This scene, which was mentioned more frequently than any other in reviews, was the most stylized and abstract, yet moving in performance.

Moeller devoted little attention, however, to the use of sound, which was, according to O'Neill, put off until the last moment, with less than desirable results.[78] Offstage sound was important only in the final two scenes. An airplane-motor effect was mounted on each side of the stage in the flies for Gordon's departure in act IX and caused no difficulties.[79] For the boat race in act VIII, however, last-minute collections of whistles, sirens, bells, and buckets of water did not suggest believably the slow-building cacophony of sound which was meant to rise to "perfect pandemonium" as Gordon won his crew race.

Although five of the six settings of the production fitted into the four pilasters, the designs can be categorized as four types: shallow interior,

75. Helburn, "Staged," p. 59.

76. Atkinson, "Strange," Jan. 31, 1928, p. 28.

77. "Light Equipment" and "Light Plot" in O'Neill, *Strange Interlude* promptbook, NYPL.

78. O'Neill letter to Theatre Guild (1928 or 1929) in Roy S. Waldau, *Vintage Years of the Theatre Guild, 1928–1939* (Cleveland: Case Western Reserve University, 1972), p. 46.

79. "Light Plot" and "Property Plot" in O'Neill, *Strange Interlude* promptbook, NYPL.

deep interior, shallow exterior, and shipboard. Shallow interiors appeared in acts I-VI (all of part 1 and the first act of part 2). The first of these, the Leeds' library, which was used in acts I, II, and IV, was a rectangle, the walls of which were lined with books. All of the shelves and books, however, were simply painted on the flats, despite the fact that the two high windows which divided the wall of books upstage had practical drapes and shades. The walls continued up into the flies out of sight, as did the walls of all interiors. Furniture was scattered across the stage in a gentle arc resulting in horizontal emphasis of the space, which was further pronounced by recessed doors on the right and left walls. It was in the furniture arrangement throughout the production, incidentally, that the designs most frequently departed from O'Neill's directions. The flatness of this setting was obvious, but Moeller did not have grouping difficulties, since no more than three actors appeared at a time. The very symmetrical arrangement of scenery and furnishings was repeated in most of the settings and emphasized the formality of the world of the characters.

Only in act III did an interior have three entrances, but the rectangular space of the Evans' dining room matched that of the library. The right and left doors were in the same locations as the library, but the upstage door and window are farther right and left than the library windows according to the ground plan. In photographs, however, their location seems the same. The deliberately tasteless room was painted a "repulsive brown" and dressed with furniture placed at extreme right and left stage, leaving center stage open—a significant shift from the library. Although this scene had little physical activity, and never more than two actors at once, Moeller created a dynamic stage picture with Nina on her knees at the feet of Mrs. Evans as the mother-in-law made her dreadful announcement of mental illness in the Evans family.

Despite the fact that only four characters appeared in acts V and VI, Moeller produced some of his most memorable staging in the third shallow interior, the sitting room of a Long Island cottage. As in act III, Moeller and Mielziner left the stage bare at center, with furniture scattered over the right and left sides. Although some of the furniture was changed for more tasteful items in act VI to demonstrate the change in fortune for Evans, the furniture arrangement differed only slightly, leaving even more open space at center. The wallpapered flats remained the same in both acts, and the upstage wall was dominated by a central curtained archway which allowed different traffic patterns from those possible in preceding acts.

Moeller was intrigued by the final exchanges of act V which closed part I. "Three rhythms of mood," he said, "cross each other physically as well as psychologically."[80] These were three duets featuring Nina with Darrell, Darrell with Evans, and Evans with Nina. Each conversation revealed desperation in a different character, and together the scenes encapsulated the dilemma of Nina. Moeller closed the action with a kind of pietà as Nina held Evans in both resignation and despair, much as Cybel had held the dying Brown two seasons earlier.

Moeller's "most memorable scene,"[81] however, was the close of act VI, where Nina gathered all three of her men for the first time in the play (this was also the first time in the play that more than three characters appeared on stage at once). Although O'Neill's direction called for Nina to remain "standing, dominating them" as they sat around the table stage left, Moeller had her sit among them, but kept her on a higher level. According to the promptbook, she still dominated in this position and ended the group reverie by rapping on the table. Moeller said that the lights changed (amber spot up on Nina) as the action lapsed "into an unreal world" with arrested motion for all until Nina broke the spell.[82]

The sitting room of the Park Avenue apartment in act VII was the production's only deep interior (see illustration 12). Still using the four pilasters to mount left and right walls, Mielziner continued the walls upstage to almost twice their depth, using tapestries hung from battens instead of wall units. The upstage wall had two sets of double doors separated by a large tapestry which disappeared into the flies. Although this room was nearly twice as large as the previous rooms (ostensibly to indicate the Evans' wealth), the elegant furniture was spread across the stage in a pattern similar to the library arrangement. The furniture pieces were so distanced from each other that no conversational groupings are evident in the impersonal room, which suggested a presentational style.

The final act of *Strange Interlude* presented the only exterior, a garden terrace of the Evans' estate, which was a completely open space bounded by a garden wall covered with vines upstage and an entrance at center, opening upstage onto a low ground row and sky drop. At the stage-right side was an arbor entrance matched on stage left by steps and a door to the house. These walls fitted into the four pilasters, creating a rectangular space identical to the shallow interiors. The only set properties in the playing space were two low benches down left and up right; again the central space was open. Although this design was practical and in keeping with the interior scheme, the setting was the starkest and most uninteresting of all.

80. Moeller, in Hutchens, "Miss," p. 8.
81. Atkinson, *Lively*, p. 62.
82. Hutchens, "Miss," p. 8; O'Neill, *Strange Interlude* promptbook, Yale, act VI, pp. 42–45.

In sharp contrast, the bright afterdeck of the yacht in act VIII was completely independent of and inside the four pilasters, which were masked downstage by curtains and upstage by the walls of the setting (see illustration 13). This was the most realistic of all designs while maintaining the stark mood which pervaded the other five, darker designs. Only the yacht setting had no walls parallel and perpendicular to the curtain line. The ship's rail ran from down right to up left center and opened out onto a sky drop. The cabin of the ship was set perpendicular to the rail, leaving a strong wall running from down left to left center. The resultant playing space was triangular, but once again the deck furniture was scattered across the stage almost in a straight line left to right. Aboard ship, however, the wicker pieces did not seem stylized in arrangement. Most striking of all in act VIII was the predominance of white in the ship's walls, beams, railing, and trim and the men's yachting pants. The brightness of the scene was further accentuated by strong daylight streaming in from stage right through the rail openings.

The most dynamic use of this space was the staging of Evans' stroke just after Gordon won his race. As Nina and her men crowded around the dying Evans, only the youthful Madeline continued to stare off right into the blazing light, oblivious to the turmoil at her back.

Although some of the sets failed to live up to the magnitude of the dramatic experiment, the acting was subject to so much praise that "acted as it was last night, this play might almost take place on a bare stage."[83] Working with a cast of only nine, Moeller was lauded in particular for his apparent trust in the actors to develop freely within a flexible interpretive method. Credited with "watchful impassivity" in directing the actors, he was congratulated for "keeping obtrusive hands off"[84] the actors and giving them the freedom to create sensitive characterizations. The actors, although very uneasy about the play, appeared to be relaxed with the roles, as they interpreted "without appearing to do so" and avoided the "'pointing' [and] straining after effect"[85] which Clark often found in Guild productions.

Commended for "extraordinary skill"[86] and "the finest acting,"[87] the cast was also cited for intelligence and alertness in assuming the task of such wordy roles, multitudinous asides, and arrested motion. Several critics found the asides virtually superfluous, since the actors made so much of this secret material clear in their performance.[88] Moeller himself

83. Nichols, "New," Jan. 31, 1928, p. 12.
84. Sayler, "Play," Feb. 11, 1928, p. 590.
85. Clark, "Eugene," Mar. 1928, p. 170.
86. Hammond, "Theaters," Jan. 31, 1928, p. 18.
87. Littell, "O'Neill's," Jan. 31, 1928, p. 18.
88. For example, John Mason Brown, "Intermission," *Theatre Arts* 12 (Apr. 1928): 240.

noted "the brilliant intuition of my players"[89] in attacking the roles, while even O'Neill told an interviewer that many of his textual cuts were due to the actors' ability to project the subtextual material without the assistance of words.[90]

Despite apparent honesty of acting interpretation, however, the actors spoke "a bastard sort of British English, an accent that sounds too much like Broadway trying to ape Piccadilly. O'Neill's characters," Clark continued, "are American, and no honest-to-God American says, 'bean' when he means 'been.'"[91] This use of pseudo-British stage speech was reportedly typical of many Guild productions in the 1920s.[92]

Surrounding the stunning Nina Leeds of Lynn Fontanne was an effective "symphony of devoted males from whom she draws weirdly fascinating but inevitably discordant harmonies."[93] Moeller skillfully helped Glenn Anders, Tom Powers, and Earle Larimore to maintain a tense but varied tempo and pace with their "repressed intensity,"[94] dottiness, and effective physical aging, respectively, all of which defined their shifting orbits around their mutual object of desire.

It was Fontanne's performance, however, which captured the fascination of so many theatergoers. Years later Atkinson still remembered vividly her aggressive, magnetic characterization as a "cool, detached, menacing *femme fatale* (the American flower of evil)."[95] The tall, forty-year-old actress, who always looked much younger than her years, had not appeared in an O'Neill play since the ill-fated *Chris Christophersen*. Although *Strange Interlude* would be her last production with O'Neill, she worked frequently with Moeller, who understood her intellectual character evaluation, delicate artistic temperament, and approach to the play text (which did not include reverence for the playwright's dialogue). While Moeller persuaded her to adhere to O'Neill's words, he did not prevent her from some impulsive, unannounced cutting of lines, especially asides, which irritated her.[96]

Fontanne was nevertheless producing some of the best work of her career. Extraordinarily efficient in the presentation of her asides as well as making the transitions between the two styles of delivery, Fontanne

89. Moeller, "Some Notes," p. 26.
90. Watts, "Realism," Feb. 5, 1928, p. 2.
91. Clark, "Eugene," Mar. 1928, p. 170.
92. Interview with Marion Thompson, MCNY, Dec. 28, 1982.
93. Sayler, "Play," Feb. 11, 1928, p. 590.
94. Anderson, "Strange," p. 59.
95. Atkinson, *Lively*, p. 4.
96. Jared Brown, *The Fabulous Lunts* (New York: Atheneum, 1986), p. 167; Zolotow, *Stagestruck*, p. 156.

shifted moods gracefully, sensitively, and delicately. De Casseres summed up the effect of her performance: "Subtle, defiant, tigerish, sweet, amoral, cajoling by turns, she plays her difficult part in a minor key of prolonged intensity."[97] In Fontanne Moeller fortunately had a remarkable actress with whom the audience remained enchanted, their weariness notwithstanding.

Despite difficulties with sound and several unmemorable settings, most of Moeller's work with *Strange Interlude* was clearly outstanding. Seldes failed to imagine "how his direction could have been bettered,"[98] and Helburn later recalled that in 1928 Moeller "was at the peak of his brilliance as a director."[99] In his first attempt with O'Neill's "structural aberrations"[100] Moeller demonstrated that he was a fitting director to join O'Neill on his theatrical odyssey of experiment. With his next O'Neill production, Moeller demonstrated the same care as with *Strange Interlude*, but he could not turn *Dynamo* into a popular or critical success.

Dynamo

The undiminishing desire of O'Neill to experiment led Sayler when reviewing *Strange Interlude* to wish that the playwright "would linger with a new form . . . before he plunges on to fresh adventures."[101] With regard to the most significant device in *Strange Interlude*, the asides, O'Neill seemed to follow Sayler's advice with his next production. When *Dynamo* appeared, however, on Monday, February 11, 1929,[102] O'Neill demonstrated once again that each new play would break new theatrical ground, even in failure.

In his positive review of *Dynamo* Atkinson observed that O'Neill had clearly "cut loose from the realistic drama, perhaps for all time."[103] An overwhelming majority of critics, however, lamented the squandering of such a stunning production on poor dramatic material. Skinner, for example, called *Dynamo* "a case of immense talent in playwriting, acting and production all being wasted on the immature profundities of a man whose intelligence cannot catch up with his chaotic and intense feelings."[104] Once again Moeller and the Guild served O'Neill well with dynamic,

97. Benjamin De Casseres, "Broadway to Date," *Arts & Decoration*, Apr. 1928, p. 103.
98. Seldes, "Theatre," Apr. 1928, p. 350.
99. Helburn, *Wayward*, p. 259.
100. Smyser, "Temporary," p. 1.
101. Sayler, "Play," Feb. 11, 1928, p. 590.
102. "Theatrical Notes" and advertisement, *New York Times*, Feb. 11, 1929, p. 27. The first reviews appeared on Tuesday, Feb. 12, 1929.
103. Brooks Atkinson, "God in the Machine," *New York Times*, Feb. 12, 1929, p. 22.
104. R. Dana Skinner, "The Play," *Commonweal* 9 (Feb. 27, 1929): 490.

sensitive direction of problematic material, but *Dynamo* was a dramaturgical blunder.

After his triumph with *Strange Interlude* Moeller was evaluated as a more serious theater artist. In an interview which appeared the day before *Dynamo* premiered, for example, Moeller was now described as "this intense and deeply mystical interpreter of O'Neill's tragedies."[105] Subsequent reviews of *Dynamo*, after expressing bitter disappointment with O'Neill's work, praised Moeller's effectiveness, imagination, picturization, resourcefulness, and clarity. Garland, for example, wrote that Moeller's direction was "so skillful . . . so *fortissimo* with the good spots, so *piano* with the poor, that Mr. Moeller's mind would be interesting to read."[106] Intending praise, Atkinson remarked that the dedicated performance and its direction were "as broad and audacious as [O'Neill's] story."[107] Moeller not only captured the style of the play but also sustained an emotional commitment to *Dynamo* throughout the rehearsal period which kept the actors likewise enthusiastic.

Although in retrospect O'Neill blamed himself entirely for rushing the play to production and failing to attend any rehearsals (since he had left the country with Carlotta Monterey),[108] his absence may have helped to keep Moeller dedicated to the script, which needed much cutting and nursing. O'Neill began composition of the play in 1927, but it was not completed until the fall of 1928, when he immediately submitted it to the Guild by mail and was never present to work on cutting or revision with Moeller despite the fact that the play was not quite ready for production.[109]

Cutting and revision were necessary, however, and O'Neill's notes and guidelines which accompanied the script gave Moeller and the Guild no specific instructions about cutting.[110] As Langner later wrote, "We greatly missed Gene at rehearsals for clarification and cutting, and had to do the best we could."[111] Moeller, of course, tried to be as faithful as he

105. Barnes, "Moeller," p. 5.

106. Robert Garland, "Eugene O'Neill's 'Dynamo' Displayed in 45th Street," *New York Telegram*, Feb. 12, 1929 in Miller, *Playwright's*, p. 63.

107. Atkinson, "God," p. 22.

108. O'Neill letter to Guild, in Langner, *Magic*, pp. 241–42; O'Neill letter to Banjamin De Casseres, in Gelbs, *O'Neill*, p. 689.

109. When O'Neill left for Europe in Feb. 1928 he thought that the Guild could "very well put on my stuff for a couple of years without me." He later changed his mind. O'Neill letter to Macgowan, Feb. 22, 1928, in Bryer, *Letters*, p. 171. See also George Jean Nathan, "The Theatre," *American Mercury* 63 (Oct. 1946): 463; Sheaffer, *Artist*, pp. 305, 324; Gelbs, *O'Neill*, pp. 677, 680.

110. Eugene O'Neill, manuscript notes, outline, and drawings for *Dynamo*, Sept. 1928 in Yale Collection of American Literature, Beinecke, Yale.

111. Langner, *Magic*, p. 241.

practically could be to O'Neill's intentions, but without the playwright for conference and approval, the director was forced to revise the play according to his own predilections with the approval of the Guild board.[112]

While Moeller made extensive cuts throughout the play for length and streamlining, most of the eliminated material came from acts II and III. Nevertheless, the promptbooks are much longer than the first edition, especially acts I and III. The production included another character, Rocco, a floorman at the power plant, who is not in the published version. O'Neill kept the plant operator Jennings in the published play but eliminated his dialogue; both Rocco and Jennings had several pages of dialogue in act III in production. Reverend Light was also included in act III in production, but O'Neill eliminated him from this act in the revised script. Moeller therefore had several more actors on stage in the final act than is suggested by the published play.[113]

The most significant changes which affected dialogue and staging occurred in act III. Moeller and his designer, Lee Simonson, eliminated the exterior of the powerhouse and created a large open construction which revealed all portions of the plant at once. As a result, O'Neill's two exterior and three interior scenes of act III were played continuously, with no scene changes.[114] This alteration necessitated minor cutting, changing and movement of some events, and occasional creation of entrance or exit lines to facilitate melding of the scenes.[115]

Moeller became obsessed with the ideas of *Dynamo* and managed to infect both the cast and the production team with his verve. "Phil seemed almost to hypnotize himself with the mood of the play," Helburn recalled. "He became possessed by the unreal, mystic values."[116] During preproduction preparations in December, and throughout rehearsals in January and early February, Moeller took Simonson and his stage manager, Herbert Biberman, on numerous field trips to power plants all over New York and Connecticut (Stevenson, Connecticut, was the specific site O'Neill had in mind when writing the play). In the first week of February Moeller even took the principal actors to Connecticut to get a first-hand

112. After the failure of the production O'Neill severely cut and reworked the material for publication. Thus the first edition (Oct. 1929) is considerably different from the produced play.

113. *Dynamo* program, MCNY; Eugene O'Neill, *Dynamo,* bound promptbook, Theatre Guild Collection, Beinecke, Yale; Eugene O'Neill, *Dynamo,* bound promptbook, Theatre Collection, Performing Arts Center, NYPL, copyrighted 1929 by Yale University; Eugene O'Neill, *Dynamo* (New York: Horace Liveright, 1929).

114. For publication O'Neill changed act III to one exterior and two interior scenes.

115. "Scene Designs of Latest Art Used by Guild," *New York Herald-Tribune,* Feb. 24, 1929, sec. 7. p. 2.

116. Helburn, *Wayward,* pp. 184–85.

sense of a modern electrical power plant.[117] The director clearly wanted to pursue all available preparation avenues in the absence of O'Neill.

As an experimental work *Dynamo* used asides as in *Strange Interlude* and simultaneous staging as in *Desire Under the Elms*, but the effects of these devices were considerably different. In addition, the use of sound, especially nonmusical sound, was more extensive than in any previous O'Neill play. The production's "continuous and generous use of sounds and noises"[118] was specifically desired by O'Neill as recurring dramatic motifs meant to enhance the onstage action. He even considered sound a significant structural device for *Dynamo* and stressed in his instructions to the Guild that the sound effects were "not incidental noises but significant dramatic overtones that are an integral part of . . . the whole play."[119] Moeller and Simonson responded enthusiastically to O'Neill's plea by creating an impressive network of sound devices beneath and above the stage.

Throughout act I O'Neill wanted occasional thunder and lightning warning of a brewing storm, which finally broke at the end of the act. O'Neill's notes said the thunder should have "a menacing, brooding quality as if some Electrical God were on the hills impelling all these people."[120] In production the thunderstorm was properly managed and effectively performed, for Moeller and Simonson answered with a five-by-five-foot thunder drum mounted beneath the stage and amplified with a microphone. In addition, they used a motor-driven wind whistle below and a rainbox at stage level. All sound effects were manipulated from a control panel and executed periodically at special, often ironic points in the script.[121]

More impressive in the theater, however, was the manipulation of the powerhouse sounds in act III. Although Moeller introduced the ominous dynamo sound early in act I ("its whirring rhythm sets the pace for all the proceedings"),[122] the most dynamic uses of this sound occurred when the powerhouse setting was onstage. Seeking a background of rushing water and the "harsh, throaty, metallic purr of the dynamo,"[123]

117. "The New 'Dynamo' as Seen by O'Neill, *World*, Jan. 27, 1929, p. M-3; "Mr. O'Neill and the Audible Theatre," *New York Times*, Mar. 3, 1929, sec. 8, p. 4; photograph, *New York Herald-Tribune*, Feb. 3, 1929, sec. 9, p. 15.

118. "Mr. O'Neill," *New York Times*, Mar. 3, 1929, p. 4.

119. O'Neill, in Simonson, *Stage*, pp. 117–18. See also Waldau, *Vintage*, p. 46.

120. O'Neill, in Simonson, *Stage*, p. 118.

121. O'Neill's directions for thunder cues were generally followed with occasional additional cues. "Sound Effects," plot in O'Neill, *Dynamo* promptbook, NYPL; "Mr. O'Neill," *New York Times*, Mar. 3, 1929, p. 4; Francis R. Bellamy, "The Theatre," *Outlook and Independent* 151 (Feb. 27, 1929): 331.

122. Moeller, in Barnes, "Moeller," p. 2.

123. O'Neill, *Dynamo* promptbook, Yale, act III, pp. 1–2.

O'Neill found this special sound "symbolic and mysterious and moving."[124] Furthermore, he wanted the powerhouse sounds not just to provide an aural environment but to seem to control or incite much of the onstage action. Moeller reported that the results provided "an unconscious accompaniment to the dialogue,"[125] a device which was continuously at work in the background, varying in intensity to accent the action of act III.

These numerous sound cues were marked throughout the promptbooks and became more numerous as the play built to a climax in the final scene. Littell verified that at frequent intervals the dynamo sounds became more noticeable.[126] The effects were manipulated by adjusting the amplifier from the control board, since the dynamo and water sounds were created by a small generator and a low-pressure vacuum line, each equipped with its own microphone. Furthermore, the speakers for the dynamo's "siren hum"[127] were mounted inside the onstage dynamo,[128] thus enhancing the immediacy of the effect.

Once again O'Neill gave all characters asides, usually initiating scenes with interior monologues and often inserting back-to-back asides in a manner similar to that in *Strange Interlude*. This time, however, the asides were less provocative, less vital, and, most significantly, less contradictory in relation to the spoken words. As Wyatt noted, "The two families in *Dynamo* are very simple folk, their words and their thoughts usually tally." In consequence, the device became "dull and repetitious."[129] Littell found that the asides "served rather more as necessary autobiography than as illumination of the secret places of the heart."[130] *Dynamo* lacked the individualized "subjective responses"[131] of intelligent people which made *Strange Interlude* fascinating.

O'Neill himself eventually realized the unsuitability of asides for *Dynamo*, recognizing that they were a "special expression for a special type of modern neurotic, disintegrated soul . . . [and that they were] quite alien to [the] essential psychological form of *Dynamo*'s characters."[132] This,

124. O'Neill letter to Guild, in Waldau, *Vintage*, p. 46.

125. Moeller, in Barnes, "Moeller," p. 2.

126. Robert Littell, "The Theatre Guild Presents 'Dynamo.'" *New York Evening Post*, Feb. 12, 1929, p. 12.

127. Percy Hammond, "The Theaters: Dynamo," *New York Herald-Tribune*, Feb. 12, 1929, in Miller, *Playwright's*, p. 64.

128. "Mr. O'Neill," *New York Times*, Mar. 3, 1929, p. 4; "Sound Effects" plot in O'Neill, *Dynamo* promptbook, NYPL.

129. Euphemia Van Rensselaer Wyatt, "The Drama," *Catholic World*, Apr. 1929, p. 81.

130. Robert Littell, "The Land of Second Best," *Theatre Arts* 13 (Apr. 1929), 246–47.

131. Moeller, in Barnes, "Moeller," p. 2.

132. Eugene O'Neill, "Working Notes and Extracts from a Fragmentary Work Diary," in Barrett H. Clark, ed., *European Theories of the Drama* (New York: Crown, 1947), p. 534.

more than production problems, seemed to O'Neill a chief failing of the play.

Moeller, on the other hand, admired the structure of *Dynamo*, the asides of which served as "a sort of contrapuntal melody"[133] to the dialogue. The director's method for delivery of the asides was similar to the arrested motion of *Strange Interlude*, but his description in the promptbook seems more obvious and abrupt than his gentle approach to physical quiet in *Strange Interlude*. "Whenever a thought is being said," he wrote, "all other people are static . . . and the person beginning the thought has the liberty of movement. When a person finishing a thought begins a speech to the others, all move out of their held positions simultaneously and the person speaking begins with an attack to emphasize the change in character of his or her speech. The held positions are not only normal repose, an extended hand or a gesture is held thru another persons [sic] thought."[134] Furthermore, the actors were spread all over the stage on different levels, making the simultaneous reanimation seem more pervasive.

As in *Desire Under the Elms*, O'Neill wanted simultaneous exterior and interior action, often in three or four different areas of the stage, but this time he needed a pair of two-story houses on stage at once, with a playable area between. He even sent sketches of possible settings[135] which clearly demonstrated what he had in mind (another removable wall scheme), but Moeller and Simonson constructed a very different environment while maintaining in principle the basic plan submitted by the playwright.

Always more interested in setting designs as architecture than as painting, in designs which achieved "the balance of structural surfaces and the play of light upon them,"[136] Simonson produced a pragmatic but stunning design which offered Moeller more freedom to manipulate and design onstage action than would have been possible in O'Neill's scheme. With *Dynamo* Simonson and Moeller worked according to Simonson's ideal of director and designer as alter egos. They harmoniously complemented one another's conceptions by producing and using a space which expressed the essential rhythms and moods of the play.

Dynamo was mounted in the four-year-old Martin Beck Theatre, on the then "unfashionable" side of Eighth Avenue, a standard house with a beautiful Byzantine interior (in remarkable contrast to the settings it

133. Moeller, in "Mr. O'Neill," *New York Times*, Mar. 3, 1929, p. 4.

134. "Production note" in O'Neill, *Dynamo* promptbook, Yale, act I, before p. 1.

135. O'Neill, "Manuscript Notes," Yale. The drawings are reproduced in Floyd, *Eugene Work*, pp. 142–148.

136. Simonson, *Stage*, p. 16; Simonson, *Part*, p. 47.

housed) but a shallow stage.[137] The production had two basic settings, which varied markedly according to the selective lighting incorporated. Although O'Neill's suggested plans were realistic in appearance, he wrote the Guild that it would not be necessary to maintain a realistic format.[138] Taking the playwright at his word and following his own principle of elimination of detail to heighten scenic effect, Simonson produced a constructivist design which served Moeller quite well but troubled the playwright when he saw photographs. In retrospect O'Neill believed that *Dynamo* was too dependent upon director and stage designer to be effective as drama.[139]

Critics, however, were impressed by the settings and Moeller's use of them. Moeller and Simonson boldly employed "a full stage—height and breadth"[140]—to fashion an environment which was "half symbol, half real,"[141] but sweepingly effective, inventive, and imaginative. Moeller created "many unforgettable pictures"[142] utilizing the variety of levels provided by Simonson and incorporating the frequent simultaneous activity suggested by O'Neill.

Given the demands of the settings, Moeller needed the actual stage and finished sets earlier than usual, so the Martin Beck was cleared by about February 3 or 4. Although Simonson had the two stage houses ready in time for the move, the power plant came late. In order to get the four levels and unusual height necessary to rehearse the scenes of act III, Moeller and Simonson stacked additional platforms atop one of the flat-roofed houses and connected the levels with rehearsal stairs while the complicated setting was being constructed.[143]

For the first two acts *Dynamo* needed two houses in contrasting styles, houses which could be opened to reveal upstairs and downstairs interiors while suggesting very different life styles and value systems (see illustration 14). Seeking a few details to suggest the whole, Simonson built what Benchley labeled "erecto-houses,"[144] outlines of houses with "skele-

137. Henderson, *City,* p. 257; Pichel, *Modern,* p. 64.

138. "Scene," *New York Herald-Tribune,* Feb. 24, 1929, p. 2.

139. O'Neill letter to Macgowan, June 14, 1929, in Bryer, *Letters,* p. 191.

140. Brooks Atkinson, "Concluding a Dramatic Cycle," *New York Times,* Feb. 17, 1929, sec. 9, p. 1.

141. Percy Hammond, "The Theaters," *New York Herald-Tribune,* Feb. 17, 1929, sec. 7, p. 1.

142. Littell, "Land," Apr. 1929, p. 246.

143. "What 'Dynamo' Looked Like During Rehearsals," clipping with drawing by Eugen Fitsch, Theatre Collection, MCNY; "New," *World,* Jan. 27, 1929, p. M-3.

144. Robert Benchley, "Dynamo," *Life* (New York), Mar. 8, 1929, in Cargill, *O'Neill,* p. 188.

tonized walls but practical doors."[145] Photographs and ground plans[146] reveal that neither house was shown in its entirety, as each unit was slightly raked with the offstage end of the house closer to the proscenium line. Each house disappeared right and left into the wings, suggesting that more lay beyond line of sight.

Although the houses at first viewing seemed to offer little differentiation in their uniform incompleteness, matching door, stair and window placement, and identical color (a nondescript gray-brown), closer examination reveals that the house of the Fife family at stage left was flat-roofed with a curving, pseudo-Spanish facade along the downstage and stage-right roof lines, whereas the Light family house stage right had a peaked, gabled roof. Furthermore, the furnishings were very distinct in style and color. Dark Victorian furniture in the Light house was upholstered in gray, black, and dark red, while the Fife furniture was of modern design, primarily wicker, colored in green, brown, pink, and flowered patterns. To contrast with the stark Light interior, the Fifes also had many more furnishings, including a gilt mirror and a living plant. Most significant, however, was the contrast of the Lights' oil lamps with the electric illumination of the Fife house.[147] Overall, Carb found that the houses expressed "the temperament of the people who live in them exactly, [were] excellent for the purpose, and [were] pictorially effective."[148]

The most striking aspect of this setting was the open space below and between the houses contrasted by the tiny, confining, low-ceilinged rooms inside the structures. Only two set properties appeared onstage outside the houses: a thin, low, gray picket fence running perpendicular to the curtain line and defining the property line (O'Neill had asked for a hedge), and a tall telephone pole up left center strung with power lines and watching over the Fife house, not unlike the trees of *Desire Under the Elms*. Otherwise the stage was bare and backed by a transparency for daytime scenes; a dark-blue cyclorama was used for nocturnal scenes. The transparency was lit from behind, with the projection of a powerhouse in the distance, and the entire stage picture was outlined by black drapes just inside the proscenium arch.

The greatest service such a set provided for the play was the capability of simultaneous staging and scene changing by simply raising and lowering light intensity instead of shifting panels. Therefore, the

145. "Scenery Plot" in O'Neill, *Dynamo* promptbook. NYPL, p. 3.
146. Nine photographs, Yale and MCNY; three ground plans in O'Neill, *Dynamo* promptbook, Yale.
147. "Scenery Plot" in O'Neill, *Dynamo* promptbook, NYPL.
148. David Carb, "Seen on the Stage," *Vogue*, Mar. 30, 1929, p. 102.

scenes of act I which O'Neill meant to be played as if no time lapsed between them were done with no interruption. Atkinson verified that the action in the four rooms moved "in quick succession;"[149] indeed, here were the smoothest scene transitions in an O'Neill play to date. To facilitate the changes Simonson mounted numerous lighting instruments inside the houses as well as in standard positions. Strip lights were placed on each story and hidden by the framework of the houses. Throughout act I the lighting intensity levels were changed twenty-five times as the primary focus shifted from room to room or outside. The brewing thunderstorm frequently accented the lighting as carbon sticks were operated offstage from a gallery high above the lighting switchboard. Thus, intense flashes of bright white light periodically inundated the stage.[150]

One of Moeller's biggest staging problems with this setting was creating interesting compositions despite the small, confining rooms of the houses. When looking at the rooms, the possibilities for significant movement or interesting composition seem all but impossible. Therefore, Moeller gave very specific movement direction to actors when inside the houses but allowed them his usual freedom when outside. For example, a typical direction of Moeller's in another promptbook will read "cross right," whereas for *Dynamo* the cross may read "cross 3 steps right."

This problem was of course mollified by the director's ability to display action simultaneously in different rooms and houses as well as outside. Moeller not only followed O'Neill's indications of simultaneous action but, by showing all areas at once, continued with additional domestic action which would have been unseen had O'Neill's wall scheme been used. Stage directions indicate that actors in both houses were always onstage and in view. Lights were brighter on the scenes with dialogue and asides, but no area was entirely extinguished. Accordingly, when individual characters or a family were not in the written scene, they assumed "a semblance of living naturally in their quarters;"[151] as the promptbook states, "small business may be engaged in by those in the dimmed areas."[152] When a character began an aside, however, all characters on all parts of the stage froze.

Moeller often had actors at work in all areas of the setting at once. In the first scene, for example, the Reverend Light was in his house downstairs while Mrs. Light worked upstairs, Reuben lingered outside at the

149. Atkinson, "Concluding," Feb. 17, 1929, p. 1.
150. "Light Plot" in O'Neill, *Dynamo* promptbook, Yale; "Sound Effects" in O'Neill, *Dynamo* promptbook, NYPL.
151. "Scene," *New York Herald-Tribune*, Feb. 24, 1929, p. 2.
152. "Production Note" in O'Neill, *Dynamo* promptbook, Yale.

fence, and the Fife family were in their house both upstairs and down. Asides were delivered from three different locations, so the freezes moved about the stage.

Simonson's powerhouse setting of act III remains one of his most memorable achievements (see illustration 15). Clark called this design and Moeller's use of it "a remarkable piece of stage setting and directing."[153] Nearly all critics echoed these sentiments, finding the three-dimensional metal, glass, and wooden structure which extended high into the air beyond the proscenium arch imaginative and accurate, modern and beautiful, clean and gleaming, "satanic and awesome"[154] in its reality as the literal was heightened to an impressive stage symbol.

The setting had four different acting levels which Moeller and Simonson called A, B, C, and D. Stage level (A) had a large gray dynamo stage right backed by a high wall with narrow windows extending up to the proscenium arch. The stage-left side was filled with a tri-level switch gallery (B, C, and D). B could be reached by stairs from A or a door on the upstage wall of B. Another staircase rose from B to C and a third stairway rose from C to D. The playable space grew progressively smaller as the actors climbed, and actors could leave the performance area from D and exit upstage to the unseen water dam. Nearly all construction was metal pipe and aluminum sheeting, or wood painted to resemble metal. Everything was painted gray, black, or white, except for a green plate-glass floor for C, the underneath side of which could be seen by much of the audience. The size and apparent accuracy of the setting was awe inspiring.[155]

When working on the upper platforms, Moeller found again that he had to be specific with movement directions, especially since areas were often isolated with lights. The two most dynamic moments in staging and lighting in act III occurred with the seduction of Reuben by Ada and Reuben's suicide. In a volatile moment which led to a "scarlet interlude hidden by a virtuous curtain," as Hammond would have it, Ada, who was costumed provocatively "in a leggy red dress,"[156] first distracted Reuben before growing frightened as he grabbed and kissed her passionately and bent her backward toward the floor, ending on top of her just before a blackout. The action took place high on level C and was accentuated by

153. Barrett H. Clark, "O'Neill's 'Dynamo' and the Village Experiments," *Drama* 19 (Apr. 1929): 222.

154. Benjamin De Casseres, "Broadway to Date," *Arts & Decoration*, Apr. 1929, p. 118.

155. Ground plan and isometric drawing in O'Neill, *Dynamo* promptbook, Yale; "Scenery Plot," in O'Neill, *Dynamo* promptbook, NYPL.

156. Hammond, "Theaters," Feb. 12, 1929, pp. 64–65.

the green glass through which some of the audience could watch the couple sinking to the floor. This was the only point within the act where Moeller interrupted the action with a curtain.

At the climax of the play Reuben killed himself by climbing on top of the dynamo and thrusting his hands into the open top in a "vivid . . . exhibit of electrocution."[157] Critics found this representation graphic and realistic, "a blue, sparkling suicide"[158] which required the careful and imaginative coordination of several special effects. The head of the dynamo was equipped with a spark-gap mechanism with two points just visible on top. An eight-inch spark jump was created at this point and was heightened by red and blue strip lights mounted inside the dynamo, which had many openings through which the colored light could stream out. When Glenn Anders as Reuben seemed to shove his hands into the dynamo, his hands were actually about a foot or so away from the two rods. As his hands went in, a bluish-white spark was fired for approximately ten seconds. At the same time the dynamo's red and blue lights came up and the regular set lighting dimmed to below half. The dynamo humming sounds stopped abruptly. When the spark ended and Reuben fell dead, all was deathly quiet for about one page of dialogue and action. Then the dynamo sound started up again, lights were restored, and the dynamo built to a very loud humming which ended the play.[159]

Of the six principal actors in *Dynamo* all but Claudette Colbert (Ada Fife) had considerable previous experience under Moeller's direction, and three, Helen Westley (Mrs. Light), Dudley Digges (Mr. Fife), and Glenn Anders (Reuben Light), had acted in *Strange Interlude* or *Marco Millions.* As a result, the cast was basically well chosen in order to approach O'Neill's material and create an ensemble without constant explanation from Moeller, who was preoccupied with finalizing the script in O'Neill's absence.

In general the acting was highly praised for believable, human characterization, even if it sometimes became rather rhetorical and homiletic in vocal delivery. This was especially true in act III when the play suddenly became more mystical and hysterical. "Charged with a mad fury,"[160] the characters relentlessly pursued their devastating goals as the actors performed "in bold, free strokes and booming voices."[161] Moeller

157. Hammond, "Theaters," Feb. 12, 1929, p. 65.
158. Charles Brackett, "The Theatre," *New Yorker,* Feb. 23, 1929, p. 27.
159. O'Neill, *Dynamo* promptbook, Yale, act III, pp. 56–58; "Sound Effects" and "Light Plot," in O'Neill, *Dynamo* promptbook, NYPL; "Mr. O'Neill," *New York Times,* Mar. 3, 1929, p. 4; Littell, "Theatre," Feb. 12, 1929, p. 12.
160. Atkinson, "God," p. 22.
161. Atkinson, "Concluding," p. 1.

had inspired his actors and carried "the cast with him on a wave of enthusiasm"[162] which resulted in powerful and dedicated performances.

Three performances especially demonstrated the verve of production, the actor's freedom granted by Moeller, and the desire of the director to inject or allow comic relief when possible. Although O'Neill demanded that the dreamy character of Mrs. Fife never become comic, Catherine Doucet's soft, sentimental performance both captured the dreaminess effectively, and sometimes through slight, amusing exaggeration in vocal drawling, "moon-gazing,"[163] and evasive, "wistful vagaries [provided] the only comedy relief to the unhappy mental ejaculations of her neighbors."[164] Without O'Neill on hand to complain, Moeller was free to provide mellow contrast to the strident frenzy which dominated so much of the play.

The young flapper of Claudette Colbert was distressing to some reviewers, who found her displaying herself self-consciously with her vibrant, flippant energy and alluring physical charms, but again Moeller achieved useful contrast in mood by essentially leaving the actress to her own devices except for basic movement and compositional placement. She imbued the role with "tingling, invigorating femininity"[165] and often posed in a straightforward and vivid manner which bespoke a commonness of character and lack of sophistication which was nonetheless enticing. Fittingly described by Wyatt as a "Gee-but-you're-a-peach young woman,"[166] Colbert's characterization served to set in stark relief the religious and fervent depiction of Reuben Light. Brief lines of doggerel by Arthur Guiterman (misquoted elsewhere) captured a popular response to *Dynamo* and Colbert:

> Eeny, meeny, mynamo,
> I have been to 'Dynamo.'
> All except that girl in red,
> It is worse'n what you said."[167]

Glenn Anders, who quietly performed the reserved Doctor Darrell in *Strange Interlude*, created a sincere, passionate, confused young man in *Dynamo*. His Reuben, who was alternately powerful and lachrymose, commanding and whining, frequently brooded, cried, and tore his hair, and remained intense and defiant throughout[168] with "sweeping earnest-

162. Helburn, *Wayward*, p. 185.
163. Littell, "Theatre," Feb. 12, 1929, p. 12.
164. Wyatt, "Drama," Apr. 1929, p. 81.
165. Carb, "Seen," Mar. 30, 1929, p. 102.
166. Wyatt, "Drama," Apr. 1929, p. 82.
167. Arthur Guiterman, *New Yorker*, March 9, 1929, p. 19.
168. [Jack] Lait, "Dynamo," *Variety*, Feb. 13, 1929, p. 56; Arthur Ruhl, "Second Nights," *New York Herald-Tribune*, Feb. 17, 1929, sec. 7, p. 5.

ness" and "extraordinary fiery passion."[169] Ultimately the role was the devastated product of obsession and religious adoration, which theatergoers usually found admirable for the actor's stirring commitment but absurd within the world of the play. Littell, for example, wrote that Anders played "with a fine, cutting sincerity and passion . . . in a part which seemed to me often quite foolish." But the critic went on the say, "I do not see how it could have been played better."[170] Despite the leading actor's ardor and zeal in the midst of spectacular staging, O'Neill's hero and his dramatic situation were deemed silly and ridiculous.

Young complained that both play and production attempted to make too literal a story and conflict which should have remained ethereal and mystical.[171] Most critics, however, agreed with Boyd's assessment: "Neither the excellent acting . . . nor the fine production could conceal the essential shallowness and adolescent pretentiousness of the play."[172] Moeller nevertheless remained "blind to the obvious faults of the play"[173] while in production and managed to mount an impressive, trenchant spectacle. Perhaps O'Neill cast his material in the wrong dramatic form and Moeller was close to the truth when he said that *Dynamo* "would make a magnificent modern opera."[174]

Mourning Becomes Electra

Understandably disturbed by the failure of *Dynamo*, O'Neill did not allow another Guild production of a new play without his presence and thorough participation during the rehearsal and cutting process. When *Mourning Becomes Electra* premiered at the Guild Theatre more than two years after the close of *Dynamo*, O'Neill had attended nearly every rehearsal and worked closely with Philip Moeller in preparing the performance script.[175]

This repressive, often lurid exploration of "the immemorial religion of the dead"[176] was reviewed by many as a stark tragedy, by others as a sensational melodrama. Whatever generic label seems most appropriate, the dynamic play in production was found by most to be a nearly perfect actuation of the play's "smothered desires, smothered screams, smothered

169. Atkinson, "God," p. 22; Littell, "Theatre," Feb. 12, 1929, p. 12.

170. Littell, "Land," Apr. 1929, p. 246.

171. Young, *Immortal*, pp. 85–86.

172. Boyd, "Eugene," Apr. 1929, p. 180.

173. Helburn, *Wayward*, p. 185.

174. Moeller, in Barnes, "Moeller," p. 2.

175. Brooks Atkinson, "Acting at the Guild," *New York Times*, Apr. 10, 1932, sec. 8, p. 1.

176. Hugh Dickinson, *Myth on the Modern Stage* (Urbana: University of Illinois, 1969), p. 147.

action."[177] Ruhl, for example, reported that all concerned in production worked "knowingly and without waste word or gesture toward the perfect orchestration of a threnody of uninterrupted foreboding and gloom."[178] O'Neill himself later wrote that the production was splendid, "a great Guild achievement against great odds," and contributed significantly to his Nobel Prize.[179]

This play and production lay completely outside the economic tribulations and emergence of left-wing theater which had escalated since October 1929. After *Dynamo* more than a dozen proletarian theaters such as the Workers Laboratory Theatre and the Prolet Bühne arose in New York. The Group Theatre was well underway and opened *The House of Connelly* a month before *Mourning Becomes Electra* stunned theatergoers on Monday, October 26, 1931, at the Guild Theatre.[180] Despite the economic and political troubles of the Great Depression, the personal anxieties and furies of O'Neill's dramatic world took center stage.

The success of Moeller with this production lay primarily in his patience, taste, and understanding with an almost unwieldy, voluminous play text and a volatile, temperamental cast. In addition, to much general praise Moeller was applauded for creating a malevolently majestic production, which slowly worked on the audience with a relentless, sustained presentation of depressing mood and careful revelation of suffering and anxiety. "Finely disciplined restraint"[181] is how Skinner described Moeller's results with tempo and pacing, which many critics found measured and exacting but slowly escalating, and appropriately so. Hutchens, for example, wrote that Moeller gave "to the performance as a whole a background of slowly increasing force and deliberate quietude from which it draws an additional starkness of outline."[182] Although Carb and Young found the pace a bit too slow—perhaps the product of excessive reverence for the play—they nonetheless admired Moeller's taste, evenness, and clarity.[183]

Although O'Neill commenced serious composition of *Mourning Becomes Electra* soon after *Dynamo* opened, he did not have it ready for the Guild for more than two years. After accepting the play in April 1931 the Guild board rejected Moeller's request to direct it. Perhaps they were

177. Benjamin De Casseres, "Broadway to Date," *Arts & Decoration*, Jan. 1932, p. 52.
178. Ruhl, "Second," p. 1.
179. O'Neill letter to Helburn (between 1932 and 1941), in Helburn, *Wayward*, p. 278.
180. Advertisement and "Theatrical Notes," *New York Times*, Oct. 26, 1931, p. 22. Reviews first appeared on Tuesday, Oct. 27, 1931.
181. Richard Dana Skinner, "The Play," *Commonweal*, Nov. 11, 1931, p. 47.
182. John Hutchens, "Greece to Broadway," *Theatre Arts* 16 (Jan. 1932): 16.
183. David Carb, "Seen on the Stage," *Vogue*, Jan. 1, 1932, p. 76; Stark Young, "Eugene O'Neill's New Play," *New Republic* 68 (Nov. 11, 1931): 354.

concerned that the failure of *Dynamo* marked Moeller as unsuitable despite his success with *Strange Interlude*. O'Neill was of a very different opinion, however, and was very insistent with the Guild until they relented and provided the director with whom O'Neill knew he could work effectively.[184]

Returning to New York from abroad in late summer of 1931, O'Neill began meeting with Moeller to cut the script before rehearsals began. Although the play's length was reduced during preproduction, Moeller and O'Neill continued to streamline the trilogy throughout rehearsals in order to produce a playable text. Changes in the dialogue occurred almost daily from the first readings through opening day—and reportedly into the first week of the run. Alice Brady, who played the leading role of Lavinia, told an interviewer that "O'Neill kept changing and changing the lines at every rehearsal. He even made some minor changes on the day of the opening performance."[185] Most of the cuts, which O'Neill would usually make only after considering them overnight, were for purposes of shortening and reducing repetition which O'Neill did not find vital. After hearing early readings, O'Neill and Moeller were convinced that severe reductions and some rearrangement of material would be necessary, but the playwright went about it slowly and methodically.[186] Although the final acting text was much shorter than the manuscript as well as the published play, the surviving promptbooks demonstrate that no entire scenes were cut, no notable events eliminated, or any characters significantly altered.[187]

When rehearsals began on Monday, September 7, 1931, the leading role of Lavinia was still unfilled.[188] Although Alice Brady was soon added to the cast, Moeller had several readings of the play without her. Granted a full seven weeks of rehearsal time by Actors' Equity, Moeller did not allow the actors to work on their feet until the second week,[189] a practice which was not unusual for this director who liked to allow the actors to make many discoveries about the text before movement began.[190] Also,

184. Waldau, *Vintage,* p. 125; O'Neill rehearsal notes in Floyd, *Eugene Work,* p. 209.

185. Alice Brady, in Morton Eustis, "Backstage with Alice Brady," *New York Evening Post,* Oct. 31, 1931, p. 4–D.

186. Helburn, "O'Neill," p. 10; O'Neill rehearsal notes, in Floyd, *Eugene,* p. 209.

187. Eugene O'Neill, *Mourning Becomes Electra,* bound promptbook, Theatre Guild Collection, Beinecke Rare Book and Manuscript Library, Yale University; Eugene O'Neill, *Mourning Becomes Electra,* bound promptbook, Theatre Collection, Performing Arts Center, NYPL, copyrighted 1931 by Yale University; Eugene O'Neill, *Mourning Becomes Electra* (New York: Horace Liveright, 1931).

188. "O'Neill Trilogy Plans Omit All Matinees," *New York Times,* Sept. 9, 1931, p. 25.

189. O'Neill rehearsal notes, in Floyd, *Eugene,* p. 209.

190. Moeller, in Ormsbee, "Philip," p. 3.

due to his slow working methods and the size of the trilogy, Moeller was unable to have a complete runthrough of the production until about October 8 or 9,[191] only seventeen or eighteen days before opening.

Since O'Neill wanted no more catastrophes like *Dynamo*, he made himself available daily not only to Moeller but also to the performers (an unusual practice for the dramatist). He normally sat quietly and impassively at rehearsals, talking through the director but occasionally offering suggestions directly to the actors, especially in an attempt to keep the characters free of sentiment. O'Neill attended nearly every rehearsal, although he never witnessed a performance.[192]

O'Neill's telegram to the actors on opening night suggests that he was expecting a critical backlash to the production's relentless gloom and horror. He charged them to "remember the Mannon dead cheer for those" critics who "may not like what we have done."[193] Otis Chatfield-Taylor indeed complained of "gruesome and unnecessarily revolting" action,[194] but such remarks were in a minority for the play, which seemed to many reviewers surprisingly free of O'Neill's "bag of theatrical tricks"[195] and obvious experimental devices. O'Neill and Moeller were nonetheless experimenting with an external approach to acting, inordinate play length, the chorus, and the use of space.

When preparing *Mourning Becomes Electra*, O'Neill considered using masks as he had in five previous productions (especially half masks, as with the major characters in *Lazarus Laughed*) and the extended aside, as in *Strange Interlude* and *Dynamo*, but he rejected these by the time he sent the script to the Guild. Although long soliloquies remained in the acting script, few unfocused secret thoughts remained from his early drafts.[196] On the other hand, O'Neill wanted the actors to suggest a "masklike quality of the Mannon faces in repose."[197] Without obscuring the charac-

191. "O'Neill's Trilogy Set for One Day," *New York Times*, Oct. 13, 1931, p. 26.

192. Seymour Peck, "Talk With Mrs. O'Neill," *New York Times*, Nov. 4, 1956, sec. 2, pp. 1, 3; Langner, "Eugene," p. 91; Gelbs, *O'Neill*, p. 747; Alice Brady, in Eustis, "Backstage," p. 4–D; Helburn, "O'Neill," p. 10.

193. Eugene O'Neill, unpublished draft of a telegram to cast (of *Mourning Becomes Electra*, Oct. 26, 1931), Yale Collection of American Literature, Beinecke, Yale.

194. Otis Chatfield-Taylor, "The Latest Plays," *Outlook and Independent* 159 (Nov. 11, 1931): 343.

195. Skinner, "Play," Nov. 11, 1931, p. 47.

196. See especially the chantyman's soliloquy at the beginning of act IV of "The Hunted," Lavinia's soliloquy at the top of act III of "The Haunted," and Lavinia and Orin's frequent remarks to the Mannon portraits or Ezra's body when alone with them. O'Neill, *Mourning* promptbook, Yale, "The Homecoming," act II, p. 2; "The Hunted," act III, pp. 1–2; act IV, pp. 1-4; "The Haunted," act II, p. 1; act III, pp. 1–2. The pages of the promptbooks are renumbered for each act.

197. Eugene O'Neill letter to Theatre Guild, Apr. 1931, in Helburn, *Wayward*, p. 263.

ters' suffering with a changeless device, O'Neill wanted the actors to assume through their performance "a dramatic arresting visual symbol of the separateness, the fated isolation of this family."[198] This is precisely what Moeller tried to achieve with the actors. As many critics testified, the effect was evident in the Mannon family, who often kept their faces "rigid and motionless,"[199] while still revealing the characters' suffering and repressed passion.

Moeller selected his actors in consultation with the Guild board, but O'Neill was given final approval of all major roles. Although O'Neill found the casting of the play somewhat safe, stereotypical, and leaning toward "old standbys" (Alice Brady was an exception), the final acting company he felt was justifiably selected, since *Mourning Becomes Electra* is such an emotional play. He was especially pleased with the casting of the passionate Alla Nazimova as Christine.[200]

While granting his usual creative freedom to actors, Moeller coaxed a temperamental cast into a methodical manner of presentation which seemed to engage the audience as if a spell had been cast over the proceedings.[201] Careful delivery was necessary anyway in the Guild Theatre because of its peculiar acoustics,[202] but Moeller encouraged unusually slow delivery as well as movement, which suggested classic formality without departing completely from modern realism in approach to character.[203] Harry Evans described the effect in his review:

> The players subjugate themselves to the value of the smoothly flowing current of the O'Neill dialog at all times, and this repression of their actions accentuates the significance of their words, until you finally view the players as physical manifestations of ideas. . . . and in this restraint, with every inflection of the voice high-lighted, you have the impression that their efforts are being presented to you through a huge microscope.[204]

Without violating an ostensibly possible world, nearly all that was seen and heard on the stage was removed from the immediacy that theatergoers had come to expect from modern realistic production.

Although this manner of presentation was consistent with all major

198. O'Neill, "Working," p. 535.
199. Young, "Eugene," p. 354.
200. Eugene O'Neill, unpublished letter to Philip Moeller, Aug. 19, 1933, Yale Collection of American Literature, Beinecke, Yale; Moeller, in Borton, "Philip," p. 28.
201. De Casseres, "Broadway," pp. 52, 68; Atkinson, "Acting," p. 1; Ormsbee, "Philip," p. 3.
202. Robert C. Benchley, "O'Neill's *Mourning Becomes Electra*," *New Yorker*, Nov. 7, 1931, in Moses, *American*, p. 263.
203. Francis Fergusson, "A Month of the Theatre," *Bookman* 74 (Dec. 1931), 445; Young, "Eugene," p. 354.
204. Harry Evans, "Theatre," *Life* (New York), Nov. 13, 1931, p. 19.

performers in *Mourning Becomes Electra*, two actresses especially described opposite poles. Alice Brady as the cold Lavinia Mannon and Alla Nazimova as her fiery mother, Christine, not only opposed one another in their roles but represented the emotional extremes of the acting style produced by Moeller's interpretation.

Before *Mourning Becomes Electra* the attractive, thirty-nine-year-old Alice Brady had appeared for twenty years in many popular melodramas such as *The Bride of the Lamb* and *A Most Immoral Lady*, often guided by her popular producer and father, William A. Brady. Because she was often associated with "neurotic dramatics,"[205] as Atkinson would have it, many theatergoers were amazed by her cold, calculating control, physical and vocal power, emotional restraint, and brooding presence. With "quiet dominance"[206] she managed "to convey a torrent of interior emotions through an exterior of calm austerity."[207] Her ability to sustain such cold and brittle but driving and unyielding power which suggested passion without clamor was ultimately overwhelming in its command of and emotional impact on the audience.[208] She effected a "stony mask of implacable hatred"[209] and moved about the stage with a severe and rigid stateliness which insinuated an air of foreboding. From the living mask emanated a big, full voice which frequently barked commands almost in a military manner—but ominously and mysteriously, without sounding forced or contrived. The result was something of a tour de force, as her emotional fervor always seemed to lie just beneath the surface presentation. With what Atkinson called "demoniac splendor,"[210] Brady's performance was a moving, if exhausting, explication of O'Neill's living mask and the slow, controlled, pictorial, repressed style Moeller selected for this production.

In vivid contrast to Brady, yet within the measured approach of Moeller, Alla Nazimova's Christine reflected both the free spirit of the volatile actress as well as her acceptance of Moeller's interpretation. This short, emotional, fifty-two-year-old Russian performer was sometimes undisciplined in learning lines exactly and often resented directors, but her emotional exploration of character and remarkably responsive body, especially when playing Ibsen's women, were rarely paralleled in her own time. Not surprisingly, her presentation of the emotional upheaval of

---

205. Brooks Atkinson, "Mourning Becomes Electra," *New York Times*, Oct. 27, 1931, p. 22.

206. Wyatt, "Agamemnon," p. 331.

207. Skinner, "Play," Nov. 11, 1931, p. 47.

208. Only once, when Ezra lay dead across the bed and Christine lay unconscious on the floor, did Brady's Lavinia break and cry out. Rush, "Mourning Becomes Electra," *Variety*, Nov. 3, 1931, p. 54; Ruhl, "Second," p. 1; Carb, "Seen," p. 76; Brown, *Dramatis*, p. 57.

209. Ruhl, "Second," p. 1.

210. Atkinson, "Mourning," p. 22.

Christine was violent and devastating, yet Moeller convinced her to mini-mize movement and adhere to a deliberate tempo.

Compared to all others on stage, Nazimova's characterization was fiery and passionate as she allowed her emotions to surface fully before suppressing them again. She therefore seemed perpetually wounded in her almost omnipresent, quiet despair broken periodically by short out-bursts of terror. Her passion, however tortured, was regularly held in check by her "preternatural grace."[211] She moved about the stage with ease and charm, always giving impetus to the attraction which Captain Brant felt for Christine. Hammond wrote that "Nazimova glides to and fro with now and then a graceful dart of her cobra head, more mesmerically reptilian than ever."[212] As in so many of her characterizations, Naz-imova's movement suggested elegant exoticism.

Nazimova frequently produced a sibilant, hissing sound with "s" and "sh" which helped her to maintain a slow delivery. Although this accented her ever-present Russian dialect,[213] which most American audiences did not seem to mind, the actress' languid tempo and diction only heightened her exoticism and the insidious sinister bearing which she maintained throughout her machinations with Ezra and Orin. Although her manner of performance seemed almost diametrically opposed to Brady's stiff and cruel resolve, Nazimova's tempo and control enabled her Christine to share the same austere dramatic world as Brady's Lavinia. As Atkinson wrote, "Mr. Moeller has molded the parts into a measured, fluent perfor-mance."[214] Stylistic continuity was preserved.

Certainly the most obvious feature of *Mourning Becomes Electra* was the extravagant length of performance, which exceeded that of *Strange Interlude.* Originally intended to be performed on three different nights,[215] *Mourning Becomes Electra* was cut so significantly that by the time a complete runthrough of the plays was held Moeller and O'Neill realized that a long single presentation was possible and preferable to three separate evenings. As with *Strange Interlude* no matinees were feasi-ble, but Moeller was certain that "the unity and suspensive action" of the play would benefit notably by a single performance.[216]

Although the premiere showing began at 4:00 P.M. to accommodate newspaper critics' deadlines, subsequent performances commenced at

211. Atkinson, "Tragedy," p. 1.
212. Hammond, *This Atom,* p. 156.
213. Robert Garland, untitled review, *World-Telegram* clipping, in *Mourning Becomes Elec-tra* folder 2, MCNY.
214. Atkinson, "Mourning," p. 22.
215. "O'Neill Trilogy," Sept. 9, 1931, p. 25.
216. "O'Neill's Trilogy," Oct. 13, 1931, p. 26.

5:00 until the production settled into a predictable and shorter running time resulting in a 5:15 opening and 11:20 closing curtain.[217] The advertisements, reviews, and newspaper notes make it clear that Moeller and the cast used the first week of performances much like an out-of-town tryout to hone the playing time to an acceptable length. After an opening night of almost six hours of playing time, the show was reduced within a week to just over five (including a fifteen-minute intermission between "The Hunted" and "The Haunted"), plus an additional hour for a dinner break around 7:00 P.M. after "The Homecoming."[218]

Once again O'Neill incorporated a chorus in his work, introducing each of the three plays with four or five common townsfolk who appeared outside the Mannon house to comment on the action which occurred within. Although this was a conscious use of chorus by O'Neill,[219] the device was less stylized than earlier plays, since each grouping had realistic dialogue and only sang if drunk. The choruses, however, were drastic departures in appearance and sound from the Mannon family. Bowen's review mentioned "cackling yokels around the front porch,"[220] and photographs demonstrate that their costumes, makeup, and posturing made them look like caricatures when compared to the Mannons. The contrast was almost startling.

Not unlike the shifting patterns of the earlier *Beyond the Horizon* and *Desire Under the Elms*, the scenic requirements of *Mourning Becomes Electra* vacillated throughout from exterior to interior, but the action was framed by the house exterior which appeared in six scenes; none of the other five settings appeared more than three times, and two settings were used only once. O'Neill intended the action to return continually to the house, which stood as a symbol of the Mannon power, wealth, and mask.[221]

For the designs of the settings and costumes Robert Edmond Jones was engaged for his eighth venture with an O'Neill play. Just a year earlier Marya Mannes could have been addressing this production when she commented that "if there is one salient and invariable quality in Jones' work, it is aristocracy."[222] It was with *Mourning Becomes Electra*, however, that such aristocracy was particularly apparent. Atkinson said that

217. Advertisements, *New York Times*, Oct. 26, 1931, p. 22; Oct. 29, 1931, p. 26; note, *New York Evening Post*, Oct. 31, 1931, p. 4–D; "O'Neill's Trilogy," Oct. 13, 1931, p. 26.

218. *Mourning Becomes Electra* program (Nov. 2, 1931), MCNY; Stirling Bowen, "The Theatre," *Wall Street Journal*, Oct. 28, 1931, p. 4; Atkinson, "Mourning," p. 22; Fergusson, "Month," 1931, p. 445; Rush, "Mourning," p. 54; Benchley, "Mourning," p. 262.

219. O'Neill, "Working," p. 533.

220. Bowen, "Theatre," Oct. 28, 1931, p. 4.

221. O'Neill, *Mourning* promptbook, Yale; O'Neill, "Working," pp. 530–33.

222. Mannes, "Robert," p. 15.

these settings reflected an "incandescent vitality" born of Jones' "inspired idealism," which thoroughly comprehended and vibrantly represented the essence of the play.[223] Likewise, Francis Fergusson found that the settings demonstrated Jones' "special gift: a gift of sympathy" with the playwright's intentions, which could sometimes express more than the play itself.[224]

Jones' designs were at once bold and strong in line, simple and selective in detail, ominous and malevolent in mood. The settings united "realism with an overpowering atmosphere"[225] and in conjunction with Moeller's work provided many theatergoers with the sense of a real location, as well as "the feeling of unreality and nightmare."[226] The gloom and foreboding of the written play were reflected visually at every turn.

Mounted in the Guild Theatre, the five settings[227] were a clipper ship's exterior with removable bulkhead set in a hazy, misty void (used only once), the exterior facade of the Mannon mansion and three interior rooms of the mansion—bedroom, sitting room, and study. All interiors were austere, somber rooms,[228] delineated by "a classic coldness of line and furnishing that fits the mood of the play and the exactions of the frigid natives."[229] All rooms were nearly rectangular and set parallel to the apron. Each featured a field of gray walls trimmed with white woodwork and pierced with large windows and black fireplaces and doors. Jones surrounded all settings with a black velvet cyclorama so that characters would enter from or exit to a mysterious, unlit void. John Mason Brown later described the effect as "sullen black doors which . . . stood out like wounds from the dull grey walls."[230]

A few feet above the proscenium line Jones mounted sliding tormentors which met the walls of interiors and kept the stage environment distanced from the audience. To enhance formality further the expensive furniture was spread across each room, almost in a straight line much like the ceremonious pattern of *Strange Interlude.* The arrangement was clearly intended to discourage conversation.

Jones used color accents to align the rooms with specific characters.

223. Brooks Atkinson, "Tragedy Becomes O'Neill," *New York Times,* Nov. 1, 1931, sec. 8, p. 1.

224. Francis Fergusson, "A Month in the Theatre," *Bookman* 75 (June-July 1932): 291.

225. Skinner, "Play," p. 47.

226. Leon Edel, "Eugene O'Neill: The Face and the Mask," *University of Toronto Quarterly,* Oct. 1937, pp. 32–33.

227. The descriptions and use of all settings are based on the promptbooks, five ground plans, eighteen photographs, and "Scene," "Lighting," and "Property" plots. When other sources are used they will be noted.

228. Lee Simonson, "Scenic Design in the U.S.A.," *Studio* 127 (June 1944): 199.

229. Burns Mantle, untitled review New York *Daily News,* clipping, MCNY.

230. John Mason Brown, *Letters from Greenroom Ghosts* (New York: Viking, 1934), p. 203.

In the study, for example, he identified the room with Mannon and Lavinia by giving it a masculine look with heavy brown drapes and no other significant color (see illustration 16), whereas the sitting room became Christine's space with her green color in curtains, cushions, and a potted palm. Furthermore, the sitting room, although formally arranged, was a bit more welcome to conversational groupings than the study.

While the study and sitting room were each used in three scenes, the bedroom interior was shown only at the close of "The Homecoming" (see illustration 17). The room was dominated by a large four-poster bed with its head against the wall up left center. This created an arcing traffic pattern between the doors. A small table and chair were placed stage right near the windows to bring Christine away from the bed before she murdered her husband, Ezra. For this nocturnal murder strong blue light spilled through the windows and created a sharp windowpane effect across the bed where Ezra lay. Strong chiaroscuro effects, emphasized by using footlights selectively, were created throughout the room and set the mood dynamically.

Using much more stage depth than any other setting was the aft section of a docked clipper ship used only in act IV of "The Hunted" (see illustration 18). In order to create a mysterious environment, a gauze scrim was placed between the setting and audience at the tormentor line a few feet above the proscenium opening. The ship was placed parallel to the apron far upstage, leaving a large expanse of open stage which represented the dock. Only a barrel and piling left center appeared in this space for the use of the drunk chantyman. The left and right sides of the ship were cut off by black portals, and a border was lowered from above and bunched to represent a furled sail on a spanker boom. The ship's deck was elevated nine feet above the stage and included side railings and a large skylight at center through which Lavinia and Orin could spy on Christine and Captain Brant in the cabin below. Utilizing only two strong pools of light in the nighttime setting (one on deck, seemingly emanating from the skylight, and one at the piling, supposedly originating from a porthole), Jones and Moeller confined most of the action to these two small areas surrounded by darkness. Director and designer created another nocturnal "visible wake of ghosts"[231] (so popular in O'Neill's work) to accentuate the eeriness and sea fog of this waterfront scene.

Midway through this act the action shifted to the cabin below deck, at which time the lights were blacked out for a few moments while a large panel on the center of the bulkhead of the ship was removed to reveal a small interior directly beneath the skylight. The space was crowded with

231. Mannes, "Robert," p. 15.

cabin furniture and lit by strip lights mounted in the ceiling and the skylight above. Strong blue light coming through the skylight created patterned shadows on the wall below when Orin murdered Brant, an effect which recalled the bedroom murder of "The Homecoming."

Opening and closing the play as well as appearing in four other acts was the exterior facade of the Mannon mansion, which was well distanced from the audience (see illustration 19). With this setting Jones was said by Wyatt to have "shadowed the austerity of Atreus."[232] Here was a setting which bespoke the play's unrelieved gloom,[233] which complemented the action and "moods of the play and [closed] it exactly on the note it [had] sought and gained by turns."[234] One reviewer responded to the setting in precisely the manner wanted by O'Neill, who requested a mansion suggesting a classic mask disguising ugliness. Ruhl thought the facade resembled a mask which was trying to conceal "the dark, pursuing horrors of its inner life."[235]

Like all other settings, the templelike facade of the two-story mansion was placed parallel to the proscenium line. The stark gray walls were interrupted by a large green central door trimmed in white and five large white windows with green shutters. Below the house front was an elevated portico, four wide steps, and four tall, broad columns, painted to represent round, fluted, Doric construction. The portico, columns, and steps were all painted white. The entire picture was framed with black, and all backing, of course, was black velvet. Therefore, behind the windows and door lay only impenetrable darkness.[236]

The perfect symmetry of this imposing design was broken by lilac bushes and a bench placed at stage level and just right of the central steps. Although this feature, which was balanced by a pine branch extending from the flies up left center, is attractive in the rendering and seems appropriate in a photograph, the ground plan reveals that the placement of the bench for some scenes created traffic problems for actresses due to their wide skirts and the nearness of the bench to the downstage tormentor.[237]

The effect of this setting was further enhanced by a beautiful

232. Wyatt, "Agamemnon," p. 331.
233. Fergusson, 1932, p. 291.
234. Hutchens, "Greece," p. 16.
235. Ruhl, "Second," p. 1.
236. Atkinson, "Tragedy," p. 1; Fergusson, 1931, p. 445; Wyatt, "Agamemnon," p. 331.
237. For the last play, "The Haunted," Moeller moved the bench fifteen inches farther onstage and the problem was alleviated. This was probably done to facilitate the drinking scene. Why this was not done for all acts is not clear. Mary Arbenz, who played the supporting role of Hazel Niles, complained of the awkwardness of the placement of the bench without explaining why. See Arbenz, "Plays," p. 312.

"funereal" downstage drop which depicted a long view of the entire Mannon mansion as seen from the street, separated from the viewers by a dark iron fence. This drop was used in conjunction with the grand drape for covering scene shifts as well as helping to establish mood before the beginning of each of the three plays.[238]

John Mason Brown described much of the design work of Jones as "a world fashioned by Mr. Jones' invention, but intended for our dreams."[239] His stark yet graceful settings, enhanced by Moeller's pictures and direction, captured and extended the dark and stony moods and sometimes nightmarish atmosphere of *Mourning Becomes Electra* which periodically (often without warning) released the tormenting, shadowy furies of O'Neill's temperament and conception. The designs were enthusiastically admired by not only the critics but O'Neill himself, who also appreciated Moeller's use of these settings in both movement and picturization.[240] Critics likewise extolled Moeller's "fine eye for pictorial values,"[241] his striking compositional groupings, and sensitive placement of action within the space. After seeing a second performance one viewer was struck especially by "the visual beauty of the performance. A painter, we think, would like to catch almost any moment in those fourteen acts and fix it on canvas; there are few indeed which are not pictorially fine."[242] Atkinson also credited Moeller's use of the space with providing "some of the stately spectacle of Greek classicism,"[243] an opinion echoed by Mantle, who found that Moeller's composition caught "the heavier mood of the Greeks without too great a sacrifice of modern naturalness."[244]

Actual movement was not extensive and was often measured, thus matching Moeller's approach to vocal tempo. In fact the director reduced the amount of movement called for in the script and worked for long moments of held positions, virtually in tableau, almost as if he were trying to impress on the viewers strong photographic images which could sometimes be more telling than dialogue. De Casseres called this a "wax-like

238. It is not clear if this painted drop was used as an act drop for every shift or only at the beginning of each play of the trilogy.

239. John Mason Brown, *Upstage: The American Theatre in Performance* (New York: Kennikat, 1969), p. 151.

240. O'Neill rehearsal notes, in Floyd, *Eugene*, p. 209.

241. John Mason Brown, "'Mourning Becomes Electra,' Eugene O'Neill's Exciting Trilogy," *New York Evening Post*, Oct. 27, 1931, in Miller, *Playwright's*, p. 70.

242. Although this was a contribution to a Theatre Guild publication, the opinion was supported by nonpartisan critics as well, e.g., Atkinson and Ruhl. "A Playgoer's Afterthought," *Theatre Guild Magazine*, Mar. 1932, p. 10.

243. Atkinson, "Mourning," p. 22.

244. Mantle, New York *Daily News* clipping.

mobility"[245] which was meant to heighten the haunting death themes of
the play. The strongest uses of such movement occurred on the Mannon
portico with Lavinia and Christine's long moments of glaring at or away
from one another. Especially elongated were the final moments of the play
when Lavinia was left alone on stage, staring and unmoving, for a long
silence. At a word from Seth at the stage-left window she exited up center
into the house, but the stage remained empty and silent for five seconds
before the final, slow curtain began to fall.[246]

Many particular stage pictures created by Moeller with the mansion
facade and interiors were recalled by critics, noted in the promptbooks,
and preserved in photographs, especially the scenes with Lavinia sitting in
her sable dress against the white steps, with Christine stealing in behind
her or brooding above her in green velvet. Also memorable was Christine
cradling Orin in a pitiful pietà in the sitting room at the conclusion of act
II of "The Hunted." Reviewers were particularly stricken by the vision of
both women in mourning black against the stark white steps and Lavinia
in her habitual dark costume posed in the jet-black rectangle of the open
front door.[247] This use of black on black recurred several times throughout the production. In act II of "The Hunted," for example, Lavinia,
dressed in black, appeared and stood framed "with sepulchral dignity"[248]
in the large black door opening up center of the sitting room. At every
opportunity Moeller and Jones managed to create simple but stately visual
splendor.

Atkinson's Sunday column summarized the critical response accu-
rately. "Philip Moeller," he wrote, "has assimilated 'Mourning Becomes
Electra' completely. For pace and coherence, for the prescience of doom in
the acting and the spectacle, for climaxes and flow, the performance he
has directed is superb."[249] "Here is tragedy in the grand manner," Ruhl
declared.[250] Propelled by critically acclaimed playwriting, acting, design,
and directing, *Mourning Becomes Electra* became an artistic landmark in
the American theater. In an audacious performance of more than five
hours which seemed "saturated with terror and death,"[251] *Mourning Be-*

245. Although De Casseres grew weary of this slowness, he acknowledged that it was a
deliberate approach of Moeller's direction. De Casseres, "Broadway," p. 68.

246. O'Neill, *Mourning* promptbook, Yale, "The Hunted," act IV, p. 12.

247. Hammond, *This Atom*, pp. 155–56; Ruhl, "Second," p. 1; "Playgoer's," p. 10; Brown,
Letters, pp. 203–04; Brown, *Dramatis*, p. 57; Benchley, "Mourning," p. 264.

248. Wyatt, "Agamemnon," p. 331.

249. Atkinson, "Tragedy," p. 1.

250. Ruhl, "Second," p. 1.

251. Ruhl, "Second," p. 1.

comes Electra was an exacting visual and aural product of careful and sympathetic preparation by Moeller and Jones working closely and earnestly with O'Neill. "You have two plays there," a playgoer wrote, "one for the eye, and one for the ear and brain. And they match, at every moment, completely."[252]

252. "Playgoer's," p. 10.

CHAPTER XII

Eumenides:
Ah, Wilderness! and *Days Without End*

> Nary an aside, divil a bit of a mask, no Freudian undertones,
> overtones, or semi-tones, no sinister probings, void of allegories,
> symbolism, intellectual gew-gaws, sans artiness, it might be a
> combination of "Another Language," interlarded with episodes
> from Booth Tarkington's "Seventeen."[1]

> These two plays will, I know, set you to wondering what sea
> change has come over me.[2]

In the season of 1933–1934, as political theaters like the
Theatre Union and the Workers Laboratory Theatre became forceful
dramatic weapons presenting agitprop protest plays and socialist realism
with leftist, proletarian messages, the Theatre Guild embarked on the
production of two comparatively quiet O'Neill plays: *Ah, Wilderness!* and
Days Without End. After the furious themes and experiments of *Strange
Interlude*, *Dynamo*, and *Mourning Becomes Electra*, these new plays seemed
a respite, a peaceful period of Eumenides.

Although both plays were dramatic experiments for O'Neill, only
Days Without End was an experiment in production. Yet the realistic
staging, humor, gentleness, and nostalgia of *Ah, Wilderness!* also displayed
another facet of the versatility of O'Neill. Feeling (temporarily) after
Mourning Becomes Electra that he had gone "as far as it was in me to go
along my old line,"[3] the dramatist laid aside "his adventures in form"[4] and
surprisingly created characters which represented "normal and whole-

---

1. Harvey Gaul, in "Garment of Repentence," *Literary Digest*, Oct. 28, 1933, p. 24.
2. O'Neill letter to Macgowan (Oct. 16, 1933), in Bryer, *Letters*, p. 204.
3. O'Neill letter to Macgowan (Oct. 16, 1933), in Bryer, *Letters*, p. 204.
4. Leon Edel, "Placid and Amiable," *Canadian Forum* 14 (Feb. 1934): 188.

some people."[5] In Bowen's view, O'Neill "was merely taking a vacation"[6] when he wrote *Ah, Wilderness!*

As the final curtain fell on the premiere performance of Monday, October 2, 1933, at the Guild Theatre,[7] the audience (usually "notoriously indifferent" at Guild first nights), actually cheered,[8] probably as much in surprise that this was an O'Neill play as in appreciation for the play and production. *Ah, Wilderness!* emerged as a great success under Moeller's expert comic direction, with designs by Robert Edmond Jones and with a strong cast of principals led by George M. Cohan—another surprise, since Cohan almost always worked exclusively in his own plays and was considered a song-and-dance man, not an actor likely to appear in either a Guild or an O'Neill production. Praising Moeller's direction as "supple, alert and sagacious,"[9] Atkinson was not alone in noting the expertise of the director with comic timing, sensitive treatment of character, interesting stage composition, and effective depiction of period and mood, both aurally and visually.[10] Moeller, who was always adept with comic plays, could use his inspirational approach with this material, which most of all needed extensive cutting rather than careful interpretation of experimental theatrical devices and acute emotional suffering of character.

Written very quickly in 1932 when O'Neill interrupted his composition of *Days Without End,* and given only one major revision before rehearsals began in late August 1933,[11] *Ah, Wilderness!* was well constructed but much too long for such lightweight material. All of O'Neill's seven scenes were shortened by cutting dialogue, but none was eliminated. Moeller altered the act-scene numbering, however, in order to reduce O'Neill's three intermissions to two. O'Neill's act I became I.1 and II became I.2. Accordingly, the two scenes of the original and published act III became act II, while act IV became III.[12]

Throughout the rehearsal period and during the out-of-town tryout

5. Mary M. Colum, "Life and Literature," *Forum* 94 (Dec. 1935): 359.

6. Stirling Bowen, "The Theatre," *Wall Street Journal,* Jan. 11, 1934, p. 3.

7. Advertisement and "Theatrical Notes," *New York Times,* Oct. 2, 1933, p. 22. Reviews first appeared on Tuesday, Oct. 3, 1933.

8. John Mason Brown, "George M. Cohan in Eugene O'Neill's Comedy," *New York Evening Post,* Oct. 3, 1933, p. 26.

9. Brooks Atkinson, "Ah, Wilderness!," *New York Times,* Oct. 3, 1933, p. 28.

10. Cy Caldwell, "To See or Not to See," *New Outlook,* Nov. 1933, p. 42.

11. Atkinson, "George," p. 1; Floyd, *Eugene Work,* pp. 159–60.

12. Moeller's three-act numbering utilized in the three promptbooks will be used in this evaluation. Although the promptbooks are consistent, each contains material not included in the others. Eugene O'Neill, *Ah, Wilderness!,* bound promptbook, Theatre Guild Collection Beinecke, Yale; Eugene O'Neill, *Ah, Wilderness!,* bound stage-manager's promptbook, Theatre Collection, MCNY; Eugene O'Neill, *Ah, Wilderness!,* bound promptbook, Theatre Collection, Performing Arts Center, NYPL, copyrighted 1933 by Yale University.

in Pittsburgh, O'Neill and Moeller made streamlining cuts in dialogue which in the end were extensive but did not significantly disturb events or characters. Both strident and sentimental, farcical and expositional lines were excised, so that the final effect seemed virtually unchanged in mood—only shorter.[13] Occasional new lines (not published) were added, but always to facilitate stage action such as getting a character offstage for a long exit. After all cutting was completed the play still ran for nearly three hours.[14] This led the Guild to begin the play "at the rather unearthly hour of 8:20"[15] to get the audience out before 11:30 P.M.

Attempting to assemble a cast in mid-August, Moeller looked for strong stage personalities and was successful in casting George M. Cohan in the role of Nat Miller. Although O'Neill warned Moeller that he should be seeking fresh rather than strong personalities, the playwright was pleased with the casting of Cohan as well as the fourteen other actors until well after the play opened, when Cohan began to stray from directions and text.[16] The casting of a star of Cohan's almost legendary fame also overshadowed the importance of the play's protagonist, Richard Miller, played by young Elisha Cook.[17]

As with *Mourning Becomes Electra*, O'Neill was almost always in attendance at rehearsals, much to the amazement of Cohan. Unlike the playwright's seven-week ordeal with the trilogy, however, the normal four weeks with *Ah, Wilderness!* proved a pleasant, even refreshing experience. Although O'Neill continued to work quietly through the director and avoided the actors, the kinds of pressures and problems inherent in his earlier work and the stress on director and actors were not operative with this production.[18]

Moeller's largest concern as he entered rehearsals was working with Cohan, who was accustomed to directing himself as well as writing his own material. Moeller approached him carefully and humbly offered

13. Eugene O'Neill, unpublished draft of letter to Warren Munsell [regarding *Ah, Wilderness!*], n.d., letter 1, Yale Collection of American Literature, Beinecke, Yale.

14. Notes preceding first numbered page reads: "Running time: 8:25 to 11:22." O'Neill, *Ah, Wilderness!* promptbook, MCNY; "A Playgoer's Discoveries," *Stage*, Nov. 1933, p. 8.

15. Although opening-night curtain was 8:10, the starting time was 8:20 beginning with the third performance. W. G., "The Theatre," *New Yorker*, Oct. 14, 1933, p. 30; advertisement, *New York Times*, Oct. 4, 1933, p. 27.

16. O'Neill unpublished letter to Moeller, Aug. 19, 1933, Yale; O'Neill letter to Macgowan (October 16, 1933), in Bryer, *Letters*, p. 204; Ward Morehouse, *George M. Cohan: Prince of the American Theater* (Philadelphia: J. B. Lippincott, 1943), p. 188.

17. O'Neill clearly identified Richard as the central character. Reviews and even the Guild marquee presented Cohan as the star. O'Neill unpublished letter to Moeller, Aug. 19, 1933, Yale.

18. S. J. Woolf, "Four Decades on the Great White Way," *New York Times Magazine*, Oct. 1, 1933, p. 9; O'Neill letter to Macgowan (Oct. 16, 1933), in Bryer, *Letters*, p. 204.

Cohan the invitation to object to anything which disturbed him. This proved a wise maneuver, because Cohan proceeded to take Moeller's directions without argument.[19] He even agreed to yield strong stage positions to other actors, a practice which surprised some of the critics.[20] Although the actor fought spiritedly with the Guild Board during this period, he trusted Moeller and created no difficulties in rehearsal.[21] Most puzzling to him, however, was Moeller's lengthy reading period and slow manner of working. The cast read and discussed *Ah, Wilderness!* with Moeller for about eight days before working on their feet.[22] Cohan, on the other hand, was accustomed to approximately two weeks of preparation, but he was patient with Moeller's need "to go slow and finish the job right,"[23] as Cohan put it.

Moeller's final stage directions were very detailed, but they were the product of inviting the actors to try many different bits of business in order to create a believable sense of the active though not hectic home life of the large family. Most of O'Neill's directions remained, but they usually had additional explicit movement and business (the reverse of Moeller's blocking with *Mourning Becomes Electra*). When Mildred tripped Richard soon after his first entrance in I.1, for example, Moeller added specific preparation moves and destination directions for Mildred. Wint Selby in I.2 was to glance specifically up right and up right center to make sure he was not being overheard before arranging Richard's "date" with Belle.[24] Such exacting business and directions (Moeller even numbered the chairs to keep the shifting movement clearly delineated) appear in no other Moeller promptbook of an O'Neill play.

This production was much more energetic, busy, and buoyant than the other Moeller-O'Neill collaborations. With abundant business and movement, simultaneous activity, and rapid act curtains accented by considerable curving, arcing movement and tempered by an occasional silence and an unrushed performance tempo, the production maintained a light-hearted and nostalgic mood amid its realistic presentation. The action always seemed to be moving but was never frantic.

Although the added pauses, business, and milking of audience laughter by Cohan in performance eventually added twenty to thirty minutes to

19. Moeller, in Ormsbee, "Philip," p. 3; John McCabe, *George M. Cohan: The Man Who Owned Broadway* (Garden City, N.Y.: Doubleday, 1973), p. 227.

20. For example, John Mason Brown, "Mr. Cohan in *Ah, Wilderness!*," in Brown. *Two on the Aisle* (New York: W. W. Norton, 1938), p. 236; Hammond, *This Atom*, p. 234.

21. Helburn, *Wayward*, p. 132.

22. Moeller, in Ormsbee, "Philip," p. 3; Cohan, in Atkinson, "George," p. 1.

23. Cohan, in Atkinson, "George," p. 1.

24. O'Neill, *Ah, Wilderness!* promptbook, Yale, pp. I-1–11, I-2–10 (pages are numbered in all three promptbooks by act-scene-page).

running time, Moeller's directions and the extensive cutting of O'Neill had reduced the production, despite its three-hour length, to a tightly played presentation by the time it opened in New York.[25] Their success was due primarily to the Pittsburgh tryout (beginning September 25) which enabled Moeller to experiment with an audience—a practice he and the Guild believed vital for the preparation of comedy. Although O'Neill was opposed to such tryouts, he made many more cuts after the cool reception which met *Ah, Wilderness!* in Pennsylvania.[26] There was nothing chilly about the New York response.

Except for the extensive use of music and offstage sound and Richard's long soliloquy on the seashore in a very dark and dreamy scene, there was little about production which suggested earlier O'Neill plays or lay outside the techniques of many other American domestic comedies. Production experiment was not to be found here. Critics and audiences were unprepared for such nostalgia and simple presentation of character and story from O'Neill. As Cohan predicted before opening in New York, "the psychological, psychoanalytical crowd will think we're all daffy."[27]

Once again designing for the Guild Theatre, Robert Edmond Jones provided costumes and four settings which were accurate depictions of the "stuffy refinement"[28] of New England styles of 1906. The greatest difficulty caused by the scenic scheme was "the cruel length of time it takes to shift" the settings.[29] The fault lay primarily with the play, which demanded realistic settings yet called for a complete set change with every scene change except from II.2 to III.1.[30]

Of the three interiors the sitting room, which was used in four scenes, featured the most period detail in a rather tasteless, cluttered manner. Papered with a vivid but ugly blue on white with heavy brown brocade draperies, the three-walled design, like all the interiors, had an upstage wall parallel to the curtain line with raked side walls. All interiors had ceilings, and each setting was placed just a few feet above the proscenium arch. All available wall space was filled with heavy cherry-mahogany furniture.[31] Almost any movement of a few steps in this setting necessitated moving to or around a piece of furniture. In consequence, the

25. O'Neill unpublished drafts of letters to Warren Munsell, n.d., 1 and 2, Yale Collection of American Literature, Beinecke, Yale; Helburn, *Wayward*, p. 132; Langner, *Magic*, p. 284.

26. "Pittsburgh Hails New O'Neill Play," *New York Times*, Sept. 26, 1933, p. 26.

27. "Pittsburgh," p. 26.

28. Atkinson, "Ah," p. 28.

29. Brown, "George," p. 26.

30. Descriptions of settings and their use are from the three promptbooks, twelve photographs, Yale and MCNY, four ground plans, "Property Plot," and "Light Plot."

31. Gilbert Gabriel, "Personal Element," *New York American*, Oct. 3, 1933, in Miller, *Playwright's*, p. 77.

space always seemed alive, and movement could not be aimless. The sitting room was an excellent design for the brisk family action sought by the director.

Less cluttered but in keeping with the style of the sitting room, the dining room, used just in I.2, was similar in shape and only slightly smaller. The walls were papered in red and brown with reddish-brown brocade curtains. Dominated by a large dining table and chairs on the stage-left side of the space, the room was virtually open from center stage to the right wall, allowing long exits and entrances for Nora, the serving woman. The space also allowed dynamic separations of Nat and Sid from the rest of the family during dinner.

Much smaller in depth and width yet similar in shape, the dingy back room of the roadhouse bar (II.1) was adorned with stained, dirty saffron-colored wallpaper. The scummy walls enclosed three round tables with bentwoods spread across the room. An open playing space was created center stage and down left for the rhetorical displays of Richard after he becomes intoxicated. Young reported that the drab, depressing room only pointed up the romance at work in the mind of Richard.[32]

The single exterior of the play stood in stark contrast to the three crowded interiors. Jones created a beach with a very large sand-colored ground cloth which faded into deep green on the upstage edges. The cloth was bunched unevenly on the stage floor. Backing the sand was a long, narrow, curving platform bearing realistic-looking willow trees and shrubs set at a slight angle from stage right to up left. The open playing space was bare save for a dark rope running across the sand attached to an upturned white rowboat up left center near the shrubs. All was backed with black velvet for the quiet nocturnal scene, which included stars in the sky and a slow, gradual dim up of moonlight through the first five minutes of the scene. This opening sequence included offstage music and featured Richard's lengthy monologue revealing his inner anxieties. Moeller had a wide, open stage and considerable depth to allow Richard to wander during his soliloquy. Young described this scene as beautiful, "a sky fretted with stage stars such as only [Jones] knows how to employ."[33]

The simple beauty of the beach scene was matched by two unforced and honest yet contrasting performances by Cohan and Elisha Cook as Nat and Richard Miller. Although he was twenty-six years old and had played numerous young punks and hoodlums in a number of productions like *Lost Boy* and *Jimmy's Women*,[34] Cook was an excellent choice for the

32. Stark Young, "Variegated Hits," *New Republic* 76 (Oct. 18, 1933): 280.

33. Young, "Variegated," p. 280.

34. Euphemia Van Rensselaer Wyatt, "A Great American Comedy," *Catholic World* 138 (Nov. 1933): 215.

sixteen-year-old, troubled, starry-eyed dreamer. In casting Cook, Moeller may have been responding to O'Neill's appeal for an "all American male boy" with no effeminate characteristics.[35] Fortunately, Cook—already an experienced performer—captured Richard's humor and nervousness, angularity, awkwardness, and quickness which served as effective counterpoint to Cohan's depiction of his father.[36]

Moeller's patience and compliant manner coaxed a very cooperative mood and moving performance from the often flippant, jaunty Cohan. Performing with no makeup, the fifty-five-year-old Cohan created a "slightly stooped, hesitant, wise, kindly *paterfamilias*."[37] With great ease in movement preserved from his dancing days, he seemed a model of relaxation and subtlety. Having discarded his familiar sharp rhythms and pert mannerisms, Cohan managed nonetheless to maintain a gentle teasing manner which mixed humor with tenderness.[38] Overall, his performance was proclaimed "masterly in its understatement, unfailing in its command of the stage, and irresistible in its high spirits."[39]

Moeller's direction of these actors in their final scene together was especially moving. Both men, so different in temperament and style, came together in almost "inarticulate affection,"[40] as neither character could utter his true feelings, but revealed through pauses, stuttering and brief touching, what could not be said. The results were said to be "amusing, true, indescribably tender and heartwarming."[41] This was the essence of what O'Neill sought and what Moeller and his company graciously provided.

Soon after the production opened, O'Neill wrote to Macgowan that the performers "really make it live very close to what I imagined it,"[42] high praise indeed from this playwright. For a few months it appeared that nostalgia had conquered O'Neill, who had turned "his back on experiment."[43] As he had demonstrated so many times before, however, a new direction did not signify a trend.

Days Without End

O'Neill's experimental religious play owes much as a dramatic composition to the medieval morality play, to August Strindberg, and to German

35. O'Neill unpublished letter to Moeller, Aug. 19, 1933, Yale.
36. Edith J. R. Isaacs, "Good Plays A-Plenty," *Theatre Arts* 17 (Dec. 1933): 909–10.
37. Isaacs, "Good," p. 909.
38. Joseph Wood Krutch, "Mr. O'Neill's Comedy," *Nation* 137 (Oct. 19, 1933): 459.
39. Brown, "George," p. 26.
40. Wyatt, "Great," p. 215.
41. Caldwell, "To See," p. 42.
42. O'Neill letter to Macgowan (Oct. 16, 1933), in Bryer, *Letters*, p. 204.
43. Edel, "Placid," p. 188.

expressionism, especially the work of Georg Kaiser. In the theater, however, the play as interpreted by Moeller demonstrated an eclectic mèlange of fascinating devices and methods—none of which managed to save the play from critical salvos. *Days Without End*, which O'Neill glibly called a "mask, pseudo-Faustian, 'modern miracle play' opus,"[44] signaled a full-fledged restoration of experiment, though the hopeful spirit of *Ah, Wilderness!* persisted in *Days Without End* despite the intense suffering of the characters and the play's sinister moods.

With Lee Simonson, Moeller created dramatic moments and bold stage pictures as provocative as any others in the theaters of New York. *Days Without End*, with its low, sleek, modern designs, controlled movement and stage composition, and spectacular final scene, engaged the audience regardless of a rejection of the play's ideas. Furthermore, Moeller's utilization of the split character John Loving should be recognized as one of the director's most effective uses of the stage. Unfortunately, the financial failure of production and scathing critical attacks on the play overwhelmed Moeller's achievement.

After *Days Without End* opened on Monday, January 8, 1934, at Henry Miller's Theatre,[45] Atkinson marveled at O'Neill's "capacity for seasoning his valiant career with bad plays."[46] Despite very negative critical assessments of the dramatic material, many theatergoers and critics were fascinated by O'Neill's central experimental device and Moeller's treatment of the play. Direction and experiment, however, were not sufficiently strong to overcome the didactic religious message (although O'Neill claimed this is not what he meant to do) and the weakly argued debate of the play. Only a collection of Catholic publications stated that with this play "O'Neill's days of greatness have begun. May they be 'Days Without End.'"[47] It is curious in retrospect that so many critics of O'Neill throughout his constantly vacillating, experimental career so frequently assumed that a new experiment or message indicated a trend.

Now fifty-three, Philip Moeller entered his final O'Neill production with something less than enthusiastic dedication. Although he did not protest his assignment, Moeller was never convinced that the play was a good theater piece.[48] He nonetheless pursued his task intent on solving its problems and mollifying its dramatic debility. Once again Moeller was

44. O'Neill letter to Macgowan (Oct. 16, 1933), in Bryer, *Letters*, p. 204.

45. Advertisement and "Theatrical Notes," *New York Times*, Jan. 8, 1934, pp. 20, 21. Reviews first appeared on Tuesday, Jan. 9, 1934.

46. Brooks Atkinson, "Eugene O'Neill's 'Days Without End' Staged by the Theatre Guild," *New York Times*, Jan. 9, 1934, p. 19.

47. Fred Eastman, "O'Neill Discovers the Cross!," *Christian Century* 51 (Feb. 7, 1934): 192; "Editorial Comment," *Catholic World* 138 (Feb. 1934): 517.

48. Moeller, in Borton, "Philip," p. 28.

credited with overcoming difficult production challenges and infusing his actors with enthusiasm and his unusual insight into O'Neill's work. The director was said to draw from the actors a commitment and dedication to the project which lent the production "substance and spirit" not only appropriate to the seriousness of the play but perhaps superior to it.[49]

Looking for production keys through externals which might help reveal internal suffering of character, strident mood, and near-tragic consequences before the ultimate redemption of the play, Moeller sought movement and composition which reflected straight lines, sharp angles, stark pictures, and almost monotonous tone in some speeches. The result was solemnity alternating with frenzy in mood, acute, sometimes exaggerated contrasts in visual and aural effects, and an almost bare, austere environment as an appropriate breeding ground for rejection and recovery of faith.

The effect of Moeller's work on tempo was a very slow pace in delivery and movement which gradually gathered momentum as Moeller attempted to interpret the play's development like a building musical piece and to underscore emphatically O'Neill's ideas throughout the play. By the final two scenes the pace was very rapid compared to the opening, but the tempo never became frantic or out of control.

Audiences in both the Boston tryout and the New York run were attentive, patient, and somewhat reverent with this tempo but usually not moved until the final moments when they were sometimes caught up briefly with the climactic scene in the church.[50] Although the audience response was much slighter than he desired, O'Neill expressed satisfaction with the production and laid no blame on Moeller or the Guild.[51]

Days Without End was begun in 1932 and went through at least seven major drafts before the Guild went into production.[52] During rehearsal it was overhauled again with restructuring of scenes, significant alteration of characters and events, rewritten dialogue, and new scenic conclusions. John's outline for his proposed novel, for example, was originally related in act III, but during rehearsals much of his story was shifted to act I.[53] As

49. H. T. P., "In New Vein the New Play from O'Neill," *Boston Evening Transcript*, Dec. 28, 1933, p. 13.

50. Euphemia Van Rensselaer Wyatt, "A Modern Miracle Play," *Catholic World* 138 (Feb. 1934): 602; Percy Hammond, "The Theaters," *New York Herald-Tribune*, Jan. 9, 1934, p. 16; "The Theatres," *Boston Daily Globe*, Dec. 28, 1933, p. 16.

51. O'Neill letter to Macgowan, Feb. 14, 1934, in Bryer, *Letters*, p. 208.

52. Tornqvist, *Drama*, p. 263; Floyd, *Eugene Work*, pp. 157, 161; Miller, *Eugene*, p. 31.

53. Eugene O'Neill, *Days Without End*, bound promptbook, Theatre Guild Collection, Beinecke, Yale, pp. 1–26 (this promptbook is numbered continuously, not by acts or scenes); Eugene O'Neill, *Days Without End*, bound promptbook, Theatre Collection, Performing Arts Center, NYPL, copyright 1934 by Yale University; H. T. P., "In New," p. 13; Arbenz, "Plays," pp. 367–68.

with *Ah, Wilderness!* Moeller also reorganized the act and scene numbering to eliminate an intermission. Act I remained the same, but II, III.1
and III.2 of the play as it would be published became three scenes of act II
in production. Similarly, the two scenes of published act IV became act
III, scenes 1 and 2.[54] Also, John's wife, Elsa, through cutting and alterations in act II became less self-motivated and more under the control of
John and his evil side, Loving,[55] or she became more of an innocent device
to escalate John's guilty collapse and recovery.

Rehearsals began on or just before December 1,[56] but they did not
proceed as smoothly as in previous O'Neill-Moeller productions. The
director was never satisfied with revisions, while O'Neill, who was in
frequent attendance, was usually frustrated or angry with alterations
which often did not solve problems. Although O'Neill protested, the Guild
and Moeller wanted a tryout week in Boston, since the play seemed so
unstable in preparation. Moeller, who was reportedly close to quitting,
grew distressed with O'Neill, who nevertheless wanted him to remain in
charge.[57] The director's difficulties were further complicated by theater-
union disruptions, but he weathered the storm, and *Days Without End*
commenced its tryout on Wednesday, December 27, 1933, at Boston's
Plymouth Theatre.[58] Although the play suffered a "fumbling opening" in
the first act due to last-minute changes, it recovered in subsequent
scenes,[59] and it was soon evident that the production at least was imaginatively staged.

While *Days Without End* had a running time of approximately two
hours,[60] the time of performance did not seem brief, due not only to a slow
deliberate tempo but also to a relentless, static, "metaphysical debate"[61]
laced with guilt and anguish, and very little physical action. This debate
was made immediate through the unusual device of a split character and
the use of only one mask, experiments given dynamic interpretation by
Moeller's mysterious and stark visual presentation.

O'Neill asked for the character of John Loving to be played by two
actors at once. The disintegrated person about whom O'Neill wrote so

54. Eugene O'Neill, *Days Without End* (New York: Random House, 1934).
55. This is especially evident in II.2 and Elsa' reentrance in II.3. O'Neill, *Days Without
End* promptbook, Yale, pp. 70–74.
56. On Jan. 1 Moeller referred to five weeks of rehearsal, and O'Neill in October told
Macgowan that rehearsals were scheduled to begin about Dec. 1. Moeller in Sheaffer, *Artist*, p.
429; O'Neill letter to Macgowan (Oct. 16, 1933), in Bryer, *Letters*, p. 204.
57. H. T. P., "In New," p. 13; Waldau, *Vintage*, p. 173; Wiley, "Philip," pp. 552–53;
Sheaffer, *Artist*, p. 429; Gelbs, *O'Neill*, pp. 778–79.
58. "Theatres," *Boston Globe*, p. 16; note in *Boston Herald*, Dec. 27, 1933, p. 15.
59. Elinor Hughes, "The Theatres," *Boston Herald*, Dec. 28, 1933, p. 14.
60. H. T. P., "In New," p. 13.
61. Moeller, in Borton, "Philip," p. 28.

often here was literally so, but became integrated at the play's conclusion when John was healthy and whole once more.[62] With two actors demonstrating the conflict within one man—"soul dust twins,"[63] as Brown christened them—Moeller's chief difficulties lay in avoiding a comic or silly effect while keeping both actors onstage close together and visible to the audience. Nevertheless, only one body (John) could be acknowledged by other characters, whereas both John and Loving were heard by everyone.

Loving, the dark side of the split character, wore the only mask in what was to be O'Neill's final experiment with literal masks. Atkinson found this aspect of production the most successful as well as being melodramatic, because it revealed "the villain and the hero of the play in bold strokes of theatre."[64] Stanley Ridges as Loving wore a half mask of a "hideous wraith" with deep-furrowed features colored in gray and purplish tones which suggested to Hammond "the dead hues of decomposition."[65] Although the effect was grotesque, the mask closely resembled Earle Larimore's John in essential features: hairline, cheek bones, bridge of nose, and broad, high forehead. Both the mask and Larimore's makeup created matching heavy, angular eyebrows.[66]

Moeller established several onstage distinctions for separation of the two characters while maintaining their unity. Besides the mask the greatest differentiation was achieved vocally. While John spoke normally, if often emotionally, Loving's voice was strident, somewhat sinister, and Mephistophelean. Sometimes speaking between clenched teeth, Ridge's delivery was frequently theatrical and obviously in pursuit of a powerful and satanic intonation.[67] Atkinson, for example, described his vocalization as "a dry, biting tone of voice like a devil's advocate."[68] According to Motherwell, Ridges "exactly sets the spooky overtone which the play seeks to establish."[69] The promptbooks and reviews verify that it was with movement and placement, however, that Moeller's work was most effective. Even though Loving and John were never allowed to touch, Loving

62. Colum, "Life," pp. 358–59.

63. John Mason Brown, "The Theatre Guild Presents Earle Larimore and Stanley Ridges in Mr. O'Neill's 'Days Without End,'" *New York Evening Post*, Jan. 9, 1934, in Miller, *Playwright's*, p. 80.

64. Brooks Atkinson, "On 'Days Without End,'" *New York Times*, Jan. 14, 1934, sec. 9, p. 1.

65. Percy Hammond, "The Theaters," *New York Herald-Tribune*, Jan. 14, 1934, sec. 5, p. 1.

66. Two close-up photographs, Yale and MCNY.

67. Edith J. R. Isaacs, "Parents and Other People," *Theatre Arts* 18 (Mar. 1934), 169; Hammond, "Theaters," Jan. 9, 1934; p. 16; Hughes, "Theatres," p. 14.

68. Atkinson, "Eugene," Jan. 9, 1934, p. 19.

69. Hiram Motherwell, "Days Without End," *Stage*, Feb. 1934, p. 18.

nevertheless remained close to John nearly all the time, "always at John's elbow,"[70] as several critics observed. Usually placed just above John, either sitting or standing, Loving seemed to lurk over John's shoulder or serve as his shadow—an unseen observer of all the proceedings. Although in a position to watch John and the other characters, Loving usually stared toward the audience, looking past any character next to him, a posture which accentuated the frequent cold, motionless stature of the malevolent character. Except when crossing to follow John, who alone initiated all large movements, Loving remained austerely stationary and almost never gestured except for an occasional "quick opening and closing of the hand."[71] Even the lower, exposed portion of Ridges' face remained impassive throughout. The burden of characterization fell to the use of voice.[72] Only in the final church scene were some of these rules violated in order to heighten the emotional impact of the climax.

By literally elevating Loving, Moeller also sought to stress moments in which Loving's power was at its peak. The director instructed the actor to stand high on his toes or mount a low block hidden from audience view by furniture. The greatest use of this device was in II.3 after Elsa fled into the rainy night.

Contrasts in the two characters were startling, especially when Larimore's John was hysterical with grief and groping almost blindly in his confusion while Loving stood next to him like an immobile automaton. In response to such opposition Atkinson wrote that Moeller "designed a performance that [was] fully aware of the visual and audible opportunities the mask affords."[73] Yet the dual presentation was effectively integrated and often subtle while exploiting the obvious dynamic differences of the stage dichotomy. Isaacs, for example, found that Loving seemed "separate from John and yet within him."[74] Both actors gave emotionally committed or stoically controlled performances which never wavered in their seriousness and prevented the physicalization from ever becoming absurd, avoiding a result which some reviewers saw as possible in less talented hands. Brown, for example, suggested that Loving's trailing after John was faintly reminiscent of "going to Jerusalem"[75] (musical chairs).

The thirty-five-year-old Earle Larimore was a favorite actor of Moeller, who had directed him in seven productions since 1926. *Days Without End* was the eighth, and more would follow. In this, his third original O'Neill production, Larimore was praised for his sincerity in the

70. Jack Pulaski, "Days Without End," *Variety*, Jan. 16, 1934, p. 48.
71. Isaacs, "Parents," p. 169.
72. Hughes, "Theatres," p. 14; H. T. P., "In New," p. 13.
73. Atkinson, "Eugene," Jan. 9, 1934, p. 19.
74. Isaacs, "Parents," p. 169.
75. Brown, "Theatres," Jan. 9, 1934, p. 81.

emotionally overwrought role, much as Glenn Anders had been as Reuben Light in *Dynamo*. Exhibiting power and exaltation in the midst of frenzy and hysteria, Larimore's characterization proved successful not only with audiences and critics[76] but also with O'Neill himself.[77]

The sustained physical and vocal control of forty-two-year-old British actor Stanley Ridges until his sudden outburst of anxiety, despair, and destruction in III.2 was almost universally praised. Credited with providing the role simultaneously with "a demoniac reality and unreality,"[78] Ridges' Loving seemed to present perpetually a psychological abstraction and a living "malevolence of the spirit"[79] while communicating with and functioning within the real world as defined by the play. In short, the audience accepted Loving and the duality of character thanks to Moeller's sensitive and imaginative staging and these two actors' committed performances which *News-Week* labeled "triumphs of virtuosity. Had either of them relaxed for a second," the review continued, "illusion would have been shattered."[80]

Moeller and his approach were well served by Simonson's five severe settings, which fittingly suggested affluence as well as austerity. "The more one shows the less one reveals,"[81] Simonson once wrote, a declaration appropriate for the style of his designs for *Days Without End*. Mounted in Henry Miller's Theatre, an older-style standard house with an upper gallery,[82] the low, sleek, modern designs of the first four settings stood in marked disparity to the traditional theatrical surroundings.

The performance space[83] developed by Moeller and Simonson was a fairly open area, but unlike most previous spare designs in O'Neill productions, the five interiors were all placed close to the audience, just inside the proscenium line, with most furniture close to that line. Therefore, most of the action which featured little movement took place close to the audience.[84]

---

76. For example, Richard Dana Skinner, "The Play," *Commonweal* 19 (Jan. 19, 1934): 329.

77. O'Neill letter to Macgowan, February 14, 1934, in Bryer, *Letters*, p. 208.

78. Isaacs, "Parents," p. 42.

79. Atkinson, "Eugene," Jan. 9, 1934, p. 19.

80. "The News-Week in Entertainment," *News-Week*, Jan. 20, 1934, p. 34.

81. Simonson, in Eaton, *Theatre Guild*, p. 189.

82. Henderson, *City*, p. 242.

83. The description of the settings and their use is based on the two promptbooks, five ground plans, fourteen photographs, "Light Plot," and "Property Plot," Yale, NYPL, and MCNY.

84. When preparing the play, O'Neill drew possible ground plans. Although they do not resemble Simonson's designs, the furniture is placed very far downstage. Perhaps the playwright requested such furniture placement. Eugene O'Neill, manuscript notes, outline, and drawings for *Days Without End*, Yale Collection of American Literature, Beinecke, Yale.

O'Neill admired the designs,[85] as did most of the critics who responded favorably to the appropriateness of the selectively completed rooms and furnishings, which seemed to combine unobtrusively modern realism with impressionism. Described as "an intelligent compromise between representation of place and abstraction of mood,"[86] the settings had doorways but no doors or ceilings, nor were any masking returns used to give the impression of construction continuing out of sight beyond the proscenium. As a promptbook describes them, "the rooms . . . just seem to fade into the black cyclorama that encloses them."[87] The settings looked like islands surrounded by darkness, an effect reminiscent of *The Great God Brown*.

The use of lighting magnified this appearance by isolating the action, sometimes in a smaller pool of light than that defined by the setting. Quite often the brightest light would appear on John in a strong stage position with Loving close by but just on the edge of shadows or at least in less intense light. This occurred, for example, just after Lucy's exit in II.1 as John and Loving prepared to pretend for Elsa that nothing was amiss. Lights were also used very obviously for accenting important emotional shifts onstage, and occasionally different colors were used to highlight different characters during dramatic moments. In II.2, for example, when Elsa asked John if she were supposed to put herself in the wife's unfortunate place in his novel, a major light cue was executed to shift the intensity to Elsa from John.

Most important of all, however, the settings were designed to allow and encourage the characters to keep their distance from one another. The furniture was spread out and few conversational units were incorporated into the arrangement of chairs. The overall feeling one gets from photographs, ground plans, and promptbook stage directions is very frigid. The production exploited the play's intense psychological conflict but insisted upon rigid, reticent physicality.

Days Without End was the first O'Neill production since *All God's Chillun Got Wings* which did not repeat a setting once it had been struck.[88] As a result, *Days Without End* reflected a scenic progression in the spirit of morality-play journeys. Moving from commercial to domestic to religious surroundings, the settings became progressively more personal until the final spiritual revelation. It was almost as if the audience were supposed to

85. O'Neill letter to Macgowan, February 14, 1934, in Bryer, *Letters*, p. 208.
86. Atkinson, "Eugene," Jan. 9, 1934, p. 19.
87. O'Neill, *Days Without End* promptbook, Yale, p. 1.
88. One could argue that *Lazarus Laughed* had such a progressive set development, but a flexible unit set was utilized. *Days Without End*, like *All God's Chillun Got Wings*, had complete scenic changes and additions throughout.

be approaching the inner man. Through the entire advancement, however, the actual stage environments never became intimate.

The first setting (act I) represented one "ghostly"[89] corner of the interior of John's New York office. The set was framed by a large dark arch which served as an inner proscenium for all scenes and suggested a Gothic arch which would appear again in the doorways of the church setting. This stage-wide arch was set only about a foot or so above the proscenium line and reduced the proscenium opening by several feet on each side. Also permanent to all settings was a twenty-by-forty-foot green carpet, the downstage edge of which touched the line of the arch. The color green was repeated in other parts of all settings except the final one.

The two walls of the small office setting met at a ninety-degree angle, the apex of which created the upstage extremity of the setting. In consequence, the audience looked into this corner just right of a large open doorway (the only entrance). The right and left ends of this scenic unit were anchored by file cabinets, and all was surrounded by black velour. The setting seemed almost suspended in space. Furthermore, nothing appeared among the office furniture to suggest life within the room except for papers and a telephone. Nothing decorated the stark walls.

The restricted playing space was further accentuated by the lighting. At first concentrated around Loving and John at the desk, the light slowly spread as the scene progressed until the set was completely illuminated. At the conclusion of the scene, however, when John and Loving were again alone, the lights returned to the opening pool of illumination in the midst of darkness.

Movement within this setting was very limited, and almost any significant cross would have taken an actor to the edge of the carpet/arch line or to the left or right limits of the room. Since most of the scene included two or three actors (four briefly) and involved much sitting, the space was not taxed. Although the promptbooks indicate more specific movement than the published play, primarily for entrances and exits, the characters essentially remained seated for nearly all the conversation.

Representing the living room of an expensive New York duplex apartment, the second setting (II.1 and 2) was placed parallel to the curtain line (see illustration 20). Because the side walls were not raked, they met the upstage walls at ninety-degree angles. Although the living room was wide and shallow, Simonson gave the space depth by placing a foyer up right center with perpendicular entranceways left and right. No stage-right wall was used at all, only a low four-fold screen. The stage-left side wall, however, had a wide window with a light-green venetian blind which

89. Hammond, "Theaters," Jan. 9, 1934, p. 16.

enhanced austere modernity. The walls were painted a pale Nile green and again featured no decoration other than molding along the top of the walls. Even the books in a large bookcase up left were dummy units without titles or distinctive colors—simply generic books. The surrounding blackness was emphasized not only by the doorways but also by the space above the folding screen and darkness behind the open venetian blind.

Small, delicate, narrow-legged furniture with elegant curves, which was spread across the room, provided vivid contrast for all the straight lines in the setting. Coldness was maintained with this furniture, however, since it appeared uncomfortable and impractical for normal use. This was especially pointed in II.2 when the characters sat around the room mostly staring into space as they spoke and drank from demitasse cups.

With John, Loving, and Elsa on stage in this setting, Moeller created numerous striking pictures, usually with Loving lurking behind and just between them. In an unusual moment at the conclusion of II.2 Loving and John were actually separated briefly as Loving lingered behind John's exit and seemed to will the solitary Elsa to flee into the rain. Earlier in II.1, however, Moeller created a tableau with Elsa, John, Loving, and Lucy (Elsa's friend and John's mistress) just before Lucy's exit. "John is holding Lucy's hand as Lucy holds Elsa around the shoulders," a promptbook reads. "Loving stands above and between John and Lucy, staring coldly out front."[90] Most of the action in both scenes, however, was conversation with all characters seated, including Loving.

The third scene of act II, like the office, featured a room corner, displaying part of John's study. Using two walls meeting at an approximate one-hundred-degree angle, the corner of this angle was placed directly on the upstage center line. This symmetrical set had two ceiling-high bookcases with blank dummy books meeting at the corner, and each case was flanked by dark doorways right and left. The extremities of the walls stopped well within the proscenium archway, creating an isolated picture. With undecorated walls and molding at the top painted to match the green of the living room, the stark feeling of the previous scenes was continued. This setting was placed deeply enough to allow considerable freedom of movement compared to the office, but Moeller and Simonson positioned a large table at center running parallel to the curtain line. The dominance of the table forced all other furniture downstage. An interesting angular traffic pattern, however, connected the two doorways. The resultant playing area was very small.

90. O'Neill, *Days Without End* promptbook, Yale, p. 46.

Moeller made dynamic use of the limited space for powerful effects. By seating Loving on a high stool placed at the head of a chaise stage left where John was reclining, Moeller could seat both characters yet seem to have Loving hovering over John. Moeller also placed a twelve-inch-square, four-inch-high wooden block on the floor on the upstage-right end of the chaise for Loving to stand on and physically dominate John during their confrontation near the end of the scene. Without the block Moeller achieved a similar effect earlier in the scene when John confronted Elsa after her flight into the rain. Loving stood above the couple but elevated himself high on his toes to dominate them. All of these juxtapositions reinforced Loving in his most powerful moments of control over John.

The fourth setting of the production (III.1), a two-room environment, was actually an addition to the study, which was moved three or four feet stage left and rotated counterclockwise until the stage-right wall almost reached the downstage edge of the carpet. The new space stage right was then filled with a corner of Elsa's bedroom, and the study's stage-right doorway became an entrance to the bedroom.

The undecorated bedroom walls, also green and topped by molding, were incomplete like those of the living room, with the abrupt upstage void partially filled in by a low three-fold screen. Dominating the new room was Elsa's bed stage right, which filled most of the downstage area. The bed was balanced stage left by the study's chaise, and at one point in this scene Elsa and John lay unconscious on both pieces facing each other across the stage. This scene was the busiest of the play, with simultaneous action and six characters usually spread across both rooms or occasionally crowded into the bedroom. Moeller's most interesting use of this space occurred with his split characters. When John fled the study through the up-left study door at the end of the scene apparently going to the church, instead of following him as usual, Loving backed out ahead of him, being forced out by John's intensity. John did not actually touch Loving, however.

The impressive final setting (III.2) was a small portion of a large Catholic-church interior (see illustration 21). Although approximately the same width as John's study, the gray church walls extended up into the flies beyond the line of the downstage arch. The walls were three narrow panels, with the central section parallel to the curtain line and the left and right sections raked about forty-five degrees beyond the downstage perpendicular. Each side panel had an arching Gothic doorway ten to twelve feet high opening onto black, and the central panel had a matching arch motif nearly twice as high as the doorways. Against this central facade Simonson placed a life-size wooden Christ on a large black cross. The crucifix was mounted with the foot just above head height and was approachable by a one-step platform up center. The entire setting, which Hammond found "spectacular,"[91] was placed only a few feet upstage, leaving an open but shallow playing area.

The lighting was generally dim except for two strong shafts of white and amber light from stage left and directly overhead which highlighted the crucifix and the space directly beneath. It was here that John knelt in prayer and rose to face gloriously his future with new faith and optimism. Moeller brought John and Loving into this space as he had them exit from the study with Loving entering first, "retreating backward before John whom he desperately, but always without touching him, endeavors to keep from entering the Church."[92] Loving was ultimately backed into the cross, where he dropped his impassivity and after much gesticulating and agonizing, unlike any other moment in the production, crumpled to the floor dead while John discovered redemption. Many critics found the scene beautifully staged and emotionally moving, but, understandably, few reviewers were willing to accept it.[93]

Although Robert Loraine's priest was almost everywhere lauded for naturalness, benignity, and authority,[94] and while the Elsa Loving of Selena Royle (Larimore's real wife) was found to be beautiful but artificial and cold,[95] these and other supporting acting performances seemed to have little impact on critical rejection of the play and ecstatic praise for the direction, design, and success with experimental problems. At the center of what was successful in production was Moeller's staging of the split character and the two actors' inspired performances, the one emotional and the other almost emotionless.

Throughout the production Moeller maintained a heightened sense of suppressed passion, except when John and Loving were alone on stage—and even then, save for the final moments of the play, Loving sustained a stoic, evil presence. Interaction among characters was aloof and cold, accentuated by indirect conversation and literal distancing of actors. When passionate displays were allowed to surface, they seemed to arise from intensely restrained emotionality. Moeller effected this leashed passion by dominating the action with seated conversation driven by a slow, deliberate tempo and by providing only occasional but then dynamic movement and direct confrontation. The resultant contrasts were startling and undoubtedly theatrical.

91. Hammond, "Theaters," Jan. 14, 1934, p. 1.

92. O'Neill, Days Without End promptbook, Yale, p. 90.

93. For example, "News-Week," p. 34; Hughes, "Theatres," p. 14.

94. For example, Stark Young, "Days Without End," New Republic 77 (Jan. 24, 1934): 312.

95. For example, George Jean Nathan, "The Theatre," Vanity Fair, Mar. 1934, p. 42.

Although Moeller staged *Days Without End* with insight and perception as he had done with his four previous sojourns with O'Neill's drama, and although the playwright was praised for his experimental character which displayed in Atkinson's words O'Neill's mastery of "the architectonics of the theatre,"[96] the production and experiment were unable to help the play to a reasonable run. One of the Guild's "finest productions"[97] closed after the short subscription run, and Moeller's artistic partnership with O'Neill was over.

For more than twelve years the theater saw nothing new from O'Neill, and when he did return in 1946 with *The Iceman Cometh*, directors were faced with fascinating characters, dark dramatic situations, depressing mood, and realistic form, but no more experimental devices, forms, and characters. With *Days Without End* O'Neill's long voyage with theatrical experiments came ironically to an inglorious end.

96. Atkinson, "On 'Days,'" p. 1.
97. John Anderson, "O'Neill's *Days Without End*," *New York Evening Journal*, Jan. 9, 1934, in Moses, *American*, p. 289.

Afterword

Without the bold and emphatic efforts of Eugene O'Neill the American theater of the 1920s and 1930s would have offered much less both as dramatic experiment and as a field of exploration for direction and design. O'Neill's insistence upon forging new paths for the usually conservative New York theater and his intrepid eclecticism of styles, forms, and devices not only offered new directions for other dramatists but also made exciting demands on and created formidable challenges for his contributing theater artists. Of course without O'Neill the American artist-director would have appeared and influenced the performing arts, but this entrance would have been much less dynamic and the impact on the theater between the wars much less forceful and lasting in value. Unfortunately, O'Neill's demands on acting style were difficult to meet and did not bear significant fruit in his experimental productions, but after the generation of the Group Theatre, performers began to return to O'Neill and apply new lessons to the creations of an older generation. In this respect at least O'Neill's impact was delayed, although his promise was ultimately fulfilled. Albeit stubborn and single-minded at times, both in reputation and in fact (one could argue that he was almost paranoid or at least excessively protective of some of his ideas and dramaturgy), O'Neill remained a collaborator with his directors and designers in most of his theatrical outings. He not only created and gave but listened and received, often taking impetus for exciting experiments from the suggestions of others.

Fourteen years of professional theatrical experiment for O'Neill and his directors, designers, and actors produced an eclectic array of devices, forms, and subjects which not only affected the most mature work of O'Neill but also helped to expand the artistic boundaries of the American professional theater. With the coming of O'Neill to Broadway, experiment was no longer suitable merely to the little theaters or imported European productions. Serious native excursions into the worlds of expressionism, symbolism, and surrealism drew Broadway theatergoers to large, uptown theaters which a decade earlier would have housed safe, escapist dramatic fare.

The dynamic changes which professional directors underwent in this era are nowhere more explicitly demonstrated than in the work of the directors who attempted to meet the challenges, innovations, and novelties of O'Neill's plays. As must be true of any career dedicated to experiment, many failures were inevitable. Failure was more frequent, however, when the plays were entrusted to old-line directors and managers who were accustomed to realistically staged American melodrama and comedy. Of the first ten O'Neill productions beginning in 1920, five (*Chris Christophersen*, *Gold*, *Straw*, *The First Man*, and *Welded*) failed utterly, four of which were given ill-conceived or very literal productions by directors who were not prepared to interpret effectively the new American drama. The fifth, *Welded*, was directed sensitively by Young but was badly managed in casting and design. None of the failures had New Stagecraft designs. Of the five successes, three (*The Emperor Jones*, *Anna Christie*, and *The Hairy Ape*) benefited from New Stagecraft designs by Jones and Throckmorton as well as intrepid directors who represented new trends in American direction (Cook, Hopkins, and Light). The surprising dramatic intensity, effective tragic structure and unusual subject matter of *Beyond the Horizon* caught the fancy of the public and the admiration of the critics despite the slipshod production, which failed to accommodate satisfactorily O'Neill's experiment with shifting location. *Diff'rent*, which was intriguing to audiences for the novelty of a huge gap in time between acts I and II, received rather ordinary but serviceable staging by Kennedy and enjoyed a modest run both uptown and down.

This four-year epoch appears now as a testing period for O'Neill, who attempted various styles and methods with numerous directors while establishing an international reputation. Although the experiments would continue for more than ten years, the plays usually seemed to follow in a more orderly fashion, with more time spent on composition and revision. Furthermore, O'Neill worked with only four professional directors in the eleven remaining productions (five directors in twelve productions if *Lazarus Laughed* is included). Between 1924 and 1934 the playwright settled down to sustained seasons of growth with a few collaborators rather than the comparatively hurried, omnivorous activity preceding the Triumvirate years. The result was dramatic experiment which was more meaningful in its own time and beyond, plus the opportunity for individual directors to become more sensitive to and practical with the theatrical problems posed by the dramatist.

All but two of the twelve later productions had New Stagecraft designs and all twelve had directors who developed in the little-theater and art-theater movements. The domestic comedy of *Ah, Wilderness!* was suited to realistic settings, but *Strange Interlude* would have benefited stylistically from New Stagecraft designs. Fortunately, the uninspired settings by Jo Mielziner did not undermine the popular intrigue created by the unusual performance length and extensive asides of the play. Three of the four failures in this group were highly praised for direction and design, which nevertheless failed to salvage weak dramatic material. Overall, then, one can say that the directors and designers were never responsible for failure after 1924 but usually served O'Neill admirably as the playwright seemed to fall into stylistic synchronization with Jones, Moeller, and Simonson especially.

Although *The Ancient Mariner* was a significant scenic experiment which exploited masks, projections, and the open playing space, the dramatic material was not suitable for the stage in a form so close to the original lyric creation of Coleridge. Failure of the self-conscious "dramatic arrangement" which was neither play, dance, or reading was understandable. For Jones, Light, and O'Neill, however, it was an important trial which propelled them toward more dynamic theatrical exploration where serious text could meet visual experiment effectively.

The preeminent directing figures were obviously Philip Moeller and Robert Edmond Jones, who mounted most of the imaginatively staged O'Neill productions. Furthermore, they demonstrated unusual sensitivity to the themes and styles of the playwright's always changing experiments. All five of Moeller's productions (although two failed to generate a significant audience) were honest presentations of the work of the dramatist, and all were exciting in the use of space and acting performances. Especially in *Strange Interlude* and *Mourning Becomes Electra* Moeller solved production difficulties and enhanced the most dynamic elements of the monolithic plays. The combined efforts of Moeller and O'Neill resulted in two of the American theater's most important and lasting achievements.

Intrigued by the double length and extensive repetition of *Strange Interlude*, Moeller orchestrated this play as though it were a symphony with recurring themes and startling shifts in mood and intensity. More important, perhaps, was his solving the most difficult problem of the play: a clear and effective method for executing the hundreds of extended asides. Significantly, his solution for a vocal problem was arrested motion. Strong visual effects were vitally important throughout most of O'Neill's work, and Moeller's staging exemplified significantly the reliance of O'Neill on strong picturization and imaginative direction for efficacious presentation of many of his experimental plays. Moeller was able to achieve powerful picturization despite a mediocre design.

With *Mourning Becomes Electra* Moeller's sensitivity to O'Neill's characters, themes, and language, manifested most notably in mood, tempo, and tableaux, was united vividly with the beautiful and haunting designs of Jones. The repression of the dramatic Mannon family was everywhere expressed, but primarily in the masklike faces of the actors, careful movement, brooding stage pictures, and ghostly surroundings. The results were spectacle, but extremely tasteful, atmospheric, and measured spectacle, a characteristic of Moeller's work when the director was at his best, and he was always so when mounting his interpretations of O'Neill.

Even in failure (*Dynamo* and *Days Without End*) Moeller with Simonson created dramatic moments and bold stage pictures as provocative as any others in the theaters of New York. Moeller's simultaneous staging in the confining houses of *Dynamo* as well as Simonson's towering, majestic powerhouse and the director's economical use of the limited playing space on each of the four levels provided O'Neill with a stunning production. The commitment of director, designer, and actors to the play kept theatergoers interested and often fascinated despite tedious events and stilted language.

Similar criticism is appropriate for the production of *Days Without End* with its low, sleek, modern designs, controlled movement and placement, and spectacular final scene, which engaged the audience despite a rejection of the play's ideas. Moeller's utilization of the split character was clearly one of this director's most effective uses of the stage. Only *Ah, Wilderness!* had little to offer as experiment, but Moeller gave it a gentle and effective presentation which engaged critical and popular theatergoers enthusiastically.

Moeller worked equally well and creatively with both Simonson and Jones, two designers as different temperamentally as one can imagine despite some of their common artistic goals. Moeller seemed to inspire most of the theatrical personnel who came within his circle, probably because he gave them so much freedom while maintaining artistic control of the production. Perhaps Moeller's most important contribution to the plays of O'Neill was finding and sustaining the nearly perfect tempo for each production, an accomplishment which is difficult to explain given the director's inspirational methods.

Furthermore, Moeller was not surpassed as an interpreter of O'Neill's stark environments, intense mood and passion, and disintegrated, foundering characters. Without Moeller as a kindred spirit (at least artistically), O'Neill's plays from 1928 to 1934 would have offered much less to the New York theater. In terms of staging efficiency and stylistic consistency Moeller was first among O'Neill's directors of the experimental era. It is unfortunate that Moeller's sensibilities and talents could not have been brought to bear on *Beyond the Horizon* in 1920. He was probably the perfect director for this tragedy of longing.

Although Moeller was imaginative, as an artist he could not reach some of the stunning creative accomplishments of Jones, who designed the most evocative, atmospheric environments for O'Neill. When Jones was at his best as both director and designer, he manipulated mood and stage pictures in unforgettable theatrical moments. Jones could be inconsistent in his work as a director, especially when allowing gross stylistic irregularities among the actors while mounting beautiful visual designs and moving compositions with the performers, as in *The Fountain*. He was nevertheless masterful in his best directorial work, notably *The Great God Brown* and *Desire Under the Elms*.

As an unsurpassed purveyor of mystery and mood, and an artist unusually sympathetic to the struggles of O'Neill, Jones was virtually the consummate director for *The Great God Brown*. Jones captured the psychological struggles and heavy symbolism of this play with his adroit use of masks and revelation of hidden personae. With simplicity, sparseness, and selectivity, Jones mounted emblematic scenery which captured a sense of modernity and isolation yet left much open space for performance. Although Jones worked to clarify some of the puzzles of the play, the director enhanced and deepened some of its mysticism. This was especially evident in his staging of Brown's assumption of Dion's mask and life. The audience, if confused, nonetheless remained intrigued by the presentation.

Desire Under the Elms in the care of Jones was one of the most important American experiments in simultaneous staging and utilization of the unit set. Nowhere was Jones more powerful and poignant in his stage composition where he had joint control of design and actors. The production became a stark but mysterious exercise in hiding and revealing. Literal concealment of rooms corresponded to the family secrets, and all was intensified by the tiny rooms which crowded the action and suggested the horrible oppression of O'Neill's imagined environment and rural characters.

While the work of Jones could inspire and enthrall both audiences and performers, his imagination and dreams often needed a rational, controlling hand to keep his creations within the bounds of practical theater. Perhaps that is why Jones and Moeller worked together so splendidly, especially in *Mourning Become Electra*, arguably the most complete and perfect first presentation of an O'Neill play.

James Light emerged as a faithful and sometimes exciting interpreter of O'Neill's plays when the playwright began to move away from old-school directors. Light's adherence to the intent of O'Neill and his willingness to take risks in multiracial casting (*All God's Chillun Got Wings*) and expressionistic staging (*The Hairy Ape*) mark him as a significant transitional director. His brave efforts helped O'Neill to enter the world of free experiment in form and style, particularly in the use of masks. Light's work with both Throckmorton and Jones served as a significant exponent of American expressionism. With his codirection of *The Ancient Mariner* in the spring of 1924, Light helped to prepare Jones for solo direction of O'Neill's plays beginning in the fall.

Although Light was uneven in his production results, his presentation of nightmarish, discordant sound, realistic character, mechanical humanoids, and distorted stage pictures in *The Hairy Ape* on the limited Provincetown stage demonstrated trenchantly O'Neill's proclivity for mixed styles and unmitigated horror. Such stylistic eclecticism and abrasiveness in mood, sights, and sounds were typical of most of the plays of O'Neill which lay ahead. More than any other before it, this production seems a hallmark for O'Neill's depiction of isolated, divided characters adrift in society and the playwright's furious assaults on the senses of the theatergoer.

The direction of Arthur Hopkins in 1921 and 1922 was more important for the career of the dramatist than for that of the director. With the Barrymores, Nazimova, and Jones, Hopkins had staged many productions important for acting, design, and directing before *Anna Christie*. He would mount many more after assisting Light with *The Hairy Ape*. Besides serving O'Neill's experiments well with these sensitive and exciting excursions into the New Stagecraft, Hopkins was invaluable to the training and inspiration of Light and especially Jones as directors. Hopkins' controlled manner and hands-off policy with actors were in turn practiced diligently by both of these directors when staging the plays of O'Neill. If *The Straw* had come under the direction of Hopkins, who was so suited for this style of drama, rather than Tyler it is likely that O'Neill would have had one more important success in the early years.

With the design assistance of Jones, Hopkins provided O'Neill with an impressively modulated, controlled, and dreamy production of *Anna*

Christie. This presentation not only brought O'Neill's plays to the attention of a much larger audience but remained the most stirring O'Neill production originally mounted for an uptown theater prior to the Theatre Guild productions of 1928. A masterful display of mood and stylized realism, Hopkins' production could have been the first of many ventures with O'Neill had the playwright not severed professional relations after Hopkins rejected *The Fountain* as unsuitable for production. The director's rejection has been shown, however, to be a wise decision. Although the loss of Hopkins as director and producer for O'Neill was unfortunate, had the two continued their association, Experimental Theatre, Inc., may never have been established. The ultimate development of the work of O'Neill may then have taken a very different direction under the guidance of Hopkins.

O'Neill's debt to George Cram Cook cannot be properly gauged. One can assume that Cook's primary contributions to the direction of the plays of O'Neill were his inspirational ideas and insistence upon experiment. Certainly Cook was responsible for giving Light his first opportunities to direct as well as for bringing O'Neill's plays to the stage in the first place. As the guiding spirit of Provincetown, Cook provided an exciting, experimental environment for the playwright's early development. The sky dome, which enabled dynamic presentation for some of O'Neill's most memorable early work, would never have been built without the insistence of Jig Cook. In *The Emperor Jones*, the first O'Neill production mounted with settings inspired by the New Stagecraft, Cook with Throckmorton's first stage designs graced the Playwrights' Theatre with a matchless world of fauvist visions in a stylized jungle. Bravely casting a black actor in the leading role, staging silent, pantomimic action in silhouette against the glittering dome, and aurally supporting the nightmare with the slowly escalating offstage drumming, Cook was faithful to the concept of the dramatist. The efforts of the director, however, were catastrophic to his own beloved amateur spirit by bringing Provincetown to the attention of the professional theater.

The direction of Tyler, Saint-Gaudens, Williams, Bennett, and Kennedy came to little. None was prepared with the imagination or daring necessary to meet O'Neill's experimental tasks or the most appropriate visual expression of his plays. Unlike Hopkins, Moeller, Jones, Light, and Cook, these old-school directors lacked exposure to or an admiration for current European methods and devices. Only Stark Young shared the sensibilities of the younger generation, though he lacked the practical ability to execute effectively as director. His efforts with *Welded* remained sadly deficient and literal. The failure of Augustin Duncan to meet O'Neill's requirements remains a mystery in light of the other successful efforts of the director with experimental work and European methods. Perhaps *The First Man* would have failed in the hands of any director, but Duncan seems almost deliberately to have denied the production an opportunity to succeed.

The work of Rouben Mamoulian stands apart from that of the other directors. With his attraction to rhythmic experiments, Mamoulian served O'Neill well with dynamic, large-scale staging in *Marco Millions*. His remarkable ability to coax individual performances from actors in crowd scenes could have helped to salvage such productions as *The Straw*, which suffered from poor execution of crowds as directed by Tyler. If *Lazarus Laughed* could have been granted a professional production, Mamoulian would have been the logical choice to execute such a colorful, crowded, musical experiment.

Under the guidance of Mamoulian, *Marco Millions* captured both the splendor of oriental royalty and the openness of nonwestern theatrical playing spaces. Mamoulian bombarded the audience with music, pageantry, opulence, vibrant color, dynamic contrasts, stylized movement, and frequently shifting, large-scale, human compositions. With his extravagant theatrical flair, Mamoulian did not just impress the audience with alien, eastern environments and activities; he moved the viewers emotionally with dynamic manipulation of actors and space. Most of his efforts enhanced O'Neill's play which needed vivid visual presentation to support a sometimes brittle text. Although many critics were not favorably inclined to the play, few could dismiss the spectacular staging of this inventive director.

Gilmor Brown also experimented with some success with crowds, rhythmic movement, and masks at Pasadena. His production of *Lazarus Laughed*, however, with a host of extras, amateurs in the leading roles, and huge community support in technical preparation, was not representative of the possibilities of professional production in 1928. Brown's work was nevertheless an important experiment with New Stagecraft and an imaginative interpretation of an O'Neill play which was almost too vast for the stage.

Without such directors and designers as O'Neill fortunately encountered for fifteen of twenty-two productions, many of the playwright's difficult experiments would not have been staged intelligibly or executed at all. Despite inventive directors, O'Neill frequently complained about the productions of his plays, but he was usually preoccupied with what he found to be the deplorable condition of American acting. For his more radical experiments O'Neill had imaginative directors, and in some cases the experimental devices originated with a director or designer, rather than the playwright (for example, masks in *The Hairy Ape* were suggested by the costumer, and the director devised arrested motion in *Strange Interlude*). During most of the fourteen-year experimental period O'Neill borrowed freely from his best directors and designers, just as they took many of their most exciting innovations (such as the simultaneous staging in *Desire Under the Elms*) from the dramatist. All of these artists, however, frequently looked to Europe for inspiration and methods, most pointedly expressionism. Without the skills, dedication and creativity of his production collaborators, O'Neill's dramatic work would have developed in a markedly different manner and it is not likely that he would have suggested nearly so much theatrical experiment without the regular successes and innovations of his compatriots.

Imaginative staging and design were vital to the success of most of his work. As a general rule, O'Neill's experimental plays were served best when they were mounted with New Stagecraft designs and when the directors were capable of creating unusual and dynamic stage pictures. His most effective directors were unafraid to experiment with any technical device which seemed possibly appropriate and were willing to give actors the freedom to explore their characters in their own way so long as they adhered to the pictorial interpretation of the play. The direction which Cook, Hopkins, Jones, Light, Mamoulian, and Moeller furnished for O'Neill helped to establish and perpetuate the director as artist in the American theater. These sensitive, artistic directors who could meet the challenges of dramatic departures from realism prepared the way for the next wave of independent, creative directors like Clurman, Strasberg, and Kazan who would continue to work with the second generation of New Stagecraft designers like Mielziner and Gorelik while exploring and developing a new, internal acting style and a fresh generation of playwrights like Williams and Miller, who would combine realism with stylization and demand evolving staging methods which began in earnest with the experiments of O'Neill.

The dramatic works of O'Neill in his experimental era were very uneven and caused his directors occasional insurmountable problems. The erratic nature of his dramaturgy was reflected in production, as a series of directors of widely different temperaments and abilities attempted to realize O'Neill's ideas and dreams. The experimental demands of O'Neill were difficult, sometimes all but impossible to meet, and frequent failure was probably inevitable. When the demands were not only reached but exceeded, the results for American playgoers were extraordinary and unforgettable theatrical experiences.

Disparate treatment of O'Neill's plays corresponded to the growing pains of American theater in the 1920s. As exciting directors like Moeller, Jones, and Mamoulian matured in their work, it became increasingly clear that the modern director was a significant artist in the American theater, no longer just a producer, star maker, or stage manager. Some of the best new American directors worked with O'Neill, and their interpretations and experiments with that playwright remain emblematic of the emerging ascendant role of the professional director as well as of a volatile and exciting period of American theater. In the final analysis it should be said that the cooperative work of O'Neill with his directors and designers, especially in its diversity and longevity at the center of New York activity, went further than the work of any other playwright, theater or collective toward liberation of predictable practices on the American stage. Perhaps more importantly, the plays and record of experiments of Eugene O'Neill continue to inspire ongoing and expected experiment and growth in serious American style and dramatic form.

Bibliography

UNPUBLISHED MATERIALS

Light, James. "The Mask." *The Ancient Mariner* program, 1924, Province-town Players folder, Theatre Collection, Museum of the City of New York.

"*Marco Millions* Entre Act Music." Typed manuscript, Box 13, Theatre Guild Collection, Beinecke Library, Yale University.

O'Neill, Eugene. *Ah, Wilderness!* Bound promptbook, Theatre Collection, Performing Arts Center, New York Public Library, copyrighted 1933 by Yale University.

———. *Ah, Wilderness!* Bound promptbook, Theatre Guild Collection, Beinecke Library, Yale University.

———. *Ah, Wilderness!* Bound stage manager's promptbook, *Ah, Wilderness!* Folder #1, Theatre Collection, Museum of the City of New York.

———. *Beyond the Horizon.* Typescript, 1918, Rare Book and Manuscript Collection, Library of Congress.

———. *Days Without End.* Bound promptbook, Theatre Collection, Performing Arts Center, New York Public Library, copyrighted 1934 by Yale University.

———. *Days Without End.* Bound promptbook, Theatre Guild Collection, Beinecke Library, Yale University.

———. *Desire Under the Elms.* Bound promptbook, Theatre Collection, Performing Arts Center, New York Public Library, copyrighted 1924 by Yale University.

———. Drafts of two letters to Warren Munsell regarding *Ah, Wilderness!*, n.d., Yale Collection of American Literature, Beinecke Library, Yale University.

———. Draft of telegram to cast (of *Mourning Becomes Electra*, October 26, 1931), Yale Collection of American Literature, Beinecke Library, Yale University.

———. *Dynamo*. Bound promptbook, Theatre Collection, Performing Arts Center, New York Public Library, copyrighted 1929 by Yale University.

———. *Dynamo*. Bound promptbook, Theatre Guild Collection, Beinecke Library, Yale University.

———. *The Fountain*. Bound promptbook, Theatre Collection, Performing Arts Center, New York Public Library, copyrighted 1925 by Yale University.

———. *The Fountain*. Typescript, 1921, Rare Book and Manuscript Collection, Library of Congress.

———. *Gold*. Typescript, 1920, Rare Book and Manuscript Collection, Library of Congress.

———. *The Great God Brown*. Bound promptbook, Theatre Collection, Performing Arts Center, New York Public Library, copyrighted 1926 by Yale University.

———. Letter (photocopy) to Philip Moeller regarding *Ah, Wilderness!*, August 19, 1933, Yale Collection of American Literature, Beinecke Library, Yale University. Original held by the Humanities Research Center, University of Texas.

———. Letters (26 photocopies) to George C. Tyler, 1919–1921, William Seymour Theatre Collection, Firestone Library, Princeton University.

———. Manuscript notes, outline, and drawings for *Days Without End*, Yale Collection of American Literature, Beinecke Library, Yale University.

———. Manuscript notes, outline, and drawings for *Dynamo*, September 9, 1928, Yale Collection of American Literature, Beinecke Library, Yale University.

———. *Marco Millions*. Bound promptbook, Theatre Collection, Performing Arts Center, New York Public Library, copyrighted 1928 by Yale University.

———. *Marco Millions*. Bound promptbook, Theatre Guild Collection, Beinecke Library, Yale University.

———. *Mourning Becomes Electra*. Bound promptbook, Theatre Collection, Performing Arts Center, New York Public Library, copyrighted 1931 by Yale University.

———. *Mourning Becomes Electra*. Bound promptbook, Theatre Guild Collection, Beinecke Library, Yale University.

———. *The Ole Davil*. Typescript, 1920, Rare Book and Manuscript Collection, Library of Congress.

———. *Strange Interlude*. Bound promptbook, Theatre Collection, Performing Arts Center, New York Public Library, copyrighted 1928 by Yale University.

———. *Strange Interlude*. Bound promptbook, Theatre Guild Collection, Beinecke Library, Yale University.

———. *The Straw*. Typescript, 1919, Rare Book and Manuscript Collection, Library of Congress.

———. *Welded*. Typescript, 1923, Rare Book and Manuscript Collection, Library of Congress.

Production contracts and account books, George C. Tyler Papers, William Seymour Theatre Collection, Firestone Library, Princeton University.

Production photographs, notes, advertising materials, clippings, Eugene O'Neill folders, Theatre Collection, Museum of the City of New York.

Production programs for all O'Neill productions, 1920–1934, Eugene O'Neill folders, Theatre Collection, Museum of the City of New York.

"Provincetown Players Scrapbook," Theatre Collection, Performing Arts Center, New York Public Library.

Theatre Collection of Photographs, Beinecke Library, Yale University.

Thompson, Marion. Personal interview, December 28, 1982. Museum of the City of New York.

Tyler, George C. Letters (18 photocopies of office carbons) to Eugene O'Neill, 1919–1921, George C. Tyler Papers, William Seymour Theatre Collection, Firestone Library, Princeton University.

Yale Collection of American Literature Photographs, Beinecke Library, Yale University.

ARTICLES AND PUBLISHED INTERVIEWS

"Adolph Klauber, Producer, Dies." *New York Times*, December 8, 1933, p. 25.

"Alice Brady Dead; Stage, Film Star." *New York Times*, October 30, 1939, p. 17.

"Alla Nazimova, 66, Dies in Hollywood." *New York Times*, July 14, 1945, p. 11.

Atkinson, Brooks. "Acting at the Guild." *New York Times*, April 10, 1932, sec. 8, p. 1.

———. "Alfred Lunt, 1893–1972, Joy Was His Gift to the Stage." *New York Times*, August 14, 1977, sec. 2, p. 3.

———. "George M. Cohan at Home." *New York Times*, September 10, 1933, sec. 10, p. 1.

———. "Laurels for 'Strange Interlude.'" *New York Times*, May 13, 1928, sec. 9, p. 1.

Baker, George Pierce. "O'Neill's First Decade." *Yale Review* 15 (July 1926): 789–92.

"Banton Would Stop Two Plays as Unfit." *New York Times*, February 17, 1925, pp. 1, 13.

Barnes, Djuna. "The Days of Jig Cook." *Theatre Guild Magazine*, January 1929, pp. 31–32.

Barnes, Howard. "Moeller of the Theatre Guild." *New York Herald-Tribune*, February 10, 1929, sec. 7, pp. 2, 5.

Borton, Elizabeth. "Philip Moeller Discusses Bridge and the Staging of Plays." *Boston Herald*, December 31, 1933, p. 28.

Boulton, Agnes. "An Experimental Theatre." *Theatre Arts* 8 (March 1924): 184–88.

Brown, Gilmor. "A Dream on a Dime." In *Ten Talents in the American Theatre*. Ed. David H. Stevens, p. 170.

"Charles Kennedy, Ex-Actor, 79, Dies." *New York Times*, September 9, 1958, p. 35.

Cheney, Sheldon. "The Art Theatre—Twenty Years After." In *The New Caravan*. Ed. Alfred Kreymborg, pp. 426–45.

"The Chorus as Used in 'The Ancient Mariner.'" *Sun*, April 23, 1924, p. 24.

Colum, Mary M. "Life and Literature." *Forum* 94 (December 1935): 354–59.

Corbin, John. "O'Neill and Aeschylus." In *Essay Annual, 1933*. Ed. Erich A. Walter, pp. 159–170.

"Court Asked to Suppress 'Hairy Ape' as Indecent." *New York Tribune*, May 19, 1922, pp. 1, 5.

Cowley, Malcolm. "A Weekend with Eugene O'Neill." In *O'Neill and His Plays*. Ed. Oscar Cargill, pp. 41–49.

Dell, Floyd. "A Seer in Iowa." In George Cram Cook, *Greek Coins*. New York: George H. Doran, 1925.

"Direction by Moeller." *New York Times*, May 7, 1933, sec. 9, p. 2. Downer, Alan S. "Eugene O'Neill as Poet of the Theatre." In *O'Neill and His Plays*. Ed. Oscar Cargill, pp. 468–71.

"E. J. Ballantine, 80, Actor and Director." *New York Times*, October 22, 1968, p. 47.

"Earle Larimore, Actor, Dies at 48." *New York Times*, October 24, 1947, p. 23.

Eaton, Walter Prichard. "The Economics of Experiment." *Shadowland*, January 1923, pp. 26–27.

Edel, Leon. "Eugene O'Neill: The Face and the Mask." *University of Toronto Quarterly* 7 (October 1937): 18–34.

"Edgar Selwyn, 68, Producer, Is Dead." *New York Times*, February 14, 1944, p. 17.

"Editorial Comment." *Catholic World* 138 (February 1934): 513–17.

Eustis, Morton. "Backstage with Alice Brady." *New York Evening Post*, October 31, 1931, p. 4–D.

Fagin, N. Bryllion. "Eugene O'Neill." *Antioch Review* 14 (1954): 14–26.

Flory, Claude R. "Notes on the Antecedents of *Anna Christie.*" *PMLA* 86 (January 1971): 77–83.

Ford, Torrey. "From Pullman Car Porter to Honor Guest of Drama League." *New York Tribune*, March 13, 1921, sec. 7, p. 7.

Freedman, Morris. "Success and the American Dramatist." In *American Theatre.* Ed. John Russell Brown, pp. 109–25.

Gabriel, Gilbert. "The Newer O'Neill." *Vanity Fair*, April 1928, p. 52.

Gale, Zona. "The Colored Players and Their Plays." *Theatre Arts* 1 (May 1917): 138–40.

Gallup, Donald. "Eugene O'Neill's 'The Ancient Mariner.'" *Yale University Library Gazette* 35 (October 1960): 61–62.

"George Marion, 85, Ziegfeld Aide, Dies." *New York Times*, December 2, 1945, p. 46.

"Gilmor Brown, 73, Headed Theatre." *New York Times*, January 12, 1960, p. 47.

Gorelik, Mordecai. "Life with Bobby." *Theatre Arts* 39 (April 1955): 30–32, 94–95.

"Granville Barker, the New Art of the Theater and the New Drama." *American Review of Reviews*, April 1915, pp. 498–99.

Harold J. M'Gee, 55, Long a Stage Actor." *New York Times*, February 24, 1955, p. 27.

Helburn, Theresa. "O'Neill: An Impression." *Saturday Review*, November 21, 1936, p. 10.

———. "Staged by Philip Moeller." *Theatre Guild Magazine*, May 1929, pp. 27–29, 58–59.

Hopkins, Arthur. "Capturing the Audience." In *Directors on Directing.* Ed. Toby Cole and Helen Krich Chinoy, pp. 205–13.

———. "Producer and Play." In *Our Theatre Today.* Ed. Herschel L. Bricker, pp. 177–81.

Hutchens, John K. "Miss Fontanne on How It Feels to Play Nine Acts." *New York Evening Post*, March 3, 1928, sec. 3, p. 8.

"Irving Pichel as Lazarus in 'Lazarus Laughed.'" *Drama* 18 (May 1928): 243."J. A. Physioc Dead; Stage Designer, 86." *New York Times*, August 5, 1951, p. 73.

"James Light Dies; O'Neill Associate." *New York Times*, February 12, 1964, p. 33.

"John Westley." *New York Times*, December 18, 1948, p. 21.

Jones, Robert Edmond. "Art in the Theatre." In *Contemporary Attitudes.* Ed. Kendall B. Taft, pp. 458–67.

———. "Fashions in the Theatre." *Theatre Arts* 3 (April 1919): 115.

Kantor, Louis. "O'Neill Defends His Play of Negro." *New York Times*, May 11, 1924, sec. 9, p. 5.

Kemp, Harry. "Out of Provincetown." *Theatre Magazine*, April 1930, pp. 22–23, 66.

Kenton, Edna. "Provincetown and Macdougal Street." In George Cram Cook, *Greek Coins*. New York: George H. Doran, 1925.

———. "The Provincetown Players and the Playwrights' Theater." *Billboard*, August 5, 1922, pp. 5–6, 13–14.

Langner, Lawrence. "Eugene O'Neill." In *A Pictorial History of the Theatre Guild*. Ed. Norman Nadel. New York: Crown, 1969.

Leslie, Frank. "Letters from the Drama Mailbag." *New York Times*, September 14, 1958, sec. 2, p. 5.

Lewisohn, Ludwig. "Eugene O'Neill." *Nation* 113 (November 30, 1921): 626.

Loving, Pierre. "Eugene O'Neill." *Bookman* 53 (August 1921): 511–20.

Macgowan, Kenneth. "Enter the Artist—As Director." *Theatre Magazine*, November 1922, pp. 289–92.

———. "Eugene O'Neill as Realist." *New York Times*, March 23, 1924, sec. 8, p. 2.

Mannes, Marya. "Robert Edmond Jones." *Theatre Guild Magazine*, November 1930, pp. 15–19, 62.

"Mary Blair, Star of Stage for Years." *New York Times*, September 19, 1947, p. 23.

"Men and Their Shadows, Mamoulian Deals in Both." *New York Herald-Tribune*, December 16, 1928, sec. 7, p. 6.

Merrill, Flora. "Fierce Oaths and Blushing Complexes Find No Place in Eugene O'Neill's Talk." *World*, July 19, 1925, p. M-4.

Miller, Jordan. "Expressionism: The Waste Land Enacted." In *The Twenties: Fiction, Poetry, Drama*. Ed. Warren French, pp. 439–54.

Mindil, Philip. "Behind the Scenes." *New York Tribune*, February 15, 1920, sec. 3, p. 1.

———. "Behind the Scenes." *New York Tribune*, February 22, 1920, sec. 3, p. 1.

Moeller, Philip. "Silences Out Loud." *New York Times*, February 26, 1928, Sec. 8, p. 4.

———. "Some Notes on the Production of O'Neill's Strange Interlude." *Theatre Guild Quarterly*, February 1928, pp. 9, 26.

Moses, Montrose J. "O'Neill and 'The Emperor Jones.'" *Independent* 105 (February 12, 1921): 158–59.

"Mr. O'Neill and the Audible Theatre." *New York Times*, March 3, 1929, sec. 8, p. 4.

Mullett, Mary B. "The Extraordinary Story of Eugene O'Neill." *American Magazine*, November 1922, pp. 34–35, 112, 114, 116, 118, 120.

Nathan, George Jean. "The Theatre." *American Mercury*, 63 (October 1946), 462–466.

———. "The Theatre." *American Mercury* 63 (December 1946): 713–19.

"The New 'Dynamo' As Seen by O'Neill." *World*, January 27, 1929, p. M-3.

"The New Plays." *New York Times*, February 1, 1920, sec. 8, p. 2.

"The New Plays." *New York Times*, March 5, 1922, sec. 6, p. 1.

"Object to 'The Hairy Ape.'" *New York Times*, May 19, 1922, p. 20.

O'Neill, Eugene. "A Dramatist's Notebook." In *O'Neill and His Plays*. Ed. Oscar Cargill, pp. 120–22.

———. "A Letter from O'Neill." *New York Times*, April 11, 1920, sec. 6, p. 2.

———. "The Mail Bag." *New York Times*, December 18, 1921, sec. 6, p. 1.

———. "Memoranda on Masks." In *O'Neill and His Plays*. Ed. Oscar Cargill, pp. 116–18.

———. "O'Neill Talks About His Play." In *O'Neill and His Plays*. Ed. Oscar Cargill, pp. 110–12.

———. "The Playwright Explains." *New York Times*, February 14, 1926, sec. 8, p. 2.

———. "Second Thoughts." In *O'Neill and His Plays*. Ed. Oscar Cargill, pp. 118–20.

———. "Strindberg and Our Theatre." In *American Playwrights on Drama*. Ed. Horst Frenz, pp. 1–2.

———. "Working Notes and Extracts from a Fragmentary Work Diary." In *European Theories of the Drama*. Ed. Barrett H. Clark, pp. 530–36.

O'Neill, Eugene and Oliver M. Sayler. "The Artist of the Theatre." *Shadowland*, April 1922, pp. 49, 66, 77.

"O'Neill and His Plays." *New York Times*, January 8, 1928, sec. 8, p. 2.

"O'Neill Appeals for His 'Chillun.'" New York *Morning Telegraph*, March 19, 1924, pp. 1, 12.

"O'Neill on Strindberg." *New York Times*, January 6, 1924, sec. 7, p. 1.

"O'Neill Play Theme Unknown to Mayor." *Sun*, May 16, 1924, p. 3.

"O'Neill Trilogy Plans Omit All Matinees." *New York Times*, September 9, 1931, p. 25.

"O'Neill's 'Hairy Ape' Escapes Charge of Talking 'Indecently.'" *New York Tribune*, May 20, 1922, p. 18.

"O'Neill's Play Tonight." *New York Times*, March 9, 1920, p. 18.

"O'Neill's Trilogy Set for One Day." *New York Times*, October 13, 1931, p. 26.

Ormsbee, Helen. "Philip Moeller, Director, Hollywood and Here." *New York Herald-Tribune*, September 9, 1934, sec. 5. p. 3.

Parker, Robert Allerton. "An American Dramatist Developing." *Independent* 107 (December 3, 1921): 236.

Pawley, Frederick Arden. "Theatre Types: A Comparative Study." In *Architecture for the New Theatre*. Ed. Edith J. R. Isaacs, pp. 41–70.

Peck, Seymour. "Talk With Mrs. O'Neill." *New York Times*, November 4, 1956, sec. 2, pp. 1, 3.

"Philip Moeller, Director, Is Dead." *New York Times*, April 27, 1958, sec. 1, p. 86.

"Pittsburgh Hails New O'Neill Play." *New York Times*, September 26, 1933, p. 26.

"Play Juries Acquit 2 Shows As Clean." *New York Times*, March 14, 1925, p. 15.

"Plays on the Road." *New York Times*, March 9, 1924, sec. 8, p. 2.

Powers, Edward J. "What Next for the Small Theatre?" *Arts & Decoration* 15 (October 1921): 374–407.

"Prologue of 'All God's Chillun' Is Read." *World*, May 16, 1924, p. 13.

"Public Protests Ignored." *World*, March 3, 1924, pp. 1, 4.

Quinn, Arthur Hobson. "The Significance of Recent American Drama." *Scribner's Magazine*, July 1922, pp. 97–108.

"Reading of O'Neill's Play." *New York Times*, November 19, 1928, p. 19.

"Records of a Tragedy." *Literary Digest*, August 8, 1925, pp. 23–24.

Rhodes, Russell. "Robert Edmond Jones Says It Was O'Neill Who Really Did Designing for 'The Iceman.'" *New York Herald-Tribune*, December 29, 1946, sec. 5, pp. 3–4.

Robeson, Paul. "Reflections on O'Neill's Plays." *Opportunity* 2 (December 1924): 368–70.

"S. C. Ridges, 59, Actor on Stage, Screen, TV." *New York Times*, April 23, 1951, p. 25.

"Scene Designs of Latest Art Used by Guild." *New York Herald-Tribune*, February 24, 1929, sec. 7, pp. 2, 4.

Seldes, Gilbert. "Profiles: The Emperor Jones." *New Yorker*, May 9, 1931, pp. 25–28.

Simonson, Lee, "Moving 'Marco.'" *New York Times*, January 22, 1928, sec. 8, p. 2.

———. "Scenery and the Drama." *Atlantic Monthly* 143 (May 1929): 639–45.

———. "Scenic Design in the U.S.A." *Studio* 127 (June 1944): 196–200.

Smyser, William Leon. "A Temporary Expatriate Again Views Broadway." *New York Times*, July 1, 1928, sec. 8, p. 1.

"The Stage Door." *New York Tribune*, November 7, 1921, p. 8.

Sweeney, Charles P. "Back to the Source of Plays Written by Eugene O'Neill." *World*, November 9, 1924, p. M-5.

Taylor, Laurette. "In the Mail Bag." *New York Times*, November 20, 1921, sec. 6, p. 1.

"Three Strange Interludes." *Vanity Fair*, February 1929, p. 63.

Throckmorton, Cleon. "Scenic Art." In *Our Theatre Today*. Ed. Herschel L. Bricker, pp. 269–77.

"The Trouble With Brown." *Time*, December 7, 1953, pp. 77–78.

Valgemae, Mardi. "Eugene O'Neill's Preface to *The Great God Brown*." *Yale University Library Gazette* 43 (July 1968): 24–29.

Vandamm. "Master of Stage Illusion—Mr. Simonson." *Theatre Magazine*, February 1931, pp. 42–43.

"The Violation of Theatrical Neutrality by the Experimental Amateur." *Current Opinion*, May 1915, pp. 334–35.

Waterman, Arthur E. "From Iowa to Greece: The Achievement of George Cram Cook." *Quarterly Journal of Speech* 45 (1959): 46–50.

Watts, Richard, Jr. "Realism Doomed, O'Neill Believes." *New York Herald-Tribune*, February 5, 1928, sec. 7, p. 2.

"What 'Dynamo' Looked Like During Rehearsals." Clipping, *Dynamo* folder, Theatre Collection, Museum of the City of New York.

"What News on the Rialto?" *New York Times*, June 1, 1919, sec. 4, p. 2.

"Willard Mack, 56, Actor, Author, Dies." *New York Times*, November 20, 1934, p. 21.

Wilson, Edmund. "Eugene O'Neill and the Naturalists." In *The Shores of Light*. Ed. Edmund Wilson, pp. 99–104.

"Wolheim, 'Bad Man' of Movies, Is Dead." *New York Times*, February 19, 1931, p. 25.

Woodbridge, Homer E. "Beyond Melodrama." In *O'Neill and His Plays*. Ed. Oscar Cargill, pp. 307–20.

Woolf, S. J. "Four Decades on the Great White Way." *New York Times Magazine*, October 1, 1933, pp. 8–9.

———. "O'Neill Plots a Course for the Drama." *New York Times Magazine*, October 4, 1931, p. 6.

Woollcott, Alexander. "The Coming of Eugene O'Neill." *New York Times*, February 8, 1920, sec. 8, p. 2.

"You Fail If Bored Says Doris Keane." New York *Daily News*, March 5, 1922, p. 21.

Young, Stark. "The Art of Directing." In *The Context and Craft of Drama*. Ed. Robert W. Corrigan and James L. Rosenberg, pp. 365–79.

———. "The Art of Directing." *Theatre Arts* 9 (April 1925): 227–44.

———. "Eugene O'Neill: Notes from a Critic's Diary." *Harper's Magazine* 214 (June 1957): 66–71, 74.

REVIEWS

A. K. "The New Plays." *World*, March 18, 1924, p. 11.

A. S. "The New Play." New York *Globe*, March 6, 1922, p. 8.

"After the Play." *New Republic*, November 20, 1915, p. 74.

"After the Play." *New Republic*, May 10, 1919, p. 55.

Allen, Kelcey. "Marco Millions Is Poignant O'Neill Satire." *Women's Wear Daily*, January 10, 1928. In *Playwright's Progress*. Ed. Jordan Y. Miller, pp. 55–57.

"American Music Enters the Theatre." *American Review of Reviews* 78 (October 1928): 439–40.

"An American Tragedy." *Literary Digest*, February 28, 1920, p. 33.

"The Ancient Mariner." *New York Evening Post*, April 7, 1924, p. 13.

Anderson, John. "O'Neill Writes a Romance About Ponce de Leon." *New York Evening Post*, December 11, 1925, p. 12.

———. "O'Neill's *Days Without End*." *New York Evening Journal*, January 9, 1934. In *The American Theatre as Seen by Its Critics*. Ed. Montrose Moses, pp. 287–89.

———. "O'Neill's Newest Play Opens at the Greenwich Village." *New York Evening Post*, January 25, 1926. In *Playwright's Progress*. Ed. Jordan Y. Miller, pp. 51–52.

———. "'Strange Interlude' Profound Drama of Subconscious." *New York Evening Journal*, January 31, 1928. In *Playwright's Progress*. Ed. Jordan Y. Miller, pp. 57–59.

Andrews, Kenneth. "Broadway, Our Literary Signpost." *Bookman* 54 (January 1922): 463–67.

———. "Broadway, Our Literary Signpost." *Bookman* 55 (May 1922): 278–84.

"'Anna Christie' Has Its Premiere at Vanderbilt." *Sun*, November 3, 1921, p. 20.

"'Anna Christie' New Triumph for O'Neill." *New York Evening Journal*, November 3, 1922, p. 18.

Atkinson, Brooks. "After the Battle." *New York Times*, January 22, 1928, sec. 8, p. 1.

———. "Ah, Wilderness!" *New York Times*, October 3, 1933, p. 28.

———. "Concluding a Dramatic Cycle." *New York Times*, February 17, 1929, sec. 9, p. 1.

———. "Eugene O'Neill's 'Days Without End' Staged by the Theatre Guild." *New York Times*, January 9, 1934, p. 19.

———. "Eugene O'Neill's Gorgeous Satire." *New York Times*, January 10, 1928, p. 28.

———. "God in the Machine." *New York Times*, February 12, 1929, p. 22.

———. "Ibsen and O'Neill." *New York Times*, January 31, 1926, sec. 7, p. 1.

———. "Mourning Becomes Electra." *New York Times*, October 27, 1931, p. 22.

———. "New O'Neill Aspects." *New York Times*, December 20, 1925, sec. 7, p. 3.

———. "On 'Days Without End.'" *New York Times*, January 14, 1934, sec. 9, p. 1.

————. "Pauline Lord in 'Strange Interlude.'" *New York Times*, December 18, 1928, p. 37.

————. "Strange Interlude." *New York Times*, February 5, 1928, sec. 8, p. 1.

————. "Strange Interlude Plays Five Hours." *New York Times*, January 31, 1928, p. 28.

————. "Symbolism in an O'Neill Tragedy." *New York Times*, January 25, 1926, p. 26.

————. "Tragedy Becomes O'Neill." *New York Times*, November 1, 1931, sec. 8, p. 1.

B. D. "Second Thoughts on 'The Fountain.'" New York *Morning Telegraph*, December 13, 1925, sec. 2, p. 8.

Barretto, Larry. "The New Yorker." *Bookman* 62 (February 1926): 704–08.

Bellamy, Francis R. "Lights Down." *Outlook* 148 (February 22, 1928): 304–05.

————. "The Theatre." *Outlook and Independent* 151 (February 27, 1929): 331.

Benchley, Robert C. "Drama." *Life* (New York) 77 (June 16, 1921): 876.

————. "Drama." *Life* (New York), November 24, 1921, p. 18.

————. "Drama." *Life* (New York), December 8, 1921, p. 18.

————. "Drama." *Life* (New York), March 30, 1922, p. 18.

————. "Drama." *Life* (New York), April 3, 1924, p. 26.

————. "Drama." *Life* (New York), December 11, 1924, p. 18.

————. "Drama." *Life* (New York), December 31, 1925, p. 18.

————. "Drama." *Life* (New York), February 11, 1926, p. 20.

————. "Drama." *Life* (New York), February 16, 1928, p. 21.

————. "Dynamo." In *O'Neill and His Plays*. Ed. Oscar Cargill, pp. 187–89.

————. "O'Neill's *Mourning Becomes Electra*." *New Yorker*, November 7, 1931. In *American Theatre as Seen by Its Critics*. Ed. Montrose Moses, pp. 262–65.

"'Beyond the Horizon,' a Frank Tragedy, Is Very Interesting." *New York Clipper*, February 11, 1920, p. 21.

"Beyond the Horizon Seen." New York *Morning Telegraph*, February 3, 1920, p. 14.

Bonte, C. H. "'Chris' and the Modernist School," Philadelphia *Public Ledger*, March 21, 1920, sec. 1, part 2, p. 9.

Bowen, Stirling. "The Theatre." *Wall Street Journal*, October 28, 1931, p. 4.

————. "The Theatre." *Wall Street Journal*, January 11, 1934, p. 3.

Boyd, Ernest. "Eugene O'Neill and Others." *Bookman* 69 (April 1929): 179–81.

Brackett, Charles. "The Theatre." *New Yorker*, January 21, 1928, pp. 25–26.

————. "The Theatre." *New Yorker*, February 11, 1928, p. 24.

————. "The Theatre." *New Yorker*, February 23, 1929, pp. 27–28.

"Broad." *Philadelphia Inquirer*, March 21, 1920, sec. 2, p. 21.

Bromfield, Louis. "The New Yorker." *Bookman* 60 (January 1925): 620–24.

Broun, Heywood. "Beyond the Horizon by Eugene O'Neill a Notable Play." *New York Tribune*, February 4, 1920, p. 9.

———. "The Emperor Jones." *New York Tribune*, November 4, 1920. In *O'Neill and His Plays*. Ed. Oscar Cargill, pp. 144–46.

———. "'Gold' at Frazee Shows O'Neill Below His Best." *New York Tribune*, June 2, 1921, p. 6.

———. "The Hairy Ape." *World*, April 2, 1922, sec. CC, p. 4.

———. "The New Play." *World*, April 7, 1924, p. 9.

———. "The New Play." *World*, May 16, 1924, p. 13.

———. "The New Plays." *World*, November 12, 1924, pp. 15–16.

Brown, John Mason. "The Director Takes a Hand." *Theatre Arts* 10 (February 1926): 73–85.

———. "Doldrums of Midwinter." *Theatre Arts* 10 (March 1926): 146.

———. "George M. Cohan in Eugene O'Neill's Comedy." *New York Evening Post*, October 3, 1933, p. 26.

———. "Intermission." *Theatre Arts* 12 (April 1928): 237–48.

———. "'Mourning Becomes Electra,' Eugene O'Neill's Exciting Trilogy, Is Given an Excellent Production at the Guild." *New York Evening Post*, October 27, 1931. In *Playwright's Progress*. Ed. Jordan Y. Miller, pp. 67–71.

———. "Mr. Cohan in *Ah, Wilderness!*" In John Mason Brown, *Two on the Aisle*, p. 236.

———. "New York Goes Native." *Theatre Arts* 12 (March 1928): 163–78.

———. "Sermons in Plays." *Theatre Arts* 11 (December 1927): 904.

———. "The Theatre Guild Presents Earle Larimore and Stanley Ridges in Mr. O'Neill's 'Days Without End.'" *New York Evening Post*, January 9, 1934. In *Playwright's Progress*. Ed. Jordan Y. Miller, pp. 80–82.

Caldwell, Cy. "To See or Not to See." *New Outlook* 162 (November 1933): 42.

Carb, David. "Seen on the Stage." *Vogue*, March 1, 1928, pp. 82–83.

———. "Seen on the Stage." *Vogue*, April 1, 1928, pp. 82–83, 140.

———. "Seen on the Stage." *Vogue*, March 30, 1929, pp. 61, 102.

———. "Seen on the Stage." *Vogue*, January 1, 1932, pp. 57, 76.

———. "To See or Not to See." *Bookman* 59 (May 1924): 329–33.

Castellun, Maida. "Eugene O'Neill's 'Anna Christie' Is Thrilling Drama, Perfectly Acted with a Bad Ending." *New York Call*, November 4, 1921, p. 4.

———. "The First Man." *New York Call*, March 9, 1922. In *O'Neill and His Plays*. Ed. Oscar Cargill, pp. 157–59.

———. "O'Neill's 'The Emperor Jones' Thrills and Fascinates." *New York Call*, November 10, 1920. In *Playwright's Progress*. Ed. Jordan Y. Miller, pp. 22–23.

———. "The Plays that Pass." *New York Call*, March 12, 1922, p. 4.

Chatfield-Taylor, Otis. "The Latest Plays." *Outlook and Independent* 159 (November 11, 1931): 343.

"Chris." *Dramatic Mirror* 81 (March 27, 1920): 577.

"'Chris,' a New Play by Eugene O'Neill." *Philadelphia Record*, March 16, 1920, p. 6.

"'Chris' at Broad." *Philadelphia Inquirer*, March 16, 1920, p. 6.

"'Chris' Sailor Play at Broad." *Philadelphia Press*, March 16, 1920, p. 12.

Clark, Barrett H. "Eugene O'Neill and the Guild." *Drama* 18 (March 1928): 169–71.

———. "The New O'Neill Play." *Drama* 16 (February 1926): 175.

———. "O'Neill's 'Dynamo' and the Village Experiments." *Drama* 19 (April 1929): 199–201, 222–23.

Clark, Norman. "New Play by O'Neill at Auditorium." *Baltimore News*, March 4, 1924, p. 9.

Colum, Padraic. "The Theatre." *Dial* 86 (April 1929): 349–52.

"Convocation of Woe in 'The First Man,' O'Neill's New Play." *New York Tribune*, March 6, 1922, p. 6.

Corbin, John. "The Holy Bonds or Welded by Hate." *New York Times*, March 23, 1924, sec. 8, p. 1.

———. "A New Provincetown Playbill." *New York Times*, April 7, 1924, p. 15.

———. "The Right Word." *New York Times*, November 23, 1923, p. 20.

———. "Romantic Marriage." *New York Times*, March 18, 1924, p. 24.

———. "A Sensation Manque." *New York Times*, May 16, 1924, p. 22.

———. "What Boys Will Be." *New York Times*, April 13, 1924, sec. 8, p. 1.

Crawford, Jack. "Broadway Sheds Tears." *Drama* 12 (February 1922): 152, 181.

"Current Bills at the Theatres." Philadelphia *Evening Bulletin*, March 16, 1920, p. 24.

Dale, Alan. "Eugene O'Neill's New Play Given Artistic Settings." *New York American*, December 12, 1925, p. 6.

———. "'The First Man,' Eugene O'Neill Play Staged." *New York American*, March 6, 1922. In *Playwright's Progress*. Ed. Jordan Y. Miller, pp. 13–14.

———. "With Alan Dale at the New Plays." *New York American*, February 8, 1920, sec. CE, p. 7.

De Casseres, Benjamin, "Adrift in the Roaring Forties." *Theatre Magazine*, June 1922, p. 370.

———. "Broadway to Date." *Arts & Decoration*, March 1928, pp. 62, 96.

———. "Broadway to Date." *Arts & Decoration*, April 1928, pp. 65, 103.

———. "Broadway to Date." *Arts & Decoration*, April 1929, pp. 72, 118.

———. "Broadway to Date." *Arts & Decoration*, January 1932, pp. 52, 68.

De Foe, Louis V. "Another Play by Eugene O'Neill." *World*, March 6, 1922, p. 9.

————. "New O'Neill Play." *World*, June 2, 1921, p. 9.

————. "O'Neill's Triple Extract of Gloom." *World*, November 12, 1921, p. 15.

————. "Two Plays." *World*, November 6, 1921, p. M-2.

Decker, Karl, "'Mariner Thrills Fail to Register." New York *Morning Telegraph*, April 8, 1924, p. 7.

Dickinson, Thomas H. "The Theatrical Interpreter." *American Review* 3 (March-April 1925): 216–21.

"Drab Life of the Sea in O'Neill's 'Anna Christie.'" *New York Herald*, November 3, 1921, p. 15.

"'The Dream Play' Not in a Key of Reality." *New York Times*, January 21, 1926, p. 18.

Eastman, Fred. "O'Neill Discovers the Cross!" *Christian Century* 51 (February 7, 1934): 191–92.

Eaton, Walter Prichard. "The Hairy Ape." *Freeman* 5 (April 26, 1922): pp. 160–61. In *Playwright's Progress*. Ed. Jordan Y. Miller, pp. 32–35.

Edba. "Desire Under the Elms." *Variety*, November 19, 1924, pp. 18–19.

Edel, Leon. "Placid and Amiable." *Canadian Forum* 14 (February 1934): 188.

"Eugene O'Neill's 'Gold' Tells a Weird Tale." *New York Times*, June 2, 1921, p. 14.

"Eugene O'Neill's New Play, 'Gold,' Not Without Alloy." *New York Herald*, June 2, 1921, p. 9.

"Eugene O'Neill's 'The Straw' Is Gruesome Clinical Tale." *Sun*, November 11, 1921, p. 12.

"Eugene O'Neill's 'The Straw' Profoundly Impressive Play." *New York Herald*, November 11, 1921, p. 6.

"Eugene O'Neill's Tragedy Played." *Sun*, February 4, 1920, p. 13.

Evans, Harry. "Theatre." *Life* (New York), November 13, 1931, p. 19.

Fergusson, Francis. "A Month in the Theatre." *Bookman* 74 (December 1931): 440–45.

————. "A Month of the Theatre." *Bookman* 75 (June-July 1932): 288–91.

Firkins, O. W. "Drama." *Review* 2 (February 21, 1920): 185–86.

————. "Drama." *Weekly Review* 4 (March 2, 1921): 207–09.

————. "Drama." *Weekly Review* 4 (June 18, 1921): 584–85.

————. "Eugene O'Neill's Remarkable Play." *Weekly Review* 3 (December 8, 1920): 567–68.

————. "O'Neill and Other Playwrights." *Yale Review* 17 (October 1927): 173–75.

"'The First Man,' New O'Neil [sic] Play, at the Playhouse." *New York Clipper*, March 15, 1922, p. 2.

"'First Man' Presented at Neighborhood Playhouse." *Sun*, March 6, 1922, p. 16.

Gabriel, Gilbert W. "De Leon in Search of His Spring." *Sun*, December 11, 1925. In *Playwright's Progress*. Ed. Jordan Y. Miller, pp. 15–16.

———. "The Great God Brown." *Sun*, January 25, 1926. In *O'Neill and His Plays*. Ed. Oscar Cargill, pp. 175–77.

———. "Personal Element." *New York American*, October 3, 1933. In *Playwright's Progress*. Ed. Jordan Y. Miller, pp. 76–77.

[Gabriel] G. W. G. "The Theatre." *New Yorker*, February 6, 1926, pp. 26–27.

Garland, Robert. "Eugene O'Neill and This Big Business of Broadway." *Theatre Arts* 9 (January 1925): 3–16.

———. "Eugene O'Neill's 'Dynamo' Displayed in 45th Street." *New York Telegram*, February 12, 1929. In *Playwright's Progress*. Ed. Jordan Y. Miller, pp. 62–64.

———. Clipping. *World-Telegram*, n.d., *Mourning Becomes Electra* folder #2, Museum of the City of New York.

"Garment of Repentance." *Literary Digest*, October 28, 1933, p. 24.

Gilliam, Florence. Clipping. *Quill*, November 1920, pp. 25–26. In "Provincetown Players Scrapbook," Theatre Collection, Performing Arts Center, New York Public Library.

"'Gold' a Triumph for Willard Mack." *Journal of Commerce*, June 2, 1921, p. 7.

"'Gold' O'Neil's [sic] New Play Interesting But Far from Writer's Best." *New York Clipper*, June 8, 1921, p. 19.

"'Gold' Opens at Frazee Theatre." New York *Morning Telegraph*, June 2, 1921, p. 14.

Grady, Louis. "Eugene O'Neill's 'Beyond the Horizon' Is One of the Great Plays of the Modern American Stage." *New York Call*, February 5, 1920, p. 4.

H. J. M. "Critique." *New Yorker*, December 19, 1925, p. 17.

H. T. P. "In New Vein the New Play from O'Neill." *Boston Evening Transcript*, December 28, 1933, p. 13.

Hackett, Francis. "Anna Christie." *New Republic*, November 30, 1921. In *O'Neill and His Plays*. Ed. Oscar Cargill, pp. 152–54.

"The Hairy Ape." *New York Evening Post*, March 22, 1922, p. 8.

"'The Hairy Ape' a Logical Tragedy." *World*, March 10, 1922, p. 14.

"'The Hairy Ape,' O'Neil [sic] Play, Is Dull and Tiresome." *New York Clipper*, March 22, 1922, p. 22.

Hammond, Percy. "'Anna Christie' by the Acrid Mr. O'Neill, Is Presented at the Vanderbilt." *New York Tribune*, November 3, 1921, p. 10.

———. "Eugene O'Neill in 'The Straw' Depicts the Joys and Sorrows of the Tubercular." *New York Tribune*, November 11, 1921, p. 8.

———. "Eugene O'Neill's 'Welded.'" *New York Tribune*, March 18, 1924, p. 12.

———. "'The Hairy Ape' Shows Eugene O'Neill in a Bitter and Interesting Humor." *New York Tribune*, March 10, 1922, p. 8.

———. "The Theaters." *New York Herald-Tribune*, May 16, 1924, p. 10.

———. "The Theaters." *New York Herald-Tribune*, November 12, 1924, p. 14.

———. "The Theaters." *New York Herald-Tribune*, December 11, 1925, p. 22.

———. "The Theaters." *New York Herald-Tribune*, January 10, 1928, p. 28.

———. "The Theaters." *New York Herald-Tribune*, January 31, 1928, p. 18.

———. "The Theaters." *New York Herald-Tribune*, February 17, 1929, Sec. 7. p. 1.

———. "The Theaters." *New York Herald-Tribune*, January 9, 1934, p. 16.

———. "The Theaters." *New York Herald-Tribune*, January 14, 1934, Sec. 5, pp. 1, 5.

———. "The Theaters: Dynamo." *New York Herald-Tribune*, February 12, 1929. In *Playwright's Progress*. Ed. Jordan Y. Miller, pp. 64–65.

Hersey, F. W. "Lazarus Laughed." *Drama* 18 (May 1928): 244–46.

Hornblow, Arthur. "Mr. Hornblow Goes to the Play." *Theatre Magazine*, March 1920, pp. 181–85.

———. "Mr. Hornblow Goes to the Play." *Theatre Magazine*, April 1921, pp. 261–64.

———. "Mr. Hornblow Goes to the Play." *Theatre Magazine*, August 1921, pp. 97–98.

———. "Mr. Hornblow Goes to the Play." *Theatre Magazine*, January 1922, pp. 29–32.

———. "Mr. Hornblow Goes to the Play." *Theatre Magazine*, May 1922, pp. 305–08.

———. "Mr. Hornblow Goes to the Play." *Theatre Magazine*, May 1924, pp. 15–19.

———. "Mr. Hornblow Goes to the Play." *Theatre Magazine*, June 1924, pp. 15–19.

Hughes, Elinor. "The Theatres." *Boston Herald*, December 28, 1933, p. 14.

Hutchens, John. "Greece to Broadway." *Theatre Arts* 16 (January 1932): 13–24.

Isaacs, Edith J. R. "Good Plays A-Plenty." *Theatre Arts* 17 (December 1933): 908–21.

———. "Parents and Other People." *Theatre Arts* 18 (March 1934): 164–72.

James, Patterson. "Off the Record." *Billboard*, April 15, 1922, p. 18. In *Playwright's Progress*. Ed. Jordan Y. Miller, pp. 35–37.

Jolo. "Anna Christie." *Variety*, November 11, 1921, p. 17.

Kalonyme, Louis. "Delectable Mountains of Current Drama." *Arts & Decoration*, February 1926, pp. 66, 82, 84, 86.

———. "Dramatica Dionysiana." *Arts & Decoration*, March 1926, pp. 62, 96, 98.

Kaufman, S. Jay. "Gold." *Dramatic Mirror* 83 (June 11, 1921): 1001.

———. "Round the Town." New York *Globe*, March 1, 1920, p. 14.

———. "The Straw." *Dramatic Mirror* 84 (November 19, 1921): 737.

Krutch, Joseph Wood. "Desire Under the Elms." *Nation*, November 26, 1924. In Hewitt, *Theatre USA*, pp. 360–62.

———. "Marco Millions." *Nation* 126 (January 25, 1928): 104–05.

———. "Mr. O'Neill's Comedy." *Nation* 137 (October 18, 1933): 458–59.

———. "Our Electra." *Nation* 133 (November 18, 1931): 551–52.

———. "The Tragedy of Masks." *Nation* 122 (February 10, 1926): 164–65.

Lait, [Jack]. "Dynamo." *Variety*, February 13, 1929, pp. 55–56.

———. "Gold." *Variety*, June 10, 1921, p. 15.

Lewisohn, Ludwig. "An American Tragedy." *Nation* 110 (February 21, 1920): 241–42.

———. "The Development of Eugene O'Neill." *Nation* 114 (March 22, 1922): 349–50.

———. "Diversions." *Nation* 118 (April 23, 1924): 486.

———. "Drama." *Nation* 116 (January 10, 1923): 48.

———. "Drama." *Nation* 118 (June 4, 1924): 664.

———. "Gold." *Nation* 112 (June 22, 1921): 902.

———. "Native Plays." *Nation* 112 (February 2, 1921): 189.

———. "Welded." *Nation* 118 (April 2, 1924). In *O'Neill and His Plays*. Ed. Oscar Cargill, pp. 163–65.

Littell, Robert. "The Land of Second Best." *Theatre Arts* 13 (April 1929): 240–55.

———. "Mr. O'Neill Pillories a Venetian Babbitt. *New York Evening Post*, January 10, 1928, p. 20.

———. "O'Neill's Strange Interlude." *New York Evening Post*, January 31, 1928, p. 18.

———. "The Theatre Guild Presents 'Dynamo.'" *New York Evening Post*, February 12, 1929, p. 12.

"Lounger in the Lobby." *Philadelphia Press*, March 21, 1920, part 4, p. 1.

Macgowan, Kenneth. "America's Best Season in the Theatre." *Theatre Arts* 4 (April 1920): 91–104.

———. "Broadway at the Spring." *Theatre Arts* 6 (July 1922): 179–90.

———. "Crying the Bounds of Broadway." *Theatre Arts* 8 (June 1924): 355–64.

———. "Curtain Calls." New York *Globe*, February 7, 1920, p. 6.

———. "Diff'rent." *Vogue*, March 15, 1921. In *O'Neill and His Plays*. Ed. Oscar Cargill, pp. 147–49.

———. "Eugene O'Neill's 'Anna Christie' a Notable Drama Notably Acted at the Vanderbilt Theatre." New York *Globe*, November 3, 1921. In *Playwright's Progress*. Ed. Jordan Y. Miller, pp. 27–28.

———. "Eugene O'Neill's New Play." *Vanity Fair*, February 1929, pp. 62, 94.

———. "The New Play." New York *Globe*, November 4, 1920, p. 14.

———. "The New Play." New York *Globe*, June 2, 1921, p. 16.

———. "The New Play." New York *Globe*, March 10, 1922, p. 14.

———. "The New Plays." New York *Globe*, December 31, 1921, p. 7.

———. "The New Season." *Theatre Arts* 5 (January 1921): 3–14.

———. "Year's End." *Theatre Arts* 6 (January 1922): 3–10.

Mantle, Burns. Clipping. New York *Daily News*, n.d. In *Mourning Becomes Electra* folder 2, Theatre Collection, Museum of the City of New York.

———. "O'Neill's New Play Is Lustful and Tragic." New York *Daily News*, November 14, 1924, p. 30.

"Marco Polo Masquerading as Babbitt." *Literary Digest*, February 4, 1928, pp. 26–27.

Marsh, Leo A. "'Beyond Horizon' Stirring Drama." New York *Morning Telegraph*, February 4, 1920, p. 14.

———. "O'Neill's Latest Pure Experiment." New York *Morning Telegraph*, January 25, 1926, p. 3.

Martin, Linton. "Dramaless Drama." Philadelphia *North American*, March 21, 1920, p. 6.

———. "Novel Note Struck in Eugene O'Neill's 'Chris.'" Philadelphia *North American*, March 16, 1920, p. 13.

Metcalfe. "Drama." *Life* (New York), 75 (February 19, 1920): 322.

———. "Playing Theatre." *Wall Street Journal*, April 8, 1924, p. 3.

———. "The Theatre." *Wall Street Journal*, March 19, 1924, p. 3.

———. "The Theatre." *Wall Street Journal*, May 17, 1924, p. 3.

———. "The Theatre." *Wall Street Journal*, November 15, 1924, p. 3.

———. "The Theatre." *Wall Street Journal*, December 12, 1925, p. 3.

———. "The Theatre." *Wall Street Journal*, January 25, 1926, p. 3.

"Molière Satire at Village Playhouse." *Journal of Commerce*, April 8, 1924, p. 7.

"More Room Improves 'The Emperor Jones.'" *World*, December 28, 1920, p. 11.

Motherwell, Hiram. "Days Without End." *Stage*, February 1934, pp. 16–18.

"Mr. O'Neill Runs Aground on a Bleak New England Farm." *New York Evening Post*, November 12, 1924, p. 14.

"Mr. O'Neill Seeking Romance." *New York Times*, December 11, 1925, p. 26.

Nathan, George Jean. "Eugene O'Neill." In *American Drama and Its Critics*. Ed. Alan S. Downer, pp. 78–115.

———. "The Rime of the Ancient Mariner." *American Mercury*, June 1924.

In *O'Neill and His Plays*. Ed. Oscar Cargill, pp. 166–67.

———. "The Theatre." *American Mercury* 2 (May 1924): 113–19.

———. "The Theatre." *Vanity Fair*, March 1934, pp. 41–42.

"The Negro in American Drama." *Theatre*, June 1917, pp. 350, 352.

"New O'Neill Play." *New York Evening Post*, May 16, 1924, p. 13.

"New O'Neill Play Opens Downtown." New York *Morning Telegraph*, November 12, 1924, p. 5.

"The News-Week in Entertainment." *News-Week*, January 20, 1934, p. 34.

Niblo, Fred, Jr. "New O'Neill Play Sinks to Depths." *New York Morning Telegraph*, November 13, 1924, p. 3.

Nichols, Dudley. "The New Play." *World*, January 31, 1928, pp. 11–12.

"Not as Others Are, But Still Worth While." *Outlook* 126 (December 22, 1920): 710–11.

"O'Neill Play Falls Far Short of Ideal upon Its Premiere." *Baltimore Daily Post*, March 4, 1924, p. 5.

"Opening Nights." *Independent* 105 (February 12, 1921): 153.

"A Playgoer's Afterthoughts." *Theatre Guild Magazine*, March 1932, pp. 7–14.

"A Playgoer's Discoveries." *Stage*, November 1933, pp. 7–14.

Pollock, Arthur. "All God's Chillun." *Brooklyn Daily Eagle*, May 16, 1924. In *Playwright's Progress*. Ed. Jordan Y. Miller, pp. 37–39.

———. "Anna Christie." *Brooklyn Daily Eagle*, November 3, 1921, p. 6.

———. "Another O'Neill Play." *Brooklyn Daily Eagle*, June 2, 1921, p. 6.

———. "The First Man." *Brooklyn Daily Eagle*, March 7, 1922, p. 10.

———. "Plays and Things." *Brooklyn Daily Eagle*, December 11, 1925, p. 18.

———. "Plays and Things." *Brooklyn Daily Eagle*, January 25, 1926, p. 10A.

"Ponce de Leon a la Mr. O'Neill." New York *Morning Telegraph*, December 12, 1925, p. 5.

"Provincetown Bill Best They've Done for Long Time." *New York Clipper*, November 24, 1920, p. 19.

"Provincetown Players Stage Remarkable Play." *Brooklyn Daily Eagle*, November 9, 1920, p. 5.

"Provincetowners Put on 'Diff'rent,' a Really Great Play." *New York Clipper*, January 5, 1921, p. 19.

[Pulaski, Jack] Ibee. "Days Without End." *Variety*, January 16, 1934, p. 48.

———. "Marco Millions." *Variety*, January 11, 1928, pp. 50–51.

———. "Strange Interlude." *Variety*, February 1, 1928, p. 52.

———. "Welded." *Variety*, March 26, 1924, p. 16.

R. H. "The Theatre." *Wall Street Journal*, January 11, 1928, p. 4.

R. M. L. "Desire Under the Elms." *New Republic* 40 (December 3, 1924): 44.

R. S. "The Theatre." *Wall Street Journal*, February 2, 1928, p. 4.

Rathbun, Stephen. "Eugene O'Neill's 'Hairy Ape' Is One of the Most Vital Plays of the Season." *Sun*, March 11, 1922, p. 4.

———. "In the Plays." *Sun*, November 6, 1920, p. 3.

———. "January Plays." *Sun*, December 31, 1920, p. 5.

Reamer, Lawrence. "'First Man,' New O'Neill Play, Is a Gloomy Suburban Story." *New York Herald*, March 6, 1922, p. 13.

Reid, Louis R. "Beyond the Horizon." *Dramatic Mirror* 81 (February 14, 1920): 258.

Ridge, Lola. "Beyond the Horizon." *New Republic* 25 (January 5, 1921): 173–74.

Ruhl, Arthur. "Second Nights." *New York Herald-Tribune*, February 17, 1929, sec. 7, pp. 1, 5.

———. "Second Nights." *New York Herald-Tribune*, November 1, 1931, sec. 8, pp. 1, 10.

Rush. "Mourning Becomes Electra." *Variety*, November 3, 1931, p. 54.

Sayler, Oliver M. "Our Theater at Cross-Purposes." *Century Magazine* 104 (September 1922): 747–56.

———. "The Play of the Week." *Saturday Review* 4 (February 11, 1928): 590.

"Sea Story 'Chris' by Monte Cristo's Son." Philadelphia *Public Ledger*, March 16, 1920, p. 9.

"Seafaring Folk as They Really Are." *Philadelphia Record*, March 21, 1920, part 5, p. 7.

Seldes, Gilbert. "The Hairy Ape." *Dial*, May 1922. In *Theatre USA*. Barnard Hewitt, pp. 338–40.

———. "The Theatre." *Dial* 71 (December 1921): 724–25.

———. "The Theatre." *Dial* 78 (January 1925): 81–82.

———. "The Theatre." *Dial* 80 (February 1926): 166–69.

———. "The Theatre." *Dial* 84 (April 1928): 348–52.

Sisk. "The Fountain." *Variety*, December 16, 1925, p. 27.

———. "Great God Brown." *Variety*, January 27, 1926, p. 26.

Skinner, R. Dana. "Blossoms in the Arid Desert." *Independent* 116 (March 6, 1926): 275.

———. "Decay and Flowing Sap." *Independent* 114 (January 10, 1925): 51.

———. "The Play." *Commonweal* 3 (February 10, 1926): 384.

———. "The Play." *Commonweal*, February 23, 1928. In *Theatre USA*. Barnard Hewitt, pp. 371–74.

———. "The Play." *Commonweal* 9 (February 27, 1929): 489–90.

———. "The Play." *Commonweal* 15 (November 11, 1931): 46–47.

———. "The Play." *Commonweal* 19 (January 19, 1934): 327–29.

Smith, Geddes. "Three Mirrors." *Survey*, April 1, 1926, pp. 43–44.

Stechan, H. O. "Lazarus Laughed." *Billboard*, April 21, 1928, p. 11.

"Strange Interlude." *Saturday Review* 4 (March 3, 1928): 641.

"The Straw." *Brooklyn Daily Eagle*, November 11, 1921, p. 8.

"'The Straw' Is Play of Hopelessness Pain and Death." *New York Clipper*, November 16, 1921, p. 20.

T. M. C. "Eugene O'Neill's Drama, 'Welded,' at Auditorium." *Baltimore Sun*, March 4, 1924, p. 9.

———. "Retrospect Reveals 'Intellectual' Values in O'Neill's New Drama." *Baltimore Sun*, March 9, 1924, Part 2, p. 2.

"The Theatre." *Sun*, June 2, 1921, p. 14.

"The Theatres." *Boston Daily Globe*, December 28, 1933, p. 16.

"This Week's Playbills." *Philadelphia Press*, March 21, 1920, part 4, p. 1.

Torres, H. Z. "'Welded' Displays Morbid Tendency." *New York Commercial*, March 18, 1924, p. 4.

Towse, J. Ranken. "Beyond the Horizon." *New York Evening Post*, February 4, 1920, p. 11.

———. "Eugene O'Neill's Latest Effort." *New York Evening Post*, March 10, 1922, p. 7.

———. "Eugene O'Neill's Latest Play." *New York Evening Post*, March 6, 1922, p. 6.

———. "The Play." *New York Evening Post*, September 9, 1920, p. 9.

———. "The Play." *New York Evening Post*, December 29, 1920, p. 9.

———. "The Play." *New York Evening Post*, June 2, 1921, p. 7.

———. "The Play." *New York Evening Post*, November 3, 1921, p. 9.

———. "The Play." *New York Evening Post*, November 11, 1921, p. 7.

"Tragedy of Great Power at Morosco." *World*, February 4, 1920, p. 13.

"The Tributary Theatre." *Theatre Arts* 12 (June 1928): 447–48.

Vreeland, Frank. "'Ancient Mariner' Made Vivid Even for Schoolboys." *New York Herald-Tribune*, April 7, 1924, p. 8.

W. G. "The Theatre." *New Yorker*, October 14, 1933, p. 30.

Warren, George C. "'Lazarus Laughed' Produced on Coast." *New York Times*, April 10, 1928, p. 33.

[Watts, Richard, Jr.] R. W. Jr. "'The Great God Brown' Is Fascinating Enigma." *New York Herald-Tribune*, January 25, 1926, p. 13.

Whipple, Leon. "Two Plays by O'Neill." *Survey* 53 (January 1, 1925): 421–22.

Whittaker, James. "All of O'Neil's [sic] Surplus Tragedy Utilized in Gold." New York *Daily News*, June 3, 1921, p. 15.

———. "Eugene O'Neill's Play Shown at 37th Street." *New York American*, March 18, 1924. In *Playwright's Progress*. Ed. Jordan Y. Miller, pp. 14–15.

———. "O'Neill Has First Concrete Heroine." New York *Daily News*, November 13, 1921, p. 21.

"Willard Mack Scores in New Drama." *New York Evening Journal*, June 2, 1921, p. 14.

Williams, Michael. "The Play." *Commonweal* 3 (December 23, 1925): 189.

Wilson, Edmund. "All God's Chillun and Others." *New Republic* 38 (May 28, 1924): 22.

Woollcott, Alexander. "Another O'Neill Play." *New York Times*, November 11, 1921, p. 16.

———. "'Beyond the Horizon' Established." *New York Times*, March 10, 1920, p. 9.

———. "Eugene O'Neill at Full Tilt." *New York Times*, March 10, 1920, p. 18.

———. "Eugene O'Neill's Tragedy." *New York Times*, February 4, 1920, p. 12.

———. "A New O'Neill Play." *New York Times*, December 29, 1920, p. 8.

———. "The New O'Neill Play." *New York Times*, November 7, 1920, sec. 7, p. 1.

———. "The New O'Neill Play." *New York Times*, November 3, 1921, p. 22.

———. "The New O'Neill Play." *New York Times*, March 6, 1922, p. 9.

———. "Second Thoughts on First Nights." *New York Times*, February 8, 1920, sec. 8, p. 2.

———. "Second Thoughts on First Nights." *New York Times*, May 8, 1921, sec. 6, p. 1.

———. "Second Thoughts on First Nights." *New York Times*, November 13, 1921, sec. 6, p. 1.

———. "Second Thoughts on First Nights." *New York Times*, April 16, 1922, sec. 6, p. 1.

———. "The Stage." *New York Herald*, March 18, 1924, p. 11.

———. "The Stage." *World*, December 11, 1925, pp. 15–16.

———. "The Stage." *World*, January 25, 1926, p. 15.

———. "The Stage." *World*, January 10, 1928, p. 15.

———. "Through Darkest New England." *Sun*, November 12, 1924, p. 28.

Wyatt, Euphemia Van Rensselaer. "Agamemnon Turned Puritan." *Catholic World* 134 (December 1931): 330–31.

———. "The Drama." *Catholic World* 126 (March 1928): 812–22.

———. "The Drama." *Catholic World* 127 (April 1928): 76–85.

———. "The Drama." *Catholic World* 129 (April 1929): 78–88.

———. "A Great American Comedy." *Catholic World* 138 (November 1933): 214–19.

———. "A Modern Miracle Play." *Catholic World* 138 (February 1934): 601–09.

Young, Stark. "Days Without End." *New Republic* 77 (January 24, 1934): 312.

———. "Dilations." *New Republic* 53 (January 25, 1928): 272–73.

———. "Dynamo." *New Republic* 58 (February 27, 1929): 43–44.

———. "Eugene O'Neill's Latest Play." *New York Times*, November 12, 1924, p. 20.

———. "Eugene O'Neill's Latest Play." *New Republic* 68 (November 11, 1931): 352–55.

———. "The Fountain." *New Republic*, December 30, 1925. In *O'Neill and His Plays*. Ed. Oscar Cargill, pp. 172–74.

———. "The Hairy Ape." *New Republic* 30 (March 22, 1922): 112–13.

———. "'Hamlet' Reinterpreted." *New Republic*, December 6, 1922. In Barnard Hewitt, *Theatre USA*, p. 348.

———. "The New O'Neill Play." *New Republic* 53 (February 15, 1928): 349–50.

———. "The Prompt Book." *New York Times*, August 24, 1924, sec. 7, p. 1.

———. "The Prompt Book." *New York Times*, December 7, 1924, sec. 8, p. 5.

———. "Susan Glaspell's *The Verge*." In *The American Theatre as Seen by Its Critics*. Ed. Montrose Moses, pp. 252–55.

———. "Variegated Hits." *New Republic* 76 (October 18, 1933), 279–80.

DISSERTATIONS

Arbenz, Mary Hedwig. "The Plays of Eugene O'Neill as Presented by the Theatre Guild." University of Illinois, 1961.

Black, Eugene Robert. "Robert Edmond Jones: Poetic Artist of the New Stagecraft." University of Wisconsin, 1955.

Chinoy, Helen Krich. "The Impact of the Stage Director on American Plays, Playwrights, and Theatres: 1860–1930." Columbia University, 1963.

Halverson, Bruce Rogness. "Arthur Hopkins: A Theatrical Biography." University of Washington, 1971.

Hicks, Lee Roy. "Robert Edmond Jones: Stage Director." University of Colorado, 1969.

Oberstein, Bennett. "The Broadway Directing Career of Rouben Mamoulian." Indiana University, 1977.

Paparone, Joseph C. "Cleon Throckmorton: His Career as a Scene Designer in New York." Indiana University, 1977.

Sarlos, Robert Karoly. "The Provincetown Players: Experiments in Style." Yale University, 1966.

Sweet, Harvey. "Eugene O'Neill and Robert Edmond Jones: Text Into Scene." University of Wisconsin, 1974.

Vilhauer, William Warren. "A History and Evaluation of the Provincetown Players." University of Iowa, 1965.

Wainscott, Ronald H. "A Critical History of the Professional Stage Direction of the Plays of Eugene O'Neill, 1920–1934." Indiana University, 1984.

Waldo, Paul Robert. "Production Concepts Exemplified in Selected Presentations Directed by Robert Edmond Jones." University of Oregon, 1970.

Wiley, David W. "Philip Moeller of the Theatre Guild: An Historical and Critical Study." Indiana University, 1973.

BOOKS

Aiken, Conrad. *A Reviewer's ABC*. N.p.: Meridian, 1958.

Alexander, Doris. *The Tempering of Eugene O'Neill*. New York: Harcourt, Brace and World, 1962.

Allen, Frederick Lewis. *The Big Change: America Transforms Itself, 1900–1950*. New York: Harper & Row, 1952.

———. *Only Yesterday: An Informal History of the Nineteen-Twenties*. New York: Blue Ribbon, 1931.

Altman, George, et al. *Theatre Pictorial*. Berkeley: University of California Press, 1953.

Anderson, John. *The American Theatre*. New York: Dial, 1938.

Applebaum, Stanley, ed. *The New York Stage*. New York: Dover, 1976.

Barnes, Eric Wollencott. *The Man Who Lived Twice: The Biography of Edward Sheldon*. New York: Charles Scribner's Sons, 1956.

Atkinson, Brooks. *Broadway*. New York: Macmillan, 1970.

Atkinson, Brooks, and Albert Hirschfeld. *The Lively Years: 1920–1973*. New York: Association, 1973.

Atkinson, Jennifer McCabe. *Eugene O'Neill: A Descriptive Bibliography*. Pittsburgh: University of Pittsburgh Press, 1974.

Bennett, Joan, and Lois Kibbee. *The Bennett Playbill*. New York: Holt, Rinehart and Winston, 1970.

Bernheim, Alfred L. *The Business of the Theatre: An Economic History of the American Theatre, 1750–1932*. New York: Benjamin Blom, 1932.

Binns, Archie. *Mrs. Fiske and the American Theatre*. New York: Crown, 1955.

Block, Anita. *The Changing World in Plays and Theatre*. Boston: Little, Brown, 1939.

Blum, Daniel. *Great Stars of the American Stage*. New York: Greenberg, 1952.

Bogard, Travis. *Contour in Time: The Plays of Eugene O'Neill*. New York: Oxford University Press, 1972.

Boulton, Agnes. *Part of a Long Story*. Garden City, N.Y.: Doubleday, 1958.

Bowen, Croswell, and Shane O'Neill. *The Curse of the Misbegotten: A Tale of the House of O'Neill*. New York: McGraw-Hill, 1959.

Bricker, Herschel L. *Our Theatre Today*. New York: Samuel French, 1936.

Broussard, Louis. *American Drama: Contemporary Allegory from Eugene O'Neill to Tennessee Williams*. Norman: University of Oklahoma Press, 1962.

Brown, Jared. *The Fabulous Lunts*. New York: Atheneum, 1986.

Brown, John Mason. *Dramatis Personae*. New York: Viking, 1963.

———. *Letters from Greenroom Ghosts*. New York: Viking, 1934.

———. *Two on the Aisle*. New York: W. W. Norton, 1938.

———. *Upstage: The American Theatre in Performance*. 1930; rpt. Port Washington, N.Y.: Kennikat, 1969.

Brown, John Russell, and Bernard Harris, eds. *American Theatre*. London: Edward Arnold, 1967.

Bryer, Jackson. *The Merrill Checklist of Eugene O'Neill*. Columbus, Ohio: Charles E. Merrill, 1971.

Bryer, Jackson, ed. *"The Theatre We Worked For:" The Letters of Eugene O'Neill to Kenneth Macgowan*. New Haven and London: Yale University Press, 1982.

Canfield, Mary Cass. *Grotesques and Other Reflections on Art and the Theatre*. 1927; rpt. Port Washington, N.Y.: Kennikat, 1968.

Cargill, Oscar, et al, eds. *O'Neill and His Plays: Four Decades of Criticism*. New York: New York University Press, 1961.

Chabrowe, Leonard. *Ritual and Pathos—The Theater of O'Neill*. Lewisburg: Bucknell University Press, 1976.

Cheney, Sheldon. *The Art Theatre*. New York: Alfred A. Knopf, 1917.

———. *The New Movement in the Theatre*. New York: Mitchell Kennerley, 1914.

Churchill, Allen. *The Great White Way*. New York: E. P. Dutton, 1962.

———. *The Improper Bohemians*. New York: E. P. Dutton, 1959.

Clark, Barrett H. *Eugene O'Neill: The Man and His Plays*. New York: Dover, 1947.

Clark, Barrett H., ed. *European Theories of the Drama*. New York: Crown, 1947.

Clurman, Harold. *The Divine Pastime: Theatre Essays*. New York: Macmillan, 1974.

———. *On Directing*. New York: Macmillan, 1972.

Cohen, Robert, and John Harrop. *Creative Play Direction*, 2d ed. Englewood Cliffs, N.J.: Prentice-Hall, 1984.

Cole, Toby, and Helen Krich Chinoy. *Directors on Directing*. Indianapolis: Bobbs-Merrill, 1963.

Cook, George Cram. *Greek Coins*. New York: George H. Doran, 1925.

Cook, Nilla Cram. *My Road to India*. New York: Lee Furman, 1939.

Corrigan, Robert W., and James L. Rosenberg, eds. *The Context and Craft of Drama*. San Francisco: Chandler, 1964.

Crowley, Alice Lewisohn. *The Neighborhood Playhouse*. New York: Theatre Arts, 1959.

Current Biography. New York: H. W. Wilson, 1940–1955.

Daniels, Jonathan. *The Time Between the Wars*. Garden City, N.Y.: Doubleday, 1966.

Dell, Floyd. *Homecoming*. New York: Farrar & Rinehart, 1933.

Deutsch, Helen, and Stella Hanau. *The Provincetown: A Story of the Theatre*. New York: Farrar & Rinehart, 1931.

Dickinson, Hugh. *Myth on the Modern Stage*. Urbana: University of Illinois Press, 1969.

Dickinson, Thomas. *The Insurgent Theatre*. New York: Huebsch, 1917.

Downer, Alan S., ed. *American Drama and Its Critics: A Collection of Critical Essays*. Chicago: University of Chicago Press, 1965.

———. *Fifty Years of American Drama: 1900–1950*. Chicago: Henry Regnery, 1951.

Eaton, Walter Prichard. *The Theatre Guild: The First Ten Years*. New York: Brentano's, 1929.

Eustis, Moron. *Players at Work*. New York: Theatre Arts, 1937.

Floyd, Virginia. *Eugene O'Neill at Work: Newly Released Ideas for Plays*. New York: Frederick Ungar, 1981.

Foner, Philip S., ed. *Paul Robeson Speaks: Writings, Speeches, Interviews, 1918–1974*. New York: Brunner/Mazel, 1978.

Frank, Waldo. *Time Exposures*. New York: Boni & Liveright, 1926.

Freedley, George. *The Lunts*. New York: Macmillan, 1957.

French, Warren, ed. *The Twenties: Fiction, Poetry, Drama*. DeLand, Fla.: Everett/Edwards, 1975.

Frenz, Horst, ed. *American Playwrights on Drama*. New York: Hill and Wang, 1965.

———. *Eugene O'Neill*. Trans. Helen Sebba. New York: Frederick Ungar, 1971.

Fuerst, Walter René, and Samuel J. Hume. *Twentieth-Century Stage Decoration*. 2 vols. 1929; rpt. New York: Dover, 1967.

Gagey, Edmond M. *Revolution in American Dram*. New York: Columbia University Press, 1947.

Gardner, Helen. *Art Through the Ages*. 6th ed. New York: Harcourt, Brace, Jovanovich, 1975.

Gassner, John. *Form and Idea in Modern Theatre*. New York: Dryden, 1956.

———. *Masters of the Drama*. 3d ed. New York: Dover, 1954.

Gelb, Arthur, and Barbara Gelb. *O'Neill*. New York: Harper & Row, 1973.

Gilliam, Dorothy Butler. *Paul Robeson: All-American*. Washington, D.C.: New Republic, 1976.

Gillmore, Margalo. *Four Flights Up*. Boston: Houghton Mifflin, 1964.

Glaspell, Susan. *The Road to the Temple*. New York: Frederick A. Stokes, 1927.

Goldberg, Isaac. *The Theatre of George Jean Nathan*. New York: Simon and Schuster, 1926.

Goldstein, Malcolm. *The Political Stage*. New York: Oxford University Press, 1974.

Gorelik, Mordecai. *New Theatres for Old*. New York: E. P. Dutton, 1962.

Graham, Shirley. *Paul Robeson: Citizen of the World*. New York: Julian Messner, 1946.

Hamilton, Clayton. *Conversations on Contemporary Drama*. New York: Macmillan, 1924.

Hammond, Percy. *But—Is It Art.* Garden City, N.Y.: Doubleday, 1927.

———. *This Atom in the Audience.* New York: n.p., 1940.

Hapgood, Hutchins. *A Victorian in the Modern World.* 1939; rpt. Seattle: University of Washington Press, 1972.

Harding, Alfred. *The Revolt of the Actors.* New York: William Morrow, 1929.

Helburn, Theresa. *A Wayward Quest.* Boston: Little, Brown, 1960.

Henderson, Mary C. *The City and the Theatre.* Clifton, N.J.: James T. White, 1973.

Hewitt, Barnard. *Theatre USA.* New York: McGraw-Hill, 1959.

Himelstein, Morgan Y. *Drama Was a Weapon.* New Brunswick, N.J.: Rutgers University Press, 1963.

Hopkins, Arthur. *How's Your Second Act?* New York: Alfred A. Knopf, 1918.

———. *Reference Point.* New York: Samuel French, 1948.

———. *To a Lonely Boy.* Garden City, N.Y.: Doubleday, Doran, 1937.

Hoyt, Edwin P. *Paul Robeson: The American Othello.* Cleveland: World, 1967.

Hughes, Robert. *The Shock of the New.* New York: Alfred A. Knopf, 1980.

Isaacs, Edith J. R., ed. *Architecture for the New Theatre.* New York: Theatre Arts, 1935.

———. *The Negro in the American Theatre.* New York: Theatre Arts, 1947.

Johnson, Albert, and Bertha Johnson. *Directing Methods.* Cranbury, N.J.: A. S. Barnes, 1970.

Jones, Robert Edmond. *The Dramatic Imagination.* New York: Theatre Arts, 1941.

———. *Drawings for the Theatre.* New York: Theatre Arts, 1925.

———. *Drawings for the Theatre.* New York: Theatre Arts, 1970.

Kinsila, Edward B. *Modern Theatre Construction.* New York: Chalmers, 1917.

Komisarjevsky, Theodore, and Lee Simonson. *Settings & Costumes of the Modern Stage.* 1933; rpt. New York: Benjamin Blom, 1966.

Kreymborg, Alfred, et al, eds. *The New Caravan.* New York: W. W. Norton, 1936.

Krutch, Joseph Wood. *The American Drama Since 1918.* New York: George Braziller, 1957.

Langner, Lawrence. *The Magic Curtain.* New York: E. P. Dutton, 1951.

Le Gallienne, Eva. *At 33.* New York: Longmans, Green, 1934.

Lewis, Emory. *Stages: The Fifty-year Childhood of the American Theatre.* Englewood Cliffs, N.J.: Prentice-Hall, 1969.

Macgowan, Kenneth. *Footlights Across America.* New York: Harcourt, Brace, 1929.

———. *The Theatre of Tomorrow.* New York: Boni and Liveright, 1921.

Macgowan, Kenneth, and Herman Rosse. *Masks and Demons.* 1923; rpt. New York: Harcourt, Brace, 1972.

Macgowan, Kenneth, and Robert Edmond Jones. *Continental Stagecraft.* New York: Harcourt, Brace, 1922.

Mackay, Constance D'Arcy. *The Little Theatre in the United States.* New York: Henry Holt, 1917.

Mantle, Burns. *American Playwrights of Today.* New York: Dodd, Mead, 1929.

———. *The Best Plays of 1919–34; and The Year Book of the Drama in America.* 15 vols. Boston: Small, Maynard, 1920–1925; New York: Dodd, Mead, 1926–1934.

Mantle, Burns, and Garrison P. Sherwood, eds. *The Best Plays of 1909–1919; and The Year Book of the Drama in America.* New York: Dodd, Mead, 1943.

McCabe, John. *George M. Cohan: The Man Who Owned Broadway.* Garden City, N.Y.: Doubleday, 1973.

Middleton, George. *These Things Are Mine.* New York: Macmillan, 1947.

Mielziner, Jo. *Designing for the Theatre.* New York: Atheneum, 1965.

Miller, Jordan Y. *Eugene O'Neill and the American Critic: A Bibliographical Checklist.* 2d ed. Hamden, Conn.: Shoestring, 1973.

———. *Playwright's Progress: O'Neill and the Critics.* Chicago: Scott, Foresman, 1965.

Milne, Tom. *Rouben Mamoulian.* Bloomington: Indiana University Press, 1969.

Morehouse, Ward. *George M. Cohan: Prince of the American Theatre.* Philadelphia: J. B. Lippincott, 1943.

Morris, Lloyd. *Postscript to Yesterday; America: The Last Fifty Years.* New York: Random House, 1947.

Moses, Montrose J., and John Mason Brown, eds. *The American Theater as Seen by Its Critics: 1752–1934.* 1934; rpt. New York: Cooper Square, 1967.

Nadel, Norman. *A Pictorial History of the Theatre Guild.* New York: Crown, 1969.

Nathan, George Jean. *The Intimate Notebooks.* New York: Alfred A. Knopf, 1932.

———. *Passing Judgments.* New York: Alfred A. Knopf, 1935.

———. *The World in Falseface.* New York: Alfred A. Knopf, 1923.

The National Cyclopedia of American Biography. New York: James T. White, 1932–1975.

O'Neill, Eugene. *Ah, Wilderness!* New York: Random House, 1933.

———. "All God's Chillun Got Wings." *American Mercury,* February 1924, pp. 129–48.

———. *All God's Chillun Got Wings, Welded.* New York: Boni and Liveright, 1924.

———. *Beyond the Horizon.* New York: Boni and Liveright, 1920.

———. *Chris Christophersen.* New York: Random House, 1982.

————. *Days Without End*. New York: Random House, 1934.

————. *Desire Under the Elms*. New York: Boni and Liveright, 1925.

————. *Dynamo*. New York: Horace Liveright, 1929.

————. *The Emperor Jones*. Cincinnati: Stewart Kidd Company, 1921.

————. *The Emperor Jones, Diff'rent, The Straw*. New York: Boni and Liveright, 1921.

————. *Gold*. New York: Boni and Liveright, 1920.

————. *The Great God Brown, The Fountain, The Moon of the Caribbees and Other Plays*. New York: Boni and Liveright, 1926.

————. *The Hairy Ape, Anna Christie, The First Man*. New York: Boni and Liveright, 1922.

————. *Lazarus Laughed*. New York: Boni and Liveright, 1927.

————. *Marco Millions*. New York: Boni and Liveright, 1927.

————. *Mourning Becomes Electra*. New York: Horace Liveright, 1931.

————. "The Rime of the Ancient Mariner." *Yale University Library Gazette* 35 (October 1960), 63–86.

————. *Six Short Plays of Eugene O'Neill*. New York: Vintage, 1965.

————. *Strange Interlude*. New York: Boni and Liveright, 1928.

————. *Seven Plays of the Sea*. New York: Vintage, 1972.

Ormsbee, Helen. *Backstage With Actors*. 1938; rpt. New York: Benjamin Blom, 1969.

Pendleton, Ralph, ed. *The Theatre of Robert Edmond Jones*. Middletown, Conn.: Wesleyan University Press, 1958.

Pichel, Irving. *Modern Theatres*. New York: Harcourt, Brace, 1925.

Pilkington, John, ed. *Stark Young: A Life in the Arts, Letters, 1900–1962*. 2 vols. Baton Rouge: Louisiana State University Press, 1975.

Poggi, Jack. *Theater in America: The Impact of Economic Forces, 1870–1967*. Ithaca: Cornell University Press, 1968.

Quinn, Arthur Hobson. *A History of the American Drama from the Civil War to the Present Day*. Vol. 2. New York: Harper, 1927.

————. *Representative American Plays*. 7th ed. New York: Appleton- Century-Crofts, 1953.

Rice, Elmer. *The Living Theatre*. New York: Harper, 1959.

Rigdon, Walter. *The Biographical Encyclopedia & Who's Who of the American Theatre*. New York: James H. Heineman, 1965.

Robeson, Eslanda Goode. *Paul Robeson, Negro*. New York: Harper, 1930.

Sadie, Stanley, ed. *The New Grove Dictionary of Music and Musicians*. 20 vols. London: Macmillan, 1980.

Sarlos, Robert Karoly. *Jig Cook and the Provincetown Players*. Amherst: University of Massachusetts Press, 1982.

Sayler, Oliver M. *Our American Theatre*. New York: Brentano's, 1923.

Selden, Samuel, and Hunton D. Sellman. *Stage Scenery and Lighting*. New York: F. S. Crofts, 1930.

Sergeant, Elizabeth Shepley. *Fire Under the Andes*. New York: Alfred A. Knopf, 1927.

Shaw, Dale. *Titans of the American Stage*. Philadelphia: Westminster, 1971.

Sheaffer, Louis. *O'Neill: Son and Artist*. Boston: Little, Brown, 1973.

———. *O'Neill: Son and Playwright*. Boston: Little, Brown, 1968.

Sievers, David W. *Freud on Broadway*. New York: Hermitage House, 1955.

Simonson, Lee. *The Art of Scenic Design*. 1950; rpt. Westport, Conn.: Greenwood, 1973.

———. *Part of a Lifetime: Drawings and Designs, 1919–1940*. New York: Duell, Sloan and Pearce, 1943.

———. *The Stage Is Set*. 1932; rpt. New York: Dover, 1946.

Skinner, R. Dana. *Our Changing Theatre*. New York: Dial, 1931.

Skolsky, Sidney. *Times Square Tintypes*. New York: Ives Washburn, 1930.

Spiller, Robert E., et al. *Literary History of the United States*. 2 vols. 4th ed. New York: Macmillan, 1974.

Stevens, David H., ed. *Ten Talents in the American Theatre*. Norman: University of Oklahoma Press, 1957.

Taft, Kendall B., et al, eds. *Contemporary Attitudes*. Boston: Houghton Mifflin, 1929.

Tiusanen, Timo. *O'Neill's Scenic Images*. Princeton, N.J.: Princeton University Press, 1968.

Toohey, John L. *A History of the Pulitzer Prize Plays*. New York: Citadel, 1967.

Tornqvist, Egil. *A Drama of Souls: Studies in O'Neill's Super-naturalistic Technique*. New Haven and London: Yale University Press, 1968.

Tyler, George C. and J. C. Furnas. *Whatever Goes Up—*. Indianapolis: Bobbs-Merrill, 1934.

Valgemae, Mardi. *Accelerated Grimace: Expressionism in the American Drama of the 1920s*. Carbondale: Southern Illinois University Press, 1972.

Vorse, Mary Heaton. *Time and the Town: A Provincetown Chronicle*. New York: Dial, 1942.

Waldau, Roy S. *Vintage Years of the Theatre Guild: 1928–1939*. Cleveland: Case Western Reserve University, 1972.

Walter, Erich A., ed. *Essay Annual, 1933*. Chicago: Scott, Foresman, 1933.

Who Was Who in the Theatre: 1912–1976. 4 vols. Detroit: Gale Research, 1978.

Who's Who in America. Chicago: A. N. Marquis, 1924–1925.Willett, John. *Expressionism*. New York: McGraw-Hill, 1970.

Wilson, Edmund, ed. *The Shores of Light*. New York: Farrar, Straus and Giroux, 1952.

———. *The Twenties*. Ed. Leon Edel. New York: Farrar, Straus and Giroux, 1975.

Woollcott, Alexander. *Shouts and Murmurs*. New York: Century, 1922.

Young, Stark. *Immortal Shadows.* 1948; rpt. New York: Hill and Wang, 1958.

Young, William C. *Famous Actors and Actresses on the American Stage.* 2 vols. New York: R. R. Bowker, 1975.

Zolotow, Maurice. *Stagestruck: The Romance of Alfred Lunt and Lynn Fontanne.* New York: Harcourt, Brace and World, 1965.

Index

Index

Index